FIGURING DEATH IN CLASSICAL ATHENS

VISUAL CONVERSATIONS IN ART AND ARCHAEOLOGY

General Editor: Jaś Elsner

Visual Conversations is a series designed to foster a new model of comparative inquiry in the histories of ancient art. The aim is to create the spirit of a comparative conversation across the different areas of the art history and archaeology of the pre-modern world—across Eurasia, Africa, Australasia, and the Americas—in ways that are academically and theoretically stimulating. The books serve collectively as a public platform to demonstrate by example the possibilities of a comparative exercise of working with objects across cultures and religions within defined, but broad, historical trajectories.

'This remarkable book glides easily between pots and prose, tragedy and sculpture. It closely reads artistic and literary masterworks with alert perception, elegant writing, and deep scholarship. It is witty, reflective, purposeful; in conception it is a model, in execution a delight.'

Professor Gregory Hutchinson, Emeritus Regius Professor of Greek, University of Oxford

'Death is a difficult subject. Not just because of the heightened emotions surrounding dying and death, but because cultural responses to death come in so many forms—as stories and epitaphs, as paintings and sculpture, as philosophical treatises. Emily Clifford's glittering and deeply humane book explores the full range of ways in which the Greeks faced up to and figured out death, and does so with deep insight and a wonderfully light touch.'

Professor Robin Osborne, Emeritus Professor of Ancient History, University of Cambridge

'Like Dante's Virgil, Emily Clifford leads us through the thanatological landscape of Classical Athens with deep learning and sensitivity. From pots to plays, temples to tombs, this ambitious interdisciplinary exploration of the epistemology of death shows how texts and artefacts did not just illustrate Greek thinking about the end of life, but actively interrogated the challenges it poses to human knowledge, in line with the affordances and constraints of both genre and medium.'

Professor Verity Platt, Professor of Classics and History of Art, Cornell University

Figuring Death in Classical Athens

Visual and Literary Explorations

EMILY CLIFFORD

OXFORD
UNIVERSITY PRESS

Great Clarendon Street, Oxford, OX2 6DP,
United Kingdom

Oxford University Press is a department of the University of Oxford.
It furthers the University's objective of excellence in research, scholarship,
and education by publishing worldwide. Oxford is a registered trade mark of
Oxford University Press in the UK and in certain other countries

© Emily Clifford 2025

The moral rights of the author have been asserted

All rights reserved. No part of this publication may be reproduced, stored in a retrieval system,
transmitted, used for text and data mining, or used for training artificial intelligence, in any form or
by any means, without the prior permission in writing of Oxford University Press, or as expressly
permitted by law, by licence or under terms agreed with the appropriate reprographics rights
organization. Enquiries concerning reproduction outside the scope of the above should be sent
to the Rights Department, Oxford University Press, at the address above.

You must not circulate this work in any other form
and you must impose this same condition on any acquirer

Published in the United States of America by Oxford University Press
198 Madison Avenue, New York, NY 10016, United States of America

British Library Cataloguing in Publication Data
Data available

Library of Congress Control Number: 2024946946

ISBN 9780198947905

DOI: 10.1093/9780198947936.001.0001

Printed and bound by
CPI Group (UK) Ltd, Croydon, CR0 4YY

Links to third party websites are provided by Oxford in good faith and
for information only. Oxford disclaims any responsibility for the materials
contained in any third party website referenced in this work.

The manufacturer's authorised representative in the EU for product safety is
Oxford University Press España S.A. of El Parque Empresarial San Fernando de Henares, Avenida
de Castilla, 2 – 28830 Madrid (www.oup.es/en or
product.safety@oup.com). OUP España S.A. also acts as importer into Spain
of products made by the manufacturer.

ACKNOWLEDGEMENTS

Thank you above all to Felix Budelmann and Jaś Elsner, who have inspired and guided this book from its earliest stages and been so generous with their time and ideas. Thank you also to Gregory Hutchinson and Robin Osborne and to my anonymous reviewers for their comments and suggestions. This book is immeasurably better as a result. I also thank Constanze Güthenke, who has encouraged my work and career, Richard Rutherford for his kind mentorship, the Arts and Humanities Research Council for funding my doctoral work, The Christopher Tower Greek Mythology Fund for its generous support of my Junior Research Fellowship during which I completed my doctorate and this book, and Corpus Christi, Christ Church, and the Warwick Department of Classics and Ancient History for offering warm and sparkling environments within which to work and converse.

Many others have engaged with my work and offered invaluable feedback and discussion: Katherine Backler, Emily Brady, Xavier Buxton, Casper de Jonge, Olivia Elder, David Fearn, Emma Greensmith, Constanze Güthenke, Lindsay Judson, Leah Lazar, Thomas Nelson, Tom Phillips, Verity Platt, Tobias Reinhardt, Tim Rood, Hugo Shakeshaft, Michael Squire, and Carrie Vout. I am also grateful to those involved in the Corpus Christi '*Phantasia* before *phantasia*' 2019 seminar series and conference, and to the authors of the *The Imagination of the Mind in Classical Athens* volume that sprang from it, both for thoughts on my work and for exploring with me their ideas on themes that are foundational to the subject explored here. The book has benefited, too, from conversation and critique at the Oxford Early Career Academic Work-in-Progress Seminars, enthusiastically convened over the years by Olivia Elder, Leah Lazar, Thomas Nelson, and Lewis Webb, the Cambridge C and D Caucus seminars, and the OIKOS-Munich-Oxford 2019 conference. I also thank the team at Oxford University Press, including Rachel Atkins, Charlotte Loveridge, Jo North, Srividya Raamadhurai, and Bethany Williams.

Thank you, finally, to friends and family, who have made this book possible—to my parents, Joyce and Mike, Carrie, and Gaby (and the whole extended family) for time, to Andy and Venetia, who have gone beyond the call of friendship in not only reading the manuscript but also professing to have enjoyed it, to Jessica for perennial inspiration, to Matt, especially, for challenging and clarifying my thinking and spurring me on to pursue my ambitions, and to my cheerleaders Felix and Jasper, who have not yet encountered life beyond my writing on death.

PROLOGUE

'I NO LONGER EXIST'?

Faking death is hard. One reason is that it is hard to do (concealing breathing, for instance, or communicating that a head droops in death rather than sleep). Still more problematic, how can you make something realistic when 'real' itself is sketchy? How many can claim to have tried death for themselves—to know what really happens and what it is like? Death is hard to know and hard to show.

FIGURE P1. *La mort d'Alceste, ou l'héroïsme de l'amour conjugal*, by Pierre Peyron, 1785, oil on canvas. Height 327 cm, Width 325 cm. Musée du Louvre, Paris: 7175. Image: © GrandPalaisRmn (musée du Louvre)/René-Gabriel Ojeda.

X PROLOGUE

Consider the eighteenth-century painting by Pierre Peyron, *La mort d'Alceste, ou l'héroïsme de l'amour conjugal* (Figure P1). In the Greek myth of Alcestis (on which Peyron's painting is based), when Admetus reached the end of his allotted life he was reluctant to die, so his wife Alcestis volunteered to die in his place. Happily, she soon returned to the world of the living (to the joy of her regretful husband), either because she was rescued by Herakles or because the gods of the underworld permitted her to do so. At the heart of the story are people grappling psychologically, emotionally, and physically with death—whether future, present, or past; whether their own or someone else's. With that in mind, let us turn our eyes upon the painting.

The body of Peyron's Alcestis glows in the darkness. Illuminated as though from within, she lights up her painted world, irradiating those around her. The implications are ethical: this woman has sacrificed her life for her husband; she is a moral exemplar. They are also existential: like the child that directs attention, including the real beholder's attention, upon her face, Alcestis is filled with implicit vitality. She is not yet dead. But her enervated limbs say otherwise. Unlike the surrounding figures, who variously clutch at fabrics and bodies (including hers), this woman is every bit an object—an analogue for the hollow vessel (cold? rigid? empty? washed?) that gleams, enigmatically prominent, in the foreground, ready to be grasped by two handles that arc downwards like Alcestis' hands. Then there is the bearded figure shrouded in blue at the foot of the bed. This is, presumably, Death, waiting—another hint that death is close but not complete. His appearance—hunched and wrapped, turned away from the beholder, barely discernible in the shadows—articulates Alcestis' future: this body is an inversion of the one outstretched and exposed on the bed, one whose light will soon be smothered beneath the fabric suspended above her head. Or, rather, fabrics. Note the second shroud brandished like an echo in front of a statue in the painting's gloomy background—is it to cover the sculpture or to reveal it? It is significant that in Euripides' dramatic version of the myth Admetus pledges to embrace a portrait of Alcestis in his bed as a substitute for the wife he has lost: a 'cold pleasure'. Is Peyron's painted stone portrait another impression of Alcestis' demise—a cold, inert counterpart to the corpse-to-be below, soon be present only in images (mental and artistic)? The gloomy figure, the alluring object, the stony statue, and the bright, languid woman, quadrate with four visualizations of death. Death is near, but hard to pin down. Add, finally, the stagey backdrop—a dark expanse of suspended fabric that sets the whole scene within a constructed space. Has Peyron faked a death, or a performance?

Compare a rendering of the story painted approximately one century later by Frederic Leighton, *Hercules Wrestling with Death for the Body of Alcestis* (Figure P2).

Figure P2. *Hercules Wrestling with Death for the Body of Alcestis*, by Frederic Leighton, c. 1869–1871, oil on canvas. Height 132.4 cm, Width 265.4 cm. Wadsworth Atheneum Museum of Art, Hartford, CT, The Ella Gallup Sumner and Mary Catlin Sumner Collection Fund, 1982.46. Image: incamerastock/Alamy Stock Photo.

Death is, in some ways, more aggressively present. Alcestis' body is still a focal point, but her whiteness looks coldly cadaverous against the glow of the sky, and her elongated shape is unnaturally rectangular. This woman is already statue-like, reminding us of Alcestis' stone double in Peyron's version. Death himself is up and active, and the blue-black of his cloak stretches into the field above and below, tending to swallow Alcestis into its tenebrous folds. But is death any easier to conceptualize here? Alcestis' body suggests that we are already in the aftermath, whereas Death's precarious position implies that he is on the cusp of departure without her. And the scene brims with pseudo-corpses that tease out death's implications by analogy—the slumped figure of a woman in the foreground that seems devoid of life and colour (her clothes are a dull off-white) but is surely not dead; the plucked blossoms, which, for all their lustrous reds and pinks, must be dying; and the bodiless face of the defeated Nemean lion, which glares into the scene like an analogue for Death himself.

Ancient treatments of the myth also display a fascination with figuring the complexities of representing and knowing death. There is no better example than the tragedy that Euripides staged in 438 BCE, a drama that plays at length on perplexity as to Alcestis' existential status. For much of the play Alcestis is somewhere between life and death. The chorus tie themselves in knots trying to define what this means (Eur. *Alc.* 139–42):

xii PROLOGUE

ΧΟΡΟΣ

...εἰ δ᾽ ἔτ᾽ ἐστὶν ἔμψυχος γυνὴ
εἴτ᾽ οὖν ὄλωλεν εἰδέναι βουλοίμεθ᾽ ἄν.

ΘΕΡΑΠΑΙΝΑ

καὶ ζῶσαν εἰπεῖν καὶ θανοῦσαν ἔστι σοι.

Χο. καὶ πῶς ἂν αὐτὸς κατθάνοι τε καὶ βλέποι;

Chorus:
...I would like to know whether the woman
is still alive or whether she has actually died.
Female attendant:
You can say that she is living and dying.
Ch: But how could the same person both die and have the power of sight?

Alcestis is not simultaneously 'dead' and 'alive'; she is simultaneously 'living' and 'dying'. The conceptual difference is reflected in the aorist participle θανοῦσαν, which distinguishes death's event from its accomplishment (an accomplishment that would have been signalled by a perfect form, as anticipated in the chorus's use of ὄλωλεν in 140). The idea that someone could be dying but not yet dead and thus still living may seem unproblematic, especially when the verbs differ in aspect: Alcestis' dying, θανοῦσαν (aorist), is a sudden event by contrast with the continuing action of living, ζῶσαν (present). But the chorus are uncomfortable with the lack of existential clarity; they feel, instinctively, that Alcestis should be doing one or the other. Their insistence on pinning down Alcestis' existential state reveals an intellectual preoccupation with death: if death is an event, when does it occur? When is it definitive? What *is* death?

Compare the language of finality used later by the chorus: 'she is no longer' (οὐκέτ᾽ ἔστιν, 392). This is a new state, or absence of a state, and makes all the difference. But even here uncertainty lingers. How is it that Alcestis *herself* was able declare her non-existence? 'I am no longer anything' she pre-empted at 390, only to eke out her existence into at least verse 391 ('farewell')—an absurdity that anticipates Shakespeare's Quince's Pyramus ('Now am I dead, | Now am I fled, | My soul is in the sky.' *MSND* V.1.295–7). Even once she has departed (apparently from life, probably from the stage), her husband makes the extraordinary decision to pretend that she still lives, rendering Herakles in ignorance of her death until verse 821. Then, after a brief interlude in which Admetus mourns his wife, Herakles returns with a mystery woman who he goes on to claim is Alcestis. Though she looks just like his wife, Admetus must be persuaded that she is genuinely alive.

It is thus left unclear whether Alcestis ever died (a bit? completely?). And she herself says nothing, skewering fantasies that she might disclose what happened or what it was like. As we will see in Conversation One, in the concluding myth of the *Republic* Plato's Er offers more generous feedback on death—in principle at least. Here, the closest an audience gets to vicarious insight into death comes earlier in the play, when Alcestis seems to diverge in experience from everyone else, seeing differently: 'They are leading me, someone is leading me; someone is leading me—do you not see?' (259–60). The reliability of her perception is open to debate, particularly given her imprecision (blurred vision?). The situation is suffused with irony and sophistry, but makes at least one serious point, a point that reoccurs in later versions of the myth. What is death? What does it look like? What is it like? How do we know?

In the spirit of this series on 'Visual Conversations in Art and Archaeology', this prologue has opened a comparative conversation across different cultures and media. It has also taken us back to Classical Athens, the defined culture that will be my focus. In the next chapters, the conversation continues, probing visual and verbal explorations of death—in philosophy, painted objects, drama, sculpture, and history. How did figuring death help Athenians figure it out?

CONTENTS

List of Illustrations	xvii
List of Abbreviations	xxi

Conversation 1. Figuring Death in Classical Athens: Visual and
Literary Explorations | 1

    I. Hello from the Other Side | 1

    II. This Book: A History of Cultural Thinking | 4

    III. Visual and Literary Conversations | 7

    IV. Classical Athens—Golden Age, Age of Death | 10

    V. What's New About This? | 17

1. Death Comes as the End: Encountering Death in
Plato's *Phaedo* | 24

    I. The Challenge | 24

    II. Plato's Spyglass | 27

    III. A Death Foretold | 35

    IV. Swan Song | 43

    V. Conclusion | 51

2. They Do It with Mirrors?: Imagining Death with Painted Pots | 56

    I. Pots and Death | 56

    II. Drinking Cups | 60

        A. Revelations | 60

        B. Stop all the Clocks | 64

        C. Forms of Thought | 71

    III. Lekythoi | 73

        A. Where Are the Bodies? | 73

        B. Death and the Object | 83

        C. Reflections on Reflections | 91

    IV. Conclusion | 96

Conversation 2. Deaths Old and New | 100

xvi CONTENTS

3. The Extraordinary Death of Sophocles' *Oedipus at Colonus* 106

  I. Dying On/Off Stage 106

  II. Crisis 112

  III. A Messenger's Account: Something Wondrous 117

    A. Looking and Telling 119

    B. Wondrous Things 125

  IV. Oedipus: If Anyone Among Mortals is Wondrous 134

Conversation 3. Niobes 141

4. Victory, Victory, Victory?: Encountering Death in the West Frieze of the Temple of Athena Nike 146

  I. Thing of Beauty 146

  II. What Does It Take to Notice Death in a Temple Frieze? 150

  III. A Sacred Art of Death 167

  IV. Life and Death in the Balance 176

  V. Conclusion 188

5. Death and the Plague in Thucydides' *History of the Peloponnesian War* 191

  I. History, Plague, and Knowledge 191

  II. Beyond Reckoning 194

  III. Missing the Trees for the Wood 201

  IV. Fair Words 211

  V. Conclusion—And a Simile 219

Conversation 4. Figuring (Out) Death 223

  I. Visual and Literary Explorations 223

    A. Beyond the Body 223

    B. One and Many 224

    C. Virtual Reality 225

  II. Classical Athens and Beyond 225

  III. Hard to Know and Hard to Show 227

Bibliography 231

Index 283

LIST OF ILLUSTRATIONS

P1. *La mort d'Alceste, ou l'héroïsme de l'amour conjugal*, by Pierre Peyron, 1785. Musée du Louvre, Paris: 7175. Image: © GrandPalaisRmn (musée du Louvre)/René-Gabriel Ojeda. ix

P2. *Hercules Wrestling with Death for the Body of Alcestis*, by Frederic Leighton, *c.* 1869–1871. Wadsworth Atheneum Museum of Art, Hartford, CT, The Ella Gallup Sumner and Mary Catlin Sumner Collection Fund, 1982.46. Image: incamerastock/Alamy Stock Photo. xi

C1.1. Dying warrior from the east pediment of the Temple of Aphaia at Aegina, *c.* 480 BCE. Glyptothek Museum, Munich. Image: Erin Babnik/Alamy Stock Photo. 14

C1.2. Dying warrior from the west pediment of the Temple of Aphaia at Aegina, *c.* 480 BCE. Glyptothek Museum, Munich. Image: Erin Babnik/ Alamy Stock Photo. 14

2.1A, B. Getty cup (kylix), attributed to the Brygos Painter, 490–470 BCE. The J. Paul Getty Museum, Villa Collection, Malibu: 86.AE.286. Image: Getty Open Content (Creative Commons). 61, 65

2.2A, B, C. Louvre cup (kylix), attributed to the Brygos Painter, *c.* 480 BCE. Musée du Louvre, Paris: G 152. Image: © RMN-Grand Palais (musée du Louvre)/Stéphane Maréchalle. 67, 69

2.3A, B, C. Met lekythos, attributed to the Bosanquet Painter, 440–430 BCE. Metropolitan Museum of Art, New York, Rogers Fund, 1923: 23.160.38. Image: Met Open Access. 74–76

2.4. Stele of a young man and a little girl, *c.* 530 BCE. Metropolitan Museum of Art, New York, Frederick C. Hewitt Fund, 1911, Rogers Fund, 1921, and Anonymous Gift, 1951: 11.185a–c, f, g. Image: Met Open Access. 79

2.5. Anavyssos kouros, *c.* 530–520 BCE. National Archaeological Museum, Athens: 3851. Image: Peter Horree/Alamy Stock Photo. 80

2.6. Another Bosanquet lekythos, 440–430 BCE. Metropolitan Museum of Art, New York, Rogers Fund, 1023: 23.160.39. Image: Met Open Access. 88

2.7. Lekythos (overgrown grave), 475–450 BCE. Musée du Louvre, Paris: CA3758. Image: © GrandPalaisRmn (musée du Louvre)/Hervé Lewandowski. 91

2.8A, B. Lekythos (Charon at the grave), attributed to Group R, 420–410 BCE. Musée du Louvre, Paris: CA537. Image: © Musée du Louvre, Dist. GrandPalaisRmn/Hervé Lewandowski. 94

C2. The Mykonos pithos, *c.* 670 BCE. Archaeological Museum of Mykonos: 2240. Image: Brenda Kean/Alamy Stock Photo. 102

xviii LIST OF ILLUSTRATIONS

C3A, B. The Caltanissetta krater (both sides), *c.* 450 BCE. Museo Civico Archeologico, Caltanissetta: S 2555. Image: courtesy of the Regional Department of Cultural Heritage and Sicilian Identity—Gela Archaeological Park. 143

4.1. Photograph of the temple of Athena Nike taken from the northwest, showing the view of the west frieze from below. Image: Chris Hellier/Alamy Stock Photo. 149

4.2A. Corner block *h* from the west frieze of the temple of Athena Nike, 426–421 BCE. Acropolis Museum, Athens: Acr. 18143 (west side). Image: © Acropolis Museum, 2018, photographer: Yiannis Koulelis. 151

4.2B. Block *i* from the west frieze of the temple of Athena Nike, 426–421 BCE. British Museum, London: 1816,0610.160. Image: © The Trustees of the British Museum. 151

4.2C. Block *k* from the west frieze of the temple of Athena Nike, 426–421 BCE. British Museum, London: 1816,0610.161. Image: © The Trustees of the British Museum. 151

4.2D. Corner block *l* from the west frieze of the temple of Athena Nike, 426–421 BCE. Acropolis Museum, Athens: Acr. 18139 (west side). Image: © Acropolis Museum, 2018, photographer: Yiannis Koulelis. 152

4.2E, F, G, H. Details from blocks *i* and *k* (see Figures 4.2B and 4.2C). Images: © The Trustees of the British Museum. 152–153

4.3. Patras shield, mid-second century CE. Archaeological Museum of Patras: 6. Archaeological Museum of Patras/© Hellenic Ministry of Culture and Sports/Ephorate of Antiquities of Achaea. Image: © German Archaeological Institute at Athens (D-DAI-ATH-1973/2291), photographer: Hartwig Koppermann. 158

4.4. Nashville Parthenon shield by Alan LeQuire, constructed 1982–1990, gilded and painted in 2002. Nashville, Tennessee. Image: domonabikeUSA/Alamy Stock Photo. 159

4.5. Lateran relief, *c.* 125–140 CE. Lateran Museum, Rome: 10461. Image: GRANGER—Historical Picture Archive/Alamy Stock Photo. 160

4.6. Conservatori shield, 150–200 CE. Museo Nuovo Capitolino, Rome: 916. Image: Stefano Ravera/Alamy Stock Photo. 161

4.7A, B. Niobid mixing bowl (calyx-krater), *c.* 460–450 BCE. Musée du Louvre, Paris: G 341. Image: © 1994 RMN-Grand Palais (musée du Louvre)/Hervé Lewandowski. 163

4.8. Niobid relief, *c.* first century CE. British Museum, London: 1877,0727.1. Image: © The Trustees of the British Museum. 164

4.9. Red-figure mixing bowl (calyx-krater), painted by Euphronios, *c.* 515 BCE. Museo Nazionale Cerite, Cerveteri. Image: GRANGER—Historical Picture Archive/Alamy Stock Photo. 169

4.10. Red-figure mug fragments, 450–400 BCE. Liverpool, Merseyside Museum: 50.42.12. Image: © National Museums Liverpool. 169

LIST OF ILLUSTRATIONS xix

4.11A. Corner block *a* from the east frieze of the temple of Athena Nike,
426–421 BCE. Acropolis Museum, Athens: Acr. 18135 (east side).
Image: © Acropolis Museum, 2018, photographer: Yiannis Koulelis. 171

4.11B. Block *b* from the east frieze of the temple of Athena Nike, 426–421 BCE.
Acropolis Museum, Athens: Acr. 18136 (east side). Image: © Acropolis
Museum, 2018, photographer: Yiannis Koulelis. 171

4.11C. Block *c* from the east frieze of the temple of Athena Nike, 426–421 BCE.
Acropolis Museum, Athens: Acr. 18138 (east side). Image: © Acropolis
Museum, 2018, photographer: Yiannis Koulelis. 172

4.12. North slab IV from the balustrade of the temple of Athena Nike, *c.* 410
BCE. Acropolis Museum, Athens: Acr. 972. Image: © Acropolis Museum,
2018, photographer: Yiannis Koulelis. 173

4.13. Fragmentary Attic relief crowning a casualty list, 450–400 BCE.
Ashmolean Museum, Oxford: ANMichaelis.85. Image: © Ashmolean
Museum. 179

4.14. Red-figure cup (kylix), attributed to Onesimos, 490–480 BCE. Harvard
Art Museums/Arthur M. Sackler Museum, Cambridge, Bequest of
Frederick M. Watkins: MA: 1972.39. Image: © President and Fellows
of Harvard College. 181

4.15. Attic red-figure two-handled jar (pelike), attributed to the Trophy
Painter, 450–440 BCE. Museum of Fine Arts, Boston, MA, Bartlett
Collection—Museum purchase with funds from the Francis Bartlett
Donation of 1912: 20.187. Image: © 2025 Museum of Fine Arts,
Boston. 183

4.16. Attic red-figure mixing bowl (bell-krater), attributed to the Polydektes
Painter, 475–425 BCE. Museo Civico Archeologico, Bologna: inv.
MCABo 18109. Image: Courtesy of Bologna, Museo Civico
Archeologico. 184

C4. *Myself as a Specimen*, by Trevor Guthrie, 2009. Private Collection.
© Trevor Guthrie. Artwork and photograph reproduced with the
kind permission of Trevor Guthrie. 228

LIST OF ABBREVIATIONS

Abbreviations of ancient authors and texts and scholarly reference works follow those of the *Oxford Classical Dictionary*, fourth edition. Exceptions are listed below.

AVI   Attic Vase Inscriptions. https://avi.unibas.ch/.

BAPD   Beazley Archive Pottery Database. https://www.carc.ox.ac.uk/carc/pottery.

OR   Osborne, R. and P. J. Rhodes (eds.) 2017. *Greek Historical Inscriptions 478–404 BC*. Oxford.

Radt   Radt, S. 1999. *Tragicorum Graecorum Fragmenta*, volume 4, *Sophocles, editio correctior et addendis aucta*. Göttingen.

Voigt   Voigt, E.-M. 1971. *Sappho et Alcaeus. Fragmenta*. Amsterdam.

CONVERSATION ONE

Figuring Death in Classical Athens

Visual and Literary Explorations

I. HELLO FROM THE OTHER SIDE

ὅς ποτε ἐν πολέμῳ τελευτήσας, ἀναιρεθέντων δεκαταίων τῶν νεκρῶν ἤδη διεφθαρμένων, ὑγιὴς μὲν ἀνῃρέθη, κομισθεὶς δ' οἴκαδε μέλλων θάπτεσθαι δωδεκαταῖος ἐπὶ τῇ πυρᾷ κείμενος ἀνεβίω, ἀναβιοὺς δ' ἔλεγεν ἃ ἐκεῖ ἴδοι.

Once upon a time [a man called Er] died in battle. Though the other corpses gathered for burial had already been decomposing for ten days, his was carried from the field in full health. But when it had been brought home, and was about to be given funeral rites on the twelfth day, he came back to life while lying on the pyre, and upon his return to life he recounted what he had seen in the other world.

—Socrates on Er in Plato, *Republic* 10.614b4–7[1]

At the end of the *Republic*, Plato's Socrates tells the story of Er, a man permitted to return from death with his memory intact to describe the afterlife to the living (10.614b–621b). The tale is a fantasy in more ways than one.

In the first place, Er's experience, and the knowledge he acquires, breaks a general rule: death is a reality that all mortals must, at some point, face but that no one can try out in advance.[2] Death is, normally, the 'great unknown'. The possibility that someone like Er might experience and remember their own death is revolutionary: it explodes, or tends to explode, paradigms of consciousness, existence, the cosmos, theology—the very stuff of metaphysics. More germane to this book, it transforms death's knowability.

---

[1] Here and throughout this book, unless otherwise indicated, Greek text is taken from the most recent OCT, line references are to the text as printed in the OCT, and translations are my own.

[2] Adapted from Díez de Velasco (1995: 11): 'La muerte, realidad experiencial pero no experimentable...' See further McManners (1981: 1).

2 FIGURING DEATH IN CLASSICAL ATHENS

Today, we might call what happened to Er a 'near-death experience', a phenomenon that scientists are taking increasingly seriously.[3] There is no question that such experiences can be profoundly life changing for those that have them and can reset expectations for death. But what about everyone else? For all their frequency, stories such as Er's are not the norm. The many must trust the statements of the miraculous few. This raises problems of communicability, reliability, transferability, and so on. Even if one person can grasp what it was like for another to die (itself a problematic idea), how can they verify that information? And how confident can they be that their own death will be similar?

Contemporary studies are grappling with these tensions.[4] But a similarly sophisticated exploration can be found in the myth of Er, specifically in how Plato has Socrates tell the story.[5] The epistemological implications of this section of the *Republic* have received limited attention in scholarship[6] but they are central to our understanding of not just Plato's thinking on death in *Republic* 10 but also his thinking on knowability and exploratory thought.

Er represents the quintessential privileged narrator—the witness permitted a peek behind the veil of death. But his experience is explicitly and emphatically presented as a story. Socrates describes it as a tale: first as an ἀπόλογος (614b2), later as a μῦθος (621b8).[7] This tale is part of a longer one narrated by Socrates,

---

[3] Note Fischer and Mitchell-Yellin (2016: esp. 4–5 on the myth of Er); Moody (2022: 8–76, with discussion of the myth of Er at 82) [1975]; research associated with the International Association for Near-Death Studies (IANDS). On 'second-fated ones' (those who are thought to be dead but turn out to be alive), see Garland (2001: 100–1) [1985]. See further Jackson Knight (1970: 63–4, 79, 92) on evidence for belief in ancient Greece that direct experience of the other world was possible.

[4] See especially Fischer and Mitchell-Yellin (2016), with critique in, for instance, Mays and Mays (2017).

[5] Fischer and Mitchell-Yellin (2016: 5) also emphasize the myth's framing as a '[story that serves] to prepare us for rational argumentation' rather than as an insight into reality (as a similar experience might be understood today). See further Benzi (2021) on Parmenides and the truth value of katabasis narratives.

[6] Most important is Halliwell (2007: esp. 448–50, 458, 460, 471–2) on layering and diegetic ambiguity in Plato's writing of this myth and the resulting uncertainty, 'a silence that is both dramatic and metaphysical'. He notes Er's dubious claim to authority, which Socrates must take for granted (458). See further Morgan (2000: 204–10, esp. 209): Kathryn Morgan emphasizes the 'self-qualification' of the myth in part as a 'tale told by someone else' and proposes that this is 'a way of stressing the difficulty of talking about the metaphysical'. Also notable are Tarrant (1955b: 223) and Thayer (1988: esp. 369, 371, 376). Dorothy Tarrant observes (on Socrates' relation of Er's report), 'the oblique construction enhances the impression of tidings from afar'. She does not elaborate on the problems that this distance might raise. H. S. Thayer opens his article with the statement 'The myth of Er is a story within a story' and a distinction between the temporalities of different Socrateses in the *Republic*. But his purpose is to position the *Republic* and Socrates, by analogy with the myth and Er, as a reliable handbook and messenger to guide us in our pursuit of knowledge and virtue. See further Lloyd (1987: 9–11) on the explicit mythological basis to Plato's eschatological accounts.

[7] On the status of myth and μῦθοι in Plato, see especially Segal (1978); Smith (1985); Halliwell (1988: 17–19); Moors (1988); Brisson (1998) [1982]; Murray (1999); Morgan (2000: chs 5–8); Halliwell (2007: 452–6); Collobert et al. (2012). A Platonic μῦθος is an important form of argument. See further page 44, note 85.

the tale of a conversation he once had with, among others, Glaucon, during which he recounted the story of Er. The story within a story itself contains many stories: Er bases the first part of his own account on stories told by the souls that he met in the afterlife of *their* experiences and sights, stories that he has been forced to abbreviate ($\tau\grave{o}$ δ' $o\mathring{v}\nu$ $\kappa\epsilon\phi\acute{a}\lambda\alpha\iota o\nu$, 615a6) because 'they would take a long time to describe' ($\pi o\lambda\lambda o\hat{v}$ $\chi\rho\acute{o}\nu ov$ $\delta\iota\eta\gamma\acute{\eta}\sigma\alpha\sigma\theta\alpha\iota$, 615a5–6). And all these stories are told, ultimately, by the writer-narrator: Plato.

The layer upon layer of storytellers emphasizes the distance that stands between the situation of the living and experience of death. Even Er falls victim to that distance. Beyond the momentous information (given somewhat in passing) that his soul went out of him but continued to exist (614b8–c1), much of the insight into death, or what happens after death, that he offers is not based on experience but on observation: on listening and watching. In fact, this is specifically what he is instructed to do by the judges of the dead (614d1–3). The messenger from the world of the dead is, essentially, a witness, albeit of more than most mortals ever get to see. The ecphrastic set-up (whereby Plato's Socrates reports Er's account of an experience that is, in turn, marked by exteriority from the object of knowledge) reflects and models the epistemological challenge posed by death: for the living, dying and death are processes and events to be extrapolated from outside observation of another's experience.[8]

Emphasis upon the perspectives of the living is supported by the pervasive idea that death is a process—a concept emphasized in scholarship on death in ancient Greece, notably in Robert Garland's *The Greek Way of Death*.[9] Garland's principle is that the process of death in ancient Greece spanned a period from the onset of dying until the settling of the soul in the underworld. This process would include the point at which a body, such as the body of Er, was placed upon the pyre. A similar emphasis on process is given in anthropological models that explore patterns governing how the living deal with death: death and responses to it, like other rites of passage such as birth and marriage, involve phases of separation, transition, and incorporation and themes of continuation and regeneration.[10] Indeed, death is also considered a process today. A growing area of medical attention is in palliative or 'end of life' care. This development empha-

---

[8] On the difference, otherness, desire, distance, and absence that runs through ecphrasis, see Mitchell (1994: 151–81); Elsner (2004); Shapiro (2007). See further Bronfen and Goodwin (1993: 7–8) on the absence at stake in death and representation.

[9] Garland (2001: 13–20) [1985]. At 14–16, Garland cites the same examples that I explore in this book (the deaths of Socrates, Ajax, and Oedipus) but focuses on preparations for death rather than the point of transition. See further Vermeule (1979: 2).

[10] See especially Hertz (1960: 25–86); Van Gennep (2004: 146–65) [1960]. See further Bloch and Parry (1982); Metcalf and Huntington (1991) [1979]. See Engelke (2019) for a recent review of the anthropology of death (and its concern with materiality).

4 FIGURING DEATH IN CLASSICAL ATHENS

sizes that dying includes not just the final moment, the 'time of death' but also the process of reaching it. More broadly, a variety of interests and practices fall within the remit of the modern science of thanatology, ranging from what happens to a body during and after death to the psychological aspects of grief and loss. For specialists, patients, and the bereaved, death is one moment in a process of dying.

But the instance of death does matter, and to insist exclusively on the process of death dodges a vital existential question: at any given point in time is someone (Er, for instance) dead or alive? This is prima facie a simple question but people in Classical Athens (like people today) did worry about it—remember the Chorus's perplexity in the *Alcestis*.[11] Conceptually, there must be a moment of death within its process, a moment, as it were, when the scales tip.[12] This elusive moment is the sort of death, or dying, in which this book is interested—death as an event, the cessation of life,[13] the switch from living to dead, a vanishing point.[14]

The myth of Er, for instance, distinguishes between what is observable by the living and the occurrence of an essential change. It is significant that, according to Socrates' account, there was something about Er that might have suggested to the living that he had not 'died' by ordinary criteria: his body was still intact after ten days unlike the other bodies, which had visibly transformed into decomposing corpses. But absence of decay was not sufficient to dissuade his family from placing him upon the pyre for cremation. Unfortunately, death could not reliably be assessed empirically. Instead, the event of death was determined by cultural agreement. In Er's case, society's opinion was incorrect. The near miss highlights an essential point: encounters with Er's death are specifically *lived* encounters—not encounters with dying, so much as encounters with *someone else* dying. For the living, death is hard to see and hard to know.

II. THIS BOOK: A HISTORY OF CULTURAL THINKING

I have opened this chapter with an extract from Plato and an epistemological problem. This problem might, conceivably, be framed in transhistorical terms:

[11] Discussed in the Prologue. Philosophers, scientists, and lawyers still disagree on when death occurs: cardiac failure; brainstem death; 'higher brain' death...Arguably, the instance of 'death' is just as much of a mystery as it ever has been. Practically, 'time of death' is determined by a doctor (or pathologist) based on a range of observable criteria.

[12] Though Garland acknowledges that 'the "spirit" departed instantly from the body', he focuses on the 'state of transfer or flux' in which it for some time remained: Garland (2001: 13) [1985].

[13] Note Vermeule (1979: 37) on death as a cessation in early Greece.

[14] The artistic challenge of the *moment* of death is the subject of a brief chapter by Stampolidēs (2014). Nicholas Stampolidēs draws attention both to the difficulty of knowing death—and, especially, recognizing its moment—and the challenge of depicting it in art (but he does not discuss the epistemological thinking that crystallizes in such artistic representations).

how could any living person ever *know* what death is like? But this is not a philosophy book (or, at least, not a traditional philosophy book). It is a cultural history. Having said that, this is also not a collation of or enquiry into what ancient Athenians thought or believed about the event or experience of death (although I do hope that readers will glean some ideas from my discussion). Rather, my goal is to build a picture of how Athenian visual and verbal culture helped Athenians grapple with death and its knowability.

To use Plato's myth of Er as an example, this book's purpose is to probe how Plato turns attention upon the difficulty of knowing what happens when we die by presenting a myth shrouded in layer upon layer of distance. This is a different angle from that often adopted by ancient philosophers or philologists towards this section of the *Republic*.[15] What Plato might or might not have been saying about the afterlife, the soul, the cosmos, virtue, or justice is not at issue here. I am interested in the thanatological and epistemological thinking that crystallizes upon encountering death in his text, a text that is a web of messenger speeches with claims to privileged insight.[16]

Moreover—and this is crucial—I am not purely interested in philosophers' texts. The principal claim made by this book is that a whole range of visual and literary artefacts—plays, pots, temples, and histories as well as philosophical literature—mediated thanatological enquiry in the Classical period. Exploratory thought—'what is death?', 'what is it like to die?', and 'how do I know?'—was not left to the likes of Plato. It was not confined to a group of elite thinkers and to the texts that they produced, texts that were self-consciously philosophical or that made death the explicit focus of enquiry. Conceptualization of death came

---

[15] For obvious reasons, much commentary on the myth of Er has focused on how it connects to discussions in the wider *Republic* about justice and poetry and on its description of the workings of the universe and the fate and rebirth of the soul. See, for example, Richardson (1926) and Morrison (1955) on the structure of the universe; White (1979: 263–4) on the myth's message regarding the punishment of injustice and reward for justice after death; Moors (1988: 219–20, 240–7) on the lessons of the myth vis-à-vis opinion and knowledge; Bouvier (2001: 37–42) on the contribution of the myth to a discourse on mimesis and education; McPherran (2010) on the myth as an allegory for life and the ethical choices we must make (Stewart (1960: 146–78) [1905: 169–72] and Annas (1981: 351–3) similarly emphasized the educational force of the myth with respect to the choices made in life, though John Alexander Stewart, an Oxford professor, framed the myth in terms of 'liberal education' for a man's life of choices and Julia Annas criticized the 'lame and messy ending').

[16] Indeed, though Plato's audience is not overtly primed for thanatological and epistemological discourse in this myth, there are several features of the *Republic* that make death, descent, and knowledge acquisition a running theme. As others have emphasized, there is a running parallel between the katabasis of the myth of Er and the philosophical and mythical katabasis that is the wider *Republic* (and, indeed, the ascent from/descent into the cave in Book 7 and other mythological katabases such as that of Odysseus) and the dialogue opens with an old man that is close to death (Cephalus) and the word κατέβην. See especially Albinus (1998), with Segal (1978: esp. 323–4); Clay (1992: 127–8); Bakewell (2020: esp. 738–9). Geoffrey Bakewell draws out topographical details that might knit closer together the journeys made by Er and Socrates through lands of the dead (the road to the Piraeus passed through the Kerameikos).

6 FIGURING DEATH IN CLASSICAL ATHENS

out of cultural interactions, out of conversations between individuals and artefacts in a variety of contexts across Athens.[17] Artefacts shaped ideas, constructed cultural attitudes, and involved Athenians in processes of exploratory thought. These visual and literary explorations were often reflexive: they generated and shaped epistemological reflections on the imaginative nature of thinking about death—upon the immediate and wider cultural frameworks within which such imaginative processes took place.[18] This claim is, in some ways, a philosophical one: it is concerned with art and literature and the active role they play in exploratory thought. It emphasizes the reflections prompted by the formal features of visual and verbal culture, and so the ways in which different media might mediate thinking differently.

Combine this claim with my existential subject matter and things start to look increasingly transhistorical. Is Classical Athens just a case study here? My answer, in short, is no. The second claim made by this book is that, if we situate this phenomenon of artefact-mediated thanatology within a cultural-intellectual-historical framework, we can develop a deeper impression of how thinking about death is culturally defined.[19] What makes Classical Athens a fertile period for this enquiry is the sheer number of forms of art and literature that emerge (albeit not exclusively, or even first, in Athens): the range of distinctive media, several of which constitute new enduring genres, is peculiarly conducive to comparative study.[20] In this respect, the picture that I build in this book contributes to a history of what ancient Athenians, specifically Classical Athenians, were interested in *and how they thought about it*—a history of cultural thinking.

[17] This claim is in tune with Clifford and Buxton (2024a), which offers a key backdrop here. Also relevant is Lakoff and Johnson (2003) [1980] and work on object-mediated meditation.

[18] See Fearn (2024a) on the reflection provoked by Gorgias' *Helen* on the cultural media through which imaginative processes function with Clifford and Buxton (2024a) more generally.

[19] Important here is work on 'visuality'—a way of seeing that is permitted and shaped by cultural conditions. See especially Berger (1972); Baxandall (1988) [1972]; Bryson (1988). The latter is discussed in Petridou (2013: 311–12); see note 5 of Petridou's chapter for further bibliography on visuality. Petridou's discussion of 'ritual-centred' encounters with the divine (drawing upon Elsner (2007: xvi–xvii, and 1–26, esp. 25) and other work on ancient Greek visuality such as I. Rutherford (1995); Elsner (1996); Goldhill (1996: esp. 18–21); Platt (2011)), spotlights one site of encounter with death (or, rather, the afterlife) in Classical Athens—the Eleusinian mysteries: I do not discuss the mysteries in this book but they offer an important example from this period of a context in which knowability, specifically knowability of what happens after death (otherwise unknown-unseen), is explored through visuality.

[20] Nevertheless, focusing on Athens raises not just the problem of methodological exemplarity (see below) but polemics surrounding a Western tradition of exemplary classicism. The history, present, and future of the discipline of Classics is under scrutiny, with critical attention falling not just upon the hierarchies and boundaries of the discipline (questions of canonicity, for instance) but also upon its cultural, political, and ideological reverberations and its relationships with white supremacy, power structures, and colonization. See for example: Goff (2005) on Classics and colonialism; Vasunia (2013) on the relationship between the British Empire in India and the discipline of Classics; Formisano and Kraus (2018) on the implications of canonicity for the discipline; Zuckerberg (2018) on the reception of classical antiquity within an online far-right community.

III. VISUAL AND LITERARY CONVERSATIONS

How, then, did a pot, or a play, construct ideas about what death is and might be like? Did they do it differently? Were Athenians aware of the cultural and imaginative frameworks that underpinned this thinking? Did they worry not just about death but whether (and how) they could figure it out?

Over the course of this book, I respond to these questions by looking closely at a range of artefacts drawn from the Classical period of Athens. Five chapters cover five media and genres—literary philosophy, painted pots, tragic drama, temple sculpture, and historiography—homing in on one or two examples in each case. Throughout, my discussion has two strands. First, how any given artefact generates encounters with death. Second, how that artefact prompts meditation on the imaginative processes involved in exploring death from the perspective of the living.

The range of media is deliberately varied. It enables me to offer media-oriented answers to the questions outlined above and, by setting one chapter alongside another, to spotlight how each medium might mediate thinking differently. This goal underpins the arrangement of my chapters, which present the material out of chronological order—beginning with Plato's famous dialogue about the death of Socrates, the *Phaedo*, written in the first half of the fourth century (probably *c.* 380 BCE), at the end of the period that I examine. The chapter arrangement (alternating visual and literary) highlights the multi-media focus of the book and prioritizes verbal-visual dialogue, facilitated by three discursive interludes—two set amidst the chapters and one positioned at the end. These 'conversations' open space for a more integrated look at how different media might work in different ways; this is where I probe not just conversations between artefacts and people but also conversations between artefacts and across disciplines.[21] In this respect, the book offers a new angle to the focus of this 'Visual Conversations in Art and Archaeology' series on comparative conversation across different cultures by offering a comparative conversation between art and text within a defined culture—Classical Athens.

---

[21] To some extent selection and categorization by medium reinforces disciplinary boundaries by presenting, for example, Plato's Phaedo's account of Socrates' death and Sophocles' Messenger's account of Oedipus' death as different objects for analysis and comparison because the one is branded philosophy and the other theatre-literature. This shapes the cultural picture around not just matter, form, and context, but also existing specialisms within Classics, rather than, say, audience, real/mythical, public/private, male/female, or some other (in)conceivable differentiation. (I note here especially Foucault (2002: xvi) [1966] on 'what it is impossible to think' and his intellectual legacy—since Michel Foucault, it is impossible not to think of the cultural systems that order our lives and ideas. However, see Güthenke and Holmes (2018) for reflections on the parameters of the discipline and optimistic suggestions for its reconceptualization.)

Nevertheless, it is worth thinking about what might emerge were my chapters reshuffled to reflect a chronological sequence. Conceivably, we could detect changes in epistemological attitudes to death within the Classical period.[22] It is surely significant, for instance, that Plato comes at the end of the period—not least because we can situate him within a culture that thought with art and text, to which he responded in his own literary medium, rather than thinking of him as a radical pioneer of a new approach. Might it also be material that the temple of Athena Nike, covered in death, was largely (probably wholly) constructed during the Peloponnesian war and not many years after the plague? My chapter on pots, especially, offers a sense of changes in content and form over time, while my first intermediary chapter (Conversation Two) introduces an Archaic backdrop. Over the course of the book, I attend to this more historical angle and probe some ways in which we might understand the phenomena discussed as situated not just within a period known as the 'Classical' but also within tighter timeframes marked by historical events.

The possibility of telling a historical story as well as a media-oriented one draws attention to the selectivity that is multiply at play in this book. In the first place, my chapters cover only a fraction of the range of media available for study from a period of one hundred years or so, and so offer a curated sample of cultural encounters with death.[23] Moreover, in each chapter I concentrate upon one or a few examples: one of Plato's dialogues in a chapter on literary philosophy; a limited selection of cups and oil flasks; one of Sophocles' plays in a chapter on tragic drama; one bit of a temple; an extract that covers plague from Thucydides' history of the Peloponnesian War. Selectivity is essential to enable detailed probing into the interactions between visual and literary culture and its viewers, handlers, listeners, and readers. One flipside is that a rigorously chronological approach is difficult to achieve and even, conceivably, misleading, especially because much of my material clusters around a couple of decades and precise dating of the pots must be treated with caution. The chapter arrangement has advantages in this respect, in that it presents a picture of culturally mediated thinking (including epistemological thinking) as a widespread phenomenon in Classical Athens without giving the impression of a story with overly neat teleology.[24]

---

[22] Such changes need not be conceptualized as developments in an evolutionary sense. For a larger-scale evolutionary approach (spanning a period of two million years or so, and not focusing on Graeco-Roman antiquity) see Kellehear (2007), who explores how large-scale transformations in social environment have influenced the recognition and experience of dying.

[23] Noticeably missing, to name a few, are studies of funerary monuments and inscriptions, lyric poetry, archaeological sites, lawcourt speeches, and other drama such as comedy.

[24] This formulation (picture versus story) taps into a long and fraught debate on the relative properties and strengths of the visual and verbal arts, as epitomized in Lessing (1984) [1766] and his legacy (on which see Lifschitz and Squire (2017)).

CONVERSATION ONE 9

In addition, what selection puts pressure on and accentuates is the exemplarity inherent not just in studies of the ancient world but also in our relationships with antiquity and, from the point of view of my topic, our relationships with death. To what extent can one example (or a selection of examples) stand for the group, whether one pot for the corpus, or an assortment of works for the totality of Classical Athenian production? And how great is the distance between my inter-actions with a selection of texts and material culture over the last few years and the relations they have had not just in Classical Athens but in times and places since?[25] Exemplarity has different repercussions in each chapter. Whereas *Oedipus at Colonus* was designed to be performed, and was actually performed, for the polis, and so was placed under the scrutiny of thousands of pairs of Athenian eyes and ears, one pot might have been viewed by only a few.[26] And whereas a text such as the *Phaedo* was selected, preserved, treasured by generations of scholars from antiquity to the present, some pots survived by accident or, if intentionally preserved in a grave, may have resurfaced fortuitously (though some ancient plays, especially fragments of plays, have also survived by chance).[27] Then there is the selectivity inherent in looking at one part of a whole: part of a temple; part of a history (though this point could be made more extensively, since the text of *Oedipus at Colonus* represents only a part of a drama—excluding music, props, and dance, for instance—and the play itself represents one of four submitted by Sophocles, and so on, and a pot might be a part of a polymorphous set, gathered, used, or arranged for a symposium or burial).

[25] The distance between our perspectives and preconceptions and those of ancient Athenians has been much emphasized and is relevant in all areas of engagement with the ancient world. For a classic meth-odological reflection on the problem of distance in the study of ancient Greek attitudes to death, see Sourvinou-Inwood (1995: 1–9). Compare Neer (2010: 12–13) in support of comprehensive close analy-sis: 'Whose eyes should we use if not our own?' (page 13). For another evocative framing that emphasizes the imaginative nature of art and scholarship, see Vermeule (1979: 4): 'Poets, critics, historians, archae-ologists, artists spend their working lives as necromancers, raising the dead in order to enter into their imaginations and experience . . .' (Indeed, this formulation draws attention to a parallel between (imagina-tive) classical study and (imaginative) attempts by the living to know death from the outside.) See further Goldhill (2012: 3–9) on the challenge of integrating detailed readings of Sophocles with an appreciation of the rich history that shapes our reception of his work.

[26] In fact, in both cases, encounters might take place at individual and collective levels. It is widely emphasized, for example, that Greek tragedy appealed not just to the audience as individual members but also as a citizenry; see e.g. Goldhill (1987) on the Great Dionysia context and (2000) on the increasing nexus between viewing and politics of the course of the fifth century (the citizen as viewer/spectator, θεατής). See further Budelmann (2000a: ch. 1) on how Sophocles' language challenges spectators and so generates a collective response qua audience. The extent to which a pot invited a collective response would have depended, in part, upon its type; a krater, for instance, was a shared object, used and seen by symposiasts as a group as well as individually.

[27] See Elsner (2017) on the impact of transmission on our reception of the ancient world. See further Elsner (2015) on the different hermeneutic challenges presented by words and images in antiquity.

10 FIGURING DEATH IN CLASSICAL ATHENS

The disjuncture between generality and particularity is characteristic of classical study.[28] What is particularly stimulating in the context of this book is that the exemplarity at play in my methodology itself probes the epistemological problem at the heart of my subject matter by enacting the possibilities and limitations of an empirical approach. To what extent can one person's death, whether in real life or in art, stand for all deaths, for death in general? Can we compare one death with another or is every death idiosyncratic? These are anxieties raised by movement from the specific to the general; they overshadow attempts to formulate an argument based on selective evidence just as much as attempts to figure out death by studying other people.

IV. CLASSICAL ATHENS—GOLDEN AGE, AGE OF DEATH

At this point, let us turn to the focus of my study—Classical Athens (broadly conceived, to encompass late Archaic/early Classical to early fourth-century material).[29] Concentration upon this culture and period permits me to offer not just a theoretical picture of how different media mediate thinking but also a culturally situated one. What might we make of the cultural-historical story told collectively by my chapters?

The political-intellectual-cultural framework within which the media that I examine were situated is significant—in both a wide sense and a narrow one. Wide in that interest in subject–object relations, epistemology, and the irrational aspects of death had long been a feature of Greek culture.[30] Narrow in that the

[28] On exemplarity and our reception of the Graeco-Roman world, see Goldhill (1994), (2017); Güthenke (2020). For scholarship more generally on exemplarity in the Graeco-Roman world and tension between the general and particular, see Cairns (2014); Langlands (2015), (2018); Lowrie and Lüdemann (2015); Newby (2016: esp. 3–4, 320–47); Roller (2015), (2018: esp. 4–23); Rood et al. (2020: 145–68).

[29] The 'Classical period' is, in any case, a construct—useful for communication and study but ultimately more revealing of a disciplinary history than a real segment of time and practice, especially from the point of view of those who lived during it. For some recent critiques of periodization see Kotsonas (2016), an archaeologist of the early Greek world, on its political implications, and Adornato (2019), who, 'like the ancient writers', favours continuity ('development is gradual and uneven'). See further Morris (1997: esp. 96–9), (2000: 77–106); Strauss (1997). The pieces by Ian Morris are discussed by Antonis Kotsonas and cited with additional bibliography in note 14 of his article.

[30] Presocratic interest in subject–object relations and epistemology: Guthrie (1962: 395–401) on Xenophanes; Guthrie (1965: 71–7, 242–3, 319–20, 454–65) on Parmenides, Empedocles, Anaxagoras, and Democritus; Hussey (1990); Laks (1999: 255–62); Lescher (1999), (2008); Prince (2006: 436–8); Curd (2020). There has been considerable work on vision and viewing in the Greek world: see especially Blundell et al. (2013); Squire (2016b), especially chapters by Kelli Rudolph (2016), Michael Squire (2016a: esp. 13), Jeremy Tanner (2016), and Susanne Turner (2016: 149–55). The irrational aspects of death in prehistoric and Archaic culture: Vermeule (1979).

years that span the end of the Archaic period into the Classical saw new visual and literary forms, opening up new forms of subjectivity: this is the so-called Greek Revolution, a term usually (if at all) applied to a transformation in visual art but which has been linked to cultural transformations more broadly—in the theatre and lawcourts, for instance.[31] Debate between people with different perspectives (thus together staging uncertainty) features prominently not just in visual and literary media of the Classical period but also in political and legal decision-making. The fifth century was a time of intense creative and intellectual activity, interest in knowability (especially through the senses) and subjectivity and changing attitudes towards death and funerary practices. These were also years on the cusp of more explicitly theoretical enquiry into the imagination (that of Plato and Aristotle).[32] All this frames the artefacts that I discuss in this book and variously resurfaces in my chapters. Below, I elaborate upon three core aspects of the fifth-century climate—political, intellectual, and cultural.

Particularly significant in the context of this book are the implications of fifth-century politics for notional and experienced identity—especially anxieties surrounding particularity and generality. It is often emphasized, for instance, that Athenians went to the theatre as citizens of the democratic polis—in their capacity qua collective citizenry.[33] However, drama appealed to its audience not just as citizens but also as people—members of another collective known as humanity;[34] as members of other intersecting social groups such as those defined by gender, religion, status, and so on; and as individuals. Fifth-century Athens, with its emphasis upon the collective of the demos, put multifaceted identities under a new sort of stress—a particular experience of simultaneous difference and sameness, possibly one of disempowerment and invisibility.[35] And, whether for the dying or the bereaved, death is one site where these tensions come to the fore. Sophocles' *Antigone* famously staged the conflict between facets of identity (exacerbated, notably, by proximity to death), and we find a similar phenomenon

---

[31] Elsner (2006) is key here. See further Elsner and Squire (2024: 309–15).

[32] See now Clifford and Buxton (2024a). [33] See note 26.

[34] Notable here is Loraux (2002: 87–90).

[35] On the plurality of identity (and 'competing affiliations'), see Sen (2006: esp. xi–xiv, 3–5, 23–8). I also draw here on black feminist thought, specifically on 'intersectionality'—a theory of marginalized subjectivity that is, at its roots, particular to the lived experiences of women of colour (note the Crunk Feminist Collective (2010): 'intersectionality without women of colour is a train wreck'): see for example Crenshaw (1989), (1991); Collins (2000: 21–43) [1990]; The Combahee River Collective (2014) [1978]; Cooper (2016); Nash (2019: esp. 1–32). A similar theory could, more generally, give visibility to the way in which some Athenians might have been marginalized by the systems of power that purported to represent them.

12 FIGURING DEATH IN CLASSICAL ATHENS

in the Athenian lawcourts, where what was actually seen and imagined to be seen during a speech was influential upon the formation of a concept of justice in general and the just decision in particular by jurymen, individually and as a collective.[36] Indeed, laws and norms surrounding funerary practices in the fifth century threw multifaceted identities into sharp and distressing relief: emphasis upon collective celebration and burial of the war dead,[37] in contrast to the individualized, family-oriented honour granted to warriors such as Kroisos in the sixth century BCE,[38] made death a matter of politics, power, and identity.[39] For others, too, notably women and children, funerary expenditure and display were curtailed—gravestones with figural decoration reduce in number from *c.* 500 BCE and then practically disappear from the material record between *c.* 480 and 430 BCE and later sources suggest that so-called 'sumptuary laws' may have restricted fifth-century behaviours in private burials.[40] When it came to death, a crisis personal and emotional yet also communal, tensions between particularity and generality were political *and* epistemological: politics negotiated who died, who mourned, and how; epistemology negotiated whether one woman might know from another's example (in art or life) anything about death in general—thinking about death (and anxieties about that thinking) in Classical Athens was shaped by a Classically Athenian politics.

Indeed, knowability, and especially perception-based knowability, is an important theme in this period. Though interest in the senses and the role they might play in knowledge—and so in the relativity of knowledge—is discernible outside Athens and before the fifth century, it continues to perplex in this period and is a defining feature of the intellectual climate, notably among the sophists.[41]

---

[36] Explored in Westwood (2024). Consider how much was at stake in this process in a murder trial or where death might be the penalty.

[37] Stupperich (1977: 4–56); Loraux (1986a); Arrington (2015: esp. 33–8).

[38] The marble funerary monument of Kroisos, also known as the 'Anavyssos kouros', is held in the National Archaeological Museum of Athens (NM 3851) with an inscribed base that is widely believed to have belonged to it (NM 4754). Nearly two metres high, it is dated to *c.* 530–520 BCE. See Jeffery (1962: 143–4, no. 57); Richter (1963: fig. 82) [1959], (1970: 118–19, figs. 395–8, 400–1, no. 136) [1942]; Karouzou (1968: 29–30); Boardman (1978: fig. 107); Osborne (1988: 6–9); Stewart (1997: 63–70, fig. 38); Elsner (2006: 73–86); Arrington (2015: 27–33). See Figure 2.5.

[39] The interrelationship between death, politics, power, and identity in this century is not unprecedented but it is different: see Stewart (1997: 68–70) on sixth-century BCE civil strife as a backdrop to the Attic kouros.

[40] See Kurtz and Boardman (1971: 89–90, 121–32); Garland (1989: esp. 3–8), (2001: 21–3) [1985]; Arrington (2015: 51–2).

[41] See, for instance, Thumiger (2013), who argues for a shift during the Classical period, with greater epistemological anxiety surrounding the perceiving subject and the perceived world in the second half of the century (in Sophocles and Euripides, in contrast to Aeschylus). See further Segal (2019) [1971]. On the sophists and the relativity of knowledge, see Guthrie (1969: 176–203); Prince (2006: 444–7); Taylor and Lee (2020). Anxiety regarding perception-based knowability is also a major feature of Plato's philosophy: see Nightingale (2016: 58–62) for an overview.

Consider the emphasis on empiricism in Hippocratic texts and Thucydides' methodological reflections on the relationship between perception and knowledge.[42] The emphasis is laced with anxiety—an awareness, for instance, that the inner workings of a body are hidden and mysterious and that there may be a mismatch between symptom and subject.[43] Though the discipline of Classics has rightly become more cautious about articulating the intellectual climate of fifth-century Athens as a 'revolution', 'evolution', or 'birth' in any sort of teleological or instantaneous sense, it is widely recognized that the Classical period reveals acute interest in knowledge formation.[44] Such interest constitutes an essential backdrop to this book. Indeed, death is, in some respects, one prism through which to examine more widespread epistemological reflection in this period on the relationship between the knowable and unknowable. The problem posed by death is an example (albeit a particularly troubling one) of a wider existential problem: how to extrapolate experience from observation, as well as the general from the specific.

These political and intellectual circumstances in Classical Athens were embedded in a wider cultural transformation, and the combination is significant. From the sixth century onwards, Classical Athens saw the emergence and popularity of new forms of verbal and visual media such as prose, drama, and large-scale bronze sculpture (new in this period to Athens, at least), as well as developments in the style and subject matter of existing media such as lyric poetry, painted pottery, and sculpted stone.[45] New styles across the Greek world are characterized by drama and immediacy; they present opportunities to encounter, in virtual reality as it were, another's embodied experience and interiority. A striking example—and germane to this subject of this book—is offered by the different impacts of the dying warriors on the east and west pediments of the temple of Aphaia at Aigina (Figures C1.1 and C1.2).[46]

---

[42] See pages 198 and 201.   [43] See Holmes (2010), (2018).

[44] See especially Lloyd (1987) for a nuanced view of what was and was not new in the Classical period (with reference to science and thought).

[45] For a broad overview of changes in thinking, technique, and politics in the fifth century BCE, not just in Athens but across the Greek world, see Lane Fox (2020: 1–6).

[46] See especially Walter-Karydi (2015: 130). See further e.g. Furtwängler et al. (1906: esp. 206–7, 224–5, 228–9, 252–4, 353–4, with plates 95, 96, 104, 105, 106); Invernizzi (1965: plates XIII.1, XIV.1, XX.2, XXI); Ridgway (1970: 13–17, esp. 17); Stewart (1990: 137–8, esp. 138, figs. 245–8). It seems possible that the temple was reconstructed after the Persian Wars, with both warriors dating to the 470s BCE: see especially Gill (1988b), (1993); Stewart (2008b: 593–7), (2013: 135–9); Eschbach (2013). Either way, the differences between the warriors exemplify the stylistic shift that occurred between the late sixth century and the fifth.

14 FIGURING DEATH IN CLASSICAL ATHENS

FIGURE C1.1. Dying warrior from the east pediment of the Temple of Aphaia at Aegina, *c.* 480 BCE. Glyptothek Museum, Munich. Image: Erin Babnik/Alamy Stock Photo.

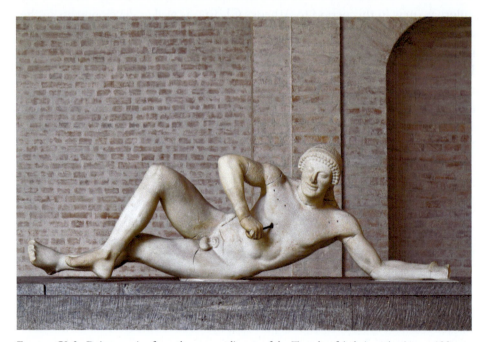

FIGURE C1.2. Dying warrior from the west pediment of the Temple of Aphaia at Aegina, *c.* 480 BCE. Glyptothek Museum, Munich. Image: Erin Babnik/Alamy Stock Photo.

The dying warrior on the east pediment of the temple of Aphaia on Aigina intrudes into the space of viewers; his muscles and veins are visible; his body is responsive; his face has turned away from viewers in apparent absorption in the reality of his situation (Figure C1.1).[47] This is, as Elena Walter-Karydi puts it, the 'bewusste Tod', the 'conscious death', and suggests an interest in embodied life and experience (including of death) that is mediated by changes in sculptural style, such as the advent of contrapposto.[48] Theatre, too, brings mythical characters to life and dramatizes their awareness of death: this is not an epic tale from the past but 'a (significant) day in the life of Oedipus', or Antigone, or Alcestis. Plato's dialogues unfurl discussions between historical figures in and around Athens.

Nevertheless, as Jaś Elsner has argued, it is possible to tell a different story by considering not just what was gained by new forms in fifth-century Athens but also what was lost (or less emphasized).[49] The changes that contribute to a heightened impression of lived experience (in that bodies appear to exist in, and to interact with, a virtual world) give sculpted, performed, painted, scripted figures and scenes an interiority that excludes the actual beholder. Viewers of the dying warrior on the east pediment (by contrast with the one on the west: Figure C1.2) are still emotionally, sensorily, ethically affected but their relationship with the 'dying' statue is also, in one important way, less direct: they are no longer invited to meet its gaze (Figures C1.1 and C1.2).[50] Their relationship is thus defined by a particular sort of exteriority, by their situation as observers ('voyeurs') of that body being in a world, rather than as acknowledged participants in that world.[51]

We might compare earlier efforts in Greek painting to show scenes realistically from the perspective of viewers by foreshortening limbs, as in Euphronios' depiction of Sarpedon's receding left leg on the red-figure calyx-krater in the Museo Nazionale Cerite (see Figure 4.9).[52] The details that make Sarpedon's

---

[47] See Neer and Kurke (2019: 70, fig. 2.23).   [48] Walter-Karydi (2015: esp. 127–34).

[49] Elsner (2006).

[50] The idea that viewers might have been invited to meet the frontal stare of a pediment statue is problematic, since the height of the pediment excludes any real possibility of meeting a gaze. Nevertheless, we can speak of the different relationships that the two warriors forge with the world of actual viewers; this would have been noticeable even from below. Indeed, the point need not be confined to the gaze; the whole body of the west warrior is frontally arranged, in contrast to that of the east warrior, which appears absorbed in its existential and physical situation without regard for viewers. Osborne (2000: esp. 230–5) emphasizes that pediments *in general* are confrontational spaces. See further Elsner (2006: 77). See, in contrast, Stewart (1997: 66–7) on how a kouros 'simply ignores you' and 'repels any direct advance'.

[51] For language of voyeurism, see Elsner (2006), with Elsner (2004: esp. 164–6) on Lacan, the desire that underpins the gaze, and the phantasized object.

[52] *BAPD* 187. See Stewart (2008a: 38–40) on the perceptual approach in Greek painting and 'the theatre of the real'.

16 FIGURING DEATH IN CLASSICAL ATHENS

body lifelike simultaneously define him as an object of observation.[53] This pot has been dated to the second half of the sixth century, demonstrating that stylistic choices, and the epistemological reflections that they raise, are not confined to a specific moment or place in time. But the point need not be that this was all new and different for all media at once and in the same way;[54] rather, the exteriority that is built into several forms that are new in the long Classical period (I am thinking not just of material culture but also the fourth wall in tragedy, layers of distance in Plato's dialogues, and the principles of empiricism that underpin historiography and Hippocratic writings) is an important part of the picture here—and might, in fact, draw closer attention to an exteriority that has long existed in other forms. Theoretically, it would have been possible to combine contrapposto with a direct interaction with the viewer: one can imagine a version of the dying warrior on the east pediment that looked outwards. Catching someone's eye (real or virtual) is existentially significant, and much of the new visual and verbal media of the Classical period does not do it.[55] Classical art invites viewers to imagine another's embodied experience—of dying, say—while grappling with the impossibility of knowing it from the outside—from the perspective of the living.

These developments spanned the Greek world, often first appearing outside Athens.[56] But the sum of Athens' parts was distinctively Athenian, and here we must also acknowledge specific historical circumstances. Death and existential risk frame this century—from the Persian invasions to the Peloponnesian War, the plague, and the execution of the notorious figure of Socrates in the wake of a bloody time under the Thirty Tyrants in 404–3 BCE.[57] Immediate historical

[53] I am grateful here to Hugo Shakeshaft, who shared his ideas on foreshortening and lifelikeness (currently unpublished) with me in conversation. See further Shakeshaft (2022: 30–1, 35).

[54] As Robin Osborne recently observed (2018: 249–50), 'real life' subject matter on fifth-century pots seems to invite *less* imaginative engagement than it did before: see further page 92, note 139. Others have complicated any sense of sudden change and questioned Athenocentric explanations for the so-called 'Greek Revolution' in art: see, for example, Borbein (2016: 141–5); Adornato (2019); Slawisch (2019). See further Vout (2014a) on key trends in scholarship on the 'Greek Revolution'.

[55] Some, of course, does, including parts of tragedy. The picture is not simple. But form matters and several forms in the Classical period seem to be in tune with intellectual interest in observation.

[56] See Lattimore (2006: 459–60) for a general overview. See further Bosher (2012), especially chapters by Kathryn Morgan (2012) and Andreas Willi (2012) on early Sicilian and South Italian performance culture. Note too Vernant (1982: 130–2) [1962] on the nexus between politics (the polis) and Greek rational thought: 'in the youthful science of the Ionians timeless Reason became incarnate in Time' (130); for Vernant, the origins of Greek thought were not peculiar to Athens or to the fifth century but to the polis. See further West (1971) on early Greek philosophy (though overstating the influence of foreign ideas—see the review in Kirk (1974)).

[57] Hanson (1989) is key here, especially part 5 on the aftermath of battle and the 'powerful, haunting image [left] in the minds of both soldier and civilian onlookers for years to come' (page xviii). See further Kern (1999: 140–54) on the increased brutality of siege warfare in the Peloponnesian War (by comparison with treatment of captured cities earlier in the century); Hanson (2005) on the distinctive, bloody,

deaths and disasters are thus a conspicuous backdrop. Moreover, though some of my material is drawn from earlier in the Classical period, the majority clusters around the tail-end of the fifth century and the beginning of the fourth. In these years death was urgently present for Athenians, both at an individual level and for the whole community. During the last decades of the fifth century, plague and war put the culture in existential crisis. All this comprises a distinctive framework within which we can locate the phenomenon of culturally mediated thinking that I explore here. It seems plausible that proximity to death brought a heightened interest in death and associated epistemological anxieties; this would also accord with the themes of war, death, resurrection, and immortality that have been observed in late fifth-century art.[58] In some ways, then, this book is a story of one culture's existential crisis, told through artefacts.

V. WHAT'S NEW ABOUT THIS?

Death has long commanded interest among classical scholars and the bibliography is wide ranging and vast.[59] Within its remit fall archaeological studies of funerary sites, material, and remains,[60] investigations into funerary rites and responses to death,[61] and histories of ancient ideas, attitudes, and beliefs, such as what happens after death.[62] Moreover, much of scholarship draws on funerary

---

desolating experience of the Peloponnesian War, especially pages 289–98 on reception of the war in classical scholarship—perceptions that it wrought the destruction of Greece/Athens/the glorious fifth century; Tritle (2007: 181–3) on the traumatic impact of war on the Greeks; Arrington (2015: 21–7) on the increased frequency and scale of military encounters in the fifth century. The account in Spiegel (1990), though largely descriptive (it explicitly treats literature 'as a faithful reflection of individual life and society'), gives an idea of how prevalent the desire for peace was in Classical Greek literature.

[58] See Palagia (2009b), especially chapters by Olga Palagia (2009a) and John Oakley (2009). Compare Griffin (2009: esp. 44–9, 90–5, 103–43) [1980] on death (and the gods) as a vibrant and dreadful fabric against and out of which the Homeric epics constitute their heroes.

[59] For an overview of trends in scholarship on death in the ancient Greek world, see Garland (2001: x–xvii, xxii–xxiii) [1985]; Mirto (2012: 155–67) [2007]. Maria Serena Mirto synthesizes a range of subjects and associated scholarship relating to ancient Greek death.

[60] For some recent archaeological approaches to death that draw on material from a range of places and times, see Tarlow and Stutz (2013). See further, on excavations of the ancient Athenian Kerameikos, Kübler (1976); Knigge (1991) [1988]; Kunze-Götte et al. (2000); Baziotopoulou-Valavani (2002).

[61] See, for example, Kurtz and Boardman (1971: esp. 91–161) on burial customs; Stupperich (1977) on the state funeral and private graves (against the political backdrop of Classical Athens); Shapiro (1991) on the iconography of mourning; Alexiou (2002) [1974] on the ritual lament. See further Garland (1989) on evidence and possible explanations for Greek funerary legislation.

[62] The focus of scholarship on ideas, attitudes, and beliefs relating to death in ancient Greece is usually not so much the event of death as its material, ritual, and other-worldly aftermath. Key studies that draw on ancient texts and material culture to explore Greek ideas about and attitudes towards death include Vermeule (1979); Sourvinou-Inwood (1987: esp. 150–1) (an interesting study in which she distinguishes images that present death from the perspectives of the self or the other), (1995); Garland (2001) [1985].

18 FIGURING DEATH IN CLASSICAL ATHENS

material not so much for what it might tell us about death but for what it might tell us about the living and socio-political-cultural discourse.[63] What all this work has in common with my focus is an interest in the living—in the relationships that living ancient Greeks had with death and the dead. In this respect, my book very much sits within this wide field, and the field provides an important backdrop to it.

One important point of difference between my study and much existing work on ancient Greek death is that I am interested not so much in what ancient Athenians did or thought about death as how they thought about it. Though the epistemological implications of death do surface in some of the above studies,

There are also more targeted monographs, such as Peifer (1989); Oakley (2004); Giudice (2015); Walter-Karydi (2015); Man (2020). Note further Sekita (2015). On belief in the 'soul' and the afterlife and ancient eschatological discourse see, for example, Rohde (1925); Bremmer (1983: 70–124); Díez de Velasco (1995); Albinus (2000); Edmonds (2004), (2011); Retief and Cilliers (2006: 44–8); Graf and Johnston (2013) [2007]; Marlow et al. (2021: esp. chs. 7, 8, 9, 10). See further Antonaccio (1995) on archaeological evidence for ancestor worship and hero cult. Notably, Radcliffe E. Edmonds III opens his book with the claim that the other world is made in a mirror image (of sorts) of the world of the living (2004: 2–3). Implicitly, what happens after death presents a similar, but not identical, epistemological challenge to the living as the event itself. Similarly, Francisco Díez de Velasco (1995) emphasizes the imaginary nature of ancient Greek articulations of the journey of the dead to the beyond; Harrisson (2019), too, approaches the afterlife as a product of the imagination but the volume is focused on *what* ancient Greeks imagined as opposed to how they went about that process and their epistemological reflections. On supernatural interactions between the living and the dead, see Johnston (1999); Ogden (2001), (2008: esp. chs. 8 and 9); Martin (2020). Sarah Iles Johnston does not delve into the epistemological anxiety that might have accompanied interactions between the living and the dead; this may in part be because she is concerned to counteract a neglect in the scholarship by embracing the possibility of irrational belief amongst the Greeks. Daniel Ogden, too, does not explore this possibility, though he acknowledges (in passing) that some might have condemned necromancy as fraudulent: Ogden (2001: 266–7).

[63] One of Ian Morris's contributions to death archaeology was a shift from more descriptive accounts of funerary material to large-scale consideration of how burial evidence (and the ritual system of which it comprised a part) might allow us to develop models of shifting social structure and perceptions of it: see especially Morris (1989) [1987], (1992). Note further Parker Pearson (2003: 3) [1999], whose book 'is not so much about the dead themselves as the living who buried them'. Compare the approach in Robb (2013), who notes 'We have not had an "archaeology of dying" or even an "archaeology of death"; we have had an archaeology of already dead persons' (page 442): John Robb's chapter proposes an archaeological approach to the problem of what dying is and means—exploring dying as a social process of collaboration between the living and dying. Some further examples that use mortuary evidence to access the (historical) living include Humphreys (1980) on what tombs and burial layouts might reveal about the priorities of the living vis-à-vis the community or the family; Houby-Nielsen (1995) on the expression of age and gender ideologies in burial practice in the Archaic and Classical Kerameikos; Snodgrass (1998: 40–1) on what rural burial might reveal about relationships between the living and the land; Gray (2011) on the insights funerary evidence might give into the experience of being Milesians, an ethnic minority community, in Hellenistic and Roman Athens; Sjöberg (2019) on how the prothesis constructed social identities. Particularly interesting in the context of this book is Loraux (1982), (1986a: esp. 328–38) [1981]: though she was more interested in life than in death (specifically in the constitution of an Athenian idea of Athens), she explored the generative power of the funeral speech and the intersection between a cultural form and the imagination.

they are rarely the focus. In Christiane Sourvinou-Inwood's study *Reading Greek Death to the End of the Classical Period*, for instance, she draws attention to the mediated nature of the account of the underworld in Book 11 of the *Odyssey*, but her purpose is to contrast it with the comparatively direct account in Book 24 (where events are recounted by the poet with no intermediary narrator).[64] The contrast supports her argument that shifting beliefs in and attitudes towards death are recoverable from the Homeric epics. A key difference between her purpose and mine, then, is that she was interested in where Athenians got to on death; I am interested in how they got there.

Specifically, I am interested in a culturally mediated epistemology of death, in the role played by culture in generating and shaping explorations of death and in provoking reflections upon that process. In this respect, it is not aspects of death, attitudes to death, or responses to death that are at the centre of this book but rather the verbal and visual culture itself and what it does. This is where a divergence in subject matter overlaps with a divergence in methodology—a difference in treatment of the material.

The driving interest of many studies of death in ancient Greece is in the representational properties of ancient material: they are interested in what it can reveal about ancient customs, attitudes, or beliefs (images and texts as reflective of norms, structures, and ideas) as opposed to the more generative role that culture has in mediating thought, in shaping ideas and involving Athenians in processes of meditation.[65] Culture is a source rather than a point of encounter. In this respect, more similar to mine in approach is work by Nathan Arrington, Nathaniel Jones, Carl Knappett, Michael Squire, and Elena Walter-Karydi on material culture, by Karen Bassi and Victoria Wohl on text, and by Seth Estrin on the two.[66]

---

[64] Sourvinou-Inwood (1995: 14–16, 99) on Homer's oblique articulation of the 'unseeable realm of death' in Odysseus' narration to the Phaeacians by contrast with the events in *Odyssey* 24, which are 'given the authority of the primary narrator'. This narrator ('the Continuator'), composing later, was unaware of the inconsistency owing to his different eschatological perspective.

[65] The nature of the relationship between content and form in a representation has been much discussed. Note especially Wittgenstein (1953: 193–229, esp. 194 (II.xi)) and Gombrich (1968: esp. 4–5) [1959] on 'seeing-as' (an experience in which viewers must alternate between seeing content and form) and Wollheim (1980: 137–51) [1968], (1998: 221–2), (2003) on 'seeing-in' (an experience in which content and form can be seen together). The chapters in Kemp and Mras (2016) discuss the relations between these approaches. See further Halliwell (2000) on an ancient discourse (notably in Plato) surrounding pictorial mimesis and the value it holds beyond naturalism, realism, or mirror-like qualities—it is, as he put it in *The Aesthetics of Mimesis*, 'world-creating' as well as 'world-reflecting' (2002: 1–33, citation at 23); Neer (2002) and (2010) on a play between presence and representation in Greek art, with shifts in emphasis over time, including towards the end of the Archaic period, and, more recently, Grethlein (2017) on tensions of immersion and reflection in classical narratives and pictures.

[66] Arrington (2015), (2018); Jones (2015); Walter-Karydi (2015: pt. 4); Estrin (2016), (2018); Bassi (2018); Squire (2018a); Wohl (2018); Knappett (2020: ch. 5). See further Turner (2016) for a bigger-picture material-culture-led discussion of 'seeing, envisioning and reflecting on death' in the Graeco-Roman world (page 160). See further Steiner (2001: 136–56) on the paradoxical associations that statues

20   FIGURING DEATH IN CLASSICAL ATHENS

Though less recent, the contributions of Françoise Frontisi-Ducroux and Robin Osborne are also key, both in approach to the material and in attention to the reflection on death that might be prompted by the formal features of verbal and visual art.[67]

As the recent flurry of publications cited in the previous paragraph indicates, the role played by funerary art in mediating thanatological meditation is an area of renewed interest, with attention increasingly turning towards Greek material.[68] This is partly driven by the flourishing of sensory, affective, aesthetic, and embodied approaches to ancient material.[69] Moreover, new materialist studies especially have sought to redress an imbalance in scholarly (and more widespread) conceptions of 'subject' and 'object' by attending to the agency and liveliness of matter and the permeability between humans and their environment.[70] Indeed, many of the pieces cited above explore culturally mediated encounters with death and reflections upon it by examining affective and sensory relations between human and non-human.[71] My focus on cultural mediation of meditation on death thus joins several wider trends in classical studies in explor-

---

carried for Archaic and Classical audiences and 'the image's versatility as cognitive tool', including in meditation on the dead.

[67] Frontisi-Ducroux (1986), (1988: 34–5), (1989: 160–1) [1984], (1995: 82–94); Osborne (1988). The work of Jean-Pierre Vernant is also important: see especially Vernant (1983: 305–20) [1965] on the κολοσσός as a cultural object that gives visible form to the invisible and so to an idea, the life of the deceased in the beyond. See further page 93, note 141.

[68] Compare the volume of work on Roman art, for example Huskinson (1998); Elsner and Huskinson (2011); Platt (2011: 335–93), (2017) [2012]; Elsner and Wu (2012); Birk (2013: 57–8); Vout (2014b); Elsner (2018a), (2018b); Trimble (2018); Clifford (2023).

[69] See Halliwell (2002), (2011); Neer (2010); Porter (2010); Peponi (2012); Gaifman (2013); Bradley and Butler (2013–19), especially the chapter by Susanne Turner (2016) within the *Sight and the Ancient Senses* volume; Cairns (2016); Grethlein (2017); Liebert (2017); Budelmann and Phillips (2018); Gaifman et al. (2018); Grethlein et al. (2020). Jonas Grethlein's claim that there has been a disparity between the enthusiasm with which different disciplines have embraced these ideas is thought-provoking in the context of this multi-media study: Grethlein (2017: 14).

[70] I note especially Meskell (1996: esp. 11–14), who engages with individuals and their lived, embodied experiences of death through death archaeology. She also outlines prior archaeological approaches to bodies (for example as artefact or reflection of society). Other work that is pertinent to death studies includes Hallam and Hockey (2001) on the relationships between death, memory, and material culture (ranging from medieval to contemporary Western societies); Newby and Toulson (2019b) on the roles played by material objects in experience of grief and expression of mourning (see the editors' introduction (2019a) for an emotion-oriented historiography of death studies and the afterword by Douglas Davies (2019) on the material- and death-turn). For further new materialist critique, see Meskell (2000); Sofaer (2006: esp. 62–88); Barad (2008) [2003]; Coole and Frost (2010), with a review of archaeologies of the body in Joyce (2005). For some encounters between ancient Graeco-Roman material and post-humanist and new materialist thinking, see Telò and Mueller (2018); Bianchi et al. (2019). Compare Hall (2018) on the ongoing value of Marxist theory.

[71] See note 66.

ing the potentialities of visual and verbal material to involve its audience in experience and thought.[72]

One striking feature of the studies included above is that they fall, predominantly, into either textual or material camps. This is often because they focus on one object type or genre (lekythoi or stelai, for example, or the lament), but even when studies are deliberately more diverse, such as Robin Osborne's 1988 article on a range of funerary pots and sculpted monuments,[73] they rarely give equal weight to verbal and visual material. This means that opportunity for comparison is lost, and with it a more nuanced picture of how culture mediates meditation. The relationship between art and text in the classical world has been extensively studied over the last few decades,[74] with insistent calls for less segregation.[75] While several publications focused on funerary topics have striven for a cross-cultural or multidisciplinary approach,[76] a balanced attention to verbal and visual material has been rarer.[77] Nathan Arrington's *Ashes, Images, and Memories: The Presence of the War Dead in Fifth-Century Athens* stands out, though literary material is primarily included as a cultural backdrop for the material culture. Meanwhile, Valerie Hope and Janet Huskinson's *Memory and Mourning: Studies in Roman Death* includes a spread of visual and verbal material and approaches to it,[78] and various chapters and articles by Françoise Frontisi-Ducroux, Seth Estrin, and Nick Brown combine visual and verbal analysis with a thanatological theme.[79] But there is room for a cohesive, extended look at what different media

[72] This topic is also of interest outside classical studies. Closest to this book in interest is D. Vance Smith's publication on how English literature of the Middle Ages prompts reflection on the impossibility of describing dying, a finitude that lies beyond experience, and on the imaginative possibilities offered by literature in the face of that problem: Vance Smith (2020). Also important here, though not focused on death, is work that explores the mediating role played by cultural artefacts from Classical Athens in processes of imagination: see especially Fearn (2024a) and other chapters in the same volume.

[73] See note 67.

[74] See for example Goldhill and Osborne (1994); Rutter and Sparkes (2000) (from a death perspective, note especially the chapters by Ruth Bardel and Karen Stears); Small (2003); Newby and Leader-Newby (2007); Squire (2009); Elsner (2015); Grethlein (2017); Capra and Floridi (2023). See further work on ecphrasis, for example Krieger (1992); Mitchell (1994: 151–81); Elsner (2002), (2010); Heffernan (2004) [1993]; Goldhill (2007); Webb (2009); Zeitlin (2013); Elsner and Squire (2016).

[75] See especially Elsner (2015) on the fragmentation of the Samos stele at Athens, not just into physical pieces but into disparate publications according to scholarly categorizations.

[76] Though each focus on material culture, Elsner and Wu (2012) offers a cross-regional collection of studies of Roman and Chinese sarcophagi (see the editorial and commentaries for comparative discussions) and Newby and Toulson (2019b) is deliberately multi-disciplinary.

[77] Compare the extensive work on art and literature by T. B. L. Webster, for example Webster (1939a), and, more recently, Platt (2011). These do not focus on death.

[78] Hope and Huskinson (2011) brings together several media and genres from the Roman world in the study of the process of death and dying, specifically through the lens of memory and mourning.

[79] Frontisi-Ducroux (1986), (1988: 31, 34–5), (1995); Estrin (2016), (2018); Brown (2019). Indeed, though the questions he asked of the material were different, Ian Morris advocated a more multi-media approach to the study of death-ritual: Morris (1992: 200–1).

22 FIGURING DEATH IN CLASSICAL ATHENS

do differently for death in the ancient world.[80] In fact, this is not just true of visual and verbal media but also of different genres within those categories such as philosophy and history, or between one pot type and another. Therefore, though my contribution here is partly one of methodology, in that this book combines a range of media with close analysis, that approach is also what contributes to scholarship on death and on the relationship between culture and thinking.

This brings me to one final but important merit of a media-centred (and multi-media) study: this book accommodates a variegated picture. In this, it again differs in purpose and product from some influential accounts of Greek attitudes to death, which sought to uncover a cohesive ancient Athenian way of thinking (albeit one that might change over time).[81] But to the extent that encounters with death are mediated, they are multiply idiosyncratic, crystallized in variable interactions.[82] They are also fractured by uncertainty. An appreciation of this uncertainty was a strength of Emily Vermeule's study: a 'derivative and arbitrary selection of aspects of Greek death' (her words).[83] Some found this uncertainty troubling. Consider the following selection from Nicholas Richardson's review in 1981:

> This is a curious book, learned and often eloquent, but somehow unsure of itself, as though the author had embarked on these strange seas of thought and let the wind take her where it would. As 'Longinus' said of the tales of Odysseus, it seems to be a kind of 'wandering in the realms of the fabulous'. For all its melancholy, Browne's *Urne Buriall* struck a note of firmness and confidence in face of death which may, after all, be closer in spirit to the nobility of classical attitudes, as mirrored in the speeches of the *Iliad*, or the quiet dignity of a fifth-century Attic tombstone.[84]

Apart from the fact that Vermeule focused not on the Classical period (or at least the period that would have included a fifth-century Attic tombstone) but on prehistoric and Archaic material, her uncertainty as to what the Greeks thought about death reflects an uncertainty that many of them appear to have felt themselves.[85] John Boardman celebrated this congruence, though he put it down to a

---

[80] In a different way (and with a broader geographic and temporal reach), Southwood and Sekita (2025) also strives to fill this gap.

[81] Consider, for example, Sourvinou-Inwood (1981), (1983), (1995); Garland (2001: esp. xv–xvi) [1985]. Compare Osborne (1988: 1) and, more recently, Arrington (2015: esp. 13–18) on individual and collective memories.

[82] Compare Potts (2002: 17, 21–2) on the idiosyncrasies of human responses to death and the merits of 'reading widely across geographical and temporal boundaries'. See further Snodgrass (2009) for words of caution against attempts to generalize even about burial in the Classical Greek polis.

[83] Vermeule (1979: x).   [84] Richardson (1981).

[85] In fact, Richardson acknowledges this from the outset: 'In the end there is not really much to say: death is the same for all, and what lies beyond remains a matter for faith or conjecture.'

Greek illogicality about death.[86] I suggest, in addition (and in opposition to Richardson), that what we are dealing with in the long fifth century is a transformation in cultural mediation of epistemological and existential anxiety in the face of death—a 'sense of self-mockery' (to use Vermeule's formulation) that becomes differently, obsessively theorized through visual and literary culture. Mock-confident illogicality is joined by anxiety-ridden attention to the bounds of knowledge,[87] greetings from the other side that are often (but not always) less weird but are thickly shrouded in distance.

Figuring Death in Classical Athens: Visual and Literary Explorations. Emily Clifford, Oxford University Press.
© Emily Clifford 2025. DOI: 10.1093/9780198947936.003.0001

[86] Boardman (1980), reviewing Vermeule's book. Vermeule (1979: 1–2) herself observes that this illogicality is 'a sense of self-mockery' in the face of the unknowable.

[87] Not least in Plato's *Phaedo*, the subject of the following chapter.

ONE

Death Comes as the End

Encountering Death in Plato's Phaedo

I. THE CHALLENGE

EX. Αὐτός, ὦ Φαίδων, παρεγένου Σωκράτει ἐκείνῃ τῇ ἡμέρᾳ ᾗ τὸ φάρμακον ἔπιεν ἐν τῷ δεσμωτηρίῳ, ἢ ἄλλου του ἤκουσας;

ΦΑΙΔ. Αὐτός, ὦ Ἐχέκρατες.

EX. Τί οὖν δή ἐστιν ἄττα εἶπεν ὁ ἀνὴρ πρὸ τοῦ θανάτου; καὶ πῶς ἐτελεύτα; ἡδέως γὰρ ἂν ἐγὼ ἀκούσαιμι.

Echecrates: *Were you yourself there at Socrates' side*, Phaedo, on the actual day he drank the poison in the prison, or *did you hear about it from someone else*?

Phaedo: I was there myself, Echecrates.

E: So then, what kind of things did the man say before his death? *And how did he meet his end*? I'd really like to hear about it.

—Plato, *Phaedo* 57a1–6[1]

At the heart of Plato's *Phaedo* is an effort to encounter death.[2] This effort is twofold: a representational (dramatic-literary) effort to provide an encounter with the death of Socrates runs alongside a philosophical effort to define encounters with death in general.[3] The driving question is: what happened/happens at the end (and, more urgently, was/is it an end at all)?

---

[1] Page and paragraph references are to Stephanus text pages. The translation of this extract is mostly from the 2017 Loeb edition, though I have made some alterations (for example, I read 'before his death' rather than 'before he died'; there is a difference between 'dying' and 'death' and the Greek reads τοῦ θανάτου). Italics indicate my emphasis.

[2] I treat the *Phaedo* as an 'independent literary artefact' following R. B. Rutherford (1995: 3) and his arguments throughout that chapter. In support, see Gill (2002: 153–61, 163–4); Long (2007: 224, 240–1); McCabe (2008: 88). See Morgan (2002: 183–4) for a flexible approach. This approach, though not universal, is well accepted.

[3] The philosophical fiction: McCabe (2008: 96–8). Plato's art: Bacon (1990), (2001). The Socrates that matters here is the written Socrates of the *Phaedo*. See R. B. Rutherford (1995: esp. 62); Michelini

DEATH COMES AS THE END   25

In this first chapter, I explore how Plato uses his literary medium to stage the challenge of exploring death. As set out in my epigraph, this is a challenge that he raises in the opening lines of his dialogue with a question that he puts into the mouth of Echecrates: 'How did [Socrates] meet his end?' (πῶς ἐτελεύτα;). With this deceptively simple enquiry, Plato establishes 'the death of Socrates' as his dramatic subject and sets it squarely within an ecphrastic discourse.[4] How close can an outsider get to the moment of Socrates' death?[5] Echecrates was not there on the day that Socrates died. Neither was Plato (see below). Phaedo was. What Echecrates wants is a clear account (σαφές τι, 57b1) of Socrates' death, a description in as much detail as Phaedo can achieve. As a result, Echecrates' desire for a missed experience, presence at Socrates' side on the very day he drank the hemlock, motivates the dialogue; an encounter with death is a goal from the start.

But death is also one of the central concerns of the *Phaedo*'s philosophical discussions, which seek to demonstrate the soul's immortality. In this respect, the equivocal framing of Echecrates' question is a red flag: πῶς ἐτελεύτα; how did he (the man, Socrates) come to an end, finish (it) off, bring (it) to pass, accomplish (it, death, life)?[6] From the beginning, Echecrates talks of endings. And indeed, engraved upon the cultural inheritance of posterity, Plato's accomplishment, 'the death of Socrates', testifies to his successful treatment of the philosopher's end.[7] But an essential purpose of the dialogue's philosophical discussion is to think of death in terms not of 'endings' but of continuities. The thought and the artistry of the *Phaedo* (if we can speak of these as separate) thus appear to be

---

(2003). Contrast Burnet (1911: ix–lvi); Hackforth (1955: 13). The 'fall' of the Socratic Problem: Dorion (2011). As a written response to and representation of death, what Plato wrote is more relevant here than what actually happened and the extent to which the historical Socrates (and/or his thoughts) overlaps with his literary counterpart is not at issue. See Blondell (2002: 8–11) and McCabe (2008: 91–2) on Socrateses. Indeed, Socrates' portrait has a certain authenticity to it insofar as it recreates what it might have been like to encounter a man who was 'unlike' other Athenians (and, indeed, unlike non-Athenians such as Simmias and Cebes). The 'artful construction' of Socrates' image as a satyr: Catoni and Giuliani (2019: citation at 713). The Socratic/Platonic division: Arist. *Soph. el.* 183b7–8, *Metaph.* 1.6, 987b1–7; Penner (1992: 122–5). Rejecting a distinct 'Socratic' period: Kahn (1997: 39–40, ch. 3); Rowe (2007: 4–6, 39–49).

[4] The importance of the Platonic prologue: Gonzalez (2003). This is not to claim that what Plato is doing here is solely, or even mostly, about Socrates' death. It cannot be ignored, for example, that the *Phaedo* contains what is generally considered to be Plato's first articulation of his so-called theory of Forms. Nevertheless, 'being there' at Socrates' death is a motivating thread.

[5] Wilson (2007: 107): 'The *Phaedo* suggests, then, that the living may not ever get complete access to the world of the dead.' Contrast the discussion in Holquist (1990: 37) of Bakhtin's view that this outside narrative of death is all that there is: see e.g. Bakhtin (1990: 104–5) [1920s].

[6] Contrast Beets (1997: 108–13, 159–60) on τελευτή as 'a non-temporal transition to the "beyond"', exceptionally attained by Socrates in life (but by most people in a coincidence of τελευτή with θάνατος).

[7] The impact of Socrates' death, as mediated by Plato and others, on Western culture: Wilson (2007). See further Lapatin (2005: 140–5).

26 FIGURING DEATH IN CLASSICAL ATHENS

in tension.[8] Though for most of this chapter I will focus on the literary challenges of encountering death in the *Phaedo*, these are densely and enigmatically intertwined with its more overtly philosophical arguments. My view, to which I will return at the end of this chapter, is that the apparent conflict between literary and philosophical imperatives draws attention to—and is designed to draw attention to—the epistemological problem of death; in both the narrative and arguments of the *Phaedo*, Plato works through the imaginative possibilities and impossibilities of meeting the challenge posed by Echecrates.[9] For now, I simply note that the ecphrastic set-up is not purely an artistic choice; it is a highly provocative one in the context of the dialogue.

In my study below, I track how Plato deals with the literary challenges of encountering the death of Socrates. I begin with two outside perspectives on death. Looking first at the external backward-facing viewpoints of reporter and writer, listeners and readers, I consider how Plato employs his mediated literary medium to meditate upon the difficulty of encountering someone else's death. How close does Plato take us? What might distance in the text suggest about the epistemological value of seeing someone die with one's own eyes? Next, I turn to the internal viewpoints of those that attended Socrates' final moments. I show how Plato harnesses the temporality of narrative to reflect upon death as a significant but asymptotic moment, a climax to dying that is anticipated by the forward-facing perspectives of the living. The question lurking behind Echecrates' 'how did Socrates meet his end?' is 'does Plato tell us?', or rather, '*can* Plato tell us?' Do we ever see Socrates die?[10] On this note, in the final part of the chapter,

---

[8] Interrelationship of Plato's form and content: Seeskin (1987: 1–22); Ausland (1997: esp. 397–406); Blondell (2002); Scott (2006: 5–6, 214–16); McCabe (2008: 88–91). The choice of characters in Plato's drama as philosophically symbolic (with focus on the *Phaedo*): Sedley (1995).

[9] The extent to which Plato's dialogues, including the *Phaedo*, are themselves open-ended is a matter of debate (and may vary between dialogues). My view is that the dialogues articulate, model, and are designed to generate, thinking, and can be read in accordance with a more object-oriented metaphysics (see page 57, note 9): for Plato, ideas (including 'death') *do* exist, and so the quest to define them is worthwhile; he makes no explicit claims to have succeeded in finding answers, only to be engaged in that vital process.

[10] By 'we' (or 'our', etc.) I include all intended and unanticipated recipients of Plato's text, contemporary, original, and in between. The original context in which Plato's writings were received is unknown. It is not impossible that they were performed, in which case we should think of an implicit dialogue along the lines of author/listener as for Greek drama. Nevertheless, while it is important to recognize the possibility that Plato's words were heard as well as read, it is known that they were eventually widely read. I therefore think of the reception of Plato's work as comprised of readers but acknowledge the possibility of listeners. Compare Charalabopoulos (2012), who favours reading Plato's dialogues as performance texts. Against this and emphasizing Plato's different aims: Kraut (1992: 25–30). See further Wilson (2012) on the lack of specific evidence for ancient performances of Plato's dialogues. Vatri (2017: 71) acknowledges the controversy surrounding the reception of Plato's dialogues and accepts the possibility that different dialogues were produced for different audiences.

DEATH COMES AS THE END   27

I explore one passage where Plato takes an imaginative vault into the mind of the dying Socrates as he, in turn, struggles to grasp the unfathomable abyss of death.

II. PLATO'S SPYGLASS

I begin with Plato's mediated literary account. Two threads run through this part of the chapter: distance (temporal, spatial, experiential, existential) and perspective. Both are characteristic of ecphrasis; they are embedded in the fabric of a verbal medium that looks back, elsewhere, through, for, and at another person.[11] In a Platonic dialogue, multiple conversations always combine in different measures at different times;[12] this constructs not only a web of viewpoints and voices but also a network of intermediaries and so a problem of power, reliability, and recession.[13] In the *Phaedo*, Plato intensifies the ecphrastic characteristics of

[11] In the language of later theorists, Plato is manipulating the written form to articulate, grapple with, and overcome the ecphrastic challenge of bringing a death of Socrates before our eyes or to recreate for us what it would be like to have been there. Plato and ecphrasis (focusing especially on his presentation of his work as poetry): Bacon (2001). See further page 3, note 8.

[12] Plato writes 'dialogues' and his dialogues contain conversation in different guises (direct and reported); we can talk of the handling and impact of the latter as something distinct from the former. It is difficult to speak of dialogue at all without the 'interference' of philosophical and literary baggage (see Greenwood (2008: 15–18)) and hard to make sense of what genre means for Plato's corpus without the circularity of explaining what he does by reference to the tradition he inspired. Plato's writings as *sui generis*: Arieti (1991: 2); Blondell (2002: 37). There is an undeniable coherence of form across his corpus: all but the *Apology* and the *Letters* can be, and have been, labelled 'dialogues' (though both these exceptions can be considered dialogic since the former anticipates an audience at his trial, including Plato himself, and the latter a recipient and the possibility of two-way correspondence). A high-level summary of characteristics of the dialogues and questions that they raise: Szlezák (1999: 14–18) [1993]. But it is also essential to recognize *variation* across Plato's writing. On the advantages of a case-by-case approach to the dialogues, see note 2.

[13] We can identify many meaningful and compelling reasons why it made philosophical and literary sense for Plato to write in the form he did. Plausible philosophical explanations abound: it most closely replicates Socratic speech; it stages philosophical debate; it avoids the dogmatism of the authorial voice. Summarizing modern approaches to Plato's form from a philosophical perspective: Gill (2002: 145–9). Some earlier discussion: Gundert (1971: 1–12, 51–63) [1968]; Meyer (1980); Stokes (1986); M. Frede (1992a); Sayre (1995: xii–xvi, ch. 1); Note further the comments in Plato's work, including Socrates' behaviour and words on misology (*Phd.* 89d1–91c6). In many explanations an anxiety is imputed to Plato whose written medium becomes an inferior representation of the spoken, lived referent. This throws us into the murky fray of Plato's views on mimesis: see note 32. Plato's writing as protreptic towards his unwritten philosophy (an approach associated more generally with the so-called 'Tübingen School'): Gaiser (1959: esp. 150–5, 192–4), (1984: 41–54). Compare Greenwood (2004) on written versus spoken words in Classical Athens (with focus on Thucydides). Much has also been written on the literary tradition to which Plato responds (including drama, epic, mime, autobiography and biography, sophistic and philosophical treatises). Summarizing the literary origins of Plato's dialogue form: R. B. Rutherford (1995: 10–15). See further Kuhn (1941); Tarrant (1955a); Bakhtin (1981: 21–6, 130–1) on the Platonic dialogues as an example of ancient literature termed σπουδογέλοιον and precursor to the novel and as an early form of autobiography; Blondell (2002: 14–37). For ancient discussion of Plato's dialogue form see

28 FIGURING DEATH IN CLASSICAL ATHENS

his writing as part of an existential meditation: literary distancing and perspectives map cognitive distance and exteriority. This unravels the imaginative nature of responding to death and makes it an object of contemplation.

Seeing Socrates' death is a problem from the outset. It is immediately clear that this is not another dialogue like the *Euthyphro* or *Crito* (or, indeed, the *Apology*): the man is already dead. This fact motivates the action and subject matter of the dialogue—death—and throws its ecphrastic ambitions, an ever-present but often unacknowledged dynamic in the dialogues, centre-stage. When Echecrates asks 'how did he meet his end?' ($\pi\hat{\omega}s$ $\dot{\epsilon}\tau\epsilon\lambda\epsilon\acute{\upsilon}\tau a;$) he issues a challenge: how to satisfy his longing for a missed experience, presence at a death that is temporally and spatially absent.[14]

This challenge permeates the structure of the *Phaedo*, which offers a striking (though not unique) example of the play-within-a-play set-up.[15] The dialogue has a double setting. The external frame is set in Phlius:[16] Echecrates (a Phliasian) talks with Phaedo, who was present at Socrates' death in 399 BCE. Echecrates wants to know about Socrates' last day in the prison: what was discussed and how he died. The main body of the work is Phaedo's account of that last day, concluding (at the end of the dialogue) with Socrates drinking the hemlock and dying. The description of Socrates' final moments and what was said is thus nar-

---

Diog. Laert. 3.18, 24, 47–51; Anonymous, on Plato's Dialogues *FGrH* 1134 (P. Oxy. XLV 3219). On Plato's use of intertextuality to define the boundaries of his philosophy (often in parody, sometimes in alliance): Nightingale (1995: esp. 1–12). Ancient dialogue more broadly: Görgemanns (2004: esp. 352–3); Goldhill (2008b); Föllinger and Müller (2013); Dubel and Gotteland (2015).

[14] Over the first few lines of the dialogue (57a), several facts of distance are established: the dialogue is set in Phlius not Athens, takes place after the events narrated within it, and occurs between two speaking parties: one, Phaedo, was there in person at Socrates' death in Athens; the other, Echecrates, was not. Echecrates emphasizes this distance in the distinction he draws between the time and place of the death and his own situation 'nowadays' in Phlius, a place that, he explains, has limited contact with Athens (57a6–b2). Indeed, if this dialogue was set in the late 380s, Phlius might have been considered particularly remote owing to its close, if complicated, relations with Sparta following the invasion of Iphicrates (Xen. *Hell.* 4.4.15).

[15] Other works that embed narrated conversation within a dramatic frame are the *Symposium*, *Euthydemus*, and *Protagoras*. Interesting variants of this structure are *Cleitophon*, which embeds an inner recollected conversation between Cleitophon and Socrates, the same characters that feature in the dramatic frame (although Plato's authorship is doubted), and *Theaetetus*, where the conversation embedded in the dramatic frame itself unfolds as a drama. Compare e.g. the *Phaedrus*, where the dramatic frame stages the philosophical conversation proper; in this respect, there is no *mise en abyme* (though the dialogue does embed a speech by Lysias). Another type is the narrative frame that embeds a reported conversation, as in the *Republic*. The important point is that the dialogue forms differ from one another: see especially Halperin (1992: esp. 95–7) on meaningful variation of representational mode in Plato's dialogues (simple/mixed narration and imitation). See further Diog. Laert. 3.49–51 on classifying the dialogues. On the presentation of dialogue in Plato's work, including in manuscript and papyrus editions and by the author: Andrieu (1954: 284–6, 288–9, 292–3, 304–8).

[16] The dialogue must be set after Socrates' death and before/at the time of Plato's writing, i.e. between 399 BCE and, probably, *c.* 380 BCE (see note 36).

DEATH COMES AS THE END   29

rated by Phaedo in the context of a conversation with Echecrates.[17] Both parts of the play-within-a-play structure, though discernible, are interwoven because the one re-presents and reflects upon the other. The exterior 'dramatic' dialogue or 'play-script' form operates as a filter on the action within and strains the death and inner dialogue through the film of Phaedo's narrating memory,[18] of seeing, listening, and responding.

Let us begin with the dramatic passage towards the end of the dialogue in which Phaedo describes Socrates' final moments and the revelation of his corpse (118a5–14):

Ἤδη οὖν σχεδόν τι αὐτοῦ ἦν τὰ περὶ τὸ ἦτρον ψυχόμενα, καὶ ἐκκαλυψάμενος—ἐνεκεκάλυπτο γάρ—εἶπεν—ὃ δὴ τελευταῖον ἐφθέγξατο—Ὦ Κρίτων, ἔφη, τῷ Ἀσκληπιῷ ὀφείλομεν ἀλεκτρυόνα· ἀλλὰ ἀπόδοτε καὶ μὴ ἀμελήσητε.

Ἀλλὰ ταῦτα, ἔφη, ἔσται, ὁ Κρίτων· ἀλλ' ὅρα εἴ τι ἄλλο λέγεις.

Ταῦτα ἐρομένου αὐτοῦ οὐδὲν ἔτι ἀπεκρίνατο, ἀλλ' ὀλίγον χρόνον διαλιπὼν ἐκινήθη τε καὶ ὁ ἄνθρωπος ἐξεκάλυψεν αὐτόν, καὶ ὃς τὰ ὄμματα ἔστησεν· ἰδὼν δὲ ὁ Κρίτων συνέλαβε τὸ στόμα καὶ τοὺς ὀφθαλμούς.

Already, then, I reckon, the parts around [Socrates'] abdomen were getting cold, and, uncovering himself (for he had been covered up), he said—indeed, this was the last thing he said—'Crito,' he said, 'we owe a cock to Asclepius; see, then, that you pay what is due and don't forget'.

'That will all happen, yes,' said Crito, 'but see if you have anything else to say...'

[Socrates] did not make any further response to [Crito's] question, but, after a short interval, there was motion, and the man uncovered him, and his eyes were in a fixed stare. On seeing this, Crito closed his mouth and eyes.

Several details make this scene immersive for both the internal and external audience. Consider the sensory details: the falling temperature of Socrates' dying body; the (mediated) sound of his final words, quoted in direct speech; the visual impression of his body's motion; the repeated veilings and unveilings of his body, alive one moment, dead the next; the fixed stare. These are combined with the viewpoints of characters at the scene: Phaedo and Crito respond to Socrates' body; they notice its coldness and the vacant gaze of his eyes and form judgements, or take actions, accordingly. The scene is powerfully, successfully brought

[17] On the frame in Plato see McCabe (2008). See further Bacon (1990: 148–9) on the 'simultaneous nearness and distance' arising from tension between the *Phaedo*'s framing scenes; McCabe (1996: 5–8) on the 'Chinese Whispers effect' in the *Parmenides* (she also notes its presence in the *Symposium* and *Phaedo*) and interaction between literary frame and argument; Clay (2000: ch. 3, esp. 23–5) on Plato's portrait frames; Wilson (2007: 104) on 'eavesdropping' in the *Phaedo*, '[Socrates'] words come to us from beyond the grave'. On frames more generally (in Graeco-Roman art): Platt and Squire (2017).

[18] For notably explicit retrospective commentary on the events that he describes: 88c1–7. For a different effect see the *Protagoras*, where a narrated conversation within a direct conversation mediates a debate on how to do philosophy, as at 348a3–6 where Socrates encourages Protagoras to put aside the poets and converse directly.

30 FIGURING DEATH IN CLASSICAL ATHENS

to life for listeners and readers: it is, in the words of later theorists, characterized by ἐνάργεια (vividness).

But the frame and punctuating discourse between Phaedo and Echecrates recalls Phaedo's mediating voice. Though real and narration worlds need not be absent for immersion (as argued by Rutger J. Allan in his categorization of linguistic and narratological immersive features), Plato does not leave them 'mentally backgrounded', undermining textual 'transparency'.[19] The features that contribute to immersion here could have been conveyed in direct speech as Plato does in the *Phaedrus*,[20] even within the play-within-a-play structure. Imagine something along the lines of 'his limbs are cold; he has fallen silent; he has moved; let us uncover him...' Instead, even as Plato brings the scene to life with details and internal perspectives, he reminds his readers of spatial and temporal distance with Phaedo's past-tense third-person narrative (the most obvious example of this is the recurrence of 'he said' throughout the narration).[21] The presence within Socrates' death scene of Phaedo's subjective self, as substantiated by what he sees, feels, says, and hears, reiterates response to death as lived experience from the outside. This does not necessarily compromise the ἐνάργεια of the scene, but it does define the offered experience as one of observing *someone else* die.[22] For the living alone, it is possible to anticipate, observe, and contemplate life's story in its entirety. One point that emerges from Plato's presentation is that to encounter death is to live and to outlive; responding to Socrates' death entails retrospective narration of that experience.

This is striking in the opening lines of the quoted extract. The line about owing a cock to Asclepius is infamously cryptic. But just before Socrates says this line (in direct speech), Phaedo comments 'he said—indeed, this was the last thing he said' (εἶπεν—ὃ δὴ τελευταῖον ἐφθέγξατο). He then observes, ' "That will all happen, yes," said Crito, "but see if you have anything else to say" ' (ἀλλὰ ταῦτα, ἔφη, ἔσται, ὁ Κρίτων· ἀλλ' ὅρα εἴ τι ἄλλο λέγεις). The amalgamation of temporalities here might lead us to wonder whether Socrates' words are deliberately

---

[19] For categorization of linguistic and narratological immersive features: Allan (2020: 18–19). Many are present in Phaedo's narrative, not just here but elsewhere (verisimilitude, perspective, interest and emotional involvement, and minimal departure).

[20] On Plato's description of background in the *Phaedrus* through characters' responses to it, see Ferrari (1987: 2–4). Note further Eucleides' comments on representational style at *Tht.* 143b5–c6.

[21] Phaedo's narrating voice repeatedly colours his quotation of others' direct speech: consider instances in this passage of ἔφη (118a7 and 9), εἶπεν (118a6), and ἐφθέγξατο (118a7). These are representative of how his account works more broadly. Insertions in Platonic dialogues and the resulting play of distance/proximity: Andrieu (1954: 316–19). On tensions of immersion and reflection and shifting modes of attention: Grethlein (2017); chapters by Rutger Allan and Felix Budelmann and Evert van Emde Boas in Grethlein et al. (2020). For more on narrative temporality see section III (A Death Foretold).

[22] This is characteristic of ecphrasis more broadly; ecphrasis offers a way of seeing, a perspective, an experience of the thing described. This makes ecphrasis appropriate for existential discourse.

meaningless, awkwardly *insignificant*, at least until retrospectively understood to be what they already are: his last ones.[23] The mismatch between Phaedo's retrospective knowledge and Crito's prospective ignorance presents an anachronistic representation of present time filtered by Phaedo's future perspective.[24] This, in turn, picks up a sense in which death, an interruption of life from the perspective of the dying, can become a conclusion when reframed by the retrospective narratives of the living. How did Socrates 'make an ending of it'? One answer is: in Plato's *Phaedo*, which shapes an exemplary—and complete—story out of remembering the end of a philosopher's life.[25]

But the problem of distance is not just one of time and space; it is also one of truth. What Echecrates asks first is not what Phaedo saw, but whether he was there (57a, cited in the epigraph to this chapter). The first word, αὐτός, asserts the purported significance of having been there in person at Socrates' side (παρεγένου Σωκράτει). This is reinforced by Echecrates' continued insistence on knowing which people were at 'the death itself' (τίνες οἱ παραγενόμενοι τῶν ἐπιτηδείων τῷ ἀνδρί;, 58c7–8); physical presence at the end is important. Phaedo's presence at Socrates' end cuts several ways: it is emotionally meaningful (it confirms that Socrates did not die 'bereft of his friends', ἔρημος [...] φίλων);[26] it operates as a benchmark against which Echecrates' desired vicarious experience may be measured; and it poses the hypothesis that there is epistemological value in the eyewitness account. Echecrates asks Phaedo how Socrates died because he is a worthy recounter: his claim to autopsy is as good as it gets.[27] But the question also unfurls the ecphrastic challenge, reporting 'something clear' (σαφές τι, 57b1),[28] and exposes its weakest link, the intermediary. For Echecrates, this not just a matter of rhetorical skill but of authority and reliability.[29]

[23] Socrates' 'final words' are hotly debated: see especially Most (1993).

[24] On Freud's masterplot, Sartre's end-determination, and 'anticipation of retrospection' in life and narrative: Brooks (1984: 23, ch. 4). On authorial perspective and the achievement of the temporal closure of death by the other (the author or reader, for instance; the significant moment cannot be perceived by the one that dies): Möllendorff (2013: 409), drawing on Bakhtin.

[25] The overlap between narrative and memory was made explicit early in the dialogue in the conversation between Echecrates and Phaedo (58d2–d9) where three different verbs for representation, description, or narrative (ἀπαγγεῖλαι, διηγήσασθαι, διεξελθεῖν) were equated with the act of remembering (μεμνῆσθαι).

[26] Echecrates seeks this reassurance at 58c9.   [27] The link is revealed by οὖν at 57a5.

[28] Consider: Ps.-Hermog. *Prog.* 10 on ecphrasis in Rabe (1913: 22–3), reproduced and translated in Webb (2009: 200–1): ἀρεταὶ δὲ ἐκφράσεως μάλιστα μὲν σαφήνεια καὶ ἐνάργεια. See further Elsner (2002: 1); notes 11, 22, and 32. Echecrates declares that, apart from the fact that Socrates died by drinking the potion, no one could tell him anything σαφές (57b1); he later reiterates that Phaedo should describe everything as clearly (σαφέστατα, 58d2) and in as much detail (ἀκριβέστατα, 58d8–9) as possible. Phaedo says he will try (πειράσομαι ὑμῖν διηγήσασθαι, 58d4–5). The 'clear' view is also important to Thucydides: see esp. 1.22.4 with discussion in Chapter Five (page 210 and note 72).

[29] See note 34. On Plato's position within a discourse on the pleasure and utility that come from a thorough and detailed narrative, see Erler (2013).

32 FIGURING DEATH IN CLASSICAL ATHENS

The adjective σαφές occurs again in the context of hearsay. At 61c8–62a2, Plato presents characters conversing about talking and listening: dialogue is the subject of dialogue.[30] Plato represents Phaedo reporting Socrates and Cebes reporting what they have heard others (Philolaus and other unknown persons) saying about suicide, which, we are to understand from Socrates' claim at 61d10–e4, is in some way reporting what they think about death or, rather, 'the life beyond' (τῆς ἀποδημίας τῆς ἐκεῖ).[31] Different opinions are expressed as to how likely we are to derive anything clear or definite, σαφές (61d8; 61e8), from what other people say.[32] Cebes is pessimistic: he has 'never heard anyone say anything definite about it'. Socrates is optimistic: 'you may hear something'. As an extended discussion on reported speech and the possibility or impossibility of hearing something 'clear' (σαφές), this passage looks back towards the motivating circumstances for the work as a whole: Echecrates' desire for a clear (σαφές) account of Socrates' death and his last words. Indeed, Socrates' switch from what he has heard (ἐξ ἀκοῆς) to the suggestion that he should examine and tell stories (διασκοπεῖν τε καὶ μυθολογεῖν) about the life beyond (περὶ τῆς ἀποδημίας τῆς ἐκεῖ) unravels the imaginative nature of encountering death, 'what sort of thing we think it is' (ποίαν τινὰ αὐτὴν οἰόμεθα εἶναι). As a *mise en abyme* for Phaedo's own account, this excursus on the perils of vicarious experience calls attention to a fault-line running through the dialogue's whole mediated account: it exposes

---

[30] See notes 12, 13, and 137.

[31] On Philolaus (*c.* 470–385 BCE), a Pythagorean philosopher, and the surviving fragments of his work, see DK 44; Huffman (1999: 78–85); Laks and Most (2016: 145–85). For discussion of Philolaus' views on suicide, see Huffman (1993: 327, 330, 405, 408–9).

[32] Compare *Symp.* 172a–173b (and throughout) on the challenge of hearing a clear account years after an event at which the source was not present. It is interesting that in this passage from the *Phaedo* we find some reassurance from Socrates as to the possibility of hearing a true account, though the comment may be facetious. Problems of hearsay open onto a Platonic dialectic on truth, language, representation, and the senses. Note especially *Resp.* 10.595a1–608b3, *Soph.* 232b1–241b8, *Phdr.* 274b6–278b6, and the enigmatic *Seventh Letter* 341b7–342a1, which, if authentic, prompts us to question whether we should expect to find truth or understanding in Plato's words, written or oral. Seventh Letter: Arieti (1991: 6); Kraut (1992: 21–3); Sayre (1995: esp. xii–xxiii, 10–17). Plato's supposed anxiety vis-à-vis the arts, specifically mimesis, has been a major topic of debate; though effort has gone into reconciling apparently contradictory views expressed across the corpus (most perplexing being the status of Plato's own art), it seems likely that respect for the arts as a powerful medium brought with it both admiration and caution. For an overview of mimesis, see Woodruff (2015: esp. 331–5). On the 'world-reflecting' and 'world-creating' facets of mimesis and its probing treatment by Plato, see Halliwell (2002: 22–4, pt. 1). See further Nightingale (2002a); Farness (2003: 117–21) on performed and instrumental mimesis in Plato's dialogues. On what mimesis meant before and in Plato, and Plato's attitude to and metaphorical use of the arts (specifically painting): Keuls (1978b); his reflections on poetry and creativity (and the quarrel between poetry and philosophy): Asmis (1992). An attempt to rehabilitate Plato's written work: Laborderie (1978: 105–14). Plato's references to his writing as a form of μουσική: Capra (2015). The problematic power of images in Plato: Destrée and Edmonds (2017b), especially the chapter by Francisco Gonzalez. For the argument that Plato was critiquing popular entertainment: Nehamas (1999: ch. 13).

DEATH COMES AS THE END   33

the narrating Phaedo as a possibly unreliable go-between.[33] Phaedo's account of Socrates' death and philosophical arguments thus sits in counterpart to the myth of Er: death's distance is in both cases overcome, but the value of each privileged narrator's claim to authority must be taken on trust.[34]

Moreover, the streaming of Socrates' death and its accompanying dialogue through the voice of a distant participant in an external conversation parades the underlying exchange between readers and author,[35] another intermediary voice that subsumes and filters the others—possibly at a later date (Plato wrote the *Phaedo* at some point within a forty-year period following the death of Socrates in 399 BCE, and probably later than 386 BCE).[36] An old debate concerns Socrates' (or any other character's) role as a mouthpiece for Plato,[37] but just as important in the *Phaedo* are Plato's and Phaedo's positions as mouthpieces for the voices they ventriloquize. The dialogue is full of appropriated, imagined, and imaginary speech and much is galvanized by the pressing context of Socrates' imminent death.[38]

[33] On this point, note Brooks (1984: 215) on 'memory and narration of failed meanings' and Flaubert's *L'Education sentimentale* as a 'book about nothing'. Perhaps Plato's combination of a retrospective account with the challenge of hearing something clear highlights the nothingness of death.

[34] See pages 1–4 for further discussion of the myth of Er. The myth of Er as a traditional θεωρία (journey to and spectatorship at a religious festival) and model for philosophical θεωρία (contemplation/theorization): Nightingale (2004: 76–7). See further Nightingale (2016: 57–62) on vision in Plato. But if sensory vision is treacherous (see Nightingale (2016: 58)), what is the value of autopsy? The rational vision of death sought in the philosophical journey of the *Phaedo* may have a better claim to authority.

[35] It is this dialogue that is at stake: Gundert (1971: 6) [1968]. The reader's conversation with Plato (and Plato's encouragement to readers to reflect not just on the weaknesses of the arguments in the dialogues but on the beliefs held by the characters and ourselves): McKim (1988). See Clay (1988) on the open dialogue's invitation to readers to think for themselves (focusing on the *Republic*); Sayre (1995: 27–32) on 'active reading' of Plato; Lamm (2005: 107) on Schleiermacher and the 'interpreter as artist'. In fact, perhaps Echecrates' plural reference at 58d7–9 to 'similar such others' who are ready to hear a detailed account of Socrates' final hours accommodates external readers as well as internal listeners. There is dramatic explanation for the plural if we envisage the *Phaedo* as taking place among a group of people in a private house, as in the *Protagoras*. However, the absence of any mention of these other listeners in the context of an otherwise richly dramatized dialogue suggests that at the very least a double meaning is intended.

[36] The absolute or relative date of the *Phaedo* within a period of about forty years (following the historical Socrates' death in 399 BCE) makes limited difference. Whereas the chronology of Plato's activity is of paramount interest to those interested in the development of Plato's thinking, the principal time reference within the constructed context of the *Phaedo* is *the past*, a past from which the author purports to absent himself. Discussion of the *Phaedo*'s relative dating: Irwin (2008: 77–84). See further Brandwood (1992) on stylometry; Kraut (1992: 6–7) on reasons for thinking it followed the *Meno*, which may be dated between 386 and 382 BCE. On orderings and their hermeneutic assumptions and consequences: Poster (1998).

[37] See especially contributions in Press (2000), together with Irwin (1992: 77–8); Kraut (1992: 2–4); Michelini (2003: 58–65); McCabe (2008: 94–6). Compare Rowe (2007: 15–20), 'Plato *is* Socrates, except, unavoidably, to the extent that Plato as author is also Socrates' creator and manipulator' (page 19). An extreme approach (Plato's dialogues are dramas; philosophical argument is subordinated to that purpose): Arieti (1991: ch. 1, esp. 5).

[38] Among other examples: Socrates is moved to put Aesop into poetry (61b2–7); Cebes urges Socrates to speak to a hypothetical frightened child that dwells within his companions (77e4–8); Socrates discusses telling stories about the beyond (61d10–e4, 110a8–110b2, 114d1–8).

34 FIGURING DEATH IN CLASSICAL ATHENS

There is an amusing example of this at the end of the hearsay discussion. Phaedo reports that 'Cebes laughed quietly at what he said and said in his own dialect: "Zeus be my witness"' (Καὶ ὁ Κέβης ἠρέμα ἐπιγελάσας, Ἴττω Ζεύς, ἔφη, τῇ αὑτοῦ φωνῇ εἰπών, 62a8–9). The narrative detail of Cebes' quiet laughter (ἠρέμα ἐπιγελάσας) brings Phaedo's, and Plato's, audiences closer to experiencing Cebes' direct speech by revealing Cebes' manner and mental process; Phaedo communicates not just Cebes' volume and tone, but his cognitive engagement with Socrates' words and his compassionate moderation of his laughter.[39] The prefix ἐπι- underscores that Cebes' emotional reaction is a response and that his utterance forms part of two-way communication. Then Plato inserts a joke: 'speaking with his own voice' (τῇ αὑτοῦ φωνῇ εἰπών). Yes, this is another realistic detail: Cebes' native Boeotian dialect.[40] But the allusion to Cebes' 'voice' might remind readers of the concinnity of voices that make this utterance: the laughing voice of the internal character Cebes; the narrating voice of the external character Phaedo; the authorial voice of the writer Plato.[41] In one sentence, Plato recreates what was said and how, filters Cebes' viewpoint through Phaedo's experience, and erases the autonomy of Cebes, Phaedo, and the others in a wink from the author's text to its reader.[42] Plato's own mediating voice is, as in all his dialogues, thoroughly present.[43]

In a different but important sense, though, and more than in any other dialogue, Plato is absent from the *Phaedo*. He quite literally writes himself out in Phaedo's overt reference to his name at 59b10:[44] 'But Plato, I think, was ill' (Πλάτων δὲ οἶμαι ἠσθένει). The natural and widely accepted interpretation of this statement is that Phaedo explains Plato's absence from Socrates' death by reference to his illness. The explicit naming of the absent friend reminds us of his tacit

---

[39] Representation of intelligent response is reinforced by the connective καί.

[40] As argued in Rowe (1993) on 62a8; Emlyn-Jones and Prendy (2017: 309, note 19). Verisimilitude as an immersive feature: Allan (2020: 18). In the light of Stephen Colvin's (2000) study of marked language in Old Comedy, we should be cautious of interpreting Cebes' Boeotian dialect as indicating, on its own, his 'substandard' philosophy here.

[41] Though note Bakhtin (1981: 47) on the 'system of languages' in the novel and the omnipresence of the author, 'with *almost no direct language of his own*'. Bakhtin elsewhere identifies Plato's dialogues as a precursor to the novel: note 13.

[42] Ecphrasis, Freud, and the collusion of speaker and listener in verbal erasure of their object: Elsner (2004: 158–63).

[43] Plato's presence in his dialogue is a major thread (often an assumption) in scholarship on Plato's corpus and raises issues akin to those in debates on biography and text: how far can we excavate an author's philosophy from what he writes? See Möllendorff (2013: esp. 405–9, 416). Roland Barthes and Mikhail Bakhtin on the author's (non-)existence: Lodge (1990: 98–9), 'Barthes says: because the author does not coincide with the language of the text, he does not exist. Bakhtin says, it is precisely because he does not so coincide that we must posit his existence.' On the author as a function of discourse ('la fonction-auteur'), see Foucault (1969).

[44] The only other reference to Plato by name is at *Ap.* 34a2.

authorial presence,[45] but it also calls his authority into question in a manner highly pertinent to the ongoing discourse on direct experience and reliability. If Echecrates, Plato, and we were not there, how close can we get to the death? The author's own absence from the represented scene reinforces the distance inherent in the dialogue's structure. Is Plato *another* Er-type character?[46] The unease that this stirs is provoking. But the point, perhaps, is less the overwhelming problem of distance than the possibility of overcoming it not by privileged narration, but by philosophy, a verbal representation that just might reveal the invisible truth.[47]

III. A DEATH FORETOLD

So far, I have explored how Plato contrives a literary foil to his existential meditation by presenting Socrates' death in a verbal medium that looks back, through, for, and at another. But the *Phaedo* is as much about looking forwards as it is about looking back. In this section, I move on to consider how Plato provokes reflection upon the exteriority that defines an encounter with someone else's death. I focus on how he aligns readers' literary expectations of a narrative climax with anticipatory internal perspectives on the ending of Socrates' life.

As soon as the *Phaedo* begins, Plato sets his readers' minds on 'the end'—or, rather, the process of reaching an ending. Echecrates' question 'πῶς ἐτελεύτα;' establishes the telos of the *Phaedo* as, in many senses of the word, a clear account of Socrates' death.[48] This writes internal and external readers and listeners into a mood of anticipation and sets an expectation that 'death' will somehow be not just a climactic moment, but an ending. The narrative longing that results is sharpened by Echecrates' insistent requests for details on the 'actual death' and by Phaedo's failed efforts to quench Echecrates' desire.[49] The concluding echo in Phaedo's ἥδε ἡ τελευτή, 'This then was the end', thus brings the literary

---

[45] Rowe (1993) on 59b6–c6: 'it also, paradoxically, reminds us of his presence as author—while also denying it (after all, he wasn't even *there*)'. See further Dubel (2015: 16).

[46] The dialogues as 'self-conscious and manifest fictions': Crane (1996: 73).

[47] The author's irrelevance in Plato for an argument's truth: Edelstein (1962); Tarrant (2000: 79–80). See further Goldhill (2002: 5, 80–98) on the fifth-century invention of prose as a 'contest of authority'.

[48] Contrast Hackforth (1955: 187) who, as part of a wider approach that privileged Plato's philosophical purpose over his literary one, made one comment on the last scene of the *Phaedo*: 'This final section needs neither summary nor comment.'

[49] See especially 57a5–b3; 58c6–9; 58d2–3; 58d7–9, among other questions as to who was there and what was said. Echecrates insists on the 'actual moment' (as at 58c6, αὐτὸν τὸν θάνατον) rather than descriptions of Socrates drinking the hemlock (57b2) and how the trial went (58a1–3). Psychoanalysis of narrative, especially the 'textual erotics' of reading plot: Brooks (1984: esp. ch. 2). An 'expectation of closure' in the *Phaedo* (though he goes on to discuss how the myth leaves things open): Clay (2000: 172). See further Halperin (1992) on erotics of narrativity in the *Symposium*.

36 FIGURING DEATH IN CLASSICAL ATHENS

narrative in full circle, and reflects how Plato's literary medium has overdetermined Socrates' death as an ending.[50]

As pointed out in the introduction to this chapter (pages 25-6), emphasis on 'endings' seems at odds with the assumptions and arguments of the so-called philosophical parts of the dialogue regarding the immortality of the soul. Does Plato's writing frame Socrates' death in terms of endings in a counter thread to the *Phaedo*'s overt philosophy? Though I will explore this problem more fully in my conclusion, it is worth noting here that the anticipation that Plato generates with his narrative simulates for readers the psychological experience of waiting for (anticipating, fearing) another's imminent death.[51] The urgency of Socrates' condemned situation (his 'appointed hour' is $\nu\hat{\upsilon}\nu$ (115a5)) motivates and intensifies not just his companions' fear of death, an inevitable journey that they will make at some indefinite point in the future ($\ell\nu$ $\tau\iota\nu\iota$ $\chi\rho\acute{o}\nu\omega$, 115a4), but the philosophical imperative of neutralizing that fear. When Plato sets his readers' minds on the 'end', he harnesses the narrative urge of the text to replicate and to reinforce that urgency, and so to impel reflection on, and conquest of, the hobgoblins of death.[52]

Consider how Plato builds narrative tension in the *Phaedo* by thematizing the condition of waiting. The moment of Socrates' departure, the final absence, is prefigured in the persistent absence of the death moment from the text. Again and again the drama of the *Phaedo* is about waiting for Socrates to die: the naval mission must return from Delos (58a6–c5);[53] the prison must open (59d4–6); the Eleven must unchain Socrates (59e3–60a1); Socrates must finish his bath and bid farewell to his family, which takes 'a long time' (116a2–b6);[54] Crito suggests that Socrates stave off the end still further—'there's still time!' ($\check{\epsilon}\tau\iota$ $\gamma\grave{a}\rho$ $\check{\epsilon}\gamma\chi\omega\rho\epsilon\hat{\iota}$, 116e6); Socrates responds 'there's no longer anything of it left' ($o\mathring{\upsilon}\delta\epsilon\nu\grave{o}s$ $\check{\epsilon}\tau\iota$ $\mathring{\epsilon}\nu\acute{o}\nu\tau os$, 117a3)—surely we are at the end? Yet, even then, the boy takes 'a long time' to get the man who will administer the hemlock ($\sigma\upsilon\chi\nu\grave{o}\nu$ $\chi\rho\acute{o}\nu o\nu$

---

[50] Note Socrates' reference to his imminent death as 'the appointed hour' ($\mathring{\epsilon}\mu\grave{\epsilon}$ $\delta\grave{\epsilon}$ $\nu\hat{\upsilon}\nu$ $\mathring{\eta}\delta\eta$ $\kappa\alpha\lambda\epsilon\hat{\iota}$ ... $\mathring{\eta}$ $\epsilon\mathring{\iota}\mu\alpha\rho\mu\acute{\epsilon}\nu\eta$) when writing himself into a tragic hero role ($\varphi\alpha\acute{\iota}\eta$ $\mathring{a}\nu$ $\mathring{a}\nu\mathring{\eta}\rho$ $\tau\rho\alpha\gamma\iota\kappa\acute{o}s$), 115a5–6.

[51] Though Socrates' death initiates an existential discussion that affects all those present; all, inevitably, await death. Emphasizing the predicament of Socrates' companions in *Phaedo* the drama: Jansen (2013: 337).

[52] 77e8: $\tau\grave{a}$ $\mu o\rho\mu o\lambda\acute{\upsilon}\kappa\epsilon\iota\alpha$. Note Dorter (1982: 4–9): Socrates defends his fourteen named companions from the fear of death as Theseus protects his twice seven companions from the Minotaur (a running theme). See further Bacon (1990) on Socrates, Theseus, and Herakles. In the text, see 89c9–10 for Socrates as Herakles and 95b7–8 for his exhortation to approach in a Homeric way. Compare *Prt.* 340a1–6 for a call by Socrates for heroic assistance; *Grg.* 473d3 where Socrates accuses Polus of trying to frighten him ($\mu o\rho\mu o\lambda\acute{\upsilon}\tau\tau\eta$) with descriptions of punishment; *Cri.* 46c3–5 on the possibility that the power of the majority might frighten like a hobgoblin ($\mu o\rho\mu o\lambda\acute{\upsilon}\tau\tau\eta\tau\alpha\iota$). The connection between Socrates' use of charms and philosophical midwifery, an idea explored more widely in Plato's corpus: *Tht.* 157c7–d5.

[53] The *Crito* is set in this gap between Socrates' trial and execution (about a month).

[54] Socrates' bath is particularly teasing in effect because Plato sets up the expectation that the moment of death has finally arrived: $\mathring{\epsilon}\mu\grave{\epsilon}$ $\delta\grave{\epsilon}$ $\nu\hat{\upsilon}\nu$ $\mathring{\eta}\delta\eta$ $\kappa\alpha\lambda\epsilon\hat{\iota}$, $\varphi\alpha\acute{\iota}\eta$ $\mathring{a}\nu$ $\mathring{a}\nu\mathring{\eta}\rho$ $\tau\rho\alpha\gamma\iota\kappa\acute{o}s$, $\mathring{\eta}$ $\epsilon\mathring{\iota}\mu\alpha\rho\mu\acute{\epsilon}\nu\eta$, $\kappa\alpha\grave{\iota}$ $\sigma\chi\epsilon\delta\acute{o}\nu$ $\tau\acute{\iota}$ $\mu o\iota$ $\mathring{\omega}\rho\alpha$ $\tau\rho\alpha\pi\acute{\epsilon}\sigma\theta\alpha\iota$ $\pi\rho\grave{o}s$ $\tau\grave{o}$ $\lambda o\upsilon\tau\rho\acute{o}\nu\cdot$ (115a5–7). Orphic symbolism to the last bath: Stewart (1972).

διατρίψας, 117a6). Most importantly, Socrates must stop talking...Crito and the man who will administer the poison wait for some time to warn Socrates that he will delay his death if he talks too much (63d4–e2). Like Scheherazade's tales, the many, lengthy, philosophical arguments that Socrates proposes to defend his companions from the fear of death stave off the climax of his own end.[55] As Socrates says, his life is not long enough to prove the truth of his final tale, but 'nothing prevents me from talking...' (οὐδέν με κωλύει λέγειν, 108e1–2); 'one should sing things like this to oneself as a charm, as it were, which is precisely why I too have been prolonging this story for so long' (καὶ χρὴ τὰ τοιαῦτα ὥσπερ ἐπᾴδειν ἑαυτῷ, διὸ δὴ ἔγωγε καὶ πάλαι μηκύνω τὸν μῦθον, 114d6–8). Words, arguments, and stories fill the time before sunset; philosophy is as much about practising death as *waiting* for it.[56]

Moreover, if to be heard is to exist,[57] discussion, narrated or otherwise, sustains the life and immortality of the soul that its participants debate. At this point, I turn briefly to a passage on mourning the dying argument (89b4–c1):

> ...Αὔριον δή, ἔφη, ἴσως, ὦ Φαίδων, τὰς καλὰς ταύτας κόμας ἀποκερῇ.
>
> Ἔοικεν, ἦν δ' ἐγώ, ὦ Σώκρατες.
>
> Οὔκ, ἄν γε ἐμοὶ πείθῃ.
>
> Ἀλλὰ τί; ἦν δ' ἐγώ.
>
> Τήμερον, ἔφη, κἀγὼ τὰς ἐμὰς καὶ σὺ ταύτας, ἐάνπερ γε ἡμῖν ὁ λόγος τελευτήσῃ καὶ μὴ δυνώμεθα αὐτὸν ἀναβιώσασθαι.
>
> ...'Tomorrow, then, Phaedo,' he said, 'perhaps you'll shear off your beautiful hair.'
> 'It looks like it, Socrates,' I said.
> 'It doesn't; not if you're listening to me.'
> 'But what do you mean?' I asked.
> 'Today,' he said, 'I'll shear mine and you'll shear yours today if our argument dies and we can't bring it back to life.'

This interchange sets centre-stage a running correspondence between argument's failure and life's end (in counterpart to narrative's climax).[58] When Phaedo agrees

---

[55] Scheherazade's 'life-giving' narration not only delays and so 'sustains', but also 'arouses': Brooks (1984: 61).

[56] One philosophical topic of the *Phaedo* is the connection between practising philosophy and practising dying and being dead: see especially 64a4–67e7. Gundert (1971: 51) [1968] comments that the idea of philosophy as an exercise in dying is 'das eigentliche Thema des *Phaidon*'.

[57] See Phillips (2021: 48–54) for discussion of Stewart (2009: 58) on 'poetry's agency in the formation of selfhood' (page 51) and, further, on the relationship between listening, self-reflection, and 'enactment of selfhood' (page 53) (pertinent here in Socrates' anticipation of Phaedo's response to his words, which constitutes Socrates' own sense of selfhood, 'not if you're listening to me'). Indeed, throughout her chapter, Susan Stewart explores the interrelationships between philosophy and lyric, for example 'both [...] are solo speakers' (page 45). Compare Bakhtin (1981: 134), 'For the classical Greek, every aspect of existence could be *seen* and *heard*.'

[58] Following Bakhtin, the chronotope of Socrates' life's course gives flesh and blood to the abstraction of philosophy: Bakhtin (1981: 250).

38 FIGURING DEATH IN CLASSICAL ATHENS

that he will cut his beautiful hair on the day after Socrates' death,[59] Socrates impresses philosophy's own fragility. For Socrates, losing his argument is a double death because it concedes the mortality of his soul. In fact, the symbiosis of philosophy and life also emerged in Xanthippe's rejected emotional outcry on seeing her husband's friends enter his cell (60a5–6):

Ὦ Σώκρατες, ὕστατον δή σε προσεροῦσι νῦν οἱ ἐπιτήδειοι καὶ σὺ τούτους.

Socrates, this is the very last time your friends will be speaking with you, and you with them.

The literary philosophy that unfolds in the dialogue thus anticipates and post-pones the end of the philosopher together with its own dialectic and narrative conclusion.

At the end of the dialogue, Socrates finally drinks the hemlock (117c3–5):

Καὶ ἅμ' εἰπὼν ταῦτα ἐπισχόμενος καὶ μάλα εὐχερῶς καὶ εὐκόλως ἐξέπιεν.

And as soon as he'd said this he put the cup to his lips and, with remarkable indifference and composure, drank it down.

This is immediately followed by a violent outpouring of grief. Phaedo's tears come in an abundant flood (ἀστακτὶ ἐχώρει τὰ δάκρυα, 117c8); Crito is over-whelmed, unable to withstand the onslaught of tears (οὐχ οἷός τ' ἦν κατέχειν τὰ δάκρυα, 117d2–3). In a gesture of surrender, both conceal themselves: Phaedo with his veil (117c8); Crito stands up and apart (117d3). Apollodorus' guttural eruption (ἀναβρυχησάμενος, 117d5) into fresh bouts of distressed weeping bor-ders on inhuman. His companions' lamentation offers the momentary possibility that Socrates has actually died: *this* is the climax for which we have waited.[60] With

---

[59] The language with which Phaedo describes how Socrates' stroked his head and played with his hair, and his subsequent words, is laced with the pain of intimacy that will be lost and beauty that will be marred. The combination of an image of mourning with an erotic theme—the imminent sunset of Phaedo's youth and beauty—may hint at Phaedo's own mortality: compare Anac. *PMG* 347 fr. 1, vv. 1–9, in which the poet grieves over the shorn head of Smerdies, envisaging his hair as a soldier, falling in the dust at a stroke of iron (separation from the beloved seen through the prism of separation in death): see Bernsdorff (2020: ii.356–72).

[60] The noisiness of burials (in contrast to the reverent silence that Socrates wants): Rowe (1993) on 117e1–2. Readers' pleasure at the narrative climax might echo the pleasure of Socrates' companions in emotional and sensory indulgence and the pleasure of philosophy. Compare *Prt.* 335d4–5 on the pleas-ure of listening to philosophical discussion; *Phlb.* 47d5–50e2 on the mixture of pleasure and pain in mournings, tragedies, and comedies, and 39c7–e6 on anticipation; *Resp.* 4.439e5–440a4, Leontius' disgusted desire to look at the 'fine spectacle' of some corpses. See Liebert (2017: ch. 3) on tragic pleas-ure in Plato's *Republic*, especially 155–70 on the pleasure of grief. Emotional impact as an important part of Plato's dialogues and argument: Blank (1993: esp. 436–7). See further Gallop (2003) on emotional power as a means of catharsis. Like him (pages 327–9), I disagree with Nussbaum (2001: 131–3) [1986], who comments on the dialogue's appeal to our intellect ('the dialogue explicitly teaches that [grief or pity] are immature and unhelpful responses' (page 131). More generally, see Rapp (2015: 444–5) on

this sensorily and emotionally intense moment, Plato prefigures the overwhelming impact of death evinced in Socrates' later ecphrasis (discussed in section IV, Swan Song). But Socrates still lives, as his blithe and gentle chiding reminds them (117d7–e2):[61]

> Ἐκεῖνος δέ, Οἷα, ἔφη, ποιεῖτε, ὦ θαυμάσιοι. ἐγὼ μέντοι οὐχ ἥκιστα τούτου ἕνεκα τὰς γυναῖκας ἀπέπεμψα, ἵνα μὴ τοιαῦτα πλημμελοῖεν· καὶ γὰρ ἀκήκοα ὅτι ἐν εὐφημίᾳ χρὴ τελευτᾶν. ἀλλ᾽ ἡσυχίαν τε ἄγετε καὶ καρτερεῖτε.

> But he said, 'what strange behaviour, you odd lot! And when it was for this reason above all that I sent the women away: so they wouldn't sound offkey like this! For I've also heard that one should die in silence. But quieten down and pull yourselves together.'

The astonishing (in Socrates' eyes) nature of his companions' response— ὦ θαυμάσιοι (117d7)—is a mirrored glimpse of what it might look like to behold the real deal: at the start of his narrative, Phaedo described the experience of being present with Socrates on his final day in the same language, as 'marvellous' (Καὶ μὴν ἔγωγε θαυμάσια ἔπαθον παραγενόμενος, 58e1–2).[62] In prefiguring what is still to come, the passion of the scene thus heightens, rather than satisfies, readers' and listeners' longing. Death the final stage must be even more astonishing... Emotional response to death is still closely bound up with the tension of waiting.

Then Plato unfolds a scene of cool, clinically precise attention to the progress of the hemlock upwards from Socrates' feet towards his heart.[63] The pace slows as the poison takes effect, and a mood of fascinated horror sets in as the narrative creeps towards its inevitable end (117e4–118a3):

---

emotions and Plato. Weeping for oneself and not the dying Socrates fits with emphasis in this chapter on the viewing or listening subject's perspective.

[61] To the extent that readers noticed echoes of Archil. fr. 13 West in this passage, Socrates' words not only affirm the sense in which his death is a 'bloody wound' that merits mourning (in moderation) by his companions but also the sense in which the occasion evokes a curious mixture of pleasure, pain, laughter, and tears, such as one might experience in the context of sympotic poetry. See further Steiner (2012) on the variegated quality and consolatory function of fr. 13.

[62] See especially Huitink (2020) for an embodied approach to ἐνάργεια. A similar bodily and emotional imaginative engagement with Socrates' death may be shown here.

[63] Bloch (2002) argues that this scene is a medically realistic exposition of the symptoms caused by ingestion of poison hemlock. While this does not change my treatment with respect to the historicity of the *Phaedo*, it is important that this is not a self-consciously poetic departure from well-known symptoms of seizure, as suggested in Gill (1973) and previously widely accepted. She also argues (pages 265–7) that Plato/Phaedo does not describe Socrates' body as cold and stiff, but as 'thick' and 'stuck' (paralysed). Below, I refer to temperature and rigidity, but perhaps we should think instead in terms of immobility and numbness. This would increase the contrast between the sensory perspective of Socrates and the anonymous man.

40 FIGURING DEATH IN CLASSICAL ATHENS

ὁ δὲ περιελθών, ἐπειδή οἱ βαρύνεσθαι ἔφη τὰ σκέλη, κατεκλίνη ὕπτιος—οὕτω γὰρ ἐκέλευεν ὁ ἄνθρωπος—καὶ ἅμα ἐφαπτόμενος αὐτοῦ οὗτος ὁ δοὺς τὸ φάρμακον, διαλιπὼν χρόνον ἐπεσκόπει τοὺς πόδας καὶ τὰ σκέλη, κἄπειτα σφόδρα πιέσας αὐτοῦ τὸν πόδα ἤρετο εἰ αἰσθάνοιτο· ὁ δ' οὐκ ἔφη. καὶ μετὰ τοῦτο αὖθις τὰς κνήμας· καὶ ἐπανιὼν οὕτως ἡμῖν ἐπεδείκνυτο ὅτι ψύχοιτό τε καὶ πήγνυτο.

[Socrates] walked around, and then, when he said his legs were getting heavy, he lay down on his back (because the man told him to do that) and at the same time the man who had given him the hemlock took hold of him and after a while he inspected his feet and legs, and then, squeezing his foot firmly, he asked if he could feel anything. He said he couldn't. And after this, he repeated the process on his shins. And moving upwards like this he showed us that he was getting cold and rigid.

Focus is still on sensory experience, but Plato sets against the appetitive experience of Socrates' companions the enervated impassivity of the moribund Socrates. The thundering inundation of their lamentation is met with a body that freezes stiffer and eventually falls silent (ταῦτα ἐρομένου αὐτοῦ οὐδὲν ἔτι ἀπεκρίνατο, 118a11). In fact, on Phaedo's presentation, the last sensation felt by Socrates is the heaviness of his legs (οἱ βαρύνεσθαι ἔφη τὰ σκέλη, 117e4–5).[64] The rest of the sensory experience of death (the touch of his foot and shins; the coldness and stiffness of his body and the areas about his abdomen) is not felt by him at all. These all appear to be sensations suffered by the anonymous man who brought Socrates the hemlock.[65] With an abundance of sensory details and reflections upon them, Phaedo shows us a man that is not only losing his sense of touch but losing his status as a person. Socrates' body is grasped, squeezed, doubly inspected beneath the professional eyes of the man who gave him the hemlock and the spectating eyes of his companions, even multiply inspected once we include Phaedo's listeners and Plato's readers. Who is the 'us' (ἡμῖν) to whom the man demonstrates what is happening to Socrates' body? Not, it appears, Socrates (who might be most interested in what is happening to his body); Phaedo has usually used 'we' to refer to himself and to Socrates' other companions.[66] The anonymous man's actions seem no longer to be directed towards Socrates, but

---

[64] Note the contrast here with the detail in 60b1–c7 where Plato/Phaedo/Socrates draws attention to Socrates' pose, legs, and sensory experience. When Socrates sits, rubs his own leg, and comments on the reciprocity between pleasure and pain, he prefigures the later scene in which he lies down, has his leg felt by someone else, and feels nothing. The narrative detail in 60b1–c7 thus not only flags one of the philosophical arguments to follow (the argument from opposites at 69e5–72d10) but also models that argument in the context of death—the process and experience of Socrates' dying in 117e4–118a3 (and, indeed, the experience of the living in response to it, 59a5–59a8) is equal and opposite to the process and experience of living in 60b1–c7. For a synoptic view of opposites in the *Phaedo*, see Ausland (1997: 397–406).

[65] On ambiguity here, see Petraki (2021: 189, with note 50).

[66] Elsewhere ἡμῖν can refer to readers of historical writings: see e.g. Polyb. 8.8.4.

DEATH COMES AS THE END   41

towards his audience. In this way, over the course of these lines, Socrates becomes, progressively, an object—a physical object of touch and sight, a notional object of discourse. With this divergence of subjectivities (represented in feeling and unfeeling bodies), Plato brings us tantalizingly close to seeing dying itself, the extinguishing of the subjective 'I' in the switch from life to death.[67]

As the hemlock nears Socrates' heart, Phaedo makes the following observation (118a6–7):

καὶ ἐκκαλυψάμενος—ἐνεκεκάλυπτο γάρ—εἶπεν—ὃ δὴ τελευταῖον ἐφθέγξατο—

and uncovering himself—for he had wrapped himself up—he said—and this was the last thing he said—

When Socrates speaks his final words, he lifts a veil.[68] Plato teeters on the brink of showing us, face to face, the moment of Socrates' death. Socrates is silent; Phaedo uses the ominously passive verb 'he was moved' ($\dot{\epsilon}\kappa\iota\nu\dot{\eta}\theta\eta$, 118a12): is *this* the moment of death?[69] But Phaedo continues 'the man uncovered him, and he presented a fixed stare' (ὁ ἄνθρωπος ἐξεκάλυψεν αὐτόν, καὶ ὃς τὰ ὄμματα ἔστησεν, 118a12–13).[70] Somehow, in between his final words and his deathly gaze, Socrates was covered once again. The moment itself, the mysterious point of change, is a point of failure, hidden behind Socrates' veil. The mask-like face of the corpse does not belong to Socrates.[71] We missed the death. Though Phaedo has drawn tantalizingly close to showing eclipsed subjectivity,[72] his collapse of the before and after suggests that, even for an eyewitness, the moment of death confounds words.

In the verbal medium of the *Phaedo*, the representation of Socrates' death continues until the end of the argument, the end of the philosopher's life, and the closing of 'the' mouth and 'the' eyes that belong naturally to Socrates but are grammatically unspecified so as to belong also to Crito or Phaedo or Plato or his readers (118a13–14):

ἰδὼν δὲ ὁ Κρίτων συνέλαβε τὸ στόμα καὶ τοὺς ὀφθαλμούς.

When Crito saw this he closed the mouth and eyes.

---

[67] Dying as change of state (between opposites): 70c4–72d10. For a rebuttal see Williams (1969).

[68] This is the first mention of Socrates' veil and is presumably introduced so that it may be removed.

[69] Gill (1973: 28) suggests that this motion might be the departure of Socrates' soul.

[70] Plato's use of the transitive aorist ἔστησεν gives Socrates, as subject of the verb, agency here even in the moment of his fixed stare.

[71] This is a point that Socrates has emphasized in the *Phaedo*, notably at 115c4–116a1.

[72] Though ἔστησεν hints at Socrates' continued, fleeting agency, raising the possibility that the veil lifts in the instant that Socrates dies, Plato's language is ambiguous; it also communicates shock—the sudden realization that Socrates is already dead.

When Crito sees Socrates' dead face with his own open eyes, he closes the philosopher's eyes and shuts his mouth.[73] And nothing more is heard from Socrates, or from Crito either, for the voice of Phaedo turns away to Echecrates to define, to objectify, and to silence the great philosopher (118a15–17):

ἥδε ἡ τελευτή, ὦ Ἐχέκρατες, τοῦ ἑταίρου ἡμῖν ἐγένετο, ἀνδρός, ὡς ἡμεῖς φαῖμεν ἄν, τῶν τότε ὧν ἐπειράθημεν ἀρίστου καὶ ἄλλως φρονιμωτάτου καὶ δικαιοτάτου.

This became the end, Echecrates, of our companion, of a man, who we would say, of the men at that time whom we put to the test, was the best and above all the wisest and most just.

In a Janus-like switch from the waiting game, Plato elides straight into memory. The narrative promise of death as the end in πῶς ἐτελεύτα is met with ἡ τελευτή, but instead of an 'end', Plato writes a memorial to the 'achievement' of Socrates the 'best, wisest, and most just',[74] treating him to the Homeric beautiful death in his celebratory response and in his blend of narrated action and dialogue.[75] With a flash of polysemy,[76] Phaedo's retreat from the moment of Socrates' death reveals another climax, Plato's *Death of Socrates*.[77]

Thus, against the fearfully expectant current of Plato's literary philosophy echoes the life of his text: Plato's written account of Phaedo's narrated representation of Socrates' demise. The anticipation of Socrates' end that unites Plato's external and internal audiences sits in mirrored counterpart to the retrospection of author and narrator, who not only remember but also memorialize Socrates with a verbal monument that stands in permanent attestation of his death even as it offers ongoing communion with him by means of its representational substitute.[78]

In this way, throughout the *Phaedo*, Plato builds a tension between anticipation and recollection, build-up and aftermath: these two conflicting temporal drives, both part of a narrative mode, dominate the lived experience of another's death.

---

[73] Closing the mouth is a standard part of ancient Greek funerary practice; prothesis scenes on pots sometimes show chin straps on the head of the deceased, used to hold the jaw closed: see Kurtz and Boardman (1971: 144 with pl. 33). Here it has the additional effect of drawing attention to Socrates' silence and the end of his discussion.

[74] See Nails (2005: 17): with this epithet, Phaedo echoes the words of the unnamed man who brought the hemlock.

[75] On the Homeric beautiful death: Vernant (1991a: esp. 57–8). Socrates as hero: note 52. I disagree with Wilamowitz-Moellendorff (1920: 179) that Plato's language here is cold and restrained.

[76] See Derrida (2003) [1968] on the φάρμακον (cure/poison) in Plato's *Phaedrus* and the volatility of writing.

[77] The death of Socrates as the climax of his life and Plato's role in creating that image for posterity: Wilson (2007). The visual appeal of Socrates' death: Lapatin (2005: 140–5). See further Burnet (1911: x), 'the likeness of a great philosopher in the supreme crisis of his life'; Gallop (1975: 74), 'a philosophical memoir rather than a biographical record'; Silverman (2003: 267, 286) on the *Phaedo* as a eulogy.

[78] Perpetuated communion through the image: see page 93, note 141. See further Estrin (2016); Arrington (2018: note 3).

DEATH COMES AS THE END   43

IV. SWAN SONG

I now turn to a passage in which Plato imagines an encounter with death from the perspective of the dying Socrates: what might it be like to face something unfathomable?[79] I explore how Plato uses literary texture to communicate ignorance and awe, and how, by spectacular failure, he comments on the imaginative nature of his writing.[80] The passage is 111c4–115a3, Socrates' fantastic ecphrasis of the regions within the earth and the land of the dead.

From the outset, Plato presents Socrates' ecphrasis as imaginative.[81] He explicitly sets Socrates' description (διηγήσασθαι, 108d5; διελήλυθα, 114d2) within a cautionary frame. At the start of his account (the geography of the earth and the experience of souls in the afterlife), Socrates opens with the comment that, while no prophetic skill is needed for description, it is too difficult even with Glaucus' skill to prove its truth (108d4–6).[82] He closes his description with the acknowledgement that it would not be suitable for any man in his right mind to rely on things being as he has described (114d1–2). Socrates suggests that the challenge of telling the truth about death lies not only in the limits of time (ὁ βίος μοι δοκεῖ ὁ ἐμός [...] τῷ μήκει τοῦ λόγου οὐκ ἐξαρκεῖν, 108d8–9), but in the confines of human knowledge (εἰ καὶ ἠπιστάμην, 108d7–8); with this he puts a question mark over mankind's ability to think inside the black box of death.

Having posited (via Socrates) the epistemological impossibility of thinking our way into the mind of someone who will and does actually die, Plato then explores the possibility of surmounting it. Socrates' narrative (μῦθος) thus emerges as a parallel for Plato's.[83] Aside from Plato's other possible motivations for including this passage,[84] one lies in the value of myth as an experiential counterpart to

---

[79] The title of this section is inspired by Socrates' words in 84e3–85b7. For a similar title, see Gallop (2003).

[80] Socrates' imaginative account has apparently come from another source; he has been persuaded by 'someone' (τινος, 108c8). This source has either been lost or else Plato has Socrates give this vague reference as part of an ongoing thread in the *Phaedo* on hearsay and the challenge of hearing something clear (σαφές). There is a running conceit that Socrates is repeating theories that he has heard from others (ὡς ἐγὼ ὑπό τινος πέπεισμαι, 108c7–8; references to Socrates' having been persuaded at 108d3 and 108e1; Socrates' use of the passive λέγεται to refer to his account at 110b5). This picks up the problem of getting a clear account from a report. Noting the anonymous/mysterious hearsay that underpins Socrates' myths of judgment in the *Gorgias*, *Phaedo*, and *Republic*: Clay (2000: 174).

[81] Imaginative in the sense of experiencing something in the absence of its physical presence. On processes of imagination in Classical Athens, see Clifford and Buxton (2024a).

[82] Critiquing six possible Glaucuses cited in the scholia and Eusebius: Clay (1985). It is plausible that Socrates refers to a seventh (the sea-god Glaucus Pontius) not least because of his prophetic powers. For other reasons, see Clay (1985: 233–6), especially on links to the imagery and philosophy of the *Republic*.

[83] Socrates and Simmias explicitly refer to Socrates' account as a μῦθος at 110b1 and b4, and 114d8. See further: Dorter (1970: 565) on the *Phaedo*'s ambiguous status as, itself, 'mythology'; note 85.

[84] At 114d1–115a3, for example, Socrates suggests that the value of his μῦθος lies in its ability to help the philosopher ward off fear and prepare for death in the best way.

44 FIGURING DEATH IN CLASSICAL ATHENS

other forms of encounter with death in the *Phaedo*: philosophy and description.[85] Consider Socrates' (enigmatic) declaration at 61d9–e4, when he offers an optimistic take on the value of description.[86] When it comes to the time before sunset (ἐν τῷ μέχρι ἡλίου δυσμῶν χρόνῳ), confrontation with an experience of maximum uncertainty and remoteness from what is familiar, 'going away from *home* to *that (unspecified) place*' (ἐκεῖσε ἀποδημεῖν), what can the dying do but 'look in different ways' and 'give an account' (διασκοπεῖν τε καὶ μυθολογεῖν)?[87] Socrates suggests that a diverse approach, looking and talking in different ways about death, is intrinsically appropriate to his situation.

This offers a hint of optimism as to the possibilities of overcoming the conceptual challenge posed by death. As a result, the spectre of ecphrastic failure that overshadows this passage indicates how not to read, or respond, to Socrates' words: what questions not to ask.[88] If we think about ecphrasis as orchestrating a way of seeing and experiencing (as opposed to effecting, as far as possible, replication of its referent),[89] Socrates' ecphrasis operates as a window into the mind of a dying man as he encounters death.[90] As Socrates says at the end of the passage (114d2–6, my emphasis):

[85] See Ferrari (1987) on the strengths of μῦθος (in complement to argument) and, in any case, the importance of attending to substance not form; Osborne (1996: 185–91, 208–11) on Timaeus' creative discourse in the *Timaeus*, 'the story is not a candidate for truth, but an example or icon; it deliberately fabricates a new likeness that only partially resembles reality' (page 186); Morgan (2000) on the interconnected nature of myth and philosophy—myth 'not just as a foil but as a mode of philosophical thought and presentation' (page 3)—and on how Socrates' recourse to myth in the *Phaedo* offers 'a discourse that acknowledges our limitations while providing emotional satisfaction' (2000: 192–201, citation at 200); Nightingale (2002a) on the value of 'fantastic' mimesis for representation of 'unseen reality' (in contrast to 'eikastic' mimesis, of which the early dialogues themselves are an example, which articulates epistemic distance from the truth); Nightingale (2002b: 235–6) on the dialogic relation of μῦθος to other genres of discourse here (μῦθος as persuasive not authoritative); Edmonds (2004: esp. 159–71, 219–20) on the traditional and authoritative contribution of myth to Socrates' arguments in the *Phaedo*; Rowe (2007: 108) on the 'soaring freedom of the philosophical soul' in contrast to ordinary non-philosophical perspectives; Martinez (2013: 37–40) on the value of the 'eikastic' μῦθος (the myth that aims to clarify philosophical truths, not to be aesthetically pleasing), especially when direct empirical experience is not possible; McCabe (2015: 83–99) on myth's dialectic opposition to argument. Myth leaves the project open: Clay (2000: 172).

[86] Socrates' voice should not be assumed to be authoritative, or a mouthpiece for Plato's own views: see note 37. Socrates gives one compelling viewpoint and a voice of optimism in circumstances that might otherwise arm the simplistic view that Plato dislikes representation and the arts.

[87] Consider a related idea (with different emphasis) at *Criti.* 107a6–e3: when it comes to a topic about which listeners are inexperienced and ignorant (such as 'the gods'), a speaker has an abundance of things to say and can get away with indistinct and deceptive illusionism.

[88] Or else we might get in a muddle: see Annas (1982: 125), 'the message is blurred'.

[89] On the different levels of attention in ecphrasis: Becker (1995: 41–4).

[90] 'A truly transcendental perspective': Clay (2000: 175).

ὅτι μέντοι ἢ ταῦτ' ἐστὶν ἢ τοιαῦτ' ἄττα περὶ τὰς ψυχὰς ἡμῶν καὶ τὰς οἰκήσεις, ἐπείπερ
ἀθάνατόν γε ἡ ψυχὴ φαίνεται οὖσα, τοῦτο καὶ πρέπειν μοι δοκεῖ καὶ ἄξιον κινδυνεῦσαι
οἰομένῳ οὕτως ἔχειν...

however, it seems fitting to me that things are like this, or else *something like this*,
as regards our souls and their dwelling places (since, at any rate, the soul is clearly
something immortal) and it seems worth someone's risk to think that things are
like this.

Let us consider the texture of Socrates' ecphrastic μῦθος of the afterlife, asking
not 'why this?' but 'why *like* this?' Though all words form part of a wider conversation between Phaedo and Echecrates, Socrates' extended speech is also a
monologue embedded within Phaedo's narrative. This begs the question, why
confront death in monologue? Four interconnected strands emerge: privilege,
poetics, isolation, and consciousness.

First, privilege. Monologue does not necessitate monophony but it can, unlike
dialogue, accommodate it. Though utterances respond and anticipate response,[91]
in monologue one speaker dominates for a period that is comparatively long,
conferring upon her words a solitary tenor.[92] The association between monologue and the sole voice is reflected in scholarship on Plato and more widely,
which has drawn links between monologue and tyrannical univocality, in contrast to the opportunity offered by dialogue for exploring different viewpoints.[93]
The political angle is less relevant here, but Socrates' sole and unimpeded voice
does provide an insight into his privileged experience of death. This sits alongside the broader relationship in Greek culture between the moment before death
and prophecy: while Socrates asserts that he needs no skill in prophecy to say
what he does, his venture into the realm of the unknown (and, it seems, his soul's
own future) hints at the sort of deathly prophecies we find elsewhere in Greek
literature.[94] As he observed at 61d10–e4 (see above), examination of the life
beyond and telling stories about it is particularly fitting for someone who is
about to die. Monologue is the right form for Socrates when he anticipates his
own encounter with death because no one apart from Socrates can speak, whether
in corroboration or disagreement. The dying voice is necessarily authoritative by

---

[91] Multi-way communication is not inevitably and entirely absent from monologue. As stressed
by Mikhail Bakhtin, uttered words are always in dialogue with one another: Bakhtin (1981: esp. 272,
276–7), (2004: 60–102, esp. 92) [1986]; Greenwood (2008: 16–18).

[92] Though, on the 'inner dialogue of the soul with itself' presented in the *Theaetetus*: Clay (2000: 161).

[93] For a brief history of dialogue as a genre and discussion of its political, social, and religious implications and associated theories: Goldhill (2008a: esp. 8–10 on Bakhtin). On the association between form
(monologue, for example) and, indeed, writing itself, and authoritarianism in Greek culture, see Blondell
(2002: 39–48). Polyphony and democratic potentialities in the 'Socratic' dialogues: Euben (1996: esp.
351–3). See note 13.

[94] For example: *Il.* 22.355–60. See further *Ap.* 39c1–d10.

46 FIGURING DEATH IN CLASSICAL ATHENS

virtue of its privileged perspective. In this respect, for Socrates to speak in monologue illustrates the obstacle that Plato encounters in imagining death from his viewpoint at all.[95]

Moreover, the opportunity to speak his mind unimpeded invites poetic language.[96] Shedding the fetters of accountability, Socrates throws wide his imagination. The poetics of Plato's passage, with its sound effect, imagery, and colour,[97] and the impression that the description operates on a figurative rather than literal level,[98] fit with a model that sees the monologue as offering a creative outlet. Plato's poetics resonate with what Kathryn Morgan calls the 'vertigo' of myth, flinging Socrates' μῦθος beyond the limits of human language and existence.[99] In this way, the mythical form and associated texture of Plato's writing at this point enact the necessity of thinking outside the bounds of familiar experience.

The sole voice is also a voice of solitude. Socrates' monologue verbalizes his (forthcoming) severance from the living world and conceptual capabilities of his companions. Impressions of distance and incoherence in his ecphrasis communicate this separation. The one certain thing about the space of death is its distance from the space of life: it is somewhere else.[100] This featured previously in 61e1 where Socrates described death as 'to go away from *home* to *that place*' (ἐκεῖσε ἀποδημεῖν).[101] Here, the space of death is imagined in the most remote terms possible (111e6–112a5):

> ἕν τι τῶν χασμάτων τῆς γῆς ἄλλως τε μέγιστον τυγχάνει ὂν καὶ διαμπερὲς τετρημένον δι' ὅλης τῆς γῆς, τοῦτο ὅπερ Ὅμηρος εἶπε, λέγων αὐτό
>
> > τῆλε μάλ', ἧχι βάθιστον ὑπὸ χθονός ἐστι βέρεθρον·
>
> ὃ καὶ ἄλλοθι καὶ ἐκεῖνος καὶ ἄλλοι πολλοὶ τῶν ποιητῶν Τάρταρον κεκλήκασιν.

> One of the gaping chasms of the earth happens to be especially enormous and bores right through the whole earth. This is what Homer is describing when he says it is
>
> > very far off, where there is the deepest gulf beneath the earth,
>
> that place which elsewhere too he and many other poets call Tartarus.

The separate space of death is a familiar idea from wider Greek thought, going back at least as far as Homer.[102] Socrates envisages Tartarus as another open

---

[95] The myth of Er is another way to do it: see pages 1–4.

[96] Plato's language and the connection between poetry, tyranny, and desire in the *Republic*: Murray (2017). Compare the despotic power of dainty beauties (οἱ τρυφῶντες) in *Meno* 76b7–c1. Conversely, on dialogue's 'ludic power': Goldhill (2008a: 9).

[97] Interaction of breath and water provides 'terrible and unbearable winds' (112b8–9); water fills the regions of Tartarus like men irrigating (112c3); rivers circle the earth like snakes (112d7); the Stygian river is described as 'wholly a sort of blue-grey colour' (113b8–c1).

[98] Dorter (1982: ch. 10).   [99] Morgan (2000: 6).

[100] On Plato's eschatological chronotopes and the distance and difference (temporal, spatial, and epistemic) that they articulate: Nightingale (2002a: esp. 239–42). See further Nightingale (2002b: 228–37) on the *Phaedo*'s chronotope as an ecological eschatology of the present, heterotopic and heterochronic.

[101] Similar language of departure: *Cri.* 54a9–10.

[102] E.g. *Od.* 24.11–14.

mouth (χάσμα) that is the biggest and deepest of all; it could not be deeper because it gapes right through the earth (διαμπερὲς τετρημένον δι' ὅλης τῆς γῆς). The more details Socrates provides, the harder it is to visualize deathly space; instead, visual details evoke a powerful impression of unimaginable deepness, downness, remoteness, separateness. Tartarus is literally 'the place called below/downwards' (τὸν τόπον τὸν δὴ κάτω καλούμενον, 112c1–2). The lowest point of Tartarus is the centre of a deep space that runs right through the earth (112d8–e3):

> δυνατὸν δέ ἐστιν ἑκατέρωσε μέχρι τοῦ μέσου καθιέναι, πέρα δ' οὔ· ἄναντες γὰρ ἀμφοτέροις τοῖς ῥεύμασι τὸ ἑκατέρωθεν γίγνεται μέρος.
>
> And it is possible to travel down either way as far as the centre, but not beyond. For the direction of both streams runs uphill on either side.

Tartarus is a Charybdis-like vortex that swallows deeper down and spews back up. All waters that enter it come in lower (κατωτέρω, 112d3) than they exit, some fall 'downwards as far as possible' (εἰς τὸ δυνατὸν κάτω, 112d7–8) before bursting back in. Vast Oceanus circles Tartarus on the 'outermost' borders (ἐξωτάτω, 112e7):[103] the space of the dead is not only cut off from the space of the living but also recedes far from that point.

The affective and sensory concentration of Socrates' description continues the impression that an encounter with death is overwhelming, visually and narratologically incoherent.[104] As observed elsewhere, Ἅιδης (Hades) is ἀϊδής (unseen).[105] For all the precision with which the landscape of death (the river network) is described, geographical features privilege emotional and sensory impact over visual specificity: Acheron is a flow of pain (ἄχος); Cocytus is a tumbling powerful, plunging, winding shrieking (κωκυτός); the Stygian-coloured lake Styx is a strangely formidable and wild (δεινόν τε καὶ ἄγριον) place of hatred (στύγος) (113b6–c2).[106] Even Pyriphlegethon, a river with vibrant visual impact as an outbreaking, out-falling, circling, winding, fragment-sprouting flaming of fire (113a6–b6), is not only muddy and clayey (θολερὸς καὶ πηλώδης, 113b1), but also 'hot and passionate' (same word: θολερός). Socrates' ecphrasis communicates a visceral emotional and sensory encounter with death.[107]

This mirrors Phaedo's aesthetic response to the whole of Socrates' final day. As Phaedo prepared for his own monologue-like description of Socrates' death, he

---

[103] Oceanos also mythically circled the earth: Emlyn-Jones and Prendy (2017: 505, note 131).

[104] See Kotin (2001) on another deliberately complex ecphrasis that represents the philosophy of the work in which it is situated: the shield of Achilles in *Il.* 18.478–608.

[105] For example: Dorter (1970: 578); Bacon (1990: 156–8), also linking ᾄδειν to find a triple pun. Also: *Grg.* 493b4–5 (but see *Cra.* 403a5–404b4 for rejection of this link).

[106] These derivations: Emlyn-Jones and Prendy (2017: 505, note 132). The terrible and fearful nature of names of this sort: *Resp.* 3.387b8–c6.

[107] The physicality of viewing death and its representations: Turner (2016: 145).

48 FIGURING DEATH IN CLASSICAL ATHENS

observed 'Well then, it was an awesome experience for me to be there' (Καὶ μὴν ἔγωγε θαυμάσια ἔπαθον παραγενόμενος, 58e1–2), and continued (59a5–9):

> ἀλλ' ἀτεχνῶς ἄτοπόν τί μοι πάθος παρῆν καί τις ἀήθης κρᾶσις ἀπό τε τῆς ἡδονῆς συγκεκραμένη ὁμοῦ καὶ ἀπὸ τῆς λύπης, ἐνθυμουμένῳ ὅτι αὐτίκα ἐκεῖνος ἔμελλε τελευτᾶν. καὶ πάντες οἱ παρόντες σχεδόν τι οὕτω διεκείμεθα, τοτὲ μὲν γελῶντες, ἐνίοτε δὲ δακρύοντες . . .

> But it was, quite simply, an extraordinary experience for me and an unfamiliar mixture of pleasure mingled with pain all at once when I reflected upon the fact that he was about to die. And all of us who were there felt more or less like this, one moment laughing, at others crying . . .

The strangeness of Phaedo's experience in the build-up to Socrates' death (θαυμάσια), and the contradictory mixture of emotions that accompanied that experience (pleasure, pain, laughter, sorrow) is a counterpart to the 'wondrous places' (θαυμαστοί, 108c6) that Socrates describes. The aesthetics of Socrates' ecphrasis articulate the somatic experience of encountering death.[108] What matters, then, is not the content but the way Socrates imagines Tartarus.

The overwhelming impact of death endures in the disorientating impression that Socrates gives of repeated movement from place to place in Tartarus. Socrates' earlier reference to death as a movement from home to an unspecified place (ἐκεῖσε ἀποδημεῖν, 61e1), persists in his picture of perpetual recession from the familiar. The waters of Tartarus flow in and out in an oscillating motion like breathing (112b3–9); rivers flow in circles (112d6–8); souls move from place to place (113d1–114c6), some borne endlessly by rivers in and out of Tartarus in hope of forgiveness by those they wronged (114b2–6). In a similar pattern, Socrates moves from one detail to the next, from Oceanos, to Acheron, to Pyriphlegethon, and so on, mimicking the move he will make himself from the familiar to the strange. Socrates extends the moment of death into a series of departures. In this way, the monologue operates as an expansion of the instant of encountering death. The temporal stagnation in the eternal present of Socrates' monologue sets his experience apart from that of his companions, which is characterized by forward and backward perspectives. By dwelling on the immediacy of the moment of encounter, Plato communicates both Socrates' experiential isolation from the living and his confrontation with the unfathomable: an eternal instant is conceptually bewildering.

Yet the adjective θαυμαστός is applied to Socrates' whole description, and therefore covers his ecphrasis not only of Tartarus but also the world of the living

---

[108] This includes a philosophical encounter with death as well as an empirical one. The wonder that accompanies Platonic contemplation (θεωρία): Nightingale (2004: 258–61). See Hunzinger (2015: esp. 432–3) more generally on the productivity and perils of wonder.

DEATH COMES AS THE END   49

and the purer world of the Forms. Strangeness is not peculiar to death, but to the human experience of confronting something outside the bounds of human knowledge. This dynamic plays throughout Socrates' ecphrasis via a paradox of negative definition.[109] Contrariness permeates Socrates' description: the four named rivers are in some way 'opposite' one another: καταντικρύ describes the relationship between Oceanos and Acheron at 112e8, Pyriphlegethon and Cocytos at 113b7. Oceanos and Acheron flow in opposite directions (ἐναντίως 112e8); neither Pyriphlegethon nor Cocytos mix their waters (οὐ συμμειγνύμενος τῷ ὕδατι, 113b2–3; καὶ οὐδὲ τὸ τούτου ὕδωρ οὐδενὶ μείγνυται, 113c5–6). Likewise, Tartarus is a prison from which those who cannot be reformed can never escape (ὅθεν οὔποτε ἐκβαίνουσιν, 113e6), but from which those who have lived piously can be 'freed' (ἐλευθερούμενοι, 114b8). This final visualization is one indication that the entire description of Tartarus is to be understood as figurative: the imaginary space of Tartarus parallels Socrates' literal imprisonment pending execution, his soul's imprisonment in his body pending death, and his soul's imprisonment by the senses of the body pending philosophical purification.[110] The prison of Tartarus is contradictory: equal and opposite to the prison of life.

Indeed, the paradox of negative definition seeps deeper through the imagery of Socrates' monologue. The clearest example of this is at 112c3, when Socrates describes the movement of water into the spaces and channels below the earth as like men irrigating (ὥσπερ οἱ ἐπαντλοῦντες). The ordinariness of the image is more startling for its presence in an imaginary world where death is a huge gaping mouth. More generally, Tartarus is full of geographic features from the living world: lakes, rivers, springs, mud, and lava. The characteristics of Socrates' imaginary world of death are weighed down by the materiality of the σῶμα.[111] On the one hand, this is not meant to be taken literally: it is a thought-experiment, a figurative illustration of the confines of human life. On the other, it is an expression of imaginative inadequacy. The probability of ecphrastic failure overshadows

---

[109] Negation holds its own branch of philosophy. See e.g. *Prm.* 161e1–166c5 and *Soph.* 236d9–241b8 on the problem of non-existence. See further M. Frede (1992b: 403–12) on the problem of 'not being' (focusing on the *Sophist*), with bibliography in his note 1. Note, too, the comment in Sekita (2015: 152), 'We may assume that [the figure of Hades] existed as a reversal, opposition and negative reflection of all that belongs to the "overground", as an embodiment of the "lack of" or "nothingness", as an inherent, irrevertible and indispensable element of the world.' Negation is also poetic: see pages 122–4, with note 71.

[110] For the body as the soul's tomb: Pl. *Grg.* 493a1–3. See further Dorter (1970: 567) on Phaedo's liberation from literal and metaphorical bondage.

[111] Compare his earlier account of the higher regions of the physical cosmos, the supposedly purer earth 'on the earth under the heavens' (110b2). Socrates conjured its wondrous beauty with recourse to spheres made of variegated colourful leather patches, colours like sea-purple, gold, chalk, snow, mountains, and rocks like gemstones. See Nightingale (2004: 141–57) on this description and, especially, on reasons to take it seriously (noting that this is not the disembodied world of the Forms, but rather a superior, beautiful realm).

50 FIGURING DEATH IN CLASSICAL ATHENS

Socrates' account which, for all its strangeness, relies on imagery drawn from the material world.[112] Death's unlikeness simultaneously articulates the sense of wonder and perplexity that Plato imagines Socrates to feel in the face of death and undercuts the privileged view offered by the monologue.

Let us move, finally, from solitude of voice to solitude of mind.[113] One feature of the monologue is the illusion of vacuum.[114] In principle, Socrates addresses a group of listeners (internal and external); in practice, his single voice performs a solitude that undermines his conscious existence. On the one hand, the opening and conclusion of Socrates' full monologue acknowledges the presence of Simmias (110b5; 114c6–9).[115] On the other, his companions do not respond to his monologue at all: Crito, the first to speak after Socrates, moves on to the practicalities of Socrates' last requests. Socrates comments on this oddity (115d2–6, my emphasis):[116]

> ὅτι δὲ ἐγὼ πάλαι πολὺν λόγον πεποίημαι, ὡς, ἐπειδὰν πίω τὸ φάρμακον, οὐκέτι ὑμῖν παραμενῶ, ἀλλ᾿ οἰχήσομαι ἀπιὼν εἰς μακάρων δή τινας εὐδαιμονίας, ταῦτά μοι δοκῶ αὐτῷ ἄλλως λέγειν, παραμυθούμενος ἅμα μὲν ὑμᾶς, ἅμα δ᾿ ἐμαυτόν.

As for the fact that I've been making an extensive argument for a while now that when I drink the hemlock I will not remain with you any longer, but will take my leave, departing for some sort of happiness that belongs to the blessed dead, *it seems to me that I'm saying all this to him in vain*, though I'm attempting to reassure you all, and myself too.

The lack of verbal response from Socrates' companions to his words (all his words, in fact, not just the monologue) intensifies the solitude inherent in the form. Insofar as Socrates' verbalized confrontation with death seeks a listening counterpart for confirmation of his subjective existence, the vacuum of the

---

[112] Ecphrastic indifference: Mitchell (1994: 152). See further Blondell (2002: 48–50) on the embodiment compelled by Plato's dramatic form; Destrée and Edmonds (2017a: 9) on 'philosophically constructed images', which remind readers of 'the limited perspective of mortals' (citing *Phd.* 114d1–6).

[113] For literary mediations of a sense of solitude (of mind as well as situation) in another place and time, the age of Virgil, see Kachuk (2021). See further Hutchinson (2007: 23–4) on Polyphemus' monologue as a medium of emotion, isolation, and intimacy; Chaniotis (2022: esp. 34–6) on night-time solitude (interesting in the context of Socrates' deathbed scene as filling the time before sunset: 61e3–4); Sekita (2022: 43–5) on ancient Greek notions of 'being alone' in the face of death.

[114] Though see note 91 on Bakhtin and the 'dialogic overtones' of every utterance.

[115] There are first person plural verbs and pronouns in Socrates' full monologue which have a similar impact, but all fall outside his description of Tartarus: 110c7; 111a8; 111a8–111b1; 111b1; 111b5; 111c7; 111c8.

[116] The surface meaning is that Socrates comments on the fact that Crito has failed to understand the arguments pertaining to the immortality of the soul that he has given over the course of the dialogue. However, his observation has especial force in a monologue that has fallen on deaf ears. Noting this silence: Clay (2000: 174). Compare Callicles' declaration that he, like many, is unpersuaded by Socrates' words despite their apparent merits (*Grg.* 513c4–6).

monologue that is left hanging teeters upon the extinguishment of identity that Socrates anticipates.[117] This imbues Socrates' reproachful observation with fresh meaning, 'For I've also heard that one should die in silence' (καὶ γὰρ ἀκήκοα ὅτι ἐν εὐφημίᾳ χρὴ τελευτᾶν, 117e1–2), and renders the affective subjectivity of his swan song a last laugh in the face of non-being.[118]

Socrates' monologue, with its poetic privilege, spatial, visual, and temporal strangeness, its contradictions and solitude, is self-confessedly imaginative. The irony is that a strangeness that can be explained in terms of cognitive unreliability is also what lends his existential perspective the tenor of authenticity.

V. CONCLUSION

Much of the philosophical discussion of the *Phaedo* circles around what death is (and what it is not). In this chapter, I have explored how this explicit philosophical enquiry intersects with the more literary side of Plato's writing to turn attention upon an epistemological challenge: the knowability of death.

Plato acknowledges and explores the challenge by choreographing the coexistence, concurrence, and contradictions of λόγος in various guises: reasoning (on the immortality of the soul); narrative account (the last day of Socrates); and imaginative description (Socrates' account of the afterlife). In Plato's Phaedo's narrative account, for example, the uncovering, covering, and uncovering of Socrates at the end of the dialogue (and his life) echoes the asymptotic frustration of getting close to the moment of death as an outsider. The offering and denial of a face-to-face encounter with another's demise then becomes a counterpart to the give and take in Plato's own mediated verbal account in which he, absent from the real and represented scene, paints a scene of death. Distance in the text reflects an implicit distance at the scene of Socrates' death; ecphrastic failure simulates the impossibility of taking an empirical approach to what death is or is like.

The fantasy of philosophy is that it can shortcut the problems associated with an empirical or mythical approach. But in the *Phaedo* the philosophical arguments in favour of the soul's immortality also prove inconclusive and unsatisfactory.

---

[117] The lonely voices of the dead souls that call out at 114a6–b1 from the Acherusian lake comprise a poetic foil to Socrates' unanswered voice. However, see note 57: Tom Phillips's discussion of the enactment of selfhood through 'the interaction between voicing and listening selves' (2021: 53) suggests that Socrates' reflection here, 'it seems to me that I'm saying all this to him in vain', constitutes his continued existence (albeit a solitary one, indicating his incipient withdrawal from the community). See further Holquist (1990: ch. 2) on the relationship between dialogue and existence in Bakhtin, including the idea that '*I author myself*' (page 28).

[118] See note 79. See Crotty (2009: 67) on Socrates' bold assertion in the face of cultural consensus on death as 'the great destabilizer of human existence': 'Do we think that death is a something?' (64c2).

52 FIGURING DEATH IN CLASSICAL ATHENS

A pessimistic response might point out that all efforts to draw close to the moment of death (have been set up to) fail. A more optimistic response might observe that all approaches, despite their ultimate failure, do a pretty good job at meeting the challenge they were set.

It might further point out the implicit congruence between some of the arguments in the *Phaedo* and the process of reading the text. Let us first address the apparent contradiction between the drive of the narrative account (which tends towards and features Socrates' 'end') and that of the philosophical enquiry (which seeks, and fails, to establish the 'endlessness' of the soul).[119] One point, perhaps, is that anyone eager to see the death of Socrates has been missing the point.[120] Does the veil hide Socrates' end because he does not end at all? If so, the narrative frustration effected by the position of the veil at the climax effects yet another argument in support of the soul's immortality (tying in with the principle that there is, put simply, one rule for the visible mortal body and another for the invisible immortal soul).[121] The blur in the text figures death as, simultaneously, an ending *and* a continuation.

More importantly, if doing philosophy is practising dying (in separating the soul from the body),[122] then perhaps practising dying (vicariously, imaginatively, through the medium of Plato's recreation of Socrates' last moments and final monologue) is the best way to grapple with what death is.[123] The more immersive and experiential the dialogue, the more successful the philosophy; virtual death and metaphorical-philosophical death go hand in hand. Moreover, death is not just a case study for a broader fascination with epistemology: death (metaphorically speaking) is *the most important thing of all*. Divesting the soul of the body's distractions is the best preparation for knowing anything,[124] and thus attaining true happiness in life as well as (perhaps) death.[125] But death (real or virtual) is also distracting—it captivates the eyes (of Leontius, memorably) and other senses; it stirs emotions (dread, grief, horror); it *invites* extrapolation from the physical world, from experience and observation of bodies. And it is thoroughly confounding, a source of wonder ($\theta\alpha\hat{\upsilon}\mu\alpha$) that needs tackling from multiple

---

[119] See Cebes' comment at 69e5–70b4.

[120] For the observation that there is irony in Echecrates' talk of 'endings' given that the 'chief conclusion' of the dialogue is that 'death is not the end', see Rowe (1993) on 57a6.

[121] See 78b4–84b7. Socrates' discussion is, in fact, more nuanced than this because he emphasizes that, while no soul is dispersed, what happens to each soul upon death depends on the extent to which it has been freed from the body's confines during a life of practising philosophy (and thus death). A happy life goes hand in hand with a happy death.

[122] See note 56.

[123] For another way, see Seneca's suggestion that the experience of fainting might offer an insight into the experience of dissolution in death: Sen. *Ep.* 77.9. This method is at once more direct (it is not vicarious) and less so (it involves fainting, not death itself).

[124] See 65a9–67b5. See further Trabattoni (2023: 19–34).   [125] See note 121.

angles. Things must get creative when Plato's Socrates or Plato's Socrates' Er talks of the beyond (a theme that will return in Chapter Five). Grappling with real death (whatever it is) is therefore hard, but the rewards—metaphorical death—are also big. In this respect, worrying about how to reconcile endings and continuities is only half the point. If one can achieve metaphorical death then life is certainly better, and death might be better too (if the soul is immortal)—or else (if the soul is not immortal) then at least a dying philosopher will not distress the living.[126] A philosopher grapples with the meaning of death because the truth matters, not because they are afraid.[127]

Temporal distance in the text, too, has much to offer philosophically because it models memory's role in knowledge acquisition. One of the key arguments for the pre-existence (and thus immortality) of the soul before birth is that learning is remembering.[128] Learning about death in the *Phaedo* involves not just the philosophical discussion through which we might recollect what death is, but also Phaedo's narrative recollection of a historical death and historical words: what Plato's Phaedo's description offers listeners and readers, then, is the opportunity not just to experience and grapple with Socrates' death, but to rehearse a process of coming to *know* it for what it is—to know not just his, but one's own. Moreover, the multiply distant qualities of the text are epistemologically reproductive: the dialogue is explicitly set both in Athens and in Phlius; it takes place both in 399 BCE and several years later; and it is directed at a mixture of Athenians and non-Athenians.[129] The diversity of times, places, and communities within which the events and conversations of the *Phaedo* do unfold model the expansive

---

[126] This is effectively what Socrates says to Phaedo at 90d9–91b7. See further Socrates' balanced contemplation of the options in *Ap.* 40c6–10 (death is either non-existence with no perception or it is a change, with the soul moving from one place to another). To me, the possibility that death is non-existence is one of the weaknesses of the *Phaedo* (which is, after all, largely focused on proving the exact opposite): while it is plausible that non-existence is better than ignorance (if Socrates does not know the truth about death before he dies and it turns out that the soul is not immortal), no one interrogates what would be best for the philosopher who, in his lifetime, comes to know that death is the end. Surely more life of metaphorical death might be better than less. Thomas Nagel (1970) wrote of death as deprivation of the good things of life. When the *Phaedo*'s Socrates argues that death is not a bad thing, he claims that there are no good things in life worth missing. But what if metaphorical death *is* a gain that might be lost in (permanent) death (unlike, from Socrates' perspective, more eating and drinking and so on: see *Phd.* 116e7–117a3)? See D. Frede (1992: 435) for the observation (in passing) that 'Although it is not impossible that Plato meant to leave room for separate pleasures of the mind [...] nothing is made here of any higher pleasures for the philosopher.' See further Feldman (1991) for a reworking of the deprivation argument, proposing that death can still be bad for the person that no longer exists.

[127] See 91b8–91c6.

[128] One argument in the *Phaedo* concerns the idea that all learning (μάθησις) is recollection (ἀνάμνησις) of knowledge that we gained at a previous time (thus proving the pre-existence of the soul in a former life and so its immortality). See 72e1–78b1. This seems to build on *Meno* 80d–86b. See note 25 on the overlap between narrative and memory.

[129] See 59b6–c6 with note 14.

54 FIGURING DEATH IN CLASSICAL ATHENS

way in which the dialogue might (and does) offer anyone, in any place and at any time, an encounter with death.[130] The explorations that might be mediated by the *Phaedo* are not, and never were, restricted to Athenians (although, for the purposes of this book, Athenians *are* included.) The distance in the text emphasizes both the challenge posed by death *and* the power of the text to meet it, again and again.

Indeed, to return to a point I raised earlier in this chapter (see page 42), the monument of Plato's text does not just memorialize Socrates; it affords him, through ongoing discourse with readers, the immortality sought in his arguments.[131] In this sense, to remember Socrates' death through the medium of the *Phaedo* is to encounter his death *and* the continuation of his life (and his apotheosis, in the literary reconstitution of the historical man as the exemplary philosopher, teacher, and martyr):[132] the text, in relationship with readers, is itself an argument for the immortality of his soul. And not just his soul but souls in general, since each reader might die (vicariously *and* metaphorically—διαφερόντως τῶν ἄλλων ἀνθρώπων, 65a2) and attain an immortality of sorts (vicariously *and* metaphorically, with freedom from care and freedom from the body),[133] and does so repeatedly on each re-reading.

The features of the dialogue that have made it so compelling as a work of literature, so renowned for its graphic description and immersive narrative, thus do work in parallel with the philosophical argument.[134] In each case, Plato stages an insurmountable problem (reclaiming a missed experience; knowing what happens when we die) and showcases how far he can, nevertheless, take us (broadly conceived) as a literary philosopher.[135] The approach (at least when it comes to death) seems both humble and optimistic: 'to look in different ways and give an account' (διασκοπεῖν τε καὶ μυθολογεῖν) about travel to/life in that other place (περὶ τῆς ἀποδημίας τῆς ἐκεῖ) (61d9–e4) and thereby (perhaps) to know the

---

[130] See page 222, note 119. For further work on the artefact as an untimely/hyper-temporal/anachronistic point of encounter, see e.g. Budelmann and Phillips (2018); Phillips (2020); Rood et al. (2020: esp. 206–11).

[131] In this respect, Socrates' death is also a beginning, a beginning of (among other things) Plato's Socrates. Compare how Alcestis' popularity in art and literature hinges on her death.

[132] Note 115c6–d2, according to Socrates, he is the Socrates of the *Phaedo*'s arguments, the talking Socrates, not the one they will see as a corpse. See Nehamas (1998: 9–10) on the life of the *Phaedo*'s Socrates as 'the best for all'. See further Petraki (2021) for the argument that Socrates' physical body is transformed in the *Phaedo* into philosophic λόγος. She argues, further, that readers are invited to sustain a more detached response to Socrates' death akin to that of Socrates himself and unlike that of the internal audience; while I agree that the emotional response of an external audience is likely to be less violent than that of the internal audience, that this is partly because of the greater distance from the scene, and that distance supports a more 'disembodied' and thus philosophical reading, I do not think this interpretation does justice to the complicated play of distance and proximity in the dialogue.

[133] See further page 52 with pages 180–1, note 106.

[134] See note 8.   [135] See further Simmias' words at 85c1–85d4.

truth.[136] All modes of thinking—logical, empirical, and imaginative—together prompt reflection on the mystery of death and the part they might each play in response to it.[137] The overall message is, then, one of challenge and possibility.

As Socrates says about suicide (62a1–2):

Ἀλλὰ προθυμεῖσθαι χρή, ἔφη· τάχα γὰρ ἂν καὶ ἀκούσαις.

'Well you must exert yourself,' he said, 'because perhaps you might even hear something.'

Death may or may not be solved but 'the readiness is all'—not just for death, for life.[138]

The sophistication of this epistemological reflection is to be expected in Plato. But it is my contention in this book that similarly complex meditation on death and its knowability is discernible in, and emerges out of, diverse texts and material culture from the Classical period that are not ordinarily categorized as philosophical. I begin, in Chapter Two, with painted pots.

Figuring Death in Classical Athens: Visual and Literary Explorations. Emily Clifford, Oxford University Press.
© Emily Clifford 2025. DOI: 10.1093/9780198947936.003.0002

---

[136] For Plato to signal imaginative representation, for instance, cannot be reduced to ongoing anxiety as regards truth or reliability, but rather emphasizes the role of the imagination where knowledge is impossible.

[137] Plato's framing devices and a resulting 'metadialogue about watching, listening, and reading': von Reden and Goldhill (1999: 265–6). See further Ferrari (1987) on how the *Phaedrus* works as a whole (including in setting and the behaviours and responses of the characters) to distinguish attention to substance (in any form) from appreciation of surface and so to stage a discourse on how to do philosophy; McCabe (2008: 97–8, 104–6) on fictionality in the dialogues and the self-conscious, active process of reading them and (2015: 3–4, 7–12) on Platonic conversations and reflective frames; Möllendorff (2013: 405–9) on Plato on authorial procedure in the *Theaetetus*. Compare the power of lyric polyphony to link real time events (via vivid illusion and emotional immediacy) with reflection via the text as a 'stylized aesthetic comparandum of the occurrence it memorializes': Phillips (2018: citation at 192). Similarly, on a double response provoked by ecphrasis (illusion and defamiliarization): Becker (1995: 84–6).

[138] Shakespeare, *Hamlet*, Act 5, Scene 2.

TWO

They Do It with Mirrors?

Imagining Death with Painted Pots

I. POTS AND DEATH

Time which antiquates Antiquities, and hath an art to make dust of all things, hath yet spared these *minor* Monuments. In vain we hope to be known by open and visible conservatories, when to be unknown was the means of their continuation and obscurity their protection [...] But the iniquity of oblivion blindely scattereth her poppy, and deals with the memory of men without distinction to merit of perpetuity.

—Sir Thomas Browne[1]

Painted pots are visible, tangible objects; they are not, ordinarily, works of philosophy. In this obvious sense they differ from a Platonic dialogue such as the *Phaedo*.[2] In this chapter, I will probe this difference: I will explore how fifth-century cups and jugs do, in their own way, mediate exploration of death—and not just with their content, with their form.

The relationship between pots and death in ancient Greece is a long one. The surfaces of pots were frequently painted with images of dying and dead bodies: this is especially notable on pots from the funerary sphere, which often evoke funerary ritual.[3] But the relationship runs deeper: pots are more than surfaces on

---

Some of the material in this chapter is adapted from 'Imagining Death with Painted Pots' in *The Imagination of the Mind in Classical Athens: Forms of Thought*, edited by E. Clifford and X. Buxton, Copyright (2024) by Imprint. It is reproduced here with the permission of Taylor & Francis Group.

[1] Browne (1958: 43, 46) [1658]. Sir Thomas Browne's seventeenth-century meditation on death responded to the discovery of bones in some pots in Walsingham, England. His writings exemplify a dynamic at the heart of my book: the possibility of imagining the unknowable from the knowable (in his case, ideas about death from mortal remains and antiquities).

[2] Note Pottier (1883: 7), who used lekythoi as evidence for funerary behaviours and 'popular' belief but distinguished them from works of philosophy.

[3] Depictions on vases from the funerary sphere through the Geometric, Archaic, and Classical periods: Kurtz (1984). See further: Shapiro (1991); Oakley (2020: 213–29); note 28.

which images of dead and dying bodies can be shown. Consider the enduring association between pots and the human body: man's mythological origins were in earth and pots can serve in urn-burials as containers for the corpse or ashes.[4] More playfully, drinking cups are sometimes given bodily features such as eyes.[5] Pots, then, do not just show bodies, they *are* bodies. And, like bodies, they are fragile; they might return to dust.[6] Or they might, paradoxically, endure, as Sir Thomas Browne mused in *Urne Buriall* (see my epigraph): like the immortality that Plato constructs for Socrates in the *Phaedo*, grave markers such as the Eleusis amphora or the monumental stone lekythoi that emerge towards the end of the fifth century BCE lay a claim to memory and to ongoing presence.[7] In this double sense, in what they show and what they are, pots are potentially powerful mediators of meditation on death.

This is the focus of my chapter. By looking closely at two painted pots made in Classical Athens, I will explore how the images and marks on their surface, their shape, and their substance, provoke reflection not just on death but on death as an imagined construct.[8] Deep-set is an emphasis on how pots are generative of thinking through their relations with humans and other objects but are not capable of being reduced to their core meaning or 'essence'.[9] In this respect, pots can operate as sophisticated models of the problem of death by virtue of being objects at all; like another person's body or bones, they are a suggestive, though ultimately inaccessible, enigma.

I focus on two popular pot types from Classical Athens: drinking cups (kylikes) and oil flasks, often used as funerary jugs (lekythoi). Looking first at a drinking cup, I consider how this sort of open vessel might offer a portal onto visualizations of death in the symposium. Although the cup that I discuss, like many from this period, was probably found in Italy, it is reasonable to think that cups of this

---

[4] See Hes. *Theog.* 571–2 on Hephaestus' formation of Pandora. An example of an urn-burial is provided by the seventh-century BCE Eleusis amphora, which held the remains of a boy: see e.g. Osborne (1988: 2–6); Grethlein (2015: 204–5), (2016: 90–4), (2018: 77–85, esp. note 14).

[5] See Boardman (1988: 172) on Greek anthropomorphization of pottery.

[6] On human bodies as transient objects that return to dust (as part of an embodied approach to Classical Attic grave stelai), see Squire (2018a: 519). See further Turner (2016: 143).

[7] See notes 4 and 109.

[8] This chapter is therefore in dialogue with scholarship in the history of classical art that attends to formal meaning and reflexivity. See especially the following. Frames: Platt and Squire (2017), especially the chapter by Clemente Marconi, with earlier discussions in Hurwit (1977), (1992). Ornament: Dietrich and Squire (2018). Reflexivity in early vase painting: Neer (1995: esp. 135–40), (2002); Grethlein (2015: esp. 203–7), (2016); Jones (2015). I follow Neer (2002: 7–8) in believing that close readings, though inevitably selective, are most illuminative of meanings produced by pots as a whole. A close reading must pull together style and subject: Elsner (2018b: 386) (equally applicable to Greek art). Formalism and aesthetic experience: Grethlein (2017: esp. 37–8). Emphasizing realism and formalism in the long Classical period: Webster (1939a: esp. ch. 5).

[9] This emphasis draws on the object-oriented ontology set out in Harman (2005: esp. 230–4) and (2012).

58 FIGURING DEATH IN CLASSICAL ATHENS

sort were used in Athens as well as overseas.[10] Indeed, they offer some of our best evidence on Athenian sympotic experience. Nevertheless, it is important that painters and potters in Attica may not only have been influenced by the preferences of (for instance) the Etruscan market but also aware that the pots that they made and sold might end up in Etruscan graves.[11] Drinking cups are not obviously functionally related to death in an Athenian context but thoughts of death may well have imbued multiple moments in their life history, from production in Attica to use at the symposium or beside an Athenian grave,[12] or else use in an Etruscan context, including eventual deposit in a tomb. Much of what I discuss here would therefore also be true in a funerary context (even intensified by increased emotional and physical proximity) though without contributions from elements such as drinking songs.

Lekythoi, by contrast, are more obviously associated with death in that, in the fifth century at least, they were often used in a funerary context.[13] Many were found in graves, where they were deposited with the dead, and images of these

[10] The initial purpose or surroundings of much Athenian pottery is uncertain. Many Attic pots were found in graves in Italy and so were ultimately viewed by non-Athenian viewers. This includes two pots that I discuss here: the Louvre cup (from Vulci) and the pelike (possibly from Chiusi). It probably also includes the Getty cup, which has an Etruscan inscription under the foot. Since I am interested in general pictures of how painters (and these were in Attica, if not necessarily Athenian) dealt with death and the nature of the visual experiences produced, it is acceptable to use these pots as evidence for Athenian visuality; the wider market and specific destination of any one example is not explored further here. A similar approach (but overconfident in dismissing influence from the 'omnivorous' Etruscan market): Osborne (2018: 40–8, citation at 48).

[11] On the 'symbiotic relationship between workshops, traders, and consumers that defined the Etruscan market for Attic figured pottery', see Bundrick (2019: citation at 209). Pots and trade: Gill (1988a), (1991); Bresson and de Callataÿ (2013). Mannack (2014: 119, 122) notes the possibility that some kalos-names may have been inspired by agents in trade: if true, this would support the idea that some painters adapted their work to suit the market. A related question is the evidence for a market in pottery and the question of value. Without raising painted pottery to anachronistically high levels of 'fine art' (though see Spivey (2018: ch. 3 esp. 57) on this point), views at the other end of the spectrum (initially championed by Vickers (1985)) are also implausibly extreme. It is probable that painted pottery held value and that there were more and less expensive examples. On the impetus towards illusion and animation on Archaic Greek vases (and their resulting aesthetic value), see Martens (1992: 368–9). See further Porter (2012) on the nexus between aesthetic and cultural value (this seems applicable to pots, to the extent that they are sites of attention). Purchasers and patrons: Webster (1972: 295–300). Potters' wealth: Wagner (2000).

[12] Though other varieties of pot were more closely associated with funerary contexts (see subsequent note), there is visual evidence that cups were used at and deposited on Athenian graves: see e.g. Figure 2.3a. Note further the fifth-century white-ground cups deposited in the 'Sotades tomb' in Athens and other graves in Attica: see Burn (1985); Tsingarida (2012).

[13] On the funerary context of white-ground lekythoi, see Oakley (2004: 9–11). In the late Archaic and Classical periods, the types closely associated with funerary contexts were the loutrophoros, aryballos, alabastron, and lekythos. Commemorative rites and ancestral tombs: Kurtz and Boardman (1971: 147–8); Parker (2005: 27–31).

vessels (appearing upon the pots themselves) show them brought to the grave or left upon it. It is possible that they were used for libations during and after the funeral and subsequently deposited as gifts or simply left behind. This context, combined with the distinct subjects and technique that emerge in the second quarter of the fifth century and bloom in the subsequent decades, generates encounters with death that are more immediate, familiar, and reflexive. Images involve fewer corpses, more graves; fewer heroes, more women and children; less black expanse, more colours and lines.[14] Death is still prominent, even central, but the focus shifts from anticipation of death, the moment of dying, and display of the deceased's corpse, to his or her memorial,[15] to encountering the dead through the intersecting prisms of memory and relations with objects.[16] In the second part of this chapter, then, I consider the contribution made by one lekythos to the collective reverie of a funerary corpus.

The two parts are bound together by a number of themes. One is a fixation on revelation and concealment of the dead: what is and is not visible? The second is the way in which engaging with the pot and its images generates reflection on death more generally, as an experience that will, at some point, belong to the viewer. My third theme comprises the epistemological meditations that are provoked by a pot's form. This is where the notion of the material world as a mediator of concept formation comes to the fore because it is the crafted substance of the pot that makes it both a canvas for thought and a commentary on the enigma of death. As an artefact, the pot stands as an aesthetic foil that simulates, or mirrors, for viewers the (im)possibility of extrapolating a subjective or objective experience from a position of outsider.[17]

---

[14] An overview of the shift in funerary scenes from the prothesis or ekphora to the tomb visit and the predominance of women: Bažant (1985: 24–6). 'An immensely increased interest in women from the time of the Persian Wars': Webster (1972: 241). The marginal figures (women, children, and adolescents) that accompany Charon: Sourvinou-Inwood (1987: 153–5).

[15] On the centrality, since the Geometric period, of remembrance and honour in Athenian attitudes to the dead (the γέρας θανόντων): Walter-Karydi (2015). On heightened emphasis in the Archaic period on the contribution made by a grave monument to memory of the deceased (the monument as no longer just a σῆμα but also a μνῆμα), see Sourvinou-Inwood (1995: 140–1).

[16] See especially Estrin (2016), (2018). Suggesting that mourners 'see differently': Turner (2016: 151).

[17] This situation might be described as a position of voyeurism in that it is characterized by desire and phantasy: see Lacan's 1964 *Seminar XI*, discussed in Elsner (2004: 164–71). See further Fowler (2000: 193–217) on monuments, desire, and instability. Opposing perspectives on the visual experience offered by Classical art: Elsner (2006) on imaginative, vicarious viewing; Osborne (2018: esp. 249–50) on Athenian pottery as a 'mirror' not a 'keyhole'. While sculpture may tell a different story from pots, 'efforts to *fragment* the picture-field' (Neer (2002: 5)) draw attention to the other-worldly site of the painted object, demanding some projection by viewers into the field.

60 FIGURING DEATH IN CLASSICAL ATHENS

II. DRINKING CUPS

A. Revelations

I begin with a red-figure cup held at the John Paul Getty Museum in Malibu (Figure 2.1a).[18] Dated to approximately 490–470 BCE, it falls at the end of what is traditionally considered to be the Archaic stylistic period, on the cusp of transition to the Classical. Though in some ways exceptional, it sits within a tradition of black- and red-figure pot painting and stands as a multivalent point of reference for visualizations later in the century.

At the centre of its interior are two figures. On the horizontal axis lies the nude figure of a man: his body extends across the tondo's field, cutting its border with his feet. His body is prostrate, both uncomfortably bent and in unfolded abandonment; his head is thrown back, pupils rolled upwards, mouth gaping open.[19] He is manifestly dead: quelling any doubts, a sword protrudes from his torso, driven through from his back. At the top right of the tondo (on this orientation) is the sword's counterpart, its ornate but empty sheath. Above him, a female figure stands at a slight angle that brings her body into a relationship with the corpse. She holds some bordered fabric, and this cloth is what the painter has depicted at the image's centre, in the middle of the circle of the cup's interior, midway between the figures. Stretched between their bodies, it disrupts a connection that was already broken by their divergent lines of sight. Below, two lines comprised of repeated arched strokes form groundlines.[20] It has been suggested that these represent a sheep skin (though many prefer to see a beach here).[21] The scene is widely accepted as representing Tecmessa covering Ajax's corpse.[22]

---

[18] *BAPD* 275946; *Para* 367.1 *bis*.; *Add*² 224. The Brygos Painter: Arias (1962: 336). A note on attribution: there has been much resistance to approaches that treat pots like Renaissance masterpieces. A historical overview of the study of Greek pots: Osborne (2018: 26–36). See further: Robertson (1992: 2–6); Sparkes (1996). Beazley versus Pottier: Rouet (2001). On approaches to classical images more generally, see Smith (2002). Though only one of a pot's important aspects, style *is* important. Disinterring an art history of style in the ancient world and highlighting the advantages of a more open approach: Elsner (1998). See further Tanner (2006). At the least, attributions provide a shorthand reference for pot identities, chronology, and stylistic traits; they also reveal common visualities and networks of interaction.

[19] Refraction of the eye in death: Geroulanos and Bridler (1994: 52–3). See further *BAPD* 202631. Saunders (2006: 151) proposes that the rolling eye might have a '"negative" value'.

[20] The challenge of the groundline in a circular object: Squire (2018b: 6–7). Tondo compositions: Webster (1939b). Images and circularity: Lissarrague (2009).

[21] See the entry at *BAPD* 275946. For a different interpretation, see CVA Malibu 8, USA 33: 33, pls. 418–20 (M. B. Moore), proposing a 'pebbly beach'. Further discussion: Williams (1980: 140).

[22] Despite the sword (visible even in the pot's fragmented state) the figures were previously interpreted as Clytemnestra and Agamemnon: *Para* 367.1 *bis*, von Bothmer (1969: 434–5, caption 11). The misidentification may have arisen on account of the rarity of stretched fabric in pot images (see note 33) by comparison with its prominence in Aeschylus' *Agamemnon*. Dyfri Williams identified a similar scene on the exterior of some cup fragments in the Louvre: Williams (1980).

FIGURE 2.1A. Getty cup (interior). Attic red-figure kylix, attributed to the Brygos Painter. 490–470 BCE. Height 11.2 cm, Diameter 31.4 cm, Width 39.1 cm. Probably found in Italy (Etruscan inscription beneath the foot). The J. Paul Getty Museum, Villa Collection, Malibu: 86.AE.286. Image: Getty Open Content (Creative Commons).

Death is horrifyingly, captivatingly visible. The shock of the face-to-face encounter is quite literally a central concern. As Susanne Turner emphasizes in her chapter on sight and death in the ancient world, there was a powerful visibility to death that was heightened by the living's responses to it.[23] And there is much to say on the striking *visibility* of Ajax's corpse here. His outstretched nude body is embedded in an iconographical tradition of the 'dead on display',[24] exemplifying a heroic-mythological trope of the beautiful dead,[25] like

---

[23] Turner (2016).

[24] Death's visuality, the prothesis, and the spectacular: Lissarrague (2001: 116–17); Turner (2016: esp. note 1, 145–6).

[25] The beautiful death (*kalos thanatos*): Frel (1984: 13–16); Vernant (1991a), (1996). But note Neils (2009b: 215–17): is beauty in the eye of the beholder or, rather, the Western tradition as influenced by the pietà image in Christian art? The wider appeal of heroic death (i.e. beyond the symposium and beyond Athens): Marconi (2004a); this is critiqued in Osborne (2004), who emphasizes that in Athens, at least, some images had a more precise meaning. Greater artistic reflection on heroic death and the fallen warrior in the late sixth and early fifth centuries: Muth (2008: 435–6).

62 FIGURING DEATH IN CLASSICAL ATHENS

Sarpedon,[26] or Memnon,[27] and a social-artistic tradition of honouring the dead with ritual spectacle in scenes of laying out the dead (the prothesis) and the funeral procession to the grave (the ekphora), which arrange the corpse and frame it with lamentation.[28] Moreover, and more specifically, the painter has apparently prioritized the frontal spectacle of Ajax's dead body on Tecmessa over a realistic depiction of his death.[29] The sword has been driven through his back, a remarkable feat for a suicide.[30]

The cup's composition maximizes the dead body's visual prominence. Unlike many other vessels, it has an interior site of display, the tondo.[31] The painted black surround forms a tenebrous circle against which the designs, reserved in red clay ground, shine like a target for the eye.[32] The surface of Ajax's corpse is a bright expanse, largely unmarked, bordered by the black outlines of his body. Add to this the border of rings and repetitive patterns, an ornamental window onto the image, and Tecmessa's open gesture as she stretches the veil, her arms a framing cradle for the corpse. Her posture, leaning towards Ajax, and her gaze direct our eyes onto his features: the visual pull of her lover's corpse on

[26] For example: *BAPD* 187 (see Figure 4.9). Thanatos in Greek art: Shapiro (1993: 132–65); Recke (2002: 60–4). There are a few other instances where Hypnos and/or Thanatos appear on cups; see 7043, 200474, 201052, 46679 (possibly: the cup is fragmentary), and 331676 (all these are dated 525–475 BCE and none show the scene in the tondo). Comparing 187 and 7043: Stansbury-O'Donnell (1999: 103–6). Examples that turn Sarpedon's corpse outwards: 201052 (cup), 17489 (mug) (see Figure 4.10), 5133 (lekythos). Compare: 330735 (lekythos), 305529 (amphora), 202217 (krater), 7309 (amphora). Others play differently with the corpse as image: e.g. 7309 opposes it with the eidolon in miniature reflection (resulting in two εἴδωλα of the deceased).

[27] For example: *BAPD* 202501 (pelike). In a cup's tondo: 46679, 205119. He is always nude (in 11 Greek examples): De Puma (1983: 294). Eos and Memnon: Recke (2002: 64–7). Achilles and Penthesilea (another sort of longing for a beloved departed): 201987, 211565. In a cup's tondo: 3881, 211565. A similar theme: 205060.

[28] For example: *BAPD* 41079. Compare 201675 and 202188, where figures reach to cradle the head of the deceased (corporeal framing that is equivalent to Tecmessa's open gesture on the Getty cup, but which more effectively succeeds in the face-to-face encounter that she misses). Prothesis in Geometric art: Walter-Karydi (2015: 30–48). In the Archaic period: Shapiro (1991: 633–9); Walter-Karydi (2015: 112–18). The ritual lament at the prothesis: Alexiou (2002: 4–7). Beauty and ornament of the dead in prothesis: Giudice (2015: 11). Prothesis on plaques: Boardman (1955). Medical and legal reasons for displaying the deceased (proposed in later sources): Kurtz and Boardman (1971: 143–4); Garland (2001: 30–1) [1985]. Rarity of prothesis scenes on lekythoi: Haywood (1997); disruption by lekythoi of the popular prothesis scene: Allen (2019). A histogram showing significant increase in preference for funerary scenes in the fifth century: Giudice and Giudice (2009: fig. 16.3). See note 14.

[29] His body but not his face: note 36.

[30] Compare: British Museum 1867,0508.1328; musée du Louvre E 635 (Eurytios krater). See further *LIMC* 'Aias I' XXV, 6. One explanation: Hedreen (2001: 110).

[31] This is revealed by its decoration and, sometimes, the presence of eyes on the exterior: the terracotta mask is a comic testament to the face behind that gazes into the pot's interior. Consider e.g. *BAPD* 4507, 7886, 9765. Though multiple pictorial areas demand numerous viewpoints and active viewing (see Lorenz (2016: esp. 169–97) on a hydria) the tondo also offers visual repose.

[32] Note early 'extramissionist' notions of vision and the active 'fiery eye', discussed in Rudolph (2016: 39).

her models the aesthetic draw of his bright, framed body on us. The threefold gaze of painter, internal viewer, and external viewer upon the deceased sets his spectacle centre-stage.

So, visibility is important here. But just as important is how the painter deals with death's *absence, invisibility*, and *unknowability*, problems that attend and are intensified by what is visible. The veil depicted in the tondo's centre both lifts to reveal the deceased and drops to conceal him from view, two coexistent potentialities.[33] Frame and fabric, envelopes that display and enclose, are in reciprocal complement, setting the mood for a play of revelation and concealment in viewing and visualizing a corpse and reflecting upon death.

On the one hand, concealment of Ajax's body has an obvious narrative imperative. His self-inflicted death is a cause for shame, a scandal to be covered up.[34] As such, Tecmessa's gesture is unambiguous: Ajax's suicide is 'absolutely not to be seen', οὔτοι θεατός (as in Sophocles' probably later rendition).[35] The natural interpretation is that she conceals. Indeed, the veil that might hide the corpse aligns internal and external viewers, but in mutual frustration: it is impossible to be sure whether Tecmessa's sight falls on her lover's face or shroud.[36] On the other hand, the empty sheath serves as a foil for the veil, a covering that has exposed the naked instrument of death.[37] The veil becomes a spatial and figurative epicentre of the tondo and the dead body, a painted analogue of the wine that fills and drains like blood, at one time exposing, at another masking the painted corpse. But the corpse itself belongs to death's aftermath not dying itself and so, visible or not, points towards an invisible concept.[38] Contradictory impulses of revelation and concealment in the tondo's image thus help sketch a

---

[33] Based on a review of 500–400 BCE tondo images in the *BAPD*, I have found only one other example with a suspended veil: 217255. On this example, display and concealment potentialities are teasingly erotic. The himation across the tondo's centre conceals the youth's nude body and the pot's only painting, and so is a double joke on viewers' expectations: draining the wine unveils a blank image.

[34] Compare how faces are covered in shame: Eur. *HF* 1159–60.

[35] Soph. *Aj.* 915.

[36] See Frontisi-Ducroux (1986), (1988: 34–5), (1989: 160–1) [1984], (1995: 82–94) on the existential significance of the frontal gaze (signifying dying: the moment before death): here, the missed connection 'diverts' ('détourne') the dead from internal *and* external viewers. Perhaps this captures the aftermath, where the dead 'no longer sees, no longer is seen' by *anyone* (citations translated from Frontisi-Ducroux (1986: 208)) (note that elsewhere she talks of how 'the dead no longer have faces' (1995: 35–44, citation at 36)).

[37] In fact, the scabbard, like the veil, has a double impact. It has exposed the weapon but also signals the possibility that it might be covered; this is enhanced by its position, hanging in mid-air as if the scene in the cup's interior takes place indoors or, at least, in private (in contrast to the scenes on the cup's exterior). For further discussion of indoor/outdoor space inside/outside another cup by the Brygos Painter (see Figures 2.2a–c), see Hutchinson (2020b: 115).

[38] See Jones (2015: 818) on Sarpedon's corpse for a similar point.

64 FIGURING DEATH IN CLASSICAL ATHENS

mental abstraction, the moment of death.[39] And in a symposium, where dead bodies and death are both visually absent, the conceptual link between what is seen and what is imagined is mediated instead by a cultural object. This object simulates, by artistic representation (pictorial and material), the double process of perceiving and creating inherent in concept-formation.

B. Stop all the Clocks

With this shift from the result of death to its concept, let us move on to the deathly visualities provoked by a cup's temporal games. Consider, again, the veil at the tondo's centre. Does it lift to display death as the awaited climax of a story, a life, and a drink? Or fall as a shroud, a signal that life and shame are over? What we see is a corpse and not the hero; no eidolon floats in the darkness above its sightless head but rather the lifeless shell of the scabbard, an artefact that acts as mirror image of the body that is only Ajax insofar as the living recreate and remember him in their minds.[40]

This is a sequential conflict that images on the pot's exterior anticipate and recall (Figure 2.1b). Imagine that the cup is full and the tondo obscured. On one side is a voting scene with draped male figures holding staffs, a quintessential image of Athenian citizenship in action.[41] Though the pot is fragmented, it is possible to identify on the left the bottom half of a female figure wearing the aegis: Athena. A scene at home in fifth-century Athens is also part of a mythological narrative, a conclusion supported by the presence of the male spectator on the right, who clutches his forehead in a gesture, perhaps of horror, concern, despair, or mourning.[42]

Another clue to the narrative and mythological significances of this scene from contemporary life appears on the other side. Male figures are again present, and the repetition of a central figure with an identical sceptre suggests that these are the same men, but the block and voting pebbles are gone. Instead, weapons have been drawn and some figures prevent others from fighting. The suspended sword and spear in the fight scene perhaps point to the quarrel's origin: the arms of Achilles. Both sides can be integrated as two moments in, or two versions of, the same story: resolution of competing claims by Odysseus (hence the presence of

---

[39] See Trimble (2018: 346) on the open door on the crane relief in the Tomb of the Haterii. On mirrors, invisibility, nothingness, and the Gorgon, see Vernant (1985: esp. 82), (1987); Frontisi-Ducroux (1988), (1989: 156–64) [1984], (1993), (1995: 65–75).

[40] On eidola see note 131.

[41] Cleisthenic resonances here: Spivey (1994); Bocksberger (2021: 167–74). Sticks and citizen iconography: Hollein (1988: 17–49); Fehr (2011: 84–91, with note 340).

[42] This figure is identified as Ajax in *CVA* Malibu 8, USA 33: 34 (M. B. Moore). Compare the seer on the east pediment of the temple of Zeus at Olympia.

FIGURE 2.1B. Getty cup (exterior). See caption to Figure 2.1a.

Athena) and Ajax for that armour.[43] The despairing, mourning, horrified figure in the voting scene looks *backward* (to Achilles' death, a narrative starting point) *and forward* (to Ajax's death, a narrative climax that remains obscured until the wine is drunk). Provided the cup is full, the moment of death remains a wine-dark blur approached obliquely from two emotional viewpoints.[44] Reflections on the liquid surface send back the face of the living observer.[45]

Now imagine that the cup is empty.[46] The exposed tondo offers respite from the temporalities of the exterior space and its imperatives to view in sequence, to compare and contrast (Figure 2.1a). The magnetic absorption of the circular field accommodates a pause for reflection, offering Ajax's corpse as the cessation

[43] Davies (1973: 68) places Odysseus on the left, Ajax on the right.

[44] Though Garland (2001: 13–20) [1985] emphasized the ancient Greek conception of death as a process, this conception did not preclude a fascination with the *moment* of dying. Late Archaic to early Classical interest in the suddenness ('Plötzlichkeit') of transition between two states: Wannagat (2003: esp. 61–4).

[45] See note 63.

[46] Conceivably, the tondo image might emerge from the wine upside down. In this respect, the 'correct' way to hold the cup is with the voting scene facing the drinker and the fight scene facing outwards.

of life and change. But then the wine that fills and covers the body performs a figurative shrouding, a funerary rite in response to death. The exterior scenes (Figure 2.1b) work once more but through the lens of memory, a past story of a death (or two) told by the living. Looking back on death, the realm of remembrance and mourning, is expressed in an intersection between the contemporary and mythological.[47] Though interpretations of scenes such as this one emphasize the difference between the pot's sides (and the implicit narrative of socio-political development from resolution by violence to resolution by vote),[48] death, as motivation for and result of both scenes, also complicates demarcations. Ajax's death, like Achilles' death, is idiosyncratic. This is exemplified by the singular spectacle of the tondo, which holds one man's death within its enclosure; its circular plane is complete and separate from the cup's other planes. But his death is also one of many; it inherits and produces a tradition of deaths.[49] Ajax dies in his own way and like Achilles (and countless others).[50] If the despairing figure mourns, he mourns Ajax and Achilles' death simultaneously. For a subject drinking at a symposium, this theme might chime with popular drinking songs in orbit, such as those to Ajax 'the best of the Greeks to come to Troy after Achilles':[51] to celebrate and remember Ajax in word or image is also to think of Achilles, two mighty warriors who died at Troy.[52] The mythological and temporal doubling effects graphically a similar conceptual link between, on the one hand, stories and images of death and corpses on a pot, and, on the other hand, the real problem of death as remembered and anticipated by a drinking subject for himself or his contemporary Athenians. On a pot that focuses on seeing the dead in its tondo, visualization of death is a construct of realities and temporalities.

Consider another red-figure cup (Figures 2.2a–c), also attributed to the Brygos Painter.[53] This provides an intriguing example of the thanatological implications of repetition. The Iliupersis scenes on its exterior are charged with duplications

---

[47] A similar idea of merged mythology and reality in the face of death: Carboni (2007: 33).

[48] See e.g. Spivey (1997: 180); Kunze (2005: 50–65). See further note 41.

[49] A similar composition on a scarab gem in the Museum of Fine Arts, Boston (21.1199) shows an outspread nude male being (un)covered by a winged deity: see *LIMC* 'Aias I' no. 141 and Odette Touchfeu's suggestion that this derives from a confusion with Eos and Memnon. The appeal of the motif appears to facilitate permeability between stories and deaths.

[50] On this point, see especially Elsner (2006: 75–7) on the referential indeterminacy of the kouros (simultaneously personal-individual and epic-universal).

[51] *Carm. conv.* 898 *PMG*. Aristophanes cites a song 'of Telamon' in *Lys.* 1236–8. Scolia of this sort were probably in circulation in the late sixth and early fifth centuries BCE: Yatromanolakis (2009: 271–5). See further Arist. 842 *PMG*, vv. 13–14.

[52] Associations between Ajax and other characters in Sophocles' play: Swift (2019). Visual links between the voting and Ajax and Achilles' game: Hedreen (2001: 104–19).

[53] *BAPD* 203900; Beazley (1925: 176.3); *ARV*² 369.1, 398, 1649; *Para* 365.1; *Add*² 224.

FIGURE 2.2A. Louvre cup (exterior, Iliupersis). Attic red-figure kylix, attributed to the Brygos Painter. *c.* 480 BCE. Height 13.8 cm, Diameter 33 cm, Width 42 cm. Found in Italy (Vulci, Etruria). Musée du Louvre, Paris: G 152. Image: © RMN-Grand Palais (musée du Louvre)/ Stéphane Maréchalle.

FIGURE 2.2B. Louvre cup (exterior, Iliupersis with Priam). See caption to Figure 2.2a.

and inversions that provoke meditation upon death as ineludible end.[54] On one side of the pot (Figure 2.2a), the central figure of a vigorously victorious Greek warrior stands astride his prostrate enemy. This figure is paired with (on the pot's other side, Figure 2.2b) the debilitated old man Priam,[55] his arms outstretched in supplication towards the warrior's double that strides in from the right. The boy Astyanax twins himself, appearing on the far right of each side's scene

---

[54] This cup, death's climax, and the 'Noch-nicht-und-doch-schon-Gestorben' (not-yet-but-already-died): Wannagat (2003: 63).

[55] Though the composition resists fragmentation into 'sides': see Robertson (1992: 94) on the fallen warrior beneath one handle, who links the action that begins and ends with a palmette beneath the other. The continuous mode: Froning (1988: 194–6).

68 FIGURING DEATH IN CLASSICAL ATHENS

(this double appearance is unusual):[56] on one side he is named and draped, his hair elegantly arranged and his body leaning out to the right in opposition to the oblique angle of his mother's body as she raises both arms bent back over her head, brandishing a pestle; on the other, he is unnamed and naked, his hair loosely outspread and his body dangling and inverted such that his arms meet at an acute angle the legs of the warrior that wields him, forming another triangle in reverse.[57] Visual switches of victor and vanquished are saturated with deaths anticipated or remembered in a relentless cycle. The boy who might escape looks back towards the left from the palmette that might mark his narrative's end. He thus looks, ultimately, towards his own death on the other side of the pot, visually past, logically future. The figure of Polyxena, as she leaves from the left towards, presumably, her sacrifice on Achilles' tomb, looks back to another sacrifice on another altar: the anticipated death of aged Priam framed by two departing descendants.[58] The pot's exterior uses visual correspondences to underwrite the narrative imperative that all men must die.[59]

As a result, the composition within the tondo (Figure 2.2c) assumes a latent bitterness, imbued with the certainty of death to come that is visualized on the exterior. At first glance, the painter has depicted Briseis serving wine to Phoenix in or outside the tent of Achilles, whose armour is suspended above.[60] The old man sits, facing to the left and extending a cup (a phiale, a vessel used for drinking and for libations). The young woman stands before him holding a jug. The image can stand as a memory, a prequel, a snapshot from the embassy to Achilles as told in *Iliad* 9.162–657 (though in the poem's version Briseis is not present

---

[56] See Robertson (1992: 95). Suggesting that the painter has mistakenly named one child because he is next to Andromache: Arias (1962: 339).

[57] And both warrior and boy are shown from the back: Rühfel (1984: 54). Compare *BAPD* 16776, 13363, 200097, and 203229 for other surviving cups (mostly fragmentary) featuring Astyanax. The Priam and Neoptolemus motif: Recke (2002: 41–50). Combinations of details and scenes: Hedreen (2001: esp. 64–90); Giuliani (2013: 171–6) [2003].

[58] Compare *BAPD* 202641, where Priam's death combines two perspectives: anticipation of his end in a climactic blow and the lament with which survivors will remember his life (the raised arms of figures about him form a substitution for mourners at his prothesis). I find it hard to see the slaughter of Priam on the Louvre cup as a, 'mildern' Sakrilege' in war, as conceded (admittedly in inverted commas) by Barbara Borg (2006: 249). The point forms part of an interrogation of what she sees as a Classical Greek perception that images tend to endorse their subject matter. See further Stähli (2005: 33–43) on how violent images of, for instance, Achilles' and Neoptolemus' exploits, more prevalent around 510/480 BCE, code such behaviour as heroic: 'Heroen setzen sich dank ungewöhnlich großer Gewalt durch—Gewalt ist natürlicher Ausfluß heroischen Verhaltens' (page 41). I am more persuaded by the conclusions in von den Hoff (2005) that, until the middle of the fifth century, images on pots of Achilles and Neoptolemus were complicated—neither entirely negative nor entirely positive. To my mind, such images raise questions about violence and war to which fifth-century Athenians might have responded in a variety of ways (especially if pots were reused over time and so encountered in multiple situations).

[59] This epic motif: Sourvinou-Inwood (1981: 20).

[60] Briseis and Phoenix are named: see *AVI* 6490.

Figure 2.2c. Louvre cup (interior). See caption to Figure 2.2a.

to pour the wine, except insofar as her presence is promised by the speakers).[61] Though the embassy's mission to persuade Achilles to fight failed, the larger end it sought, the fall of Troy, was ultimately achieved, as the outside of the pot attests. The old man within demands, motivates, and anticipates the death of the one without.

But the seated figure of Phoenix with his white hair and beard (Figure 2.2c) also looks *backwards* to his wretched analogue, Priam, another old man stretching out his hand, not for wine but life (Figure 2.2b). The echoes are remarkable—albeit with a twist. Consider their costume: bodies wrapped in a (differently) dotted cloak (himation) with a border comprised of a thick black band fringed with dots on its inner edge; heads encircled with a fillet rendered as two parallel lines in added red with four ribbons hanging at their neck. Each man has a sceptre—though Priam's is no longer in his grasp—and both sceptres feature slanting stripes along their length. Note, too, their eyes: the black pupil distinct within the circle of the iris. Only some figures on the cup have eyes that look like this: Briseis in the tondo and, on the side shown in Figure 2.2a, the prostrate

---

[61] Robertson (1992: 95) also notes that the tondo scene forms a prologue.

70 FIGURING DEATH IN CLASSICAL ATHENS

Trojan, a fleeing woman that may be Cassandra, and the escaping Astyanax; as a result, Phoenix's eyes link him both to the Trojan girl that pours him wine and to figures in distress on the exterior, figures that either die already or soon will. Indeed, any differences between the compositions serve to unite the old men as much as distinguish them, not least the difference proposed by the sacred frame: the aged figure in the interior might offer a libation from the shallow cup in his right hand;[62] the other *becomes* the offering. In addition, between each old man and the figure they face is a shield emblazoned with a powerful creature in black silhouette, in one case a bull, in the other a lion; the echo, again, both links and discriminates: the lion confronts the dying man head-on; the bull hangs idle, half out of the picture. There is a different game with the sword/scabbard. This time, the one in the tondo and the one worn by the Greek that slaughters Priam feature identical decorative motifs and neither are used. But the context for the latter imbues the former, set directly in front of Phoenix's face, with potential for slaughter. Even the bordered part of the cloth that loops beneath Priam's right arm—for which there is no direct equivalent in the interior scene—finds a faint echo in the black circle of the tondo and the concave arc of the chair at Phoenix's back.

The repetition extends a powerful invitation to draw an analogy: another double, Phoenix too confronts mortality. Indeed, in the visual climax to a symposiast's drink, his venerable image is unveiled as the culmination of a mortal life. The direction of his gaze is unclear but just might fall into the bowl of the painted cup he holds. His aged contemplation is a *mise en abyme* of the drinking subject who stares into another tondo, seeing either his reflection on the wine's surface or his painted image in counterpart.[63] Briseis, a Helen-like woman defined by successive separations (from Troy, from Achilles), throws his age, his inexorable death, into sharper relief by presenting him with the fulfilments denied him: a failure to win a girl and an argument.[64] Though she is draped, the painter has shown her body's outline, her breasts and buttocks, beneath the fabric. Perhaps she, like Anacreon's girl with the embroidered sandals, 'gapes after' another,

---

[62] Moreover, Simon and Hirmer (1976: 113) comment that the appearance of Phoenix's hair is almost like that of a priest.

[63] Compare the interiors of *BAPD* 203905, 203907, 203912 (in this final one, figures present two reflective surfaces: liquid and shield). Unusual and interesting is 217212 which features a symposium involving Hades and Persephone in the tondo, a ghostly reflection of the drinking subject's environment. Frontality, painted drinkers, and reflexivity: Frontisi-Ducroux (1995: 97–9). Wine as mirror: Frontisi-Ducroux (1997: 114–16).

[64] This scene takes on still more poignancy against the backdrop of Phoenix's words to Achilles in *Il.* 9.444–57: as a young man he slept with his father's concubine so that his old father would be hateful to her; his father then cursed him with childlessness. Other possible Briseis and Phoenix combinations: 203903, 204400. Old men excluded (perhaps): 204401 (outside a door); 209980 (tondo: old man; exterior: Dionysian revelry). Old age tears lovers apart: 217030 (Eos and Tithonus).

repelled by his white hair.[65] The explicit association on the Getty cup between the world of myth and the real world of Athens is here drawn through the handling of the pot and the conceptual link between drinking subject and object. From contemplation of age to the frightening prospect of death is not so far a leap; the drinker that gazes into the dregs of his cup and hears another singing of graceful youth departed might well respond in his own verse with tearful dread of Tartarus.[66]

C. *Forms of Thought*

Let us return to the tondo of the Getty cup (Figure 2.1a). Actual and possible layerings divide the pot's single surface into multiple imaginable surfaces of different depths and in different spatial relationships to one another. The association between surface and substance is something that painted pottery explores with especial point because it shares in both visual properties, a three-dimensional body and a two-dimensional canvas, in a manner unlike other three-dimensional or two-dimensional art such as freestanding and relief sculpture or wall paintings.[67] This is still more interesting in red-figure painting, where vacillation between image and background is built into the technique: figures are reserved background and background is added in paint.

Here, the veil talks to other surfaces that denote substance or its opposite and reveal interest in the human figure as a drawing and a person. Consider Ajax's nudity. The bare skin that covers his body's substance echoes the bodiless pelt beneath him, another corpse reduced to its surface. Moreover, though his rigid body is differentiated from the fabric that appears to fall into soft crescents above

---

[65] Anac. 358 *PMG*. Drinking, singing, and meditating upon age and mortality were familiar themes at the symposium. Death and old age in Greek lyric poetry: Budelmann (2018: 199–200). Old men feature on cups, such as *BAPD* 5361 (Pelias) and 203416 (tondo: old man singing to his lyre), though not so frequently as youths. Implied visual parallels between age and departing for war (two imminent departures in death): 204336, 211334, 217284, 211641. Meditation on age is also discernible on the temple of Zeus at Olympia: Holloway (1973: 100–1). There are also a reasonable number of deaths in tondos, though it is a less popular subject (at least in the fifth century) than, for example, symposium and athletics scenes. See, for example: *BAPD* 203224 (Achilles kills Troilus); 205060, 217201 (Amazonomachy); 204442 (death of Orpheus); 204546, 220533 (Poseidon kills a giant); 203838, 205108, 204549 (fight with Persians/archers); 201755, 204507 (Theseus and the Minotaur); as well as deaths implied by subjects such as warrior departures, a popular tondo image. On the relationship between pot images and poetry at the symposium (a form of intervisuality), see Palmisciano (2023).

[66] Anac. 395 *PMG*. Art, death, and terror management: Spivey (2005: ch. 8). On how images of the fallen in the symposium 'worked upon the viewer to internalize and accept death': Arrington (2010: 124). See further Murray (1988) on the polarity of death and the symposium, noting 'If the poetry of death has a certain place [in the symposium], it is because intimations of mortality are often most present to a man in his moments of greatest pleasure' (page 240).

[67] Perhaps the nearest point of reference is the sculpted sarcophagus or the box of Kypselos. On a larger scale, a temple's sculptural work might construct a similar interplay.

72 FIGURING DEATH IN CLASSICAL ATHENS

him, the triangular point of his right elbow and the gentle curve of his left arm and buttocks reiterate the edges and folds of the veil that will cover him. The same lines and shapes represent objects of different ontology and disrupt their distinction, even their presence. There is a coincidence of three-dimensional presence of dead body upon ground beneath veil, and its absence: a reduction of similar-looking lines, edges, surfaces, and skins. Interest in representation and decoration fits with a trend in pottery from the late Archaic period onwards.[68] But it also hints at artistic triumph in the face of death: insofar as lines and paint show depth, they represent a material corpse that will decay;[69] insofar as black perimeters surround blank space, they visualize an ex-person, an empty shell, a non-appearance.

Expressive manoeuvring of borders and space elsewhere on the pot corroborates this. At the bottom of the scene the red mass of the corpse's right arm and the red expanse of the sheepskin ground area trace the curvature of the inner red clay circle leaving a narrow gap of black paint. The effect is a lack of depth, where 'background' 'figure' and 'line' move backwards and forwards in a *trompe-l'œil* like Wittgenstein's duck-rabbit.[70] An edge that is natural for an arm is strange for a base, or a pelt, which is neither hidden by the red perimeter nor flows beyond it, but, rather, performs as frame *and* framed in its faithful tracing of the circular interior of the ornamental border.

Less faithful are the feet of the dead, which break through, or over, the inner red circle and the meandering border beyond.[71] The shift in visual category is confusing. The unusual lower edge of the woolly ground suggests this embellished circle was never a window frame. But what was otherwise a border, a decorated edge to the black canvas of the central tondo, is suddenly given substance. The artifice of the repeating motif shifts from back to foreground, taking on existential significance in the context of the scene.[72] Switching from within to over, the corpse appears to shift dimensions and float out into the black unseen of the painted perimeter. There is a similar optical glitch at the corpse's head. The circular border alternates three running meanders with a starburst square. But here there are four: the additional meander—a deliberate miscalculation?[73]—stretches

---

[68] See Neer (2002) on interest in fragmentation of the picture field in the late Archaic period, which coincides with the advent of the red-figure technique.

[69] Though this triumph of paint and line can only imply and not enact decay.

[70] See page 19, note 65.

[71] Figures, frames, and their scholarship: Squire (2018b: 7–9, esp. note 17). Boardman (2001: 186) is sceptical that overlapping the frame holds special significance.

[72] Metaphorical (and existential) significance to breaking the frame: Marconi (2017: 139–44). See further Hurwit (1977: 9–14) on the 'interrupted frame'.

[73] Observing another ornamental miscalculation: Squire (2018b: 7). Compare *BAPD* 205176, where Skiron's foot pierces excess meanders.

the perimeter thin, the miniature labyrinths of its geometric motifs yawning wider before the rolling eyes of the corpse.[74] Transformation of visual space at the border visualizes ontological transformation, a transition out of life and out of the image.

In fact, if, as Nikolaus Dietrich's study of space in Greek painting suggests, the relevant location of these figures was never 'outside' or 'the natural environment' (or even 'backstage') but rather their material support (the pot), it is not just the ground upon which Ajax lies that would 'implode' on his disappearance but also the whole pictorial-material environment.[75] In a similar way, the feet that pierce the tondo's frame imitate the sword that transfixes the corpse, transposing two bodies, two vessels. The pot's perforated body acquires a cadaverous corporality, its interior laid bare in a shedding of blood-red wine, its lifeless shell carried in the subject's hands like the bodies of Sarpedon or Memnon. Pot-turned-body disinters visually and materially the existential transformation effected by penetration of the person's frame, another body turned hollow vessel (in mirror image to the emptied sheath above).

With these hints of structural, spatial dissolution, Ajax's pictorial relationship with and rupture of his environment instantiates the loss of perception that accompanies his body's death and, in turn, dissolves the material world into darkness.[76]

III. LEKYTHOI

A. Where Are the Bodies?

We now turn to a different corpus of pots that blossoms in popularity and inventiveness in the fifth century BCE (from *c.* 470 BCE to the end of the century):[77] white-ground lekythoi. This time, I focus on an Athenian lekythos held in the New York Metropolitan Museum of Art (Figures 2.3a–c).[78] As above, I first consider how the pot explores the visibility of death and the dead, before delving deeper into the ways in which it involves viewers in meditations on death and its knowability.

---

[74] The composition appears similar at the feet: a stretch of six adjacent meanders.

[75] See Dietrich (2010: 550–2). The association of pictorial space with the spatial qualities of different media (and different material supports): Dietrich (2017: esp. paras. 15–21).

[76] For a similar idea, see Osborne (1988: 4). On the association between death and darkness, see Sekita (2024: 106–7).

[77] Oakley (2004: 215–8). [78] *BAPD* 216333; *ARV²* 1227.5; *Para* 466.5; *Add²* 350.

74 FIGURING DEATH IN CLASSICAL ATHENS

FIGURE 2.3A. Met lekythos (centre view). Attic white-ground lekythos, attributed to the Bosanquet Painter. 440–430 BCE. Height 38.7 cm. Metropolitan Museum of Art, New York, Rogers Fund, 1923: 23.160.38. Image: Met Open Access.

FIGURE 2.3B. Met lekythos (left view). See caption for Figure 2.3a.

76 FIGURING DEATH IN CLASSICAL ATHENS

FIGURE 2.3C. Met lekythos (right view). See caption for Figure 2.3a.

As on many lekythoi, two figures frame a central funerary monument.[79] On the left stands a young man displaying his nude physique in a frontal pose but with his head turned in profile to the right, looking towards the monument. A cloak and aryballos (a flask for perfumed oil but more globular in shape than a lekythos) hang from his left arm, while, in his left hand, he grasps a spear that spans the painted borders of his world, echoing the vertical lines of the stele with its shaft. Facing him on the opposite side of the monument is a woman, also in a frontal pose but with her head turned in profile to the left. She wears a peplos and carries an alabastron (a rounded but more elongated flask for perfumed oil) and a basket with funerary offerings (including garlands, fronds, and a tainia—a strip of fabric used as a headband, breastband, or girdle).[80] The tall rectangular face of the stele, honoured at the top with a headband of its own, is mounted upon a three-stepped base on which five lekythoi, one squat lekythos, and a drinking cup, each painted in solid black, together with one garland, a dotted tainia, and a frond that cascades down the steps, have been deposited. Around the upper edge of the pot's body circle two black lines within which flows a band of meanders (broken and stopt).[81] Another decorative ring—also bordered by two black lines but this time featuring egg and dart—is faintly discernible on the shoulder beneath the gleaming black neck of the jug; these were probably once accompanied by three palmettes bordered by tendrils (possibly with buds).[82] Meanwhile, at the bottom of the pictorial field, a single painted border offers a ground line that traces the black expanse at the jug's base, leaving in between a strip of thinner, more translucent paint.

The central stele is a site of death. It is also the focal point for the painted figures' attention and, in turn, the two profile gazes direct the real viewer's eyes onto the monument. In an obvious sense, the visual impact of death upon internal and external viewers alike is immediate: bare flesh and bare stone arrest with naked frontality. And this is not just a matter of visual spectacle. Proximity is sharpened by multiple sensory parallels between external and internal bodies. In the scene, as in daily life, getting close to the dead is physical: both painted figures and real mourners bring and/or handle pots,[83] and the woman seems to be holding a cloth or sponge (or else a crumpled tainia) in her right hand, perhaps for cleaning the body of the monument (or the corpse, at another time). Touch as well as sight, and implicitly other sensory stimuli such as the smell of

---

[79] Compare e.g. *BAPD* 213986; 648, 1140, 1921, 1924, 2327, 3378, 7199, 10342, 11521, 11732.

[80] The peplos now appears as white lines against the white background and so is barely visible.

[81] The meanders: Kurtz (1975: fig. 4*g*).

[82] Little of the shoulder decoration survives but see Kurtz (1975: 37–8, figs. 14, 15) on lekythoi of the Bosanquet Painter.

[83] Compare: *BAPD* 2755, 209247, 216337 (bringing pots); 209272, 212350, 217819 (Figure 2.8a) (pots on tomb).

78 FIGURING DEATH IN CLASSICAL ATHENS

perfumed oil and (if a real viewer were to hold this pot while standing beside a grave in the Kerameikos) the sound of mourning, or of reading aloud inscriptions on stelai, unite external and internal bodies in an encounter that is defined by presence and immediacy.[84] To some extent, then, viewers (both real and painted) that look at the stele (both painted and real within the painted world of the pot) encounter death directly.

But the stele also invites a more imaginative response to it by presenting itself as a *third body*. Crowned at its top with a headband, it imitates the upright bodies of the figures that stand alongside it and is of roughly comparable height. But unlike Archaic stelai on which upright figures were visibly carved in relief (a visual memory that images of monuments on lekythoi such as these might have unearthed—see Figure 2.4), the unmarked space framed by the monument's outline is evocative of a deceased that is absent and invisible.[85] The stone face presents an empty visage that mimics the blank, ungiving stare of a corpse (not unlike the stare of an Archaic kouros, in fact—see Figure 2.5).[86] Are we shown here an imaginative encounter with the deceased qua deceased, provoked by the form of the monument?[87]

And what about the figures themselves? The suggested lines of sight from their profile gazes, turned inwards onto the monument and towards one another, invite self-projection by real viewers into the eyes, minds, and memories of the painted figures. What might these figures see? A simple answer is that they see the monument. But also, perhaps, each other. Each figure looks not just upon the monument but through it and onto each other: they become, through the prism of the monument, the object of each other's gaze. In this respect, each painted figure on this lekythos might be a life-sized image of the deceased (an εἴδωλον) or might be a mourner.[88] This is not necessarily to say that they see a ghost in a literal sense but that each painted figure might join the painted stele in suggesting an encounter with the deceased at the grave—or, to put it another way, might visualize for real viewers an imaginative encounter with the deceased that might be provoked by the painted monument.

---

[84] Tactility, mourning, and remembrance in Greek funerary art: Arrington (2018). Physicality of experiencing death: Turner (2016: 154).

[85] Some examples of Archaic Attic stelai with relief figures: Richter (1944: figs. 55, 57, 60, 61, 62, 66, 71, 72, 73–5). See further pages 64–74 on the stele in the Metropolitan Museum (Figure 2.4).

[86] On the Anavyssos kouros, see page 12, note 38. See further page 41 on Socrates' eyes: ὃς τὰ ὄμματα ἔστησεν (Pl. *Phd.* 118a13).

[87] The stele as point of contact between the living and dead: Baldassare (1988: 11–12); De Cesare (1997: 192); Lissarrague (2001: 120).

[88] Identification of the dead on lekythoi is notoriously (and meaningfully) difficult. See e.g. Bažant (1986), arguing for deliberate ambiguity. See further Bergemann (1997: 55–6, 67) on the impossibility of identifying the dead on the majority of grave stelai (noting that even nudity is not conclusive).

FIGURE 2.4. Stele of a young man and a little girl. Attic marble stele. *c.* 530 BCE. Height 423.4 cm. Metropolitan Museum of Art, New York, Frederick C. Hewitt Fund, 1911, Rogers Fund, 1921, and Anonymous Gift, 1951: 11.185a–c, f, g. Image: Met Open Access.

Now, there is at least one plausible way to categorize these figures more precisely. Surely the nudity of the male figure might mark him out as dead?[89] If so, the aryballos and spear are attributes of the painted deceased—this man was an athlete and a warrior—in contrast to the woman's alabastron and basket, which

---

[89] See e.g. Oakley (1997a: 68).

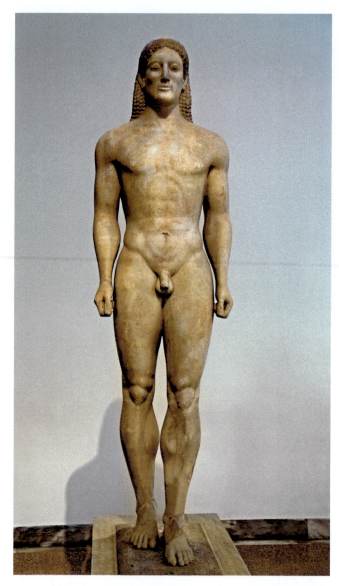

Figure 2.5. Anavyssos kouros. Attic marble kouros. *c.* 530–520 BCE. Height 194 cm. National Archaeological Museum, Athens: 3851. Image: Peter Horree/Alamy Stock Photo.

she may be bringing as a gift to his grave.[90] This is a reasonable way to pin down the image here (and is exactly the sort of argument found in leading publications on lekythoi).[91] But, though specific identities are certainly available, the object

---

[90] It need not follow that any real deceased recipient of this lekythos was necessarily a male warrior, though that is possible: lekythoi were deposited in the 'public cemetery' (demosion sema) where the war dead were buried as well as at private graves: see Oakley (2004: 215–16).

[91] See especially Oakley (2004: 165).

also invites a more creative mode of viewing and, in turn, a more exploratory approach to the concept of death.

In the first place, zooming in on presence and visibility misses the conspicuous hole at the centre of this image—a hole that is, in fact, at the centre of the fifth-century BCE material record. Though aspects of this painted monument are reminiscent of a third body, it is obviously not a body and makes little effort to resemble a body in a figurative sense—it is a σῆμα but not an εἰκών.[92] In this respect, the body-like hints (the band tied around its 'head', for instance) serve to remind us that a real (or, at least, realistic) head is missing: the tall blank box is a visual negation of the body that a fifth-century Athenian might once have expected to see in paint or in stone—whether freestanding or in relief—and longed to see in life. Whereas, as observed above, the actual body of the deceased, and the visibility of that body, played a central role both in funerary ritual and in the artistic and literary tradition.

The bodies of the dead do not disappear in the fifth century. They are prominent, for instance, in images that recontextualize the motif of the divine removal of Sarpedon,[93] in temple sculpture (see Chapter Four), and also in prothesis scenes, which were prevalent on funerary pottery in the Archaic period but also enjoy some popularity on lekythoi at a similar time to the Met lekythos.[94] Dead bodies seem, moreover, to have been a spectacular feature of Greek tragedy, displayed on the eccyclema.[95] And private funerary ritual continues, though aspects of it that were conducive to display seem to have been curtailed.[96]

On the other hand, and in several important ways, the dead and their bodies enjoy much less visibility. This is often explained politically: in democratic Athens, monumental emphasis shifted from the individual, especially an elite male indi-

---

[92] See Sourvinou-Inwood (1995: ch. 3). See further note 141.

[93] On a lekythos in the British Museum (1884,0223.2), for instance, the winged figures of Hypnos and Thanatos hold the body of a warrior in front of a stele. The image brings into view the corpse that the monument usually conceals, setting up an overt dialogue between revelation and concealment. Moreover, by recontextualizing the motif of the body's removal in a scene where the natural interpretation is that the corpse *arrives* at its final resting place, the image toys with possibilities of disappearance, whether by flight or burial. See *BAPD* 212420; *ARV²* 851.272. Compare: 216353. For a catalogue and discussion of Hypnos and Thanatos scenes on lekythoi, see Oakley (2004: 125–37). See further Bérard (1988: 167–8), emphasizing arrival not departure and arguing that the presence of Hypnos and Thanatos testifies to a 'beautiful death', free from the usual negative connotations of the corpse; Mintsi (1997) on the transformation from an epic scene to one from daily life; Giudice (2003), linking images of Hypnos and Thanatos on lekythoi with discourse in Greek tragedy surrounding female glory; Schmidt (2005: 58) for the argument that these are mythical figures but not mythological scenes; Spivey (2018: 157–9) on the reuse of Euphronios' 'stock' motif.

[94] As on a pot attributed to the Sabouroff Painter and dated to *c*. 450 BCE, held in the Metropolitan Museum (07.286.40). See *BAPD* 212338. For a catalogue and discussion of prothesis scenes on lekythoi, see Oakley (2004: ch. 3). See note 28.

[95] See page 107 with note 8.   [96] See page 12, note 40.

82 FIGURING DEATH IN CLASSICAL ATHENS

vidual such as Kroisos (see Figure 2.5), to the collective war dead.[97] The bodies of the latter were cremated and their ashes were mixed, mourned, and buried together.[98] In the private funerary sphere, too, though there were real, individual bodies available during the funeral, figured bodies disappear from the material record: from *c.* 490 BCE there are no figured stelai or kouroi of the sort that were so popular in the Archaic period (see Figures 2.4 and 2.5).[99] Stelai with figures carved in relief (but not kouroi) only reappear *c.* 430 BCE (albeit strikingly different in content and style). The blank in the centre of the image on the Met lekythos signals, then, a double absence: the absence of a figured body on the figured stele and, possibly, the absence of a real stele in the vicinity of the grave. Moreover, the invitation to notice what is not visible in the image is reinforced by the pot's brusque combination of frontal and profile views. What we have in the central monument is, as it were, a blend between the frontal body of an Archaic kouros and the rectangular frame of an Archaic stele, only here the stone bodies (whether frontal and freestanding or in profile and relief) have been removed from the frame/monument base.[100] Not only that, they have been visually set to the side: the frontal-profile figures that frame the monument echo the frontal/profile (i.e. kouros/relief) Archaic stone bodies that are missing—in fact, this is especially true of the nude male body, which is a closer approximation to the majority of sculpted bodies encountered on Archaic tombstones.

This means that the body of the deceased is *also* doubly invisible: we cannot see either a representation of the real dead body or a representation of the represented/memorialized deceased. Invisible but not forgotten: the painted bodies that frame the monument themselves remind us of the body that is doubly not there—the body that has been removed from the monument as well as from the light of day. Whether or not we see the deceased in either of the figures that frame this monument, the image draws attention to what has gone. This sort of absent presence or present absence is different from non-presence; we can compare it to the positive effect of negation in poetry.[101]

The very inclusion of a painted monument upon the surface of a lekythos is also provocative because it reminds viewers that the pot itself (in this case 38.7 cm tall)[102] neither contains nor mimics the absent dead body.[103] In this respect,

---

[97] See e.g. Neer (2010: 188).   [98] See pages 12, 136, 179–80, and 206–7.

[99] On the debate as to whether the stelai depicted on lekythoi existed or were products of painters' imagination, see Oakley (2004: 214). Arguing that questions of archaeological reality distract from the metaphorical discourse staged by the centrality of figured monuments on lekythoi: Baldassare (1988: 107–9).

[100] See further Neer (2010: 190–3) for discussion of a similar mix and appropriation of Archaic statue forms on early Classical stelai.

[101] See pages 122–4 with note 71.

[102] A fairly average height for a fifth-century terracotta lekythos. Later in the century some lekythoi become stone monuments: note 109.

[103] Compare Elsner (2012a: 179–80) on sarcophagi and reflexivity and mimesis of the body.

the traditional association between pots and human bodies throws their undeniable difference into sharper relief: even urns, containers for bodies or ashes, are inadequate substitutes; like a memory, their simultaneous association with and distance from the human form is bittersweet. Consider how, in Aeschylus' *Agamemnon*, urns and ashes of the war dead are a mockery of the men that died.[104] Or how Sophocles' Electra, holding an urn, the memorial of her brother, reflects that Orestes is nothing, a 'little substance in a little urn'.[105] But a lekythos is not even an urn; it does not and could not contain ashes, let alone a corpse, within its miniature cavity.[106] A painted monument upon a lekythos thus marks a corpse that is not just invisible by virtue of being implicitly buried in the earth,[107] but is not there at all.[108] In echoing the band that crowns the painted monument, the leafy garland that encircles the foot of the miniature lekythos placed centrally on the top step plays on this point: both these objects, pot and monument, purport to stand in for a body that has gone. But how alike are they really? Can the pot—picked out in silhouette against the white of a monument reduced to its outline—substitute the monument that substitutes the body?[109]

B. Death and the Object

So far, I have focused on themes of visibility—on how what is and is not visible on the painted pot encourages viewers and handlers to grapple with what death means for the body. This thinking is shaped not just by the object itself but also by its position in a tradition of funerary art with emphasis on visibility. In this section, I push the pot's thanatology further, probing how its formal

---

[104] Aesch. *Ag.* 433–44.

[105] Soph. *El.* 1129, 1142. The effect is compounded by irony: the urn does not contain Orestes' ashes. The play probably postdates the Met lekythos by a decade or so but seems to tap into similar concerns.

[106] In fact, false bottoms in lekythoi sometimes render the suggested interior also absent. See Oakley (2004: 7, fig. 2) for a large lekythos with a tiny interior.

[107] A lekythos in the British Museum (1842,0728.1002), dated to 460–440 BCE and attributed to the Tymbos Painter, grapples with precisely this point. See *BAPD* 209344; *ARV²* 756.66; *Add²* 285. The image shows a dead body inside its tomb: while decorated pillow, shroud, and horizontal corpse recall the prothesis, the box that surrounds the body upon a stepped base and the fillets that hang upon it evoke the tomb. Tapping into two iconographical traditions, the pot turns both on their head: the monument reveals what is usually hidden; the prothesis, scene of display and spectacle, is bereft of spectators. On the ambiguity as to whether this shows a prothesis or the corpse in the grave, see *CVA* Tübingen 5, Germany 54: 61, pl. 27.1 (J. Burow). See further Carboni (2007: 28–9) on the peculiarity of this scene. Compare: *BAPD* 16860.

[108] Compare Hardie (2002: 84–91) on cenotaphs and the absent-presence of the dead in Ovid's *Metamorphoses*.

[109] Consider examples where the monument depicted on the pot *is* a lekythos, as in *BAPD* 9024582 (image: Oakley (2004: 201, fig. 164)), and examples where the lekythos becomes a stone monument (such as Clairmont (1993) nos. 4.120, 4.150, 4.180, 4.190, 4.218, 4.421, 4.671, 4.680, 4.690, 4.710).

84 FIGURING DEATH IN CLASSICAL ATHENS

qualities—its composition; style of painting; repetition and variation of motifs—prompt meditation on the ontology of death.

We begin with the nude male figure. As introduced above, his nudity indicates that he may be dead—that the figure we see here may be an εἴδωλον. But the logic needs some unpacking: what is going on here is not merely equivalence (nude warrior = dead warrior)[110] or incongruence (surely no living mourners stood naked by a grave in real life, thus this figure is not a living mourner). *Difference* is also important here. For instance, the fact that nudity would be out of place in a real-life scene encourages viewers, who encounter the pot either at the grave or in preparation to visit it, to think in terms of negation and the unexpected: this figure is meaningful because he is not ordinary.[111] This is also true of his physical beauty: he surprises with his excellence. For reasons of beauty as well as impracticality, he is not like a real man at a real grave. Either way (and especially taking both together), he stands out; he is θαυμαστός, an object that provokes amazement and wonder. Likewise, death is unlike life and, as we have seen at Socrates' deathbed (Chapter One) and will see in Sophocles and Thucydides (Chapter Three and Chapter Five), death confounds.

The spear grasped in his left hand reinforces the invitation to set this man apart. Spanning the upper and lower painted borders of his world, it practically cuts him out of the picture. This man is compositionally beyond; he exists outside the rest of the image.[112] The visually empty lekythos that hangs behind his head in the top left area of the notional scene (empty in the sense that it is painted in outline, unlike the ones on the steps) picks up on this idea (see Figure 2.3b): it, too, is out of place, either defying gravity or else transported from the world of the gymnasium.[113] And, for that matter, note that the only lekythos on the steps on his side of the spear has toppled over. The two jugs—one pictorially hollow and the other apparently drained or draining and possibly broken—join

[110] See notes 88 and 89 and page 186, note 124. We can find support for this sort of equivalence in the visual tradition, especially the tradition of the beautiful dead: note, especially, that kouroi and male bodies sculpted in relief on tombstones were nude (see Figures 2.4 and 2.5).

[111] The polarity set up between the nude male figure holding a long (sharp? hard?) spear and the clothed female figure holding a soft cloth or sponge or scrunched tainia adds to this effect: the image invites viewers to think about difference.

[112] Likewise, consider the impact of lekythoi where the top of the painted monument impinges upon the upper border. In these it is the monument that does not fit in the scene, and the clash is appropriate: the deceased, too, is of another time and place. See e.g. an Athenian lekythos attributed to the Inscription Painter and held in the National Museum of Athens (CC1690): *BAPD* 209239; *ARV*² 748.2, 1668; *Para* 413.2; *Add*² 284. See further *BAPD* 648, 2323, 2327, 8941, 10342, 10912, 11520, 16829, 209247, with discussion above on the transgression of a cup's border by Ajax's feet.

[113] Compare especially the example in the previous note (*BAPD* 209239): two lekythoi hang in symmetrical negative mirror image (silhouette and outline) seemingly in mid-air on each side of the monument's acroterion. Perhaps needless to say, I disagree with Rhomaios's assessment in *CVA* Athens, National Museum 1: III.J.c.7 on pls. 6.3–5 (K. Rhomaios): 'leur caractère est purement décoratif'.

the nude male in an existential space that is different and divided from that on the right.

But death is not confined to the space of the pot occupied by the nude male figure. Note especially the weight of the spear that divides the picture. Its line is thick and heavy—more so, in fact, than the rest of the figured scene. In this respect, it has more in common with the border of meanders above and the ground line below (and also the miniature painted pots on the steps of the monument). In some ways, then, and bearing in mind that what we see here is much diminished from the original painting, what we encounter on this object is a framework (including the spear) of noticeably greater solidity than the figures and objects within it. The miniature pots, echoing the terracotta structure on which they are painted, belong to the world of the pot, a cosmos that is solid and enduring. It is not just the dead, then, that are insubstantial, but the *prospect of death*: after all, even if the painted woman looks like a living mourner, her mortality is reflected in the delicate lines of her body and in the body of the man that stands before her like the ghost of her future.

Let us probe this idea further. Consider now the contrast between the two figures and the monument. The simplicity of the monument's representation in outline is stark and, as observed above, plays on the absence of the deceased with the emptiness of its two-dimensional frame.[114] This flatness is set against two figures rendered in greater depth.[115] Observe the soft curves of their bodily features (the male figure's kneecaps, abdominal muscles, and clavicle; the contours of the female figure's arms), the thickness of their hair, and the overlapping folds of their drapery, falling in layered waves under the pull of gravity. Even the combination of profile and frontal views, though somewhat unnatural, puts the figures in a world with more than one point of view, a world that looks sideways as well as forwards. Thus, when they look at the monument—a cardboard cut-out, as it were—they, like external viewers, look upon an image that is *unlike* them. The difference is not merely one of living bodies versus inert matter; this is a matter of visual ontology. The composition, with its combination of dimensionalities, presents the idea that the two painted figures are real and are looking at a drawing, just like external viewers are looking at a drawing on a pot.[116] As a

[114] For similar examples, see *BAPD* 1140, 1921, 1924, 3889, 11695, 12688, 209247. Compare Platt (2017: 381) on 'the sarcophagus' function as both frame and container': here, the outline technique puts the (blank) image of death centre-stage and acknowledges the remains 'contained' nearby.

[115] Parts of the figures such as their clothing may have been rendered in colour (though, if so, the colour has not survived). Beazley (1938: 17), for instance, makes the following comment on another lekythos attributed to the Bosanquet Painter and held in Athens (Nat. Mus. 1935: *BAPD* 216329), 'The youth's cloak is brown, with a white border; the woman's garment may have been rose-red; and there is a little blue.'

[116] Other lekythoi explore this theme in even more provocative ways. See e.g. the lekythos held in the Louvre (MNB 3059): *BAPD* 209289; *ARV²* 754.14; *Add²* 285. A female figure in profile approaches a

86 FIGURING DEATH IN CLASSICAL ATHENS

whole, the composition figures, once more, the idea that death (insofar as the monument is a site of death) is ontologically different from life.[117] What is to one mind a representational flop is to another an imaginative triumph: the features that expose the monument as an image also render it a site of encounter with death as *difference*, as other than life.

In an image that takes as its subject continued communion between the living and the dead, the impact is painful as well as disorientating.[118] The monument that represents the deceased is so overtly a product of line and paint that it rejects a real relationship with both figures, an impact that is similar to the cold pleasure of Admetus' surrogate wife or the hateful charm of statues in the eyes of Menelaus.[119] However you spin it (whether an imaginative encounter is undercut by awareness that it is not real, or, as Tom Phillips suggests, the imagination thrills at its ability to produce an affective and sensory encounter in an unreal situation),[120] imaginative encounters have a double nature, real and unreal, pleasant and painful. Compare how in Euripides' *Trojan Women*, funeral honours seem, to Hecuba, a vain opportunity for the living to boast; even so, their performance stirs the bitter response ἰὼ ἰώ· | μελέα μήτηρ.[121] Seth Estrin's work on the bittersweet nature of memory images on funerary objects is important here: like monuments, lekythoi were, and to some extent still claim to be, sites of encounter with specific deceased loved ones that continue to impress their presence upon the living via the affective power of objects.[122] But this dynamic is also

---

stele, at the top of which is depicted a scene in a rectangular frame. The internal framed scene shows a second female figure seated on chair with a mirror. Behind the second figure is suspended some fabric, perhaps a tainia (though disproportionately large). In a virtuoso iteration of persons of different realities and ontologies (flesh and blood, painted, graven, reflected; real, visualized as real, visualized as image, visualized as reflection of image), the painter draws simultaneous attention to sameness and difference. The visual similarity between the figures points towards their kinship, to the lekythos and the sculpted monument as mirrors in which one might contemplate one's own death. But difference also sets each outside the image; each viewer is presented as another's voyeur, underscoring the exteriority that defines the perspective of the living on death. The play of images thus draws attention not just to mortality as a shared endpoint but also to the epistemological challenges posed by that existential situation. Compare a lekythos that features two figures looking at a monument on which are set two smaller, but in other respects naturalistic figures (a seated female figure and a child): *BAPD* 212317; Riezler (1914: pl. 22).

[117] Nathaniel Jones's (2015) study of the image theory that unfurls within the images on lekythoi is key here. Exploring the 'raw data', in his words, 'from which [the] philosophical systems [of philosophers such as Plato and Aristotle] were constructed' (page 834), he pinpoints the epistemological and ontological reflections that are and might be crystallized by a painted pot's formal properties. See further Crowley (2019: 36–9).

[118] The fragmentation of the visual field that Neer (2002) identifies in Archaic and early Classical vase-painting permeates these pots but the artistry that undercuts naturalist representation shows less 'pleasing tension' (page 183) and more painful disjuncture.

[119] Eur. *Alc.* 353; Aesch. *Ag.* 416–19.

[120] Phillips (2024: 261–5) on Menelaus' dream visions of Helen.   [121] Eur. *Tro.* 1250–2.

[122] See Estrin (2016), (2018). See further Arrington (2018: 21–3) on longing (πόθος) for the deceased and tombs as substitutes for absent bodies.

what makes lekythoi effective mediators of thanatological reflection: viewers are primed to think not just about a lost loved one but also about death more generally, a death that they will, at some point, share.

At this point, let us revisit the difference between the two painted figures. On the one hand, the polarity could not be more pronounced: to the left, a nude male figure holding a long (sharp? hard?) spear; on the right, a clothed female figure holding a soft cloth or sponge. On the other hand, the two figures are united in their mutual difference from both the flat world of the painted monument and the more substantial cosmos of the pot. In other ways, too, these figures are presented not as opposites but as mirror images. Their height and poses are similar—the main difference lies in the gestures of their arms. And they both carry pots. Again, we might emphasize difference: one (the aryballos) is round and associated with the male world of the gymnasium; the other (the alabastron) is ovular and often depicted in female environments, whether at the grave or in scenes of bathing.[123] But these pots are also similar: not only are both small, closed vessels used for perfumed oil, they are both rounded and shown in outline (in contrast, in both cases, to the miniature lekythoi and drinking cup shown in silhouette below). Do these hollow, globular shapes associate both figures not just with the insubstantial world of the monument but with the space 'beyond' to the left of the spear?

If viewers must choose, most would probably specify that the male figure is deceased and the female is mourning. But viewers do not have to choose. Instead, I would emphasize the work that this image is doing to show affinity (as well as difference) between the figures. There is little here, in fact, to suggest that the female figure might not be dead too. (At the very least, it is worth asking what we would expect this woman to look like if she were dead—we would not, for instance, expect her to be nude. The assumption that she is living thus primarily rests on the likelihood that the nude man is dead and the assumption that the grave should belong to one of them or the other.) The important point here is, I think, less who is who and more the fact that all figures—painted *and real* might be the deceased. The death(s) that viewers might encounter through the images here include not just the painted man's, or the woman's, or the deceased's (including both the deceased marked by the painted tomb and any deceased marked by a real tomb), but also their own.

Add to this the fact that it is not just one pot, or even two, that mourners see on the Met lekythos (this is true of other works attributed to the Bosanquet Painter: see Figure 2.6).[124] The *mise en abyme* of a painted lekythos on a terracotta lekythos is refracted into several miniature black pots that litter the

---

[123] Richter and Milne (1935: 16–17).
[124] On the Bosanquet Painter, see Oakley (1997b). Also: *BAPD* 216329, 216331, 216332, 216333.

88 FIGURING DEATH IN CLASSICAL ATHENS

FIGURE 2.6. Another Bosanquet lekythos. Attic white-ground lekythos. 440–430 BCE. Height 36.1 cm, Diameter 11.3 cm. Metropolitan Museum of Art, New York, Rogers Fund, 1023: 23.160.39. Image: Met Open Access.

monument's painted steps.[125] Visualization of death involves not one but many vanishing points of endless iteration. Redundancy is not just for emphasis;[126] it also performs a visual ὀτοτοτοτοῖ, each pot another silent cry of woe.[127] Like the alliteration with which Sappho's Aphrodite mourns Adonis—καττύπτεσθε, κόραι, καὶ κατερείκεσθε χίθωνας—reiterated images articulate a ritual lament, only here in a material-visual form as opposed to a verbal-sonic one.[128] Moreover, many painted black pots on one lekythos echo the numerous real ones among which this lekythos might have been seen at the grave.[129] Each pot is an individual gift (his aryballos, her alabastron); each is part of a near homogenous heap of objects of like shape and decoration, image after image of scenes at or in preparation for the grave.[130] The universality of the one among many mentality is sobering: what is one more pot on the pile?[131]

[125] These are striking against the white background. Lekythoi (when painted on lekythoi) are often rendered as painted black miniatures. Miniature lekythoi examples: *BAPD* 216332, 216329, 216331, 216332, 216333.

[126] See Steiner (2007: 10–12) on repetition as a strategy to combat entropy in the context of Greek pots. See further Hutchinson (2017) on the impact of repetition in the *Iliad*. Death, repetition, commemoration, and intermediality: Trimble (2018: 339–42).

[127] On the virtues of silence (being 'struck dumb' by the image) in the funerary sphere, see Vout (2014b: esp. 288–9). See further Sekita (2024: 111) on the sounds associated with the dead (silence and inhuman screams).

[128] Sappho 140 Voigt = 140a LP. See note 28.

[129] Many lekythoi form a group at the grave and the cemetery level. Consider one discovery of seven lekythoi in a tomb: Schmidt (2005: 53–4).

[130] Members of a visual corpus, lekythoi might participate in the sorts of visual conversations discussed in Day (2018) in relation to inscribed monuments. Moreover, while images are not identical (on which see Osborne (2012), who emphasizes the pressure that Athenian pot images put upon expectations and the questions that they raise), they are often variations on a theme. See Sourvinou-Inwood (1995: 335) for a nexus between individualization and generic persona on lekythoi; Walter-Karydi (2015: 142–3) on life-sized bodies on lekythoi as generic figures of the dead rather than representations of the deceased buried nearby; Arrington (2018: 9) on generic figural types in funerary sculpture. See further Lissarrague (2001: 120–1) on the generic nature of an unreadable inscription ('the image of a text') on a lekythos by the Inscriptions Painter (see note 112). But an unreadable painted inscription does not just '[leave] unspecified what is to be read' by the buyer (as François Lissarrague suggests); it anonymizes the deceased, whose name has dissolved into a meaningless letter-image.

[131] Consider, too, the visual resemblance of the miniature black eidolon (winged figure) and the miniature black pot. Eidola examples: 209341, 1140, 305529. On eidola, see Peifer (1989: esp. 147–81). See further Oakley (2004: 212–13) on eidola as 'marking a place where direct contact with the dead can be made' (page 213); Jones (2015: 825–6). In some scenes on lekythoi, eidola seem to evoke less the ongoing presence of the individual deceased than their absorption into a homogeneous collective of the dead (what makes one winged figure different from another or, for that matter, different from a pot?). See e.g. Díez de Velasco (1989: 309–17) on how several (but not all) instances of eidola on lekythoi indicate the mass of anonymous dead in which the deceased has been, is being, or will be included. Martin (2016), however, offers a differently nuanced interpretation of the winged figures on lekythoi, emphasizing instead the reassuring bridge that is figured on these funerary pots between the worlds of the living and the dead (the possibility of family reunion) and the individuality that might be found in an otherwise

The visual lament of iterated objects seems to perform death as much as it responds to it. Even as the repetition essays a continuation that marches against the narrative of death as climactic end, it creates a lack of development or change that expounds death's eternal nothing.[132] The pot and its pots thus offers an encounter with death as transition to a state that might lack development as well as variation.[133]

Add to this the evident vulnerability not just of the painted figures but also of the objects that surround them. On our pot (Figure 2.3a–c), two lekythoi have fallen over and one garland unravels.[134] On another unusual example in the Louvre (Figure 2.7), the painter has depicted a tomb that is untended or abandoned; the branches that descend like a final curtain over the steps of the monument will soon extinguish from sight, and from memory, even the rubbish heap of upended pots at its base.[135] Even the permanence of the object, a lasting memorial, is fragile. Compare how in *Trojan Women*, Hector's 'undying' shield, shadow of its former glory, 'will die with the body'.[136] Like the meanders that spiral again and again around the circle of the pot's exterior, every image in this scene seems to echo another. Objects stand, objects fall; garlands hold, fronds have unfurled; nothing is identical but everything repeats.

These images that look upon death sideways through the eyes and memories of survivors are also laced with anticipation of death to come in the fragility of the objects that represent and perform death in their actual or projected

ordinary winged figure by the dedicator of the pot (pages 16, 25). Both these possibilities hold and are brought out by the fact that the eidola and the miniature pots are similar but not the same. There is scope here for an encounter both with the individual remembered dead and with death as loss of individuality (and both encounters are contingent upon the viewer-handler's relationship with the pot). See further Elsner (2018b: 354) on ornamental repetition on sarcophagi and 'the repetition of death itself as an endless and unavoidable replication'.

[132] Insofar as, on an example such as the Getty cup, action and moment generate forward- and backward-looking temporal imperatives on the moment of death whereas lekythoi show an act of ongoing contemplation, this discussion sits alongside conclusions in Osborne (2018: 220–4) on changes in temporality from late Archaic to Classical images. Might we further characterize the difference between the reflections mediated by the cup (dramatic stills of the vote/fight with the aftermath in the tondo) and the lekythos (repeated instances of pots on and at graves) in terms of the 'pregnant' or 'ongoing' moment, respectively? See Bergmann (1996); Dyer (2005).

[133] Death is imagined as, as Díez de Velasco (1989: 316) put it, a moment of 'GRAN CAMBIO', great change.

[134] Fallen vessels on lekythoi: Arrington (2014).

[135] *BAPD* 3032. The tomb is not abandoned but it is fragile. By acknowledging the real risk of decay and oblivion in the absence of action, the scene concedes the engulfing power of death. (This image may also be interpreted as acknowledgement of the need to remember departed relatives with funerary rites in accordance with Athenian law: see Schmidt (2005: 45–6, fig. 10).)

[136] Eur. *Tro.* 1222–3.

THEY DO IT WITH MIRRORS? 91

FIGURE 2.7. Lekythos (overgrown grave). Attic white-ground lekythos. 475–450 BCE. Height 14.8 cm, Diameter 6.5 cm. Musée du Louvre, Paris: CA3758. Image: © GrandPalaisRmn (musée du Louvre)/Hervé Lewandowski.

fragmentation.[137] Looking back on another's death in memory collides with anticipation of one's own inevitable mortality.

C. Reflections on Reflections

On this note, let us consider the epistemological reflections on the knowability of death that are mediated by the Met lekythos. The first point to emphasize is that, for all the connections that are invited between the world of real Athenian mourners and the world of the Athenian mourners painted on the pot, the experience of death presented by this lekythos is defined by *looking*, looking at things and looking at other people absorbed in their own experiences. Real viewers

---

[137] On a similar note: Boardman (1988: 176) on pierced cups from graves as examples of 'the cancelling or killing of a practical vessel'. See further Osborne (1988: 13) on other pot images that muse on 'the fragility of human life'; Vout (2014b) on funerary objects' 'lost-ness' (page 315), their 'rhetoric of unreachability'. Compare Arrington (2014: 7): the fragility of objects contrasts with 'the stable presence of the deceased'.

92   FIGURING DEATH IN CLASSICAL ATHENS

look at painted viewers looking at a monument (and possibly at one another). This is not unusual: it is characteristic of lekythoi, which (unless we count the frontal face of the monument) do not make use of the frontal gaze that sometimes (on other pots) communicates death, sleep, or ecstasy—disconnection from the ordinary world of the living.[138] The world of real and painted viewers might be the same in that the subject matter here seems to have been drawn from ordinary Athenian funerary practice, but the points of view are not.[139] The shape of the lekythos reinforces this point: unlike the Getty cup, viewers can only engage with its outer face. Encounters with death through this pot are defined by exteriority.

Not only that, but the poses adopted by the figures are unnatural (fully frontal bodies, even the feet, with fully profile heads). No one would stand like that at a real grave. For one thing, this suggests that the bodies of the figures (who might or might not be living) are on display alongside the monument. Real viewers are offered not so much an encounter with death as an encounter with other people encountering it. Moreover, insofar as frontal views of the bodies of the monument and the figures offer external viewers and handlers a direct visual connection to match the sensory immediacy of handling the real pot, the figures' gazes, turned to the side, echo the mourner's gaze, turned away from a real corpse or grave and towards the pot and its images. Pulling external gazes towards them and so into profile (vis-à-vis a real deceased, or grave), the pot and its painted monument operate as prisms that invite viewers to look at death sideways—indirectly.

The pot thus models the epistemological problem of encountering death through observation of the external world. Whilst the drinking cup danced between revelation and concealment of Ajax's body (sheer visibility), the painted

---

[138] Note further the Ilissos stele in the National Archaeological Museum, Athens (NM 869). On the existential significance of the frontal face, see note 36.

[139] Robin Osborne (2018) emphasizes a shift in the subject matter on pots in Classical Athens, with images 'mirroring' real Athenian life as opposed to offering a window onto a separate world. He argues, further, that fifth-century scenes involve less imaginative visual engagement because the world represented is the same world inhabited by painters and purchasers of the pots. Osborne proposes this metaphor in riposte to Jaś Elsner's (2006) suggestion that the Greek Revolution was characterized by a change in viewing, from direct engagement with a gaze to vicarious experience from the outside as voyeur of an imaginary world of glances. But this seems to me to be a false opposition. It is possible for content to mirror the viewers' world but for engagement with that world to be indirect and imaginative. Even when real and represented worlds and viewpoints are knitted closer together by the invitation extended to real beholders to adopt the perspective of painted viewers, there is an emphasis upon (and, indeed, a heightened awareness of) processes of viewing and being viewed; see further notes 17 and 116. Note, further, the possibility that the very idea of an encounter at a funerary stele such as this one might be imaginative: see note 99. This chimes with Arrington (2014: 3): 'lekythos painters strove not after realism but to present the idea of a grave and the concept of a grave visit'; see further Arrington (2015: 264). Death and the limits of vision: Turner (2016: esp. 144–5, 154–5, 160).

monument is a visual reminder of the invisibility of the real corpse.[140] It self-consciously re-presents (as well as presents) the deceased.[141] When looking at the tondo of the Getty cup, viewers might imagine that Tecmessa sees the deceased beneath the shroud. By contrast, when looking at the images on this lekythos, viewers might imagine not just that the painted figures *see* the deceased but also that they *remember* the deceased, an imaginative encounter that might be just as emotionally and sensorily intense as a real one but that is qualified with awareness of the distance that characterizes its status as memory.[142] This lekythos invites viewers to imagine not just what is seen (and so represented, at least in part, in paint) but what is imagined.

Significantly, this is also true of scenes showing Charon with the dead, as on one lekythos in the Louvre (Figures 2.8a–b).[143]

A visualization of the experience of death from the perspective of the deceased? So proposed Christiane Sourvinou-Inwood while pursuing her wider argument that the greater prominence and changed appearance of Charon on fifth-century lekythoi suggests increasing awareness of and interest in an individual experience of death and continued existence in some sort of afterlife.[144] But though this

[140] On the participation of lekythoi in a discourse on the possibilities of making the dead visually present, see Arrington (2015: 253–67).

[141] On the coincidence of two representational systems (Archaic/presentational and Classical/representational) on lekythoi, see Jones (2015). On presentation, see Schnapp (1988: 571) on the κολοσσός, citing and translating Emile Benveniste (1932: 119–20): 'Through a fiction made out of wood or clay, the presence of the dead man is prolonged beyond the grave. The communion with the living of which he has deprived his bodily being, is thus perpetuated thanks to his image.' See further especially Vernant (1983: ch. 13) [1965], who brings out not just the presence of the κολοσσός but its emphasis on 'all the elements of the inaccessible, the mysterious, and the fundamentally foreign that the world beyond death holds for the living' (page 315). See too page 42, note 78. Conversely, on the image of the dead as an 'appearance [...] not even skin-deep' (discussing Republican ancestral masks): Turner (2016: 149). See further Vernant (1990) on the Classical 'invention' of the image (comparing εἴδωλον and εἰκών), critiqued in Neer (2010: 14–19) and Crowley (2019: 31–9).

[142] See Jones (2015: 832–3) on images on lekythoi as Aristotelian memory-images, or φαντάσματα.

[143] *BAPD* 217819; *ARV²* 1384.18; *Add²* 372.

[144] See Sourvinou-Inwood (1987: 150–8) on death of the other as mirror and prefiguration of the subject's self, mortality, and death and on scenes with Charon as 'des images de la mort vue de l'intérieur, du point de vue du défunt, la mort de soi du point de vue de la partie survivante, l'âme dans l'outre-tombe' (page 150); Sourvinou-Inwood (1995: 328). See further Sourvinou-Inwood (1981: 22, 37–9). Further interpretations of the Charon figure: Sourvinou-Inwood (1987: 155–8) on his ambivalence for marginal figures as reassuring (as mythological ferryman) and frightening (as metaphor for death); Díez de Velasco (1995: 56–7) on him symbolizing a more democratic form of 'good death'; Oakley (2004: 125) on how, in Classical Greek literature, 'the image of "Charon waiting" indicates approaching death'; Giudice (2015: esp. 267) on the appearance of Charon on lekythoi and the need for emotional reassurance in a time of political and social turmoil; Walter-Karydi (2015: 143) on the image of Charon and new interest in the existential boundary between life and death. See further Allen (2019), also highlighting the emphasis on an ongoing relationship between the living and the dead. For a catalogue of lekythoi with Charon, see Oakley (2004: 113–25).

94 FIGURING DEATH IN CLASSICAL ATHENS

FIGURE 2.8A. Lekythos (Charon at the grave). Attic white-ground lekythos, attributed to Group R. 420–410 BCE. Height 38.8 cm, Diameter 13.5 cm. Found in Greece (Eretria, Euboea). Musée du Louvre, Paris: CA537. Image: © Musée du Louvre, Dist. GrandPalaisRmn/Hervé Lewandowski.

FIGURE 2.8B. Lekythos detail (Charon at the grave). See caption for Figure 2.8a.

image might well reflect a heightened concern with what happens when one dies, the scene is not shown from the perspective of the deceased (or from the perspective of anyone participating in the scene); strictly, it is shown from the perspective of an external viewer. In this respect, the scene is like the one in Euripides' *Alcestis*, discussed in my prologue (though here Charon is visible to the real beholder whereas Alcestis' words in the play indicate that only she is able to see Charon).[145] More importantly, it is striking that the painted woman on the Louvre lekythos does not incline her head towards the boatman so much as towards the alabastron that she holds in her right hand.[146] Observe, too, the painted lekythos that is set prominently on the monument's base between the two painted figures. Is there a hint here that Charon is shown to the external viewer as a manifestation of the painted woman's imaginative response to the pot in her hand and the pot at the grave? If so, each of these painted pots become an analogue for the real lekythos through which real viewers must themselves imagine this sort of scene. And the painted woman becomes, in turn, an analogue for the real beholder.[147] But, crucially, to the extent that this woman invites the real beholder to share her perspective or herself echoes the beholder's perspective, both perspectives encompass not a direct encounter with death (or Charon) but rather an encounter with a pot (and conceivably, through it, Charon's visit to the grave). The images here are framed as imaginative, as conditional upon an encounter with pots.

The image on the Met lekythos is also framed as imaginative. Not only does the composition suggest that the figures are encountered through the prism of the monument, that the monument is a third body, that the pot is a substitute for the monument (and the deceased), that the space of the nude male is ontologically distinct, that the monument is 'just' a picture, and so on, but the whole

---

[145] For further discussion, see page 116, note 40.

[146] Indeed, as noted in Oakley (2004: 120), it is unclear whether the female figure shown with Charon is even deceased. Her attributes, at least, are very similar to those of the female figure on the Met lekythos: both women bring an alabastron and a basket to the grave. Kardara (1960: 157–8) observed that figures rarely interact on later lekythoi, 'the communion between them takes place through the spectator only'. To a similar effect, Osborne (1998: 194) points out that since only one figure can be seen at a time on lekythoi (because of the shape), 'the viewer has to turn the vessel to recover the full situation': though he focuses on how this underscores the relationship between the figures, it is also true that that relationship is contingent on the viewer. Compare Baldassare (1988: 110, 115) on the single point of view offered by lekythoi and elimination of the vessel's circularity, and on the apparent lack of communication between figures. It seems to me to be simultaneously true that many lekythoi purport to offer a single point of view while requiring the viewer to turn the pot to see the whole image: what we encounter on lekythoi is a tension between a possible and a frustrated encounter.

[147] In this respect, she is akin to the 'spectator' figures discussed in Stansbury-O'Donnell (2006): her presence in the image involves the real beholder in a process of not just looking at the pot and its images, but in a 'web of vision' in which they both see and are seen; her presence shapes the identity and self-conception of the real viewer.

96 FIGURING DEATH IN CLASSICAL ATHENS

scene is marked out as a pictorial field by the painted borders and the ornament of running meanders.[148] Add to this the symmetrical positioning of the two painted figures either side of the monument in near mirror reflection, their bodies, like the face of the monument, turned towards the real viewer to produce a threefold line-up. The overall impression is of a scene that has been carefully orchestrated and pleasingly arranged for the real viewer: this is a painted world not a real world, theatre not life. And if the thick line in the man's grasp contributes to the structuring of the pot's cosmos, what might be a sponge in the woman's hand hints at a time when the image might be erased (as, in fact, the woman's clothing almost has been). The fragility here—the possibility that the image might fade—echoes the image of the pots that have toppled over. It hints not just at the ontology of death as destruction but also at the creative foundations upon which that conceptualization is built, at the imaginative process of making and responding to painted objects.

IV. CONCLUSION

The symposium is not a space of death but when its painted images make death their subject the tondo's circular field invites drinking subjects to introspection, absorption in a visual and conceptual profundity. For a man in his cups, sending his eye to the bottom of a wine-dark 'sea', thoughts go deep. In the event-driven context of a drinking cup (the symposium, a delimited period of multi-sensory delight), a moment of encounter with the pot's painted interior becomes infused with the ephemerality of finite experience. In addition, the combination of multiple visual fields, interior and exteriors, invites viewers and handlers to turn the object, to compare, connect, and concoct its images, to engage with death as a temporal event and to participate in a metaphorical viewing that chimes with the mythological subject matter. Figures set in the distant past invite meditation on

[148] Compare here two lekythoi on which the mythological transportation by Hypnos and Thanatos is expressed with self-conscious artifice. One in Berlin (Antikensammlung, 3325) shows three female figures visiting a gravestone with a 'sculpted' Hypnos, Thanatos, and corpse group on its finial: see *BAPD* 46170. On the contrast (between the worlds of the living and the dead): Díez de Velasco (1995: 35); a range of readings: Giudice (2015: 43–4). Curtius (1895: 91) was on to this imaginative visuality with his interpretation of the acroterion form as 'a visionary appearance' ('einer visionären Erscheinung'), demonstrating how fourth-century art reached an apex of emotional expression. A second lekythos in Berne (Jucker Collection) shows the immortal brothers painted on a miniature hydria set upon the monument steps: see *BAPD* 9022305. On the 'jeu d'image' of the hydria as 'vase en abîme' that opens onto the mythic, heroic arena, mediating between the pot and the dead: Lissarrague (2000). On both pots, the mythological register is simultaneously an artistic one and each explicitly artistic version of the scene recalls an image with a rich iconographical and literary tradition. See further De Cesare (1997: 69–75) on replication and citation of sculptural art in vase painting, including the preface by Salvatore Settis (pages 13–15) on *mise en abyme* and the possibility that schemata and motifs migrated between art forms.

present mortality and future death: viewers see one (Phoenix) as another (Priam) and another (Phoenix) as the self, and transposability of identity reiterates an existential situation all viewers have in common. The cup, an enduring and inorganic material object, enfolds and opens onto many temporalities, including moments of transient sensory experience; in relationship with viewers and handlers, it mediates reflection on death as one and many temporal events and a timeless concept.

The specifics in each case are also important. Ajax, for instance, brings particular mythological, political, and religious connotations.[149] As an object of hero cult, his death is exceptional rather than ordinary, and there is a heightened significance to the materiality of his dead body, which will become a locus for continued influence and community attention.[150] Moreover, as an eponymous hero, his name stands for a distinct group identity, one of the ten Athenian tribes.[151] But the reverberation of associations across the multiple fields of the pot and its symposium context (Ajax, Achilles; Phoenix, Priam; painted figures, real viewers), enable conceptual movement from the exemplary to the general. This sort of associative process has also been noted in Sophocles' later play, where Ajax's character is reminiscent of Homeric Achilles, Odysseus, and Hector, and inspires the Sophoclean Odysseus, at least, to introspection, 'contemplating [Ajax's] predicament no more than [his] own'.[152] The move from observation to vicarious experience, a sense of one's own subjectivity, and the formation of some sort of general concept fits with ideas of the imagination as an interface between external and internal worlds.[153]

But the Getty cup does more than participate in the formation of a concept of death; it also prompts reflection on the imaginative nature of exploring death, making thought itself an object of contemplation. The suggested equivalence between categories of material object (corpse, pot) turns a spotlight on the process of extrapolation from singular perceptible examples to the general concept of death. But the picture of death that results is fraught with uncertainty: the falling veil, the pattern that fragments. In fact, the impossibility of knowing what dying is like is simply an urgent and anxiety-laden example of the challenges that underpin imaginative extrapolation of another's subjectivity and any generalized concept of experience. Humans are pot-like enigmas even to themselves.

Like drinking cups, lekythoi generate encounters with death and epistemological reflections upon them. However, the nature of these encounters and the

---

[149] Themes in the Archaic and Classical Athenian reception of Ajax: Bocksberger (2021: ch. 3).

[150] For more on this idea, see Chapter Three.   [151] See e.g. Williams (1980: 143–4).

[152] Soph. *Aj.* 124. Interchangeabilities and (im)possibilities of self-identification: Roisman (2019); Swift (2019).

[153] See Clifford and Buxton (2024b).

98 FIGURING DEATH IN CLASSICAL ATHENS

processes by which they are crystallized are somewhat different. I will focus here on two points of contrast. First, in Classical Athens at least, the grave (and the home, when preparations are made to visit the grave) *is* a site of death. Encounters with death through lekythoi are thus more immediate and targeted than they are through cups. Existential reflections emerge out of a situation of mourning the dead while interacting with objects (pots, wreaths, monuments). The emotional and sensory paradoxes (pleasure and pain, presence and absence, perceptibility and imperceptibility) that characterize encounters with lost loved ones are instrumental in processes of existential and epistemological reflection. This means that, from the perspectives of viewers as mourners, encounters with death in response to lekythoi are largely defined by retrospection (in contrast to the shifting temporalities evoked by a cup, with its multiple fields and narrative scenes). But lekythoi also, like cups, prompt more generalized reflection on death as an eternal concept. The sheer physical and visual abundance of lekythoi, real and painted, asserts (and unravels) a universality and anonymity.

This introduces my second point of contrast: does it matter that figures on lekythoi are *not* Ajax? One feature that makes lekythoi distinctive as a corpus of pots in the fifth century, and thus different from the cups that I explored in this chapter, is their (predominantly) real Athenian subject matter.[154] Lekythoi still invite comparisons, connections, and concoctions, and one result is still a transposability of identity. But this figurative process operates less through myth, and more through a closer mirroring between real viewers and figured images on the pots. As noted above, one seam of scholarship has proposed that the real-life content, especially the ubiquity of marginal figures such as women and children, reveals changing attitudes to death in Athens, and a growing interest in death as an individual event with a distinct afterlife.[155] More recently, Robin Osborne has argued that, in Classical Athens, real-life images operate as mirrors: images on pots increasingly share the world of their viewers.[156] This is all important, and suggests that attention in the fifth century turned towards situations (including funerary situations) closer to home.

However, as Osborne himself (and many others) emphasizes, what matters is not just what was seen but also the way in which it was seen. One central claim

---

[154] There has been emphasis on the continuum in ancient Greece between myth and reality: 'real life scenes' are not replications of reality but form part of a cultural imaginary. See e.g. Bérard et al. (1989) [1984], especially the chapter by Claude Bérard and Jean-Louis Durand; G. Ferrari (2003). Note especially the presence on lekythoi of funerary scenes that combine myth with 'real life', such as images of Charon and Hypnos and Thanatos at the grave together with an Athenian figure. It is important to acknowledge the discursive frame within which real life scenes are also set because it galvanizes their mediation of reflection on death. But the change in the subject matter that is chosen as the loam for that discussion remains significant.

[155] See notes 14 and 144.   [156] See note 139.

of this chapter has been that the formal qualities of lekythoi (including a play of visual ontologies) combine with real life content to mimic a real-life context, generate thanatological reflections, and frame them as imaginative. This draws on Nathaniel Jones's argument that, by putting pressure on the status of the image as an image, lekythoi painters not only sharpen an emotional encounter with someone that has gone but also stage a more extensive epistemological problem.[157] Indeed, Jones's argument can be positioned within Richard Neer's version of the Greek Revolution: Greek representational art, including images on pots, had long had a double impact on viewers (as both a likeness and presence), and the relations with beholders that are forged by Classical forms are an amplification of that rhetoric.[158] This formal shift both facilitates and magnifies epistemological reflection. Elena Walter-Karydi has drawn a link between the advent of contrapposto in Greek sculpture and heightened meditation on the relationships between the living and the dead and, crucially, on the death of the self and the other.[159] Likewise, in the sepulchral world of lekythoi, death makes the same imaginative demands as ever but is visualized at greater remove.

Indeed, to flip the emphasis in Jones's article, epistemological reflections might encompass not just the status and use of images but also the relationship more generally between perception and reality, knowable and unknowable. This relationship is only put under more pressure the more familiar and apparently knowable the subject matter. Perhaps, then, as attention turns more closely upon one's own condition, including in and in response to an image, it also develops more epistemological anxiety. When reflection on death gets closer to home, it becomes more acute. If the scene on a pot is a mirror, that mirror is set assertively within a painted terracotta frame.

Another story here is that *both* these pot types engage in a philosophy that is not unlike Plato's project in the *Phaedo*. This seems especially true of lekythoi which, like a Platonic dialogue, generate reflection on death out of a scene from real life (mourning the dead; discussion among friends). But Plato's Socrates' exemplary death also taps into a tradition of the beautiful dead, the exceptional figure that wins immortal renown though his death, and, in that respect, may also build on thanatological meditations at the symposium—or indeed, as we will see, at the theatre.[160]

Figuring Death in Classical Athens: Visual and Literary Explorations. Emily Clifford, Oxford University Press.
© Emily Clifford 2025. DOI: 10.1093/9780198947936.003.0003

---

[157] See note 117.   [158] Neer (2002), (2010). See further pages 13–16.

[159] See Walter-Karydi (2015: 123–34 with esp. 139–59).

[160] Sarpedon's death (for example) is more obviously relevant here. Ajax's suicide is shameful and not heroic; it is not a beautiful death. Though see Wilson (2007: 1–8) on a mixed response to Socrates' execution by suicide, which is also, by some accounts, shameful.

CONVERSATION TWO

Deaths Old and New

In the first two chapters I have examined the ways in which two different media—Plato's literary philosophy and painted pots—generated reflections not just on death but also on its knowability. I have probed the invisibility and absence of the dead, the exteriority that defines the relationship of the living with death, and the status of each literary and artistic medium as an aesthetic artefact. I have also suggested that these ways of grappling with death and its knowability are culturally significant, that there might be something distinctively Classical about the 'realistic' scenes that mediate reflection on the possibility of knowing about death and what it might be like from the outside.

It therefore seems important at this point to pull in some comparative material—the goal being to avoid an overly stark picture of what may or may not be distinctive about the material focused on in this book. In this second conversation, I take a brief look at two Archaic deaths, one verbal, one visual.

I begin with Homer. There is a startling directness to Hector's death in *Iliad* 22.361–3:

> Ὣς ἄρα μιν εἰπόντα τέλος θανάτοιο κάλυψε,
> ψυχὴ δ' ἐκ ῥεθέων πταμένη Ἄϊδόσδε βεβήκει,
> ὃν πότμον γοόωσα, λιποῦσ' ἀνδροτῆτα καὶ ἥβην.
>
> Just as he spoke these words the completion of death covered him,
> and his soul, winging from his limbs, was gone to Hades,
> weeping over its lot, forsaking manliness and youth.

Death's completion (τέλος—note similar language in the *Phaedo*) strikes in an aorist instant (κάλυψε) after Hector has spoken (εἰπόντα). The departure of the spirit is similarly rapid, gone in an aorist flutter (πταμένη) from his limbs. Hector as subject never returns, switching first to an object and then its fragmentation into spirit (ψυχή) and body parts (ῥεθέων).[1] Indeed, what the spirit ultimately

---

[1] See Sourvinou-Inwood (1995: 56–9) on the departure and ontology of the ψυχή; Garland (2001: 1–2) [1985] notes the 'loss of personality' in the Homeric separation of ψυχή from the self (αὐτός).

CONVERSATION TWO 101

leaves behind is not even a body; it is a set of abstractions, attributes of manhood (ἀνδροτῆτα) and youth (ἥβην). Identity evaporates in the instant of death, leaving a lasting idea of beauty. The immediacy of Hector's transition from speaking subject (356–60) to speaking object (μιν εἰπόντα) is marked by 'just as' (Ὥς ἄρα), which presents the event as a brusque interruption of his voice. But it is also voice that envelops us in the moment of expiration, mirroring the behaviour of the departing ψυχή. The o, o, o, ooω vowels of ὃν πότμον γοόωσα draw exhalation from the voice that sings these verses in assonance with the wailing of the spirit: the double wail involves a singer in affective response to the completion of death alongside Hector's spirit.

Consider, too, the familiarity of these lines: not just the opening sequence 'just as' (Ὥς ἄρα) but also the phrases that communicate the moment of death (τέλος θανάτοιο κάλυψε) and departure to Hades (Ἄϊδόσδε βεβήκει)—the entire three-verse sequence, in fact, which replicates the death of Patroclus (16.855–7), a death that marked the course of the Trojan War and the lives of Hector and Achilles. The sameness of these verses and their components makes them remarkable, especially in accumulation. For speakers, listeners, and readers, similar verses ring like a death knell, marking two and more men in the same way. Hector dies like other Trojan and Achaean warriors—not just violently on the battlefields around Troy but also in the same words. As in the ritual lament, a formulaic feel might carry deep emotion and grief, perhaps even a sense of impotence, in a lack of control over the choice of words or the course of life. But for Hector to die exactly like Patroclus (and somewhat like others) also strips each of their selves.[2] Whether kindred deaths absorb these men into a generalized category of 'hero', or into a generalized category of 'the dead', an identical death annihilates each man's individuality, producing an anonymous and indistinguishable ψυχή. In this respect, Iliadic deaths have something in common with the multitude of miniature images on the Met lekythos and the analogous figures on the Getty cup (a cup that might have been used against the backdrop of songs from the *Iliad*): in each case, death is strikingly de-individualized, refracted into an iterative event.

In some ways, the death of Hector seems to offer a more explicit and direct encounter with the instance of death; there is less of a sense that death is imagined from the perspective of the living. On the other hand, death remains epistemologically problematic; it is unclear, for instance, how similar the deaths of each warrior are meant to be.

---

[2] There are also echoes here of Sarpedon's death: see page 156.

Figure C2. The Mykonos pithos. Tenian-Boeotian relief pithos. *c.* 670 BCE. Height 1.34 m. Found in Chora, Mykonos. Archaeological Museum of Mykonos: 2240. Image: Brenda Kean/Alamy Stock Photo.

Let us now turn to a seventh-century BCE storage pot decorated in relief with scenes drawn from the fall of Troy—the Mykonos pithos (Figure C2).[3] This object, designed for large-scale storage of liquids or dry food, was apparently used, or more likely reused, as a funerary urn: as a container and marker of

---

[3] See Ervin (1963); Caskey (1976: esp. 36–7); Hurwit (1985: 173–6); Anderson (1997: ch. 11); Osborne (1998: 53–7); Stansbury-O'Donnell (1999: 139–42); Ebbinghaus (2005); Giuliani (2013: 57–70) [2003].

human remains. On its neck is a large horse with wheels at its hooves and square windows in its body and neck inside which can be seen warriors' heads in profile. The image, encircled with fighting warriors, is generally understood to show the wooden horse amidst fighting between Achaeans and Trojans. In addition, around the pot's shoulder and body are three rows of metope-like snapshots that also seem to have been drawn from the Trojan War: here are, again and again, doublets and triplets (often comprising a male warrior, a woman, and a child) in confrontation.

Leaving to one side questions of narrative and who is doing what in the images, one striking aspect of this pot is the discourse that it sets up surrounding the visibility of death—specifically, what is and is not visible from the outside. On the one hand, the images on this pot make a feature of revelation, the possibility of seeing through barriers. The beholder is offered a glimpse of the hidden interior of the wooden horse; the grills that fill the handles continue the theme, with repeated triangular holes arranged into fourfold clusters that resemble wheels with crossed spokes—are these yet more circular shields, but now shields that are semi-transparent? On a pot full of real and figured windows, the 'metopes' on its shoulder and body start to look less like framed images and more like holes into the clay belly: if so, scene after scene of slaughter visualizes the situation of the dead body stored within, replaying an enduring state in repeated instances of dying.

But it is just as easy to emphasize concealment. After all, the wooden horse is the example par excellence of a vessel with hidden contents. And the scenes that are spread about the pot's body are set emphatically *outside* the body of the horse, visually and narratologically. It is also unclear how the death of the one within might ever be construed from the many on the pot's surface: while motifs repeat (such as the gestures of the women, arms outstretched), there is also sickening variation in each warrior's treatment of the child. Here, as on the Getty cup and the Met lekythos, is a tension between the particular and general aspects of death.[4]

This has been the briefest of looks at two media that merit much more time and space. Even so, it raises questions surrounding the particularity of the visual and verbal explorations that I examine throughout this book. Already in these two examples, drawn from times and places beyond Classical Athens, are words and images that prompt their audience and viewers to grapple not just with what

---

[4] The single fallen figure in a central panel on the top row is significant here. See Osborne (1998: 57) for emphasis on ambiguity as to whether this man is Greek or Trojan (querying whether it makes a difference) and Giuliani (2013: 62) [2003] for the possibility that he 'represents *all* fallen Trojans'. Moreover, both Stansbury-O'Donnell (1999: 120) and Giuliani (2013: 66) [2003] emphasize, more generally, the repetition and variation on the pot.

death is, but also with the possibility of knowing it from the outside. The instant of Hector's death comes, as in the *Phaedo* and in the tondo of the Getty cup, with a cloak (τέλος θανάτοιο κάλυψε)—a cloak that not only removes Hector from sight as he dies but also turns the instant of death into a metaphor.[5] Meanwhile, on the Mykonos pithos, repeated scenes of slaughter and death are bordered by decorative motifs and neatly arranged like windows across a vessel that is in an analogous relationship with a masterpiece of carpentry. Thus, each medium figures death as a removal from sight that is culturally mediated, mediated by imagery of artefacts that smother and contain.

At the same time, there is a difference between the two encounters discussed here that is, in part, a matter of medium. For all the wrapping and veiling and burial implied by the metaphor of covering in τέλος θανάτοιο κάλυψε, any containment and concealment of the (absent) corpse is fleeting, with a rapid transition to flight, departure, dispersal, and abstraction—words flowing rhythmically onwards in a sequence of departures, one replaced by another, convey the winging away of the soul. In the case of the pot, by contrast, there is an inbuilt and ongoing dynamic of containment in its materiality as a storage object: as Carl Knappett argues, the pithos is a container (for bodies, as for produce)—a closed shape without a lid, it *mostly* conceals the body within, but not entirely (its contents visible, perhaps, through the 'window' *within* its neck—a real opening in counterpart to those figured, in this case, *upon* it).[6] In this, its materiality and function reinforce tensions of visibility and concealment in the images upon it, a dynamic that is absent from the poem.[7] Moreover, in its 'custodial' role, it preserves, holds, isolates, in a way that is, again, markedly different from the poetic fragmentation and departure of Hector.

This draws attention to one way in which the picture offered in this book *is* a culturally specific one: the particularity of the explorations of death that are proposed lie partly in the medium-specific way in which they generate reflection (pots work differently from Plato, for instance, and relief storage jars work differently from painted oil jugs). But the difference also lies in the degree of epistemological emphasis. It seems significant that each of these two Archaic examples, for all their attention to visibility and obscurity, and even to artefactuality, do not make a feature of observers. We might compare here not just the outer frame of the *Phaedo*, in which Echecrates and Phaedo explicitly reflect

---

[5] De Jong (2012: 151) on 361 notes the metaphorical nature of the language of death in Homer. See further Vermeule (1979: 37–41) on θάνατος as a negative, a qualifier, a cloud, a colour, an aspect and not an agent.

[6] See Knappett (2020: esp. 140–52) on containment of the dead, 'partial viewing', 'passive facilities and their custodial function', and more.

[7] See Elsner (2012a) on 'decorative imperatives between concealment and display' on Roman sarcophagi, a discussion on which Carl Knappett builds (see previous note).

upon on the death of Socrates (set elsewhere and at another time), but also the dynamic in the theatre where events are observed not just by the audience but also by the chorus, and where deaths are frequently communicated from a spatial or temporal distance.

Figuring Death in Classical Athens: Visual and Literary Explorations. Emily Clifford, Oxford University Press.
© Emily Clifford 2025. DOI: 10.1093/9780198947936.003.0004

THREE

The Extraordinary Death of Sophocles'
Oedipus at Colonus

I. DYING ON/OFF STAGE

ὦ παῖδες, ἥκει τῷδ' ἐπ' ἀνδρὶ θέσφατος
βίου τελευτή, κοὐκέτ' ἔστ' ἀποστροφή.

Children, there has come upon this man the divinely-ordained
end of his life, and there is no longer any turning back.

—Oedipus speaking about himself, in Sophocles, *OC* 1472–3

Greek tragedy is renowned for its bloody themes. Characters die gruesomely, miserably, in war, by suicide, by murder, by divine justice. And their deaths are presented in graphic detail: think of Aeschylus' Clytemnestra's description of Agamemnon's dying throes or Sophocles' Messenger's account of Haimon's suicide upon the body of Antigone.[1] But how close does tragedy take us? For all the captivation that death and dying seem to have had for composers and audiences, the *moment* of a character's death—the switch from living to dead—usually happens off stage, absent and unseen; what is shown to the audience is the build-up and aftermath, not the event.[2]

In this respect, ancient tragedy seems to have missed an opportunity. When it comes to representations of dying people it is difficult to think of a more 'present' genre than one that involves actual bodies (compare philosophy, pots,

---

[1] Aesch. *Ag.* 1382–92; Soph. *Ant.* 1234–43.

[2] See Macintosh (1994: 126–42) on three explanations for the rarity of death scenes in Greek tragedy (aesthetic, practical, and religious); she proposes instead that imprecision surrounding the moment of death in ancient drama mirrored the Greek conception of death as a social process. See further Macintosh (2022: 165–6). Her emphasis on the elusive nature of the moment of death on the tragic stage even in messenger speeches is highly relevant to my discussion in this chapter, though I emphasize the reflection on death (including its moment) that was generated.

sculpture, and historiography).[3] And, as observed in Chapter Two, corporeality goes hand in hand with death: it is of the body (the mortal body) to deteriorate, die, and decay. This is accepted even in philosophical arguments for *immortality*: the soul may survive; bodies normally do not. Tragedy makes use of bodies before and after their death (possibly via some sort of corpse substitute in the latter). But the event itself, the extinguishing of life, is remarkably disembodied, communicated by retrospective description or synchronous voices from behind the stage building.[4] Herakles, his pre-death agonies a visual spectacle, does not actually die on stage (at least not in any way that can be extracted from the text of Sophocles' *Women of Trachis*).[5] Expiration in full view, such as that of Alcestis and Hippolytus, is unusual (at least in the extant corpus).[6] Tragedy does not tend to do death with physical dying bodies.[7]

Instead, encounters with dying moments are characterized by a distinctive sort of phantasy (via memory and narrative experience). Before death, characters, including dying characters, are present body and soul, but the actual moment of death is physically absent; the 'presence' of that moment, a future moment, is crystallized instead by the anticipations of minds within the drama and among the audience. The moment itself might be communicated by offstage cries, or real-time reporting, again engaging the audience's imaginative faculties. In the aftermath, evidence of death (dead bodies, for example) might be present, but the moment has passed; the instance of dying might be communicated by a retrospective account from a third party.[8] Tragic encounters with death are

[3] Compare Budelmann (2006: 136–7, 141) on the key role played by the presence of an acting body in representations of pain on the tragic stage, and Goldhill (2006: 154) on the potentially explosive combination of violence with real bodies in the theatre (theatre offers, he argues, particular conditions for the representation of violence compared to, for instance, prose or epic poetry). On the representational challenges posed by death (and violence) on the stage (focusing on the notion of 'performability' in Early Modern English and French theatre): Glynn (2022).

[4] On displacement of the suffering body in Greek tragedy, its place in a literary tradition of embodiment only in wounding and death, and attempts to avoid that embodiment through language: Murnaghan (1988) (though she sees the *OC* as an exception: see note 52).

[5] I refer here to 'the text' but it is an impossible entity. See Goldhill (2012: 262–3) on the advantages of referring to Sophocles' written work as a 'script'. As Simon Goldhill observes, a reading of the script is a performance. In any given reincarnation of the script of *Women of Trachis* Herakles might be understood to die. It is, however, not stated explicitly in the words.

[6] Eur. *Alc.* 391: 'farewell!'; Eur. *Hipp.* 1458: 'Cover my face as quickly as you can with my cloak!' In any case, Alcestis' death in Euripides' play is wracked with epistemological anxiety (see my prologue).

[7] Of course, the bodies on stage are the bodies of actors, who represent the characters. They thus could and should not actually die. Perhaps the presence of real bodies in the theatre is an encumbrance. On that note, see Senelick (2022: 3–6) on the philosophical incompatibility between performance and dying and the meditation upon that point in Tom Stoppard's *Rosencrantz and Guildenstern are Dead*.

[8] See especially Bassi (2018: 37–8): 'The result is a paradoxical situation in which empirical observation (the sight of the dead body) only confirms what the observer cannot know (the state of being dead); [...] As a distinctive feature of Greek tragedy, [the eccyclema] gives prominence to the material presence of the corpse in the service of concealing the moment of death.'

108 FIGURING DEATH IN CLASSICAL ATHENS

thoroughly imaginative. As elsewhere in this book, then, my question in this chapter is not whether we encounter death in Greek tragedy at all, but what those encounters are like: how does Greek tragedy encourage its audience to explore death and to grapple with the imaginative nature of that process?[9]

I focus on one play: Sophocles' *Oedipus at Colonus* (the *OC*). As a drama in which an old man, Oedipus, arrives at the land in which his life will end,[10] this is a good play for thinking about dying and death. Oedipus also constitutes a powerful exemplum of the relationship in Greek tragedy between bodies and death. Visible for most of the play, he leaves the stage at 1555 for his death and completely vanishes at his life's completion (transition into death or heroism or both; what happens is unclear). His death and disappearance are then communicated by a Messenger. This format puts pressure on what is perceptible and imperceptible, knowable and unknowable, about death. It also puts a question mark over the extent to which what *is* perceptible is helpful: what difference would it make to see Oedipus' body during (or, indeed, after) his death? Insofar as this play stages the build-up to death but sends the moment behind the scenes, it can stand (somewhat) for the genre. It is a good choice of play for thinking not just about dying and death, but about tragic encounters with them.

It is also a curious choice. In the first place, there are several factors that make Oedipus' death unusual, both in general and by comparison with the genre: death in old age, a notional conclusion to life rather than the brutal interruption (murder or suicide) found in other dramas;[11] the foreknowledge that the dying man has of his coming demise; the disappearance of his body and absence of his corpse (and thus the lost opportunity for mourning). Can an unusual death reveal anything about tragic dying—or dying in general? Admittedly, the exemplarity of any one tragedy for a varied genre is always questionable.[12] It is then (arguably) better to select a play that is apposite and by the unexpected to throw light upon what is expected, turning a distinctive tragedy into a suggestive exemplum for how a genre deals with death.

This is all the more true because, composed towards the end of the fifth century and performed posthumously, this play was in a position to reflect on almost a

---

[9] On fifth-century drama as a form of early Greek philosophical thought, see Billings (2021: esp. ch. 2).

[10] What happens to Oedipus at the end of the play has been extensively debated, as I address below.

[11] The fact that Sorana-Cristina Man's study of death in Greek tragedy focuses wholly on violence seems indicative of this point: Man (2020). See further Reinhardt (1979: 224) [1933] on death as painful tearing from life in *Antigone* and *Ajax*.

[12] On exemplarity and our reception of the classical world, see page 10, note 28. See further Goldhill (2012: 139–65) on what is at stake in seeking an abstract notion of 'the tragic' and generalizing about tragedy. When I use 'tragic' in this chapter, I mean 'pertaining to a Greek tragedy'.

century of drama, by Aeschylus, Sophocles, and Euripides, among others.[13] And not just a century of drama—a lifetime, nearly itself a century (Sophocles was born in 496/5 BCE and died in 406/5 BCE),[14] of death and existential risk, not least the years resisting invasions from Persia, the devastating years of the plague and Peloponnesian War, the recent mass slaughter at Sicily, and the attack of the Boeotian cavalry on Athens near Colonus in 408/407 BCE.[15] By the time it was first staged in 401 BCE by Sophocles' grandson Sophocles, Athens was again reeling in the wake of her surrender and the cruelty and slaughter under the Thirty Tyrants in 404–403 BCE (one of whom was also called Sophocles—just how many deaths, distant and recent, might have occurred to an ancient audience on watching an account by a recently deceased Sophocles of an old man's death in Colonus, the playwright's native deme, an old man reviled, feared, and vengeful?).[16] The drama puts pressure on the possibility of drawing analogies between the different lives and deaths of Oedipus, Sophocles(es?), and Athenians more generally. The death in this drama might be the most exemplary of deaths because it is so familiar, so close to home. It is tragic, personal, and political.

Equally interesting for the purposes of this book, then, the questionable exemplarity of the play as a model for what it might more generally be like to die in tragedy invites audience members to confront the tenability of their expectations surrounding any one death. Is *any* individual's example transferable? Is there any such thing as an 'ordinary death' in *or outside* tragedy? Or might every death be idiosyncratic? This question compromises extrapolations of what death is and is like from observation of a dying person. It is a question that might crop up in any genre, but which seems especially pertinent in the tragic theatre, where mythical individuals such as Oedipus might have exemplary force, and where a tragic

---

[13] See especially Van Nortwick (2015: ch. 4) on 'late Sophocles' and the *OC*. See further Ringer (1998: 90–9) on Sophocles' daring and self-consciousness in the *OC*; Markantonatos (2007: 21–30) on Sophocles' art and last play; Nooter (2012: 147) on the sonic exceptionality of the *OC* and its place at the end of the fifth century; Van Nortwick (2012) on the *OC* as a late tragedy and the dramatist's 'farewell to his art' (page 150). Knox (1964: 144) comments, 'This play is a worthy last will and testament. All the great themes of the earlier plays recur; it is as if Sophocles were summing up a lifetime of thought and feeling in this demonic work of his old age.'

[14] For Sophocles' biography, see Lefkowitz (1981: 75–87). See further Ringer (1998: 97–8); Kelly (2009: 9–14); Jouanna (2018: 5–107) [2007]. On connections between Sophocles' play and biography/ historical context, see Wilamowitz-Moellendorff (1917: 368–73); Bowra (1944: 307); Reinhardt (1979: 193–4) [1933]; Burton (1980: 291–2); Segal (1981: 407–8); Edmunds (1996: 163–8); Calame (1998: 355–6); Markantonatos (2007: 10–21); Kelly (2009: 14–18); Currie (2012: 332); Hesk (2012: 174–9); Van Nortwick (2012: 141), (2015: 115–16); Scharffenberger (2017: 336–9).

[15] Diod. 13.72.3–73.2.

[16] The Thirty Tyrants' names: Xen. *Hell.* 2.3.2. On the setting of the play in Sophocles' native deme: Radt Testimonia 18.

110 FIGURING DEATH IN CLASSICAL ATHENS

performance might stand as a source of instruction to, and thus exert normative influence over, the Athenian polis.[17]

Then there is another problem: does Oedipus even die (in an ordinary sense)? Details in Sophocles' drama indicate that Oedipus' death will be far from ordinary, that he is destined to become the object of hero cult and so to remain present among the living and exert his influence upon them. This complicates our understanding of what happens to him when he disappears. Does he become a hero after or upon his death, or even over the course of the play (what is the existential status of a hero anyway?)?[18] Or does he somehow transcend his mortal existence without dying at all (is death reserved for those who do not become heroes?)? Much scholarship has circled around the nature of Oedipus' transition to and ultimate possession of cult hero status.[19] Surely, then, the *OC* is at best bewildering and at worst irrelevant for thinking about death?

What I hope to demonstrate in this chapter is that it is precisely this uncertainty that, combined with the features detailed above, makes the *OC* a product-

---

[17] On Oedipus' 'exemplary' death: Scodel (1984: 118). On drama as a source of instruction to the polis, see Ar. *Ran.* 686–7, 1008–12. See further Pucci (2007); Valakas (2009: 201–7). Note the comparative absence of death (as opposed to the dead) in Old Comedy; death is important to the genre of tragedy.

[18] The timing of a hero's recognition as such might also complicate matters here. On hero cult, see Méautis (1940: ch. 1). Heroes were human beings subject to human ethical standards: Blundell (1989: 253–4).

[19] See e.g. Rohde (1925: 430–1); Méautis (1940: ch. 3); Bowra (1944: ch. 8); Linforth (1951: 97–104), though he emphasizes that Oedipus dies and that heroization is, for him, an 'empty thing' (page 102); Rosenmeyer (1952: esp. 104–11); Knox (1964: 58) on the *OC* as a mystery play about Oedipus' transition; Burian (1974) on how the double suppliant drama format dramatizes a heroization of Oedipus on stage, paving the way for his daemonic heroization; Reinhardt (1979: 193–4) [1933]; Henrichs (1983: 93–100), (1993: 176–8); Birge (1984); Kearns (1989: 50–2, 189, 208–9); Lardinois (1992); Wilson (1997: 178–86); Calame (1998); Scullion (2000: 231–2); Markantonatos (2002); F. Ferrari (2003); Tilg (2004a) on chthonic symbolism in the play; Bowman (2007) on how Oedipus' curse effects his metamorphosis into a hero (a source of comfort to an Athenian audience at the end of the fifth century); Currie (2012: 331–3) on Oedipus' simultaneous status as Sophoclean tragic hero and cultic hero (with Sophocles dramatizing a '*process* of transformation'); Garvie (2016: 75–82) [2005]. Note especially Hester (1977: 31–2), who observes 'most of the instances show that the power of a dead hero comes precisely from being dead'. Critical to this question is the reading of the Messenger's words at *OC* 1583–4: ὡς λελοιπότα | κεῖνον τὸν ἀεὶ βίοτον ἐξεπίστασο. Two scholia accept (for different reasons) the λελοιπότα that is in the manuscripts: Xenis (2018). Many scholars instead accept Mudge's emendation to λελογχότα (he 'obtained' his immortal life): see e.g. Wilamowitz-Moellendorff (1917: 366); Kamerbeek (1984: 216); Dawe (1996: 80); Guidorizzi et al. (2008: 372). I prefer to keep λελοιπότα and to read τὸν ἀεὶ βίοτον as the ordinary life that Oedipus has had constantly and for so long. As regards a real cult and tomb of Oedipus at Colonus, I follow Scott Scullion in thinking that this was most likely a 'dramatic postulate' (2000: 232). In any case, what matters for the purposes of this chapter is the death of Oedipus that is encountered in Sophocles' play; it is possible that, even in the fifth century, this encounter would have been reinforced by external knowledge, but evidence postdates the *OC* (see e.g. Androtion *FGrH* 324 F 62, though, as Jacoby comments, it is unclear which part belongs to Androtion and the idea of the tomb is complicated (IIIb Supp. vol. 1, 169 and vol. 2, 155, note 5)).

ive case study for this book. Even if Oedipus does not die, the lack of clarity surrounding what happens to him, his new ontological status, and the way in which he reaches it, sheds light not only upon the expectations that surround death but also upon an epistemological problem. If Oedipus' death *is* extraordinary, what does that reveal about the alternative: what would it take for his death to be considered ordinary?[20] Could the mystery that shrouds what it might mean to be and become a hero simply be emblematic of a larger existential problem: what can the living know about any ontological situation beyond existence? I will not explore Oedipus' heroic status further here: hero cult has monopolized scholarship on this play. Instead, I will focus upon how Sophocles' drama encourages its audience to grapple with death. The very fact that Sophocles' dramatic account of the end of Oedipus' life has equivocal value as an example of one death, tragic death, or death in general, throws the epistemological problems that surround death into sharper relief.

The chapter falls into three parts. I begin with a scene in which there is a gear change in expectation: a shift from awareness to dread when Oedipus' death becomes imminent and a discernible splitting of perspectives as the dying man diverges from the living in knowledge and trajectory. Next, I discuss the Messenger's speech, in which an ecphrastic set-up brings ideas of distance to the fore. Finally, in a section that doubles as a conclusion, I delve into some attributes of Oedipus' death that put pressure on its potentially exemplary force: to what extent might an audience derive general ideas about what death is and is like from this play? This question is entwined with the relationship between the exemplarity of Sophocles' Oedipus' death and our reception of Oedipus and *Oedipus* as significant (from a death perspective) within the specific context of the play, the tragic, Classical Athens, or more universally for audiences then, now, and in between. In each case, my starting point is the language of the script, though, throughout, what might and might not be present and visible on stage is important.[21] My overall point is that existential reflection through Sophocles' Oedipus is epistemologically problematic; encountering Oedipus' death is characterized by distance and exteriority, and the tension between ordinariness and extraordinariness that defines him as a tragic figure has implications for a more philosophical question as to the relationship between one death and a general experience.

---

[20] Especially in the theatre: on the 'never-ending ending' of the death on stage, see Goodman (2022). See further Carlson (2001) on the 'haunted stage'.

[21] On extrapolating the 'dramatized visible event' (page 3) from the script, see Taplin (2003: 1–6) [1978].

112 FIGURING DEATH IN CLASSICAL ATHENS

II. CRISIS

Let us turn first to a scene towards the end of the play in which there is a pronounced shift in expectation (1456–1555): Oedipus' death suddenly becomes imminent. The scene mostly involves Oedipus, Antigone, and the chorus (Theseus joins towards the end) and unfolds in the interval between the exit of Polynices and the exit of Oedipus with his daughters and Theseus. Threefold thunder crashes (1456, 1463–4, 1478–9) and blazing flashes of lightning (1466–7) fulfil the thunder or lightning of Zeus that, earlier in the play, Oedipus said had been entrusted to him by Apollo as signs of the turning point of his life (94–5).[22] For Oedipus and the audience, at least, it is now probable that the moment of Oedipus' death is close.[23]

It is through the chorus, primarily, that Sophocles orchestrates the advent of a crisis in the drama.[24] The sensory explosion precipitates an emotional explosion, reflecting and reinforcing a widespread realization that something significant is imminent. The chorus speak of fear's touch as it assails the ends of the hairs on their heads (1464–5). Their hearts cower ($\check{\epsilon}\pi\tau\alpha\xi\alpha\ \theta\upsilon\mu\acute{o}\nu$, 1466), a decisive, physical shrinking within that also bursts out in repeated cries that are expressively fervent: $\check{\epsilon}\alpha\ \check{\epsilon}\alpha$ (1478)... $\mathring{\iota}\grave{\omega}\ \mathring{\iota}\acute{\omega}$ (1491). The intensity of their emotional reaction to the sensory assault reflects their heightened expectation of a dreadful event.[25]

The audience's apprehension of the dramatic event is, in turn, built upon vicarious adoption of the chorus' experience (communicated by the chorus' words, animated metrical rhythms, and movements on stage). This vicarious experience is reinforced by direct reaction to the choral spectacle (which is to say, the audience, and Theseus too, at once responds with and to the chorus) and, conceivably, staging effects such as rolls of thunder.[26] Fulfilling the prophecy that the audience, Antigone, and possibly the Eumenides heard from Oedipus at

---

[22] An earthquake does not transpire, though the Messenger later speculates that something of that sort might have occurred (1661–2).

[23] The scholiast comments that this first thunder crash at 1456 is 'the most essential moment in the drama' ($\tau\grave{o}\ \sigma\upsilon\nu\epsilon\kappa\tau\iota\kappa\acute{\omega}\tau\alpha\tau\upsilon\nu\ \tau\upsilon\hat{\upsilon}\ \delta\rho\acute{a}\mu\alpha\tau\upsilon\varsigma$) (Xenis (2018)). See especially Linforth (1951: 168–71): *this* is the moment when the audience know that the death will occur during the time span of the play. Suggesting that the audience already know the tragedy's outcome in the first scene: Wilamowitz-Moellendorff (1917: 329).

[24] This sort of heightened moment, especially as a point of sudden change, might provoke the sublime: see Porter (2016: 53) on the crisis or $\kappa\alpha\iota\rho\acute{o}\varsigma$.

[25] Wallace (1979: 46) argues that 'interruption of the ordinary flow of events' by death is characteristic of Greek tragedy; here, Oedipus is not yet dead but 'jolts' in reality communicate the proximity of that moment.

[26] Theseus' words on entering the stage draw attention to this aural phenomenon: he responds first to the 'common sound' from both chorus and Oedipus, and then immediately asks whether there is a thunderbolt or the noisy impact of rainy hail, hinting that he hears one in the other (*OC* 1500–4). On the possibility that the chorus themselves performed the thunder: Gardiner (1987: 115). Others propose a thunder-machine: see Edmunds (1996: 75); Guidorizzi et al. (2008: 362) on 1456.

94–5,[27] the theatrical climax taken as a whole represents and generates an amplification of mental vision for all parties. Attitudes towards Oedipus' death shift from awareness of its possibility (he is an old wandering man seeking rest from his journey) to expectation of its imminence, a leap forwards on a sliding scale towards proximity and presence.

Oedipus is, nevertheless, still alive and the moment of death remains absent. The confident foreknowledge of death that is realized by the audience and Oedipus is thus a strong visualization of a future event, an imaginative encounter, of sorts, with the moment itself. This sort of mental experience ordinarily only accompanies unnatural death: Hippolytus' fatal injury, Ajax's suicide, Iphigenia's impending sacrifice, or, in Oedipus' case, the hand of fate.[28] But though unnatural death and the associated anticipation of its proximity (when and where it will occur) are not the norm for mortals, they are ordinary for tragedy. It is not that characters in tragedy never die in ignorance or uncertainty,[29] but rather that when major characters such as Oedipus die, representations of their death are overshadowed by grim certainty: life's end is recognized to be close, inexorable, definite; it drags them down with dreadful magnetism.[30] This is reflected in the language with which Oedipus explains to Theseus the significance of the thunder and lightning (1508–9):

ῥοπὴ βίου μοι· καί σ᾽ ἅπερ ξυνῄνεσα
θέλω πόλιν τε τήνδε μὴ ψεύσας θανεῖν.

This is the turn of the scales of my life, and I wish to die
without disappointing you and this city of the things that I agreed to grant.

---

[27] Jebb (1900b: 227) [1886] on 1474 emphasizes that only Antigone heard Oedipus.

[28] This might suggest he is already on the route to becoming a hero: his death (or transformation) is not ordinary.

[29] I pass over descriptions of war casualties such as in Aeschylus' *Persians* where, though characters are named, their life is over in a few words; these descriptions conjoin the instant of the audience's knowledge with the surprise of sudden death.

[30] The 'dark "necessity"' of death (page 72), 'language of tragic inevitability' (page 72) and the 'fated day' (pages 56–7) in *Alcestis*. Segal (1993a: ch. 4); see further Segal (1993b: 217–19). Charles Segal argues in both publications that *Alcestis* provides a rare account of a 'normal death'. On my reading here, the grim certainty that Alcestis has of her death before it occurs makes her death comparable to that of other characters in Greek tragedy. See further Markantonatos (2013: 46) on the 'almost superhuman mental faculties' revealed by Alcestis' knowledge of the proximity of her death; he comments in note 40 on her similarity, in this respect, to Oedipus. Alcestis' death may not be violent, but as a substitution for Admetus' death it is not normal. (Though see below on the questionable normality of any death: IV. Oedipus: If Anyone Among Mortals Is Wondrous.) See further Macintosh (2022: 168) on 'dying into death', 'The tragic characters only begin to attain tragic status once they begin to die.' In fact, perhaps, in their foreknowledge of death, tragic characters are extreme examples of the human condition: see Elias (2001: 5) [1982], 'It is not actually death, but the knowledge of death, that creates problems for human beings. [...] Human beings know, and so for them death becomes a problem.'

114 FIGURING DEATH IN CLASSICAL ATHENS

When Oedipus talks of the turning point of his life (ῥοπὴ βίου μοι, 1508) the imagery he uses of sinking scales communicates a downwards momentum in counterpart to the 'overturning' (καταστροφήν, 103) that he begged from the Eumenides at the start of the play (the prefix κατα- has overtones of downwards motion).[31] The image of Hades as 'below' and death as a descent is a familiar one in Greek literature,[32] and will return in the Messenger's speech, but it is worth noting here because it is an important way in which the absent future, Oedipus' death, becomes mentally present. It also reflects one way in which the encounter with Oedipus' death is positioned as both ordinary and extraordinary, somewhat familiar and somewhat unfamiliar within the genre and the ambit of mortal experience. I will return to this duality in my conclusion.

The certainty of death that accompanies the final countdown is potent—so powerful, in fact, that edges blur between expectation of Oedipus' death and occurrence of the event itself. For Oedipus, long-fated death 'has come' (ἥκει, 1472) upon him with the fulfilment of the promised signs; in knowledge of his imminent death, in accordance with his lot, he is already dead.[33] What might be amusing in another genre and time—'Now am I dead, | Now am I fled...' (Pyramus, *A Midsummer Night's Dream* V.I)—is serious in Greek tragedy, where the nature of the deaths permits advance certainty and appreciation of death's onset. For Oedipus, the end of his story is expanded into a significant final day, allowing, paradoxically, for imperfective experience of a perfective moment:[34] the end is an instant that can only ordinarily be experienced by living observers since the dying, once death occurs, no longer exist to observe the moment's completion.

---

[31] Jebb (1900b: 232) [1886] on 1508 also notes the momentum in this word.

[32] Tragedy: Soph. *Ant.* 895–6; Eur. *Alc.* 360 and 393–4; Eur. *Hipp.* 1447; Eur. *Hec.* 205–10; Eur. fr. 638 (Loeb 506). Lyric: Anac. fr. 395 *PMG*. Indeed, one Greek word for dying is to die 'downwards' (thoroughly, away): καταθνῄσκω.

[33] This sort of language can be observed elsewhere in Greek tragedy. Alcestis, once her 'fated day' (*Alc.* 147) arrives, is dead before her death: 'you might call her both living and dying' (*Alc.* 141). Ironically, Admetus will experience the same plight: *Alc.* 241–3. Still speaking, still with more to say, she insists 'existing no longer, you would say I am nothing' (*Alc.* 387, see also 390). Alcestis' perplexing existential situation has been much discussed: see e.g. Gregory (1979: esp. 263), (1991: ch. 1, esp. 28–34); Buxton (1987: 19–23); Macintosh (1994: 70–1); Luschnig (1995: 5–6, 39); Lloyd (2007: 303–4). Likewise, with Deianeira dead indoors and dying Herakles on his way, the chorus of *Women of Trachis* do not know whom they should mourn, for 'it is the same thing to see and to wait to see' (*Trach.* 952).

[34] On perfective and imperfective time in Sophocles, and on the contrast between Oedipus' imperfective wandering from day to day and the perfective accomplishment of his life on 'this day' (*OC* 1612), see Hutchinson (1999: 58–63). On the significant day in Greek literature (ἦμαρ τόδε), marking confident recognition by a character of a decisive moment defined by the end of one state and beginning of another, see Herrero de Jáuregui (2013: esp. 62). As Miguel Herrero de Jáuregui explores, the phrase in Greek tragedy is overshadowed by the possibility that characters are mistaken or deceived (pages 64–7). On Sophocles' gods 'offering a future that is uncertain': Budelmann (2000a: 194). See further Parker (1999: 27): 'As mortals we see the Sophoclean gods through a glass darkly'.

Oedipus' reference to himself in the third person, as 'this man' ($\tau\hat{\omega}\delta\epsilon$ [...] $\mathring{a}\nu\delta\rho\acute{\iota}$, 1472), contributes to this effect. To some extent, the phrasing adds cosmic significance to the moment by suggesting that the words are spoken not just by Oedipus but by a god, the voice of fate.[35] But the phrasing also sets Oedipus implicitly outside himself. This is an out-of-body experience of sorts, a formulation that, though anachronistic, points towards a real sense in which Oedipus' language reflects a divide between the living, who respond, and the dead or dying that are the object of that discourse, and yet allows him, unusually, to straddle both.

The situation of the dying Oedipus, an existence in a temporal suspension with a downwards momentum, is a source of perplexity for the living. It is apparent that he, the one who will die, sees and knows what is to come with greater clarity than those who observe him.[36] Though the chorus (who were not yet on stage during Oedipus' prayer at 84–110, and so did not hear the prophecy) respond to the celestial portents with dread, their fear is laced with uncertainty. Will Zeus cast a bolt from the sky portending misfortune (1468–70)? Will divine power bring 'something lightless' ($\tau\iota\dots\mathring{a}\varphi\epsilon\gamma\gamma\acute{\epsilon}s$) upon the earth (1480–1), even upon them (1482–4)?[37] It is only following Oedipus' explanation that they pray with reverent certainty of his death (1556–78).[38] Even Antigone, who was on stage during Oedipus' prayer and must have overheard something to prompt her to respond 'be silent!' ($\sigma\acute{\iota}\gamma a$, 111), cannot comprehend the signs. In response to Oedipus' (correctly) confident interpretation that the thunder signifies 'the end of life that was prophesied' ($\theta\acute{\epsilon}\sigma\varphi a\tau os\mid\beta\acute{\iota}ov\ \tau\epsilon\lambda\epsilon v\tau\acute{\eta}$, 1472–3) and that there is no longer any 'turning it back' or 'turning away' ($\mathring{a}\pi o\sigma\tau\rho o\varphi\acute{\eta}$, 1473), she asks 'How

---

[35] Long (1968: 89) comments that the impersonal phrase 'shows that events are now beyond human control'. There is a similarly jarring effect later in the Messenger's speech when the god seems to speak both to and with Oedipus, 'Oh this man ($o\mathring{v}\tau os$), this man, Oedipus, why are we delaying our departure...?' (1627–8). The use of $o\mathring{v}\tau os$ here can be interpreted as emphatic deixis, giving the god's words an intimate tone; on this sort of deictic in Sophocles, see Ruijgh (2006). Note that Bernard (2001: 152–5) differed, emphasizing impatience instead.

[36] This more extensive knowledge gives irony a lesser role: Buxton (1984: 18). The opposition in the play between Oedipus' visuality (on stage) and obscurity (through his different knowledge): Edmunds (1996: 46). Bowra (1944: 344–6) comments on the different perspectives in this scene and elsewhere in the play but focuses upon mortal ignorance in the face of the divine. Markantonatos (2002: 124–5) makes a similar point (though he suggests that the perspectives begin to converge); see further Markantonatos (2007: 107–8). Charles Segal also observes, 'Where the others are confused, [Oedipus] is calm': Segal (1981: 396).

[37] Nooter (2012: 173) also notes this contrast between the chorus' fear and Oedipus' certainty.

[38] While I agree with Umit Dhuga (2005: 344) that the chorus demonstrate an appreciation of the urgency of the situation in their final stanza before Theseus' entrance (1491–9), their continued use of dochmiacs and exclamations ($\mathring{\iota}\grave{\omega}\ \mathring{\iota}\acute{o}$, $\pi a\hat{\iota}$, $\beta\hat{a}\theta\iota\ \beta\hat{a}\theta$', 1491) suggests that there has not yet been a major shift in their comprehension.

116 FIGURING DEATH IN CLASSICAL ATHENS

do you know?' (πῶς οἶσθα; 1474). Oedipus diverges from those around him in understanding.[39]

Moreover, with lucidity of insight comes remarkable clarity of sight: Oedipus alone, it appears, recognizes the presence of the two divinities that lead him to Hades (1547–8). His privileged perspective reflects a bifurcation of living and dying vision.[40] His dying powers of sight seem more than metaphorical; his clarity of sight is like a god's.[41] In a reversal that positions Oedipus as not just in control of the situation and those around him but actually adopting the role of divine escort, he turns from blind follower to solemn guide as he is led from the stage by gods that only he can see (1542–8).

The divergence in Oedipus' perception and understanding raises epistemological problems for those that observe him: the combination of clear sight with dark vision whispers of cognitive unreliability. Oedipus' eyes have long been dark: for him, light is lightless (ὦ φῶς ἀφεγγές, 1549), and its final rays must be felt not seen (νῦν δ' ἔσχατόν σου τοὐμὸν ἅπτεται δέμας, 1550). He presents an extreme, and perverse, version of the dying warrior, who, in Greek epic, gains a prophetic insight precisely at his most vulnerable, as his sensory organs fail.[42] The blindness that has defined Oedipus and heralded his identity from the start of the play must somewhat undermine the trust that others might place in his insight: how is anyone to believe and to follow a formerly helpless old man, who needed a young girl for guidance and protection?[43] From the outside perspective of the living, the divergent vision of the dying appears at once more perceptive and less sound.

Thus, in this critical scene, Oedipus' death seems more perceptible, more palpable, and the anticipation of those that observe him rises in excitement and dread. But with greater proximity comes a splitting of comprehension and vision.

---

[39] See Dunn (1992: 4–5) on another reversal in dramatic irony at the beginning of the drama (blind Oedipus recognizes the setting before the audience does so).

[40] There is a similar bifurcation in Eur. *Alc.* 259–62 when Alcestis describes the physical appearance of Hades and asks the chorus 'don't you see him?' (οὐχ ὁρᾶις;). On her dying perspective: Segal (1993b: 229–30); Sekita (2022: 43–5). Lloyd (1985: 122) argues that Euripides is interested, in the *Alcestis*, in the 'inevitable estrangement from the living of those on the point of death'. See further *Alc.* 252–6; *Hipp.* 1447.

[41] A near comparison is Apollo's sight in Euripides' *Alcestis* (and Alcestis' sight later in the drama: see previous note); Apollo not only sees but converses with Death, exclaiming, 'I am looking upon Death right here beside me' (24).

[42] Compare Alcestis' description of how her 'dark' or 'obscure' 'eye' or 'sight' 'is oppressed' (βαρύνεται, 385). Compare: *Alc.* 269; *Hipp.* 1444.

[43] See e.g. Knox (1964: 145): 'To cast an old man in the role of the hero was a bold step, and of all old men in the world this Oedipus is surely the least likely candidate.' Though this interpretation conflicts with a major thrust in scholarship, which sees this contrast as the point of the play: Oedipus' transformation from blind human to cult hero. See note 19. See further Nooter (2012: ch. 5) on Oedipus' 'strong poetic presence' for much of the *OC* (page 162); Oedipus' lyric voice gives him authority and power.

In the final moratorium between certainty that death will occur and expiration, the dying diverge from the living on a downwards trajectory, knowing differently and seeing differently, often (linguistically at least) already dead. But in a drama where the unexpected realization of crisis is signalled by the intrusion of unmistakable cosmic force, *all* parties sense in their different ways the imminence of something significant: the chorus with their heightened emotions; Oedipus with his divergent perspective. This seems to be the sort of 'intensifying of perception' that James Porter considers to be characteristic of the sublime (here, perhaps, its advent).[44] The bifurcation of sight and knowledge corresponds with a bifurcation of existence, a separation of the dead from the living—a process and event that is both momentous and mysterious.

III. A MESSENGER'S ACCOUNT: SOMETHING WONDROUS

ἄνδρες πολῖται, ξυντομωτάτως μὲν ἂν
τύχοιμι λέξας Οἰδίπουν ὀλωλότα·
ἃ δ' ἦν τὰ πραχθέντ' οὔθ' ὁ μῦθος ἐν βραχεῖ
φράσαι πάρεστιν οὔτε τἄργ' ὅσ' ἦν ἐκεῖ.

Men of the polis, I could say,
most briefly, that Oedipus is dead,
but as for what happened, there is no account that could tell it briefly
and the many actions that transpired there could not be told in a few words.

The Messenger, *OC* 1579–82

At the end of the scene just discussed, Oedipus leaves the stage with Theseus, Antigone, and Ismene. After a brief interlude from the chorus in which they pray for a painless death for 'the stranger' (1556–78),[45] the Messenger enters to give his account of Oedipus' death (1579–1666). This is the scene to which we now turn.

What is remarkable about Sophocles' choice to represent Oedipus' death by verbal description is not that it is unusual but that it is the norm for Greek tragedy. As observed in the introduction to this chapter (I. Dying On/Off Stage), death happens to bodies, and tragedy, unlike many other representational media, can use real bodies. Though rare, there are tragedies in which a character dies on stage; showing the death, not telling the death, *is* an option. The ecphrastic presentation of Oedipus' death is therefore a formal choice and, intentionally or

---

[44] Porter (2016: 54).

[45] Kamerbeek (1984: 214) on 1568–73 observes that the chorus sing of what is happening (off stage and so unseen) in terms of a katabasis; Guidorizzi et al. (2008: 367) talks of the ode's conclusive tone, almost that of a funeral song (ἐπιτύμβιος).

118 FIGURING DEATH IN CLASSICAL ATHENS

not, frames Oedipus' death in terms of distance and exteriority (these are hall-marks of ecphrasis, of which the messenger report is a classic tragic example).[46] Though familiarity with the messenger speech format might limit the extent to which it is noticeable in any one play, the format still defines how members of the audience interact with the scene and their encounters with the death described. Indeed, though the prism through which I approach this discussion is death, it is notable that the ecphrastic format per se of tragic messenger speeches has been an underexplored topic, though ecphrastic features (distance, vividity, perspective, and so on) have been discussed under different aegises. The narrative qualities of the speeches (especially questions of focalization) have been thoroughly explored,[47] for example, and there have also been targeted studies of descriptions of objects and art more generally in tragedy.[48] More recently, these two threads have been brought closer in cognitive approaches to tensions of immersion and distance in ancient narrative (including in tragic messenger speeches).[49] The latter studies form a key backdrop to the discussion that follows immediately below.[50]

This part of the chapter falls into two halves. I begin with a consideration of the messenger speech as a representation, a substitute for a missed experience (presence at the scene described). I then consider the messenger speech as an artefact in its own right: turning our eyes away from the story and towards the painting, as it were, to what extent does the Messenger's presentation of the events as 'something wondrous' (κἀποθαυμάσαι πρέπον, 1586) generate encoun-ters not just with Oedipus' death but with death more generally?[51] Distance is an important theme throughout but where the first discussion frames it in terms of immersion and subjectivity (familiar terms from recent approaches to tragic nar-rative), the second does so in terms of the object—Oedipus' death becomes an object of attention.

[46] See page 3, note 8.

[47] Markantonatos (2002: 130–47) is important here; his book-length study of narrative in the *OC* includes a detailed section on the Messenger's speech. On narrative and tragic messenger speeches, see further de Jong (1991); Barrett (2002). On narrative in/narratology 'of' tragedy more generally, see Roberts (1989); Goward (1999); Lowe (2000: ch. 8); Gould (2001: ch. 14); Markantonatos (2002); de Jong (2004), (2006), (2007); Grethlein and Rengakos (2009: pt. 4), especially the chapter by Francis Dunn.

[48] See e.g. Steiner (2001); Zeitlin (2009) [1982]; Stieber (2011).

[49] See especially Budelmann and van Emde Boas (2020). See further Rijksbaron (2006) on the pres-ence and function of historic presents in Sophocles and Euripides (reading some of these as unaugmented imperfects might reshape the immersive qualities of a messenger speech): the ὁρῶμεν in *OC* 1654, for example, could be either, with the present tense communicating greater immediacy as the Messenger turns his attention upon the man that he can see (Theseus) as opposed to the one that he cannot.

[50] On issues of epistemology and authority in tragic messenger speeches, see Barrett (2002: esp. ch. 6).

[51] See Elsner (2002: 2) on description of art as a specific (and major) ancient genre of ecphrasis. Emphasis on ancient ecphrasis as a broader category than its modern definition (description of a work of art) is correct but, in eagerness to rectify a simplistic narrowness, fails to appreciate its merits. Indeed, since ecphrasis makes a verbal artefact of its subject (of any sort) and conjures an experience of looking at that artefact, it is, to some extent, 'description as of a work of art'.

A. Looking and Telling

Oedipus' death is multiply distant. At a macro level, it is not only represented by a verbal substitute (his acting dying body is absent from the stage) but also reported after the event: the audience (and chorus) are not just missing but have *already missed* the death. The spatial and temporal absences of Oedipus' dying body are all the more stark for the fact that his living body has been so persistently present until now.[52] He has been on stage for 1555 verses (since the opening scene) and leaves the stage with the sole purpose of dying somewhere unseen and unknown to all mortals apart from Theseus.[53] The contrast between the staging of this scene and the rest of the play up to this point intensifies awareness of Oedipus' absence; he has departed from the performance as from life. If the same actor that played Oedipus also played the Messenger this effect might be compounded.[54] This could work in either direction, of course: for some members of the audience, the familiar body and voice might collapse distance and enable deeper immersion (when the Messenger quotes Oedipus, for example). But, to the extent that members of the audience did notice the repetition, the re-entrance of the same acting body after a brief interlude (22 verses from the

[52] Note the remarks upon Oedipus' appearance by characters who visit him: 75–6 (the stranger); 140–1 (the chorus); 327 (Ismene); 555–6 (Theseus); 1255–63 (Polynices). In addition, the motivation in several scenes concerns what to do with his body, which is a source of interest, fear, and desire, an object to be manipulated, positioned, and owned: the chorus worry where he should sit and, for a while, ask him to leave; Ismene reveals that the Thebans plan to control his body outside the Cadmean land; Oedipus offers his body to Theseus as a source of protection and asks for sanctuary; Creon comes to abduct his body; Oedipus demands that no one touch his body or look upon his death or corpse. Other than Oedipus, Antigone is only absent between 846 and 1099 and the chorus (as is normal) remain on stage from 117. On the foregrounding of Oedipus' living body on stage in the *OC* (arguing that, insofar as his body is not in pain, this attention is unusual not just in tragedy but in Greek culture), see Murnaghan (1988: 36–41). Oedipus' seated position on stage and visuality as a central and authoritative figure: Budelmann (2000b: 188). On the transformation of space in the theatre by acting bodies: Rehm (2002: ch. 4).

[53] The impact of his departure is significant: Jebb (1900b: 238) [1886] on 1542–55 notes 'A more splendid dramatic effect than Sophocles has created here could hardly be conceived'; Winnington-Ingram (1980: 253) calls it 'the greatest *coup de théâtre* in Sophocles'; Kirkwood (1994: 97) observes the impressive effect; Van Nortwick (2012: 141) goes further, 'one of the great exits in Western theater'. Moreover, Oedipus has been connected musically and emotionally with the chorus (Nooter (2012: 156–65); this intimacy is ruptured by the absence of his body *and* lyrical song. Staging would add to the effect: if, for instance, Oedipus departs through the central door in the stage building (σκηνή) (as argued in Wiles (1997: 146)), there would be a sense in which he moves *away* from the chorus and the audience, physically enacting an existential shift. More generally, Lowe (2000: 175) argues that the departure of each and every character from the stage is an 'endgame' of the tragic genre.

[54] The division of parts in the *OC* is problematic; it is difficult to avoid there being four actors without dividing the part of Theseus among more than one: Ceadel (1941) (proposing, instead, that an extra actor stepped in to play Antigone and Ismene in sections where no or minimal speech was required). See further Ringer (1998: 92–3) on the dramatic impact of part-sharing in the play; Rehm (2002: 31, 91, 133–5, 174–5) on role-doubling in other tragedies; Jouanna (2018: 205–7) [2007]. In many proposed part divisions, the same actor plays Oedipus and the Messenger (sometimes Theseus too).

120 FIGURING DEATH IN CLASSICAL ATHENS

chorus) might heighten awareness of Oedipus' absence by presenting a differ-ence.[55] In what he is (a different character) as much as in what he does (give a third-party report after the event), the Messenger frames the encounter that he offers in terms of distance.

This fundamental play of distance permeates the report in different ways (and to different extents) at different times, and the variation is significant. Generally, when describing the build-up to Oedipus' death, the Messenger's words make an otherwise absent scene imaginatively present for the audience. This presence is defined by immersion, by bringing the audience into the scene (rather than setting aspects of the scene vividly before the audience).[56] There are several fea-tures that make the Messenger's account of Oedipus' final moments immersive.[57] The sequence in which events are told, for instance, accords naturally with the order in which they occurred.[58] There is also an abundance of visual and spatial details, including features of the landscape that might trigger memories of seeing real sites of religious and cultural significance among internal and exter-nal audiences (even if these features were not located specifically at Colonus).[59] These features are mostly communicated without mediating markers, and the absence of a noticeable filter (retrospective comments, for example) allows the representational status of the account to recede into the background. Indeed, where the Messenger's perspective does shape the narrative, it contributes to the immersive effect precisely because it offers a perspective born of embodied pres-ence within the scene rather than an objective unfurling of events (if such a thing could ever be presented and experienced). For example, the Messenger shares his emotional and sensory responses (1624–5) and appears to provide knowledge restricted by the limits of his sensory apprehension (1598–9).[60] Also effective are

[55] See further Budelmann and van Emde Boas (2020: 60–1) on the various immersive possibilities of a tragic messenger speech and the stimuli that compete for attention.

[56] On the difference, see Grethlein (2013: esp. 117–18).

[57] I draw on the taxonomy formulated by Rutgers Allan. See page 30, note 19.

[58] In the language of narrative theory: plot and story, respectively, or *fabula* and *sjužet* (Russian Formalism) or *récit* and *histoire* (Genette). For an overview of these terms, structuralist contributions to narratological theories, and their application to ancient texts, see Schmitz (2008: ch. 3) [2002].

[59] Termed 'cognitive frames' in Allan (2020: 18). Saïd (2012: 91–2), for example, discusses the dis-placement to the play's Colonus of several known features (such as Oedipus' tomb, the location of the covenant between Peirithous and Theseus, the Thorician rock, and the hill of Demeter) from other places in and around Athens/Attica. Kelly (2009: 101–2) suggests that the polyvalence of features such as the threshold with bronze steps is deliberate.

[60] There are two (modest and inconclusive) indications of the Messenger's observing body. He notes 'the hair of all stood upright' (1624–5): is this a perceptive observation or an impression informed by his own emotional state? Earlier, at 1599, an indefinite ποθεν hangs ambiguously on the phrase and verse end, 'fetch water from a running stream... somewhere': is it part of Oedipus' indirect command to his daugh-ters (as suggested by Markantonatos (2002: 136)), or might it acknowledge limitations on the Messenger's knowledge?

features such as direct speech (1611–19; 1627–8, 1631–5, 1640–4), which contribute towards textual transparency, as well as attention to the rules of 'real life' (insofar as emphasis is placed upon the inexplicability of the miraculous disappearance). In many ways, then, the Messenger's account produces an encounter with the end of Oedipus' life that is characterized by immersion.

But for all the intensity with which distance is reduced, it is not completely collapsed. At some crucial points in the narrative, attention is drawn to the mediating role of the Messenger and the nature of the perspective that he offers. The narrative frame is important here. The Messenger opens with a brief commentary on the overall story: 'Actually, this is something you might well find amazing' (1586). He later concludes with reflection upon the interpretations that he has offered, or even the whole speech that he has given: 'And if I do not seem to be speaking in my right mind, I would not ask belief from those to whom I do not seem to be thinking straight' (1665–6). His meditation upon and response to his own discourse, and his suggestion that the appropriate response is one of amazement, pulls against the transparency of his narrative, reminding the audience that he offers a lens, a window, or even a picture, but not a portal.[61] Moreover, the sheer mass of descriptive details that he provides (as opposed to 'action-orientated' details), especially the visual specificities of the landscape at 1590–7, sustain a simultaneous awareness of the scene as an object of visual attention:[62] although the audience and the chorus are drawn into the Messenger's experience, it is an experience of watching, not participating. A highly immersive narrative is expressed as an experience of looking and framed as the object of a discourse.[63] To the extent that this might generate not only an encounter with Oedipus' death but also reflection upon the nature of that encounter, the play of proximity and distance models the voyeurism that inheres in watching someone else die: however close one gets, another's death remains a spectacle seen from the outside. That there is a play of focalization, immersion, and distance in a messenger speech is not new but the epistemological implications for reflection on death are important.

Still more significant is the fact that different descriptive modes do not simply coexist in the Messenger's speech but cluster at different points in his account. There is a noticeable shift at 1645 from a more direct mode to description that is conspicuously focalized: we suddenly encounter a flurry of references to the Messenger's perceiving eyes (ἐξαπείδομεν, 1648; ὁρῶμεν, 1654) and ears (εἰσηκούσαμεν, 1645) and his actions (ὡμαρτοῦμεν, 1647; ἀπήλθομεν, 1647;

---

[61] The reflective frame corresponds with the 'metanarrative elements' that counteract transparency: Allan (2020: 19).

[62] On the 'as-if' of narratives, which can simultaneously invite immersion and reflection (awareness of reading or hearing a story), see Grethlein (2017: chs. 2–4).

[63] Freud, triangulation, objectification, and ecphrasis: Elsner (2004).

122 FIGURING DEATH IN CLASSICAL ATHENS

στραφέντες, 1648).[64] This influx of overt markers of the speaker's filtering effect coincides with the withdrawal of his body from the scene of Oedipus' death.[65] The more direct (which is to say, less noticeably mediated) mode discussed above accompanies the section of the description that covers death's prologue (dying); by contrast, heightened focalization coincides with the realization that the Messenger does not and cannot offer a privileged perspective on the endpoint of the dying process.[66] He, like Oedipus' daughters, was instructed to leave, to turn away. By the time they turned back, Oedipus had disappeared.

What follows in the Messenger's speech is a tortuous attempt to put into words something that he did not see and cannot say. This pushes focalization to extremes, because the narrative is no longer filtered by the Messenger's perception of the scene but imaginatively shaped by the Messenger's meditation upon what he has *not* perceived, an experience (or lack thereof) that generates a distinctly elusive literary encounter with Oedipus' death (1656–66):

> μόρῳ δ' ὁποίῳ κεῖνος ὤλετ' οὐδ' ἂν εἷς
> θνητῶν φράσειε πλὴν τὸ Θησέως κάρα.
> οὐ γάρ τις αὐτὸν οὔτε πυρφόρος θεοῦ
> κεραυνὸς ἐξέπραξεν οὔτε ποντία
> θύελλα κινηθεῖσα τῷ τότ' ἐν χρόνῳ,
> ἀλλ' ἤ τις ἐκ θεῶν πομπός, ἢ τὸ νερτέρων
> εὔνουν διαστὰν γῆς ἀλάμπετον βάθρον.
> ἀνὴρ γὰρ οὐ στενακτὸς οὐδὲ σὺν νόσοις
> ἀλγεινὸς ἐξεπέμπετ', ἀλλ' εἴ τις βροτῶν
> θαυμαστός. εἰ δὲ μὴ δοκῶ φρονῶν λέγειν,
> οὐκ ἂν παρείμην οἷσι μὴ δοκῶ φρονεῖν.

But by what sort of death that man perished, not one man
among mortals could tell except Theseus.
For neither a fire-bearing thunderbolt from the god,
nor a coastal squall, stirred up at that moment,
these did not bring about his end,
but either some one of the gods as an escort, or the lightless
foundations of the world below, well-meaning in its splitting of the earth.
For the man was being dispatched, not with lament,
and not pained by disease, but (if any among mortals is)
as someone extraordinary. And if I do not seem to be speaking in my right mind,
I would not ask belief from those to whom I do not seem to be thinking straight.

---

[64] The only other explicit marker is at the narrative's beginning (the first person plural ἡμῖν at 1589).

[65] Markantonatos (2002: 145) also notes that the Messenger 'draws attention to his presence, only to signal his absence from the mystery'.

[66] Explicit references to the restricted knowledge and understanding of internal narrators as distinctively Sophoclean: de Jong (2007: 289–90). The Messenger in the *OC* as limited but not unreliable: Scodel (2009: 425).

The Messenger's description of the death is defined by negation: 'not one man among mortals could tell' what happened (οὐδ' ἂν εἷς | θνητῶν φράσειε, 1656–7); 'neither' (οὐ...οὔτε, 1658) a thunderbolt 'nor' (οὔτε, 1659) a squall brought about his end; he was called away 'not with lament' (οὐ στενακτός, 1663) and 'not pained by disease' (οὐδὲ σὺν νόσοις | ἀλγεινός, 1663–4).[67] In sum, the Messenger 'would not ask belief' (οὐκ ἂν παρείμην, 1666) from anyone who does not think he is thinking straight.

But there is not nothing here. Embedded in the negative framing are ideas as to what *did* happen to Oedipus. In the centre, a gnarled kernel of positivity (1661–2): the cause was either some unidentified escort from the gods (τις ἐκ θεῶν πομπός, 1661) or else the 'light-less' (ἀλάμπετον, 1662) foundations of the world below, kind in its splitting of the earth—a mysterious formulation that substitutes a visualized and unseeable (dark) chasm for a visual absence, a positive gap for a negative one. Couched in convoluted language of conjecture,[68] of imprecise identity and impenetrable depths, the Messenger's positive ideas are nebulous and obscure. And they are openly acknowledged to be assertions not representations: we are told that they lack a direct phenomenological basis—no mortal can *say* what happened (φράσειε) because no one *saw* anything concrete (apart from Theseus, apparently).[69] But not perceiving something can be an act as well as an omission: the Messenger can (presumably) be sure that there was no thunderbolt, squall, lament, or illness because he (presumably) did not see the sky flash, feel wind or rain, smell the sea, or hear cries and groans. Whereas he *did* see Theseus prostrate himself before the earth and sky (1654–5, discussed further below), behaviour that implies divine involvement from above or below. The logic at play here underpins the Messenger's mirroring of Theseus' pious response to the death: the details that he adds put an optimistic and reverential spin on the strange event: if the earth split, it was 'well meaning' (εὔνουν 1662); instead of beset by miseries of grief and pain (οὐ στενακτὸς οὐδὲ σὺν νόσοις | ἀλγεινός, 1663–4) Oedipus was 'on the contrary' (ἀλλά, 1664) 'marvellous' (θαυμαστός, 1665). Amidst the uncertainty and denial, there is a sense of possibility: knowledge

---

[67] Compare the third choral ode (1211–48), with its negatives and alpha-privatives: see Segal (1993a: 16–20, esp. 19) on tragic negation of song (the 'unmusical muse') and 'representation of joylessness'; Carey (2009: 124–5); Easterling (2009: 168) on 'the paradox of absence ("no strength, no interaction, no friends") being a way of stressing presence ("all evils of evils")'.

[68] Rutherford (2012: 215–16) admires the simplicity of the Messenger's style here. But stylistic simplicity is combined with conceptual complexity, not just in 1661–2 (as Richard Rutherford observes) but throughout the passage in its persistent negative expression. See further Silk (2009: 153–5) on the complexities of 1661–2.

[69] Bernard (2001: 157–9) also points to indications that the Messenger is uncertain as to whether he has correctly interpreted events; this forms part of his discussion of evidence that Oedipus' end is not meant to be seen as a good one.

124 FIGURING DEATH IN CLASSICAL ATHENS

that is out of reach but not necessarily unreachable; significance that is profoundly appreciated if not fully grasped.[70]

Note, too, the influence of the Messenger's negations on his audience's impression of what Oedipus' death was like. The fire-bearing thunderbolt from a god that did not wreak damage and the squall from the sea that was not stirred up do not just affirm what did not happen—or, at least, the sensory experiences that the Messenger did not have. They offer an imaginative encounter with the missed death that is shot with sparks and booms, with gusts and a salty taste, even in the instant of denial—these things may not have been experienced *then* but they are, however elusively, brought into re-imaginings of the event.[71] The constellation of words teases out possibility—in the wake of the sea wind ($\theta \acute{v} \epsilon \lambda \lambda a$), displaced ($\kappa \iota \nu \eta \theta \epsilon \hat{\iota} \sigma a$) in a place it never occupied ($o \ddot{v} \tau \epsilon$), is an emphatically precise caveat zeroing in on a moment in time ($\tau \hat{\omega} \ \tau \acute{o} \tau' \ \acute{\epsilon} \nu \ \chi \rho \acute{o} \nu \omega$). The precision (it was not *then* ... but was it, is it, *never?*) hollows the vacuum not filled by air on the move; even as you notice the wind that is not there comes a hint that perhaps it was or will be, another time. The death, imagined by the Messenger and re-imagined by his audience, becomes a something constructed out of an accumulation of nothings.[72]

The Messenger is both observer and recounter. The narrative he tells, a literary reshaping of what he did and did not see into a cohesive and articulate story, something 'conspicuously appropriate to be wondered at' ($\kappa \grave{a} \pi o \theta a v \mu \acute{a} \sigma a \iota \ \pi \rho \acute{\epsilon} \pi o \nu$, 1586), reflects a creative shaping in his mind in response to the scene at the time he observed it.[73] This 'making' dynamic is common to narratives, especially messenger speeches,[74] but plays out with particular subtlety in descriptions of death because imaginations and conceptualizations of 'what death is' must (ordinarily?)

---

[70] The deliberate mystery: Bowra (1944: 342). Emphasizing the 'striking tension between certainty and ignorance, or presence and absence, in his narrative': Easterling (2006: 137). See further Milbank (2024) on analogies and overlaps between 'negative capability' in Coleridgean poetics and theological apophasis: 'the frustration [of our rational knowledge] is rather to be positively embraced as an invitation to a more crucial, engaged and inexhaustible mode of understanding' (page 230).

[71] See Monthéard (2020) on how negativity is intertwined with positivity in Keats's odes and, especially, on the 'ghostly trace' left by negation (building on Oswald Ducrot's idea of 'presupposition'). See further Scarfe (1961: 8–9) (also on Keats); Hidalgo Downing (2002) on the counterfactual realities produced by poetic negation; Giora et al. (2005) on the prevailing positivity of negation; Rubenstein (2008) on the coincidence between Virginia Woolf's negative diction and a personal and cultural (modernist) despondency (might we sense in the negations of Oedipus' death not just Sophocles' outlook at the end of his life but also a wider atmosphere of end-of-the-war/end-of-Athenian-supremacy disillusion?).

[72] On death as the 'nonsignifiable "Other"' and the paradox of representing absence, see Bronfen and Goodwin (1993: 7). On how failure to represent something specific (the war) might communicate the unrepresentable and unspeakable experience of it: van Alphen (1993). On the sublimity offered by negativity (in Wordsworth): Clarkson (2017).

[73] See further Markantonatos (2002: 130–1).

[74] I include here other similar descriptive accounts which may or may not be given by 'messengers' or 'heralds'.

be constructed in ignorance from the outside, by those that observe and respond to another's death.[75] An audience's reliance upon the narrative representation of Oedipus' death by the Messenger, who holds no special privilege, replicates a more far-reaching reliance on the perceptual, interpretative, and imaginative capabilities of the living in response to death. The distance that is embedded in the Messenger's verbal representation of Oedipus' death does not compromise a direct experience that his audience missed so much as simulate the distance of encountering death from the perspective of the living.

B. Wondrous Things

I now turn to features of the speech that present what the Messenger saw in terms of spectacle. What is it about the end of Oedipus' life that invites attention, that makes it (implicitly in the Messenger's eyes and ultimately in the Messenger's speech) 'something suitable for wonder' (κἀποθαυμάσαι πρέπον, 1586)? I will examine first the landscape in which the scene is set and then the presentation of Oedipus. Finally, I will return to the Messenger's mysterious, negative-ridden account of his disappearance, approaching it from the other side of the coin (less in terms of what it reveals about the subjectivity of the Messenger's account, and more in terms of what it might reveal about the demands made by the moment of death).

Consider the Messenger's description of the landscape in which the last moments of Oedipus' life are spent (1590–7):

> ἐπεὶ δ' ἀφίκτο τὸν καταρράκτην ὁδὸν
> χαλκοῖς βάθροισι γῆθεν ἐρριζωμένον,
> ἔστη κελεύθων ἐν πολυσχίστων μιᾷ,
> κοίλου πέλας κρατῆρος, οὗ τὰ Θησέως
> Περίθου τε κεῖται πίστ' ἀεὶ ξυνθήματα·
> ἀφ' οὗ μέσος στὰς τοῦ τε Θορικίου πέτρου
> κοίλης τ' ἀχέρδου κἀπὶ λαΐνου τάφου
> καθέζετ'.

> And when he reached the down-rushing journey
> planted from the earth with bronze steps,

---

[75] See Williams (2006: 56–9) on 'stark fiction': his point that a fictional work such Sophocles' *The Women of Trachis* might support contemplation and comprehension of a real horror is transferable to the principle that one's own death (a horror?) might only be approachable from a distance. See further Roberts (1989: 175–6) on mortals' quest for coherence in their own and others' stories. Elsewhere she discusses the desire for an 'ending beyond the ending', an aftermath that makes it possible to look back upon a life in its entirety (the more enticing in literature for being impossible for one's own death): Roberts (1997: 254). But, suggesting that Oedipus 'has lived long enough to understand the meaning of his own story': Cole (1992: xxxv).

126 FIGURING DEATH IN CLASSICAL ATHENS

> he stood at one of the branching paths,
> near a hollow crater, where lies the
> ever faithful covenant of Theseus and Peirithous;
> beside this (he stood in the centre) and the Thorician rock,
> by a hollow pear tree and upon a stony tomb
> he took his seat.

The pathway at which Oedipus ends one journey and begins another has the motion of a down-rushing waterfall,[76] but is 'rooted' or 'implanted' from beneath the earth (γῆθεν ἐρριζωμένον, 1591) with bronze steps: these hard, gleaming objects spring like plants from the earth and fall like rapid water.[77] Likewise, the 'hollow crater' (κοίλου [...] κρατῆρος, 1593) can simultaneously be visualized as a naturally occurring hollow or rock basin and a mixing bowl.[78] Indeed, the latter, an artefact in its own right, would comprise a suitable memorial for another cultural artefact: the 'bringing together' of Peirithous and Theseus, a covenant that held everlasting faith (πίστ' ἀεὶ ξυνθήματα, 1594) and that may have been marked with libation and ritual death (sacrifice).[79] The landscape is a paradox of moving-stillness and nature-culture.

Moreover, together with the stone that marks Thoricus, the steps and bowl produce a landscape characterized by materiality and durability. But the bowl's cavity is also a void, and its vacuum is echoed by the hollow pear tree (κοίλης τ' ἀχέρδου, 1596); these are two empty spaces that endure in the landscape. Indeed, these hollows are beside a stony τάφος (1596), a grave or tomb with space (to contain) at its core.[80] The τάφος is an inanimate, material artefact and it partners an organism that is a shell (the tree) and a bowl with a hole that itself shifts between nature and culture. Do all these objects mark death?[81] If so, they mark

---

[76] Budelmann (2000b: 189) also comments on the paradoxical nature of Oedipus' death (an ending and a transformation). On the ὁδός as at once a physical 'way' and a dynamic and abstract one: Easterling (2011: 76–7). Similar in concept to the journey that both ends and begins is the simultaneous death and birth articulated on two fourth-century gold tablets found in tombs in Thessaly: these are discussed in Herrero de Jáuregui (2013: 53).

[77] The idea that 'roots' connect the surface of the earth to its depths can be traced to Hes. *Theog.* 726–8: Guidorizzi et al. (2008: 372–3) on 1591; a bronze threshold with roots in the earth appears in Hes. *Theog.* 748–50, 811–13: see Segal (1981: 369).

[78] The scholiast reads the crater as a natural hollow (τοῦ μυχοῦ): Xenis (2018) on 1593. See further Jebb (1900b: 245–6) [1886] on 1593; Birge (1984: 16): mention of the κρατήρ here recalls the chorus' reference to a κρατήρ at 158–60 when they described the grove of the Eumenides, not to be entered.

[79] See Jebb (1900b: 245–6) [1886] on Schneidewin's interpretation of 1593, drawing on Eur. *Suppl.* 1201.

[80] Note the 'seat belonging to dread goddesses' in Apollo's prophecy (*OC* 89–90), and the discussion in Budelmann (2000b) of the rocks upon which Oedipus took his seat in the first scene and how they foreshadowed Oedipus' death.

[81] On associations between the landscape in this passage and death, see especially Calame (1998: 339–42) on landmarks that point towards Oedipus' katabasis or 'passage vertical', such as the bronze steps that are like plunging roots, the crater (a metaphorical mouth, he suggests), and connections to the myth of Persephone's abduction by Hades; Budelmann (2000b: 189–91); Markantonatos

death as some sort of interface between transience and intransience, matter and void, nature and culture. Compare the covenant (τὰ [...] πίστ᾽ ἀεὶ ξυνθήματα) that lingers in contrast to the transience of the living, who came and went like Peirithous and Theseus (their bodies have departed but their faith endures) or like visitors at the grave (τάφος).[82] The landmarks of the place insist upon its solidity, its permanence, but at the centre is hollowed space and a path that becomes a sheer drop.

The landscape as a whole is thus a paradox: it mixes motion and stillness, presence and absence, nature and culture.[83] Andrea Nightingale might call this 'ecological eschatology';[84] James Porter might call it 'sublime'.[85] What each term and associated thinking captures is the principle that an encounter with landscape description might offer access to something fundamentally mysterious like death.[86] Much hangs upon language (upon the status of the landscape as a

(2002: 198–208) (on Colonus as a transformation of Eleusis); Guidorizzi et al. (2008: 374) on 1595–6. A scholion comments that the path is 'down-rushing' because it is thought to be the place for descent into Hades and that some said Persephone was seized there: Xenis (2018) on 1590–1. The landscape of Colonus and grove of the Eumenides has also been studied as a setting for Oedipus' transformation into a hero: see Birge (1984). See further Easterling (2006: 141–4) on the symbolic function of the landscape details given by the Messenger.

[82] Contrasting the fragility of an object with the presence and permanence of the dead: Arrington (2014: 7). On the discourse provoked by Graeco-Roman funerary monuments on the absence/presence of the deceased: Elsner (2012a); Estrin (2016), (2018); Arrington (2018: 21–4); Squire (2018a); Brown (2019). The paradox of Oedipus' departure (he is gone but remains present): Easterling (2011: 82); the liminal state of Oedipus' unburied corpse (and the roots of this concept in the *Iliad*): Van Nortwick (2012: 145–7). 'The life that is forever' as a possible metaphor for death: Currie (2012: 341) (see note 19). The 'ever-present [reality]' of a cult hero and his tomb (by contrast with his incipient heroization in Homeric epic and Sophoclean drama): Henrichs (1993: 165).

[83] See especially Guidorizzi et al. (2008: 374) on 1595 on the confusing space-time and marginality of this middle (μέσος) ground; Oedipus is positioned between natural and cultivated, living and dead. Compare Budelmann (2000b: esp. 186) on the emphasis on what is natural and unshaped in the Colonan landscape at the start of the play.

[84] 'Ecological eschatology' is a term and concept discussed by Andrea Nightingale in relation to the *Phaedo*: see page 46, note 100. This geographic threshold is also 'the threshold of existence': Reinhardt (1979: 222–3) [1933]. Compare the Colonus of the chorus' song at 668–719, full of 'végétation luxuriante' but 'paradoxalement attaché à la mort': Calame (1998: 338). 'The movement that happens at the edges of the earth marks both ends of life': Montiglio (2005: 11). See further Easterling (2009: 169) on 'darkly unknowable places' and temporal and spatial limits in the ode at 1211–48.

[85] See Porter (2016: 51–4) for a typology of causes that provoke the sublime in antiquity, including 'transgression' of 'limits' to the 'place beyond', 'lasting and everlasting qualities', 'gaps [...], especially those marked by extraordinary heights and depths', and 'contrasts'. See further Porter (2015: 401) on sublimity and recoil or pursuit and (2016: 390–7) on the material foundations of the sublime, and the 'materiality and immateriality of *experience itself*' (page 392). For James Porter (2016), 'the sublime produces profound mental or spiritual disruption, [...] a shock of the Real' (page 5); it is concerned with 'the reality of a world [...] in all of its unfathomable extraordinariness' (page 618).

[86] In this respect, the philosophical contemplation (θεωρία) discussed by Andrea Nightingale is not just a theoretical version of a political and religious cultural practice of spectatorship, but actually emerges out of encounters with the world. This includes the real world and the artefactual world (a messenger's

128 FIGURING DEATH IN CLASSICAL ATHENS

description, not nature itself): the polysemy of κρατήρ, the ability of metaphorical language and thought to 'plant' steps both neutrally and surprisingly in and out of the earth.[87] It is not just the extraordinary nature of Oedipus' death that imbues the place where he will die with existential significance but also the way that Sophocles' Messenger describes that place when he turns land into land-scape, space into setting.[88]

Let us now look closer at Oedipus' body, which arrives, stands, then takes its seat within the imagined landscape (ἐπεὶ δ' ἀφῖκτο [...] ἔστη [...] στὰς [...] καθέζετο, 1590–7) and, as in a tableau, never moves again from that place.[89] Like his environment, Oedipus' body becomes an object of attention in his final moments (1597–605):[90]

> [...] εἶτ' ἔλυσε δυσπινεῖς στολάς.
> κἄπειτ' ἀΰσας παῖδας ἠνώγει ῥυτῶν
> ὑδάτων ἐνεγκεῖν λουτρὰ καὶ χοάς ποθεν·
> τὼ δ' εὐχλόου Δήμητρος εἰς προσόψιον
> πάγον μολοῦσα τάσδ' ἐπιστολὰς πατρὶ

account or a tragic performance, for instance, as much as a real death). One sort of θεωρία mediates another. See Nightingale (2001) together with her more extensive treatment in (2004: esp. 68–71, ch. 2) on how fourth-century philosophers positioned themselves as spectator-theorists (lookers rather than listeners, spectators rather than performers), drawing upon the contemporary Greek practice of θεωρία. See further page 48, note 108 and pages 200–1, note 40.

[87] See Goldhill (2012: ch. 1, esp. 23–5, 36) on Sophoclean irony, especially on the ambiguity of λύσις and its association with death and the τέλος of life in the *OC* (see Chapter One for similar language in Plato's *Phaedo*). See Easterling (1999) on the powerful simplicity of Sophocles' language in the *OC*. Kirkwood (1994: 261) comments that the *OC* is 'less ironical in theme than any of the [other six surviving plays by Sophocles]'. This is true to the extent that Oedipus does not know less than the audience. Indeed, G. M. Kirkwood points out that, in the *OC*, the irony of sight and blindness of the *OT* is reversed. But could we go further? The divergence of perspectives in the crisis scene, discussed above, suggests that Oedipus is *more* knowledgeable not just than other characters such as the chorus, but even than the audience. Jouanna (2018: 449–50) [2007] emphasizes Oedipus' early awareness of his destiny ('a total surprise for the spectators'). The play *is* highly ironical but in a different way from that usually understood. See Goldhill (2012: 26–37) on how Sophocles 'ironizes irony' (page 26), turning attention upon the audience's misplaced sense of superior knowledge.

[88] See Fearn (2024b) on lyric contemplation of nature, landscape, and human–world relations and 'transformations of space into place' (page 113). Connected is Andrea Rodighiero's discussion of nature as a '*cultural* backdrop' in the *OC*—the Colonan landscape as a 'literary construction of a collection of spatial memories': Rodighiero (2012: esp. 57, 79).

[89] In this respect, the imagined scene replays the staged scene that lasted for much of the play. The resulting picture is another scene of temporal limbo, an expansion of the 'final hour' before death. On motion in the *OC*, see Hutchinson (2020a: 176–90, esp. 182–9): as Gregory Hutchinson discusses, the absence of motion at the end of Oedipus' life (as described by the Messenger) is striking in its denial of an audience's expectations that death will involve movement (set by the ode at 1556–78 and the god's question at 1627–8, τί μέλλομεν | χωρεῖν;) and its contrast to the unusually laboured and violent motions earlier in the play.

[90] Indeed, see Carey (2009: 128–33) on the presentation of Oedipus in the third ode as a topographical feature.

τάχει ᾿πόρευσαν ξὺν χρόνῳ, λουτροῖς τέ νιν
ἐσθῆτί τ᾿ ἐξήσκησαν ᾗ νομίζεται.
ἐπεὶ δὲ πᾶσαν ἔσχε δρῶντος ἡδονὴν
κοὐκ ἦν ἔτ᾿ οὐδὲν ἀργὸν ὧν ἐφίετο [...]

and he undid his filthy dress.
And then, calling to his daughters, he urged them to bring
flowing water from somewhere for bathing and libation;
and they both went to a crag that was sacred to fresh and green Demeter
and in full view, and brought the waters requested by their father
quickly, and they readied his body, bathing him
and dressing him in the customary way.
And when he was satisfied with the work,
and there was no longer anything left to do...

Oedipus strips his body (ἔλυσε δυσπινεῖς στολάς, 1597) and is washed and dressed by his daughters (λουτροῖς τέ νιν | ἐσθῆτί τ᾿ ἐξήσκησαν ᾗ νομίζεται, 1602–3). Though he continues, for the moment, to exert control over what happens to him (his daughters act in accordance with his instructions, τάσδ᾿ ἐπιστολάς, 1601), the emphasis on his body as an object of others' sight, touch, perhaps even smell (when he exchanges his 'filthy dress', δυσπινεῖς στολάς, for funerary clothes), prefigures his ontological transfiguration from person to corpse.[91]

The physical objectification of Oedipus is symbolically reinforced by the ritual significance of washing. As emphasized by others, the act of washing Oedipus at this point (and the libations that are offered: λουτρὰ καὶ χοάς, 1599) imparts the

[91] van Erp Taalman Kip (2006: 49) points out the role reversal towards the end of the play in that Oedipus now touches others rather than being touched (he is ἄθικτος), but her point is that he no longer *needs* the reassurance or guidance of touch. My emphasis is different: he is objectified in the Messenger's speech and by the living as he approaches death. Indeed, there is emphasis on the visuality of bodies on the brink of death more widely in Greek tragedy. Consider Alcestis' attention to surface (ἐσθῆτα) and ornament (κόσμον) at Eur. *Alc.* 161, shaping her dying body into a work of art akin to the representational substitute that Admetus promises to embrace in their bed (*Alc.* 348–54); Alcestis' wasted body, a 'burden' that retains its beauty (*Alc.* 173–4, 203–4); Iphigenia—'conspicuous as in a painting' (Aesch. *Ag.* 239–42, citation at 242); Polyxena's self-exposure, as beautiful as an ἄγαλμα (Eur. *Hec.* 560–1). In other cases, death's silent visual spectacle is like a moment of artistic creation: fr. 307 attributed to Aeschylus (Sommerstein); Eur. *HF* 990–4. See especially Bassi (2018) on the corpse in Euripides' *Alcestis*, which '[calls] attention to the divide between living beings and non-living things' (page 35) with its materiality; Wohl (2018) on Euripides' *Trojan Women* and the catastrophic merging of man and matter in the context of tragic death. See further Stieber (2011: 145–50, 215) on Euripides' 'aesthetic of transforming female suffering into a beautified spectacle' (page 215). More generally, on death, bodies, art, and beauty (ranging from the Bronze Age to Imperial Roman material), see e.g. Vernant (1991a); Treherne (1995); Parker Pearson (2003: esp. 71) [1999] on the body as a 'carefully crafted artefact'; Trimble (2018) on death, transformation, and visual ontologies. See further Tyrtaeus fr. 10 West, *IE*² (esp. v. 30) on the beauty of dying in the front ranks as a young man. On the body as an aesthetic artefact in early poetry: Zeitlin (2018). This effect would prove particularly interesting in other tragedies if the dead were displayed as an 'effigy' on the eccyclema, as Jebb (2004: 141) on 915 suggests for Ajax. See further Bassi (2018: 35, 36) on the possibility that a living human played the corpse; Jouanna (2018: 233–4) [2007].

130 FIGURING DEATH IN CLASSICAL ATHENS

significance of this moment not just in relation to Oedipus' death but also his subsequent heroization.[92] But where others have focused on mystic significance, it is also worth thinking about how the washing generates an encounter with death. The act of washing and beautifying Oedipus' body (especially at the hands of his daughters) picks up the sense in which he is already perceived by himself, and now his daughters, to be dead. When Antigone and Ismene wash their father's body they treat him like the corpse he would usually become when he dies: they bring a process that would normally follow his death (the washing of a corpse by female members of the family, part of what has been widely interpreted as the ancient Greek dying 'process') into the final moments of his life.[93] Moreover, the language in which the Messenger describes the dressing of Oedipus' body picks up on the visuality of the Greek funeral, as seen in images of the prothesis on Attic pots.[94] In one word, Oedipus' daughters 'dress' Oedipus, 'adorn' him, and 'ready' him in suitable trappings for death: ἐξήσκησαν. Extension of the normal dying process (and its associated visuality) into the final moments of Oedipus' life becomes another example of how, in tragedy, expectation of imminent demise can blur with the onset of death; extension of the spectacle of death (which is to say, a dead body's impact upon the living) into dying's longue durée is a distinctively tragic 'beautiful death', and the rewards it brings are unclear.[95] Compare Socrates' declaration in the *Phaedo*, 'But already now my

[92] See Jouanna (1995: 49–51) on the λουτρὰ καὶ χοάς as a purifying ritual. Oedipus' body has preternatural significance because it will become a source of protection for Athens and a focus for hero cult. Much of the play's drama revolves around the gift or denial of his body and the trouble or protection that will arise from its tomb. For example, Ismene's revelation that the Thebans will 'set up' or 'make stand' (στήσωσι, 399) Oedipus near the Cadmean land where they can 'exert power' (400) over him, for fear his tomb, being unlucky, will prove a grievous burden (402), hinted at an overlap of body and tomb, bringing to mind the standing Archaic kouros which replaced and represented the body of the deceased (see Figure 2.5). See also: 576–7, 581–2. See further Van Nortwick (2015: 117–18) on how 'heroic bodies as physical objects [...] on stage influence the outcome of all three [of Sophocles' late] plays'; his chapter on the *OC* (ch. 4) attends to the movement of and claims upon Oedipus' body on the stage.

[93] For a similar observation in response to Euripides' *Alcestis*, see Parker (2007) on 160–1, 'in bathing and dressing elegantly, Alcestis treats herself as a corpse'. On Greek death as a process, see note 2 above with pages 3–4. Arguing for mystic significance here: Calame (1998: 349); Markantonatos (2002: 213), (2007: 132–3). Linforth (1951: 176–7) differs. On acts of purification in ancient Greece in response to the pollution of death, see Parker (1983: 35–9).

[94] See pages 61–2, including note 24.

[95] See Vernant (1991a) on the Homeric beautiful death and epic's role in crystallizing and perpetuating it and (1991b) on Classical lyric poetry and lifetime praise. Touching on tragedy's dubious rewards for death: Soph. *Ant.* 801–52, with Jebb (1900a: 153) [1888] on 834–8. Likewise, Pelling (1997: 236–7) emphasizes that though a tragedy 'typically offers some "restitution" or "compensation" in a closing scene', it often ends in discomfort and 'cradle to grave may not be enough' (page 250). Tragedy's self-conscious reflection on the life it can bestow a story in 'the city's collective memory' (and Euripides' problematization of art's substitute for death in *Alcestis*): Segal (1993a: esp. ch. 3, citation at 6). See further Segal (1992: 107–10). On the 'material/immaterial trace that is the play's own language', see

appointed time is calling me, a tragic man would say, and it is nearly time for me to go for a bath' (115a5–7). Mock heroics and teasing aside,[96] one way in which Socrates is very much like a man out of a Greek tragedy, a man like Oedipus, is in the foreknowledge that he has of his death. Both he and Oedipus can stage a significant 'final day' for their audience because, extraordinarily, the hour of their end is known.

The impression of death before death is reinforced by the Messenger's description of the characters' responses to the last thunderclap. The sound precipitates shuddering, howling, unremitting breast-beating and prolonged wails of grief from Oedipus' daughters as they fall to their knees in a ritual lament that seems temporally premature (1606–9). But, folding his arms about them ($\pi\tau\dot{\nu}\xi\alpha\varsigma$ $\dot{\epsilon}\pi$' $\alpha\dot{\nu}\tau\alpha\hat{\iota}\varsigma$ $\chi\epsilon\hat{\iota}\rho\alpha\varsigma$, 1611), Oedipus confirms (1611–13):

> [...] ὦ τέκνα,
> οὐκ ἔστ' ἔθ' ὑμῖν τῇδ' ἐν ἡμέρᾳ πατήρ.
> ὄλωλε γὰρ δὴ πάντα τἀμά...
>
> ...Children,
> on this day your father no longer exists!
> For all that is mine is dead...

Once the final day is reached, Oedipus 'exists no longer' and everything relating to him 'is dead'. A pseudo-corpse, he still has arms with which to embrace but no more life (and in fact, following Sarah Nooter's analysis, no poetic voice).[97] This paradoxical situation is further communicated in a grammatical switch from objective to subjective perspectives, together articulating the coexistence of alive and dead Oedipuses. In 'your father no longer exists' Oedipus presents himself as a third person subject from the perspective of his daughters; in 'all that is mine is dead' the possessive pronoun communicates that the perspective is now his own. But it is surely one thing for the living to observe another's death and another for the one who is dead to do so?[98] Indeed, both statements make use of a grammatical absurdity: in each, the subject governs an action of perfected non-existence.

Wohl (2018: 33) on Euripides' *Trojan Women*. Compare the immortality offered Socrates by Plato in the *Phaedo* as part of a discourse on the epistemological challenges posed by death (Chapter One).

[96] See page 36, notes 50 and 54, and Goldhill (2012: 142).

[97] Nooter (2012: 175–7) on Oedipus' shift from poetic voice to 'object of another's narrative' (page 176).

[98] Though Keith Lehrer has argued that the final moment of life is an aesthetic moment for the dying, whose last thought will be a 'thought of what [they are], completed with [their] death': Lehrer (2011: 106). Perhaps there is something of this completed life's story in Oedipus' contemplation here of everything that is his in the moment that it ceases to be.

132 FIGURING DEATH IN CLASSICAL ATHENS

Either way, Oedipus' dying perspective concurs with the emotional response of his daughters and, once he has spoken, all three mourn his death. As such, the scene presents an extraordinary prothesis in which the living (including the dying) mourn the dying before he has gone. Still more remarkable, in this deathbed-cum-funeral scene the living and the dead 'lie upon one another' in grief (ἐπ' ἀλλήλοισιν ἀμφικείμενοι, 1620): though this phrase presumably communicates a close embrace,[99] it imports an image of piled bodies, even corpses.[100] In a variation of tropes familiar from the ritual lament (in which the living contrast their state with that of the deceased, or wish that they were dead or had never been born), each person doubles as mourner and mourned.[101]

What does this scene have in common with the landscape description discussed above? Most notable is that in both cases (the setting and the characters positioned within it), the Messenger describes what he saw before the death in terms of death's aftermath. Oedipus is washed, dressed, laid out, and mourned like a corpse; he is also seated upon a tomb, beside a tree that is already hollow. In each, the impact of a perfected state is imported to a final moment, expanding that moment (which, in reality, is gone in an instant) into a significant final day. There may be something distinctively tragic in this—in encountering a death that is so well foretold it can imbue a mysterious present with actions and images yet to come. And part of what makes this possible is the messenger-speech format: the Messenger knows what will happen because he has already seen it. Indeed, this seems to reinforce a dramatic irony to which the tragic genre lends itself: the mythological subject matter has, in a loose sense, been seen before.[102]

Let us return, finally, to the concluding section of the Messenger's speech. As discussed above, the Messenger concludes his report with an inventive and decidedly negative explanation of Oedipus' disappearance. He introduces that explanation with a description of Theseus' response to the sight of Oedipus' death (1647–52):

> [...] ὡς δ' ἀπήλθομεν,
> χρόνῳ βραχεῖ στραφέντες, ἐξαπείδομεν
> τὸν ἄνδρα τὸν μὲν οὐδαμοῦ παρόντ' ἔτι,
> ἄνακτα δ' αὐτὸν ὀμμάτων ἐπίσκιον
> χεῖρ' ἀντέχοντα κρατός, ὡς δεινοῦ τινος
> φόβου φανέντος οὐδ' ἀνασχετοῦ βλέπειν....
>
> and when we had gone away,
> after a short time we turned around, and we observed from far off

---

[99] In fact, this word seems particularly memorable when used to describe a family group marked by incest. On intimations of this 'claustrophobic intimacy' in the *OC*, see Holmes (2013: 34–5).

[100] Compare Soph. *Ant.* 1289–92.

[101] Alexiou (2002: 171–8) [1974]. See further Antigone and Ismene's words at *OC* 1683–92.

[102] See note 134.

> the man, the former no longer present anywhere,
> whereas the king, to shade his eyes,
> was holding his hand against his head, as if some dreadful
> source of fear had appeared, not endurable to see.

Though Oedipus made clear that his death should not be seen or heard by anyone apart from Theseus (1640–4), the Messenger turns back and looks (1647–52), albeit too late.[103] Theseus' pose suggests a recoiling, a shielding from the 'strange-awesome-dreadful-horrible' (δεινοῦ) 'cause of terror' or 'cause of panicked flight' (φόβου) that 'appeared to the senses' (φανέντος), an unseen vision, perhaps a moment of darkness involving the 'lightless foundation of the earth' (γῆς ἀλάμπετον βάθρον, 1662), perhaps a blinding flash of light—for Theseus responds by shading his eyes.[104] Death revealed is an unendurable sight (οὐδ' ἀνασχετοῦ βλέπειν, 1652). Like the corpses seen by Leontius in Plato's *Republic*, death's 'fine spectacle' attracts and repulses the gaze.[105] This two-way impulse is a recurrent feature of tragic death scenes (in Sophocles and more widely) where language shifts between lurid detail and the feeling that such visual horror must not or cannot be seen or told.[106] The correspondence between the draw and repulsion of death and its stirring of desire to see what is unseeable, to transgress what is forbidden (by the gods or otherwise), tips death's moment of visual impossibility into ethical non-permissibility. The unseeable nature of Oedipus' death arises from a running theme of ritual mystery and the point that his body will hold a sacred and political power. In other dramatic examples, the voyeurism of looking

---

[103] 'There is a gap or mystery—the journey's end cannot be known': Easterling (2011: 81). Alignment of the audience with the '"citizens" of whom he says "I cannot disclose it to any of these"': Reinhardt (1979: 220) [1933]. Compare Easterling (1993: 199–200), who suggests that Theseus in the *OC* might stand for the privileged spectator, a mortal chosen to witness things beyond mortal comprehension (though, as she points out, it is left unclear whether Theseus indeed manages to grasp the mystery). In fact, if the same actor played Theseus, the Messenger, and Oedipus, then he would embody those who did (perhaps) and did not see. On the division of parts in the *OC*, see note 54. On the development of Sophocles' sentence here, and the slow realization that 'the man' who was seen by the Messenger must have been Theseus not Oedipus because the latter was (paradoxically) seen to be no longer present anywhere, see Haselswerdt (2019: 630). On Sophocles' unpredictable sentences, which make spectators think and rethink their expectations, see Budelmann (2000a: ch. 1). See further Long (1968: 161–8) on Sophocles' love of abstracts, especially in his later plays; Silk (2009) on his 'magisterial elusiveness' (page 134).

[104] Nooter (2012: 176) notes that this gesture and the accompanying prayer is also how worshippers greeted the Eumenides.

[105] Pl. *Resp.* 439e5–440a4. On death's destabilizing impact on sight (and the other senses): Turner (2016: 160).

[106] Consider: Soph. *Aj.* 915 and 1004, *El.* 755–6 and 864, *Trach.* 961. Compare the paradox of beautiful horror in Aesch. *Ag.* 659 (a sea 'flowers' with corpses) and Eur. *Tro.* 1175–7 (the αἰσχρά of Astyanax's 'slaughter of shattered bones' 'laughs' from the curls his mother used to kiss, a radiant ugliness). Sophocles the honeybee, unflinching but not excessive in confrontation of horror: Buxton (1984: 8–9). On tragic pleasure as satisfaction of an appetite for affective intensity, including bodily and emotional pain, see Liebert (2017).

134   FIGURING DEATH IN CLASSICAL ATHENS

at another's death slips into erotic gratification.[107] Unseen and visually over-whelming, obscure and blinding, desired and shunned, the collisions of opposites capture a moment of unseeable magnitude.

As observed above, these are characteristic markers of the sublime.[108] The Messenger's description of Theseus' response to the moment of Oedipus' death thus represents (vicariously) an existential moment that is on the borders of conceptual possibility with poetic sublimity, and so gives form to a theory. The conceptualization of dying as involving some form of liminality is a familiar one in anthropological theory.[109] But while anthropological ideas of transition from life to death usually focus on process, and ultimately upon the return to normality (from the perspective of the living), it is also important that the liminal is an edge-point, a final border.[110] And this sense of life's farthest margin ($\tau \acute{\epsilon} \rho \mu a$, $\tau \epsilon \lambda \epsilon \upsilon \tau \acute{\eta}$, $\dot{\rho} \sigma \pi \acute{\eta}$) finds artistic expression in a dual-impact of attraction and repulsion.[111]

IV. OEDIPUS: IF ANYONE AMONG MORTALS IS WONDROUS

When it comes to the mystery of death, the *OC* takes matters to extremes. Death is, in a real, physical sense, continually absent: for most of the play, Oedipus' death is in the future, an absent object of present expectation; when his death occurs, it does so off stage, unfolding in retrospective discourse.[112] There is thus no direct encounter with the moment of death. Instead, encounters with Oedipus' death, and meditations on death more generally, are generated by

[107] Consider: Soph. *Ant.* 1234–43; *Trach.* 912–31. The psychodynamics of ecphrasis, including the gap between subject and object and the desire of the gaze: Elsner (2004: 165–6). On the transgression and taboo associated with ecphrasis (which involves a movement between media), see Scott (1994: xiii).

[108] See especially Haselswerdt (2019) on sound and the ineffable, sublimity and the abject in the *OC* and the play's 'preoccupation with perceptual distance and proximity' (page 613). As she observes (pages 629–30), Longinus cites the *OC* at *Subl.* 15.7, focusing on how skilfully Sophocles visualizes the dying Oedipus and his self-burial—i.e. the aspects of the speech that are emphatically *invisible*. Compare Halliwell (2011: 34–5, ch. 7) on the metaphysics of the sublime and 'the mind's heightened awareness of its capacity to transcend the boundaries of finite, material existence' (page 35); Costelloe (2012: 2) on 'the sublime, which, at its etymological heart, carries the long history of the relationship between human beings and those aspects of the world that excite in them particular emotions, powerful enough to evoke transcendence, shock, awe, and terror'. The sublimity of the play was also a central theme in eighteenth-century responses to the play, as explored in Ryan (2010: 30–88). See further notes 24 and 85.

[109] See page 3, note 10.

[110] Compare concern on sarcophagi with $\tau \grave{a}$ $\check{\epsilon} \sigma \chi a \tau a$: Platt (2012: 227).

[111] The continuum in Sophocles (and in other poets, earlier and contemporary) between abstract and concrete, psychological and physical: Sullivan (1999: 213). See further notes 84 and 86 on Andrea Nightingale's link between cultural and philosophical $\theta \epsilon \omega \rho \acute{a}$ and articulation of 'ecological eschatology'.

[112] Edmunds (1996: 154) also notes these temporal deferrals of Oedipus' death (for most of the play deferred from the present to the future and then, in the Messenger's speech, deferred from the past to present).

SOPHOCLES' *OEDIPUS AT COLONUS*   135

performed responses to death's prelude and aftermath. This is a familiar theme in this book but the *OC* exaggerates the imperceptibility of the instant of death by removing Oedipus bodily from the stage, a stage where he has been continually physically present, and by framing encounters with that death (when it does occur) as the object of a discourse about, among other things, knowability and visuality.

I have focused on two scenes in this chapter. The first staged different perspectives on death, those of the living and dying; Oedipus' viewpoint, characterized by distinctive vision and understanding, offered an impression of what it might be like to die but also turned attention upon the epistemological problems surrounding knowing anything from another's potentially unreliable testimony. The second staged an account of Oedipus' final moments by the Messenger. Though the account was shown to be highly immersive, it was nevertheless defined by distance in that the experience it offered was one of seeing (or not seeing), of struggling to define something unknowable from what is knowable by the senses. Indeed, seeing Oedipus approach death involved seeing him and his setting in metaphorical terms, as the lifeless, hollow body he would become after death, an object of sensory attention by the living (in ritual washing, for instance). Then, heightened emphasis on the Messenger's mediating role as his narrative approached the end of Oedipus' life brought the epistemological challenges presented by that moment into the foreground. This was corroborated by presentation of Oedipus and his surroundings as, *in extremis*, points of paradoxical attraction and repulsion, visibility and invisibility, knowability and invention.

In defining the endpoint of Oedipus' life by imperceptibility and unknowability, the *OC* prompts similar reflections on the epistemological challenges of encountering death to those generated by Plato's *Phaedo* and painted pots. In doing this by, in part, removing the moment of a character's death from the stage, it is representative of a tendency more broadly within the tragic genre (or, at least, within the surviving corpus).

However, the *OC* also, in its own way, pushes imperceptibility and unknowability further than other plays. After Oedipus leaves the stage, he is never seen again. In contrast to several other tragedies, a corpse is not produced on stage. This absence is momentous, and attention is drawn to it in the scene that follows the Messenger's speech. Of course, one essential reason for the absence of his corpse is that Oedipus' body and place of burial must remain concealed for supernatural and political reasons; provided that Theseus keeps them hidden, Athens (simultaneously Theseus' land and the fifth-century polis) will remain free from pain (1760–7).[113] But the distressed responses of Oedipus' daughters

---

[113] Markantonatos (2002: 115–60), especially, draws attention to the mystery at the heart of the Messenger's narrative but argues throughout that Sophocles' purpose is to emphasize the heroic, miraculous nature of Oedipus' death.

136 FIGURING DEATH IN CLASSICAL ATHENS

call attention to something more problematic about the absence of Oedipus' body: it denies his family the opportunity to receive, wash and dress his body, to participate in the funeral, and to sustain a connection with him by visiting his tomb.[114] The deathly landscape and premature funerary ritual in the Messenger's ecphrasis makes its real absence at the end of the play more stark.[115] 'A longing grips me,' Antigone says, 'to see the home beneath the earth' (ἵμερος ἔχει μέ τις [...] τὰν χθόνιον ἑστίαν ἰδεῖν, 1725–6). It is ambiguous whether she wishes to visit her father's tomb or to die herself (perhaps both) but she is later more explicit in her request to Theseus, 'we want to look upon the tomb of our father ourselves' (τύμβον θέλομεν | προσιδεῖν αὐταὶ πατρὸς ἡμετέρου, 1756–7). The physical presence of the corpse and the tomb is important to the living. This is not just for forensic reasons (proof of death), though perhaps the absence of a dead body is one reason why some critics have proposed that Oedipus does not die at all but instead transcends mortal life.[116] The absence of a corpse and a tomb also means a missed encounter with death and the dead.[117] Without these material objects, the living are left hanging, unable to forge a new relationship with the dead and so to continue their own lives in a new equilibrium.[118] This situation would have been familiar to many Athenians, who, for much of the fifth century, were restricted in their access to the bodies of the war dead or private tombs at which to mourn them.[119] But familiarity would surely have made the scene more raw; far from making Oedipus' death ordinary (or at least closer to ordinary), it throws the extraordinary, unsatisfactory nature of a death without a body, without a funeral,

---

[114] The problem is all the more marked because one of Oedipus' daughters is Antigone, who, in Sophocles' earlier play, demonstrated a particularly strong commitment to the burial of kin; see below with note 134. See further Chapter Two on encountering death through funerary pots.

[115] Guidorizzi et al. (2008: 371) on 1579–779 speaks of the great void ('questo grande vuoto') that Oedipus leaves behind him. Indeed, death has imbued the Colonan landscape setting from the beginning of the play. On the 'deep strain of sadness' that underlies the play's lyric celebration of Athens, see Knox (1964: 155–6). Saïd (2012: 85) also observes the literary association of the grove with death and mourning motifs. Markantonatos (2002: esp. 115–30) traces an expectation during the play of Oedipus' heroic death but focuses on the mysterious nature of the event.

[116] Note the chorus' apparent ignorance of Oedipus' death even following the Messenger's report, perhaps prompted by the absence of Oedipus' corpse: 'He is gone?' they ask Antigone (1678), as if they had not recently asked him the same question (1583). (Burton (1980: 271) differs, arguing for deletion of the question mark so that the chorus confirm, not question, Oedipus death.)

[117] See further Segal (1981: 402): Antigone is 'barred from the actual experience of [her father's] death which would give it emotional reality'.

[118] In contrast, Murnaghan (1988: 40–1) finds finality reinforced by the absence of lamentation or corpse; Markantonatos (2002: 149) emphasizes the kommos form of the narrative and comments that the medium of lamentation 'allows the girls to place the event within an emotional and chronological perspective'. But, as Emily Wilson observes (2004: 56–7), those left behind endure a living death. See further Segal (1995: 136–7).

[119] See further Currie (2012: 343) on the similar impact on families of Oedipus' heroization and heroization of the Athenian war dead (in each case distanced from their family).

SOPHOCLES' *OEDIPUS AT COLONUS*   137

without a tomb, into sharper relief.[120] In removing from the stage not just the moment of death but its aftermath, the *OC* puts its own, distinct emphasis upon the mystery that ordinarily surrounds death.

This returns us to the problematic power of the *OC* as a mediator of more general reflection on death. Oedipus' death, like Oedipus himself, sits somewhere between ordinary and extraordinary. As a man that dies in his old age, Oedipus' death seems refreshingly ordinary (at least by comparison with most deaths that occur in Greek tragedies). His death is presented from the start of the play as a welcome rest for a wanderer after a long journey, metaphorical imagery that taps into a way of conceptualizing death more broadly in Greek culture.[121] Even his blindness, though inflicted in exceptional circumstances, is representative of a universal human condition: 'LIFE IS UNCERTAIN';[122] count no man happy until he is dead.[123] In all these respects, old dying Oedipus might be every aged mortal.[124] In other ways, though, he is highly unusual, in life as well as

---

[120] See Loraux (2002: 87–90) on how tragedy provided the audience with an opportunity to mourn as individual members of humanity (as opposed to as citizens of a polis that restricted private mourning and funerals).

[121] Rest in death is 'sweet' for Oedipus (and so are the Eumenides that can grant it): Tilg (2004b). On 'wandering and the human condition' in ancient Greece and Rome, see especially Montiglio (2005: ch. 3) (though she acknowledges on page 44 that the tragic wanderer is exceptional, not everyman, 'he does not wander just because he exists'). Journeying in Sophocles, Oedipus' quest 'for an *end*', and his 'last journey': Easterling (2011: esp. 73, 78, 79). Blundell (1989: 255), too, argues that 'the emphasis of the play is on death as the end'. See further Cole on the *OC* as the 'journey of life' (in counterpoint to the ages of life in the *OT*) (1992: esp. xxxii–xxxv). The 'path' in Sophocles (emphasizing the personal path each human tracks in the world as opposed to their fate): Becker (1937: 195–212, esp. 210–12). On Oedipus' swift perfective death as set 'against the long time which has preceded it': Hutchinson (1999: 60). See further Carey (2009: 124) on how style in the ode at *OC* 1211–48 enacts the idea of 'waiting' for death (θάνατος ἐς τελευτάν, 1223, is delayed until the last verse of the strophe). On the central place of metaphor in human cognitive processes, see Lakoff and Johnson (2003) [1980].

[122] Housman (1988: 236–7), expressing, in parody, an essential principle of Greek tragedy.

[123] See Herodotus' Solon in the *Histories* 1.30–2. Note further the themes of the ode in *OC* 1211–48: life is uncertain, both youth and old age are wretched; never to be born is best, or else to die as soon as possible. On this ode, life and suffering, death and release, and overliving (both 'the worst thing of all', page 63, and 'the necessary precondition for tragedy', page 65): Wilson (2004: 58–65). See further Easterling (2009: esp. 165), 'The syntax of the whole ode brings out very clearly the fact that what is true for Oedipus is true not only for him and for them, but for all humanity'; Trivigno (2018) on the chorus of the *OC* on the goodness of death, as exemplified by Oedipus. Rutherford (2012: 280) finds a more questioning approach to Oedipus' exemplarity in the ode.

[124] Emphasizing age in the *OC*: Cole (1992: xxxiii–xxxv); Wilson (1997: 5–8) (indeed, at pages 8–11 he also argues for a theme of political 'old age', in that the *OC* 'provides an artistic closure to the era of classical Athens'); Budelmann (2000a: 80) on Oedipus' special relationship with time (he is, in this respect, unlike other men); Budelmann (2000b: 193) on Oedipus as cult-hero-to-be *and* old man; Kitcher (2018), on the *OC* as a '*human* tragedy', a struggle for serenity. Dhuga (2005), however, notes that the aged chorus of the *OC* are strikingly authoritative, which indicates that there is (in this play at least) no simple equation between age and infirmity. On a shift between general and specific meditation in the third ode, see Carey (2009: 128–9). Note especially 1239–41, where the chorus associate Oedipus' aged

138 FIGURING DEATH IN CLASSICAL ATHENS

death. Crucially, his death is not natural but preordained, and he will, ultimately, hold exceptional status as a hero.[125] In who he is and how he dies (and who he is once he is dead), Oedipus puts the porosity between ordinary and extraordinary under pressure.

But the epistemological point to which the *OC* draws attention is not just the extent to which encountering Oedipus's death specifically might illuminate a mystery. Instead, the questionable exemplarity of Oedipus' death turns a spotlight upon the desires and expectations of the living in the face of an existential problem. Why should *any* death be exemplary? After all, is any death ordinary?[126] In ancient Athens, some died in old age, some in battle, some in childbirth, some from disease. It was not just the war dead or cult heroes that disappeared without a material trace: cenotaphs might be used for a range of the dead, for people who died at sea, for example, or overseas.[127] And it was not just mythological characters whose bodies exerted supernatural force after their death: Sophocles himself became the object of hero cult.[128] Perhaps the main way in which all deaths are alike is that every death is individual.

Indeed, exemplarity is at the heart of the *OC*, not just in its eponymous character but also in the life history that the play has accumulated in the thousands of years since it came into being. From the very beginning, the play has offered itself as an influential model for thinking about theatre and death. Written by Sophocles, a titan of Greek drama (and often, for ancient and modern critics alike, the exemplary ancient dramatist),[129] at the end of his own life and performed after his death (and after the deaths of so many others), it could not help but propose analogies between the death that it contains, the death of its aged author, and death more generally.[130] Produced at the end of the fifth century, it comprises the conscious and unconscious reflections of a dramatist upon almost a century of drama and death; it holds the tantalizing promise of a lens onto the mediating role played by Greek tragedy in personal and general thanatological meditation.

condition with their own. On the exemplarity (and monstrosity) of Oedipus more generally, see e.g. Segal (1995: 141).

[125] Overliving as a human condition (and Oedipus' exceptional rehabilitation from this condition): Wilson (2004: esp. 41–2, 58–65).

[126] Death, 'the most uncertain of all certainties': Grieve (1898: 31).

[127] On disappearance as a Greek mythical-ritual model for heroic death, see Guidorizzi et al. (2008: 378) on 1649. On cenotaphs, see Kurtz and Boardman (1971: 99–100).

[128] Jouanna (2018: 65–6) [2007].   [129] Goldhill (2012: 153).

[130] See note 14. For similar themes in wider scholarship, see Neill (1997); Hutcheon and Hutcheon (2004); Curtin (2019); Vance Smith (2020); Senelick (2022). Though note Elias (2001: 3) [1982], 'The social problem of death is especially difficult because the living find it hard to identify with the dying.' See further pages 116–7 with note 40 and, in contrast, Conversation Three. Note, too, the other deaths implicated in this drama: see below, including note 134.

Since its first production, in fact, the play has continued to offer a sounding board for reflections on death.[131] Consider the echo of Oedipus' bath in Plato's *Phaedo*.[132] Regardless of whether this was intended to be a direct reference to the text or performance of Sophocles' play, the recurrence of the motif (including within this book!) is itself generative of thought on how a cultural product might engage, and continue to engage, in diffuse cultural reflections. Consider, further, the 2019 Cambridge Greek Play, in which the *OC* became 'one of the greatest plays about old age, the bearing of life's horror, and the transcendence of the ordinary'.[133] This more recent reincarnation interacted not just with a fifth-century discourse but also with a web of interactions thereafter, including, explicitly, a discourse surrounding the Chilean dictator Pinochet. Implicitly, Pinochet dies not just like Oedipus but also like Socrates, and Sophocles, and countless others. Oedipus too, in the *OC*, when he denies his daughter a corpse to bury, interacts with another situation in another play by Sophocles, when Antigone is kept from a body: the body of her brother Polynices.[134] Echoes of this kindred situation, future within the mythological world of the *OC*, past within the cultural world of fifth-century Athenian dramatic performances, juxtapose two deaths that are similar and different.[135] Two bodies go unhonoured, unburied by their family; one betrayed his city, the other offers, in his death, a city's protection; one died young and violently, the other old and apparently without suffering; both have disappeared but both live on in cultural retellings.[136]

---

[131] See especially Rodighiero (2007) on representations of Oedipus' mysterious death in the play's reception history. See further Markantonatos (2007: ch. 6); Kelly (2009: ch. 8); Scharffenberger (2017: 336–82) on the *OC*'s reception more generally. See Ryan (2010) on reception of the *OC* in the eighteenth century.

[132] See pages 130–1, note 96.   [133] The Cambridge Greek Play (2019).

[134] See Sophocles' *Antigone*. For a detailed treatment of the intertextual relationships between the *OC* and other plays, see Markantonatos (2007: ch. 5). See further Lamari (2009) on 'future reflexivity' in tragedy; Holmes (2013) on the 'volatility' (page 23) of the final scene and the relationship between the *OC*, *Oedipus the King*, and *Antigone*. On connections and contrasts between the *OC* and Aeschylus' *Oresteia* (particularly in the Furies/Eumenides and themes of retribution), see Winnington-Ingram (1954); see further Bernek (2004: ch. 3) on the *OC* as a suppliant drama (and its close relationship with Aeschylus' *Eumenides*) and Kelly (2009: ch. 3).

[135] See further Conversation Three for discussion of other analogous deaths in the *Antigone*.

[136] Note Carey (2009: 133): 'Neither [the third stasimon] nor anything else in the play is offered as the last word.' Indeed, the ongoing life of the *OC* echoes the continued presence of both Oedipus and Sophocles as cult heroes. Perhaps this is anticipated in the language of the play: see Suksi (2001) on the nightingales' music in the grove at Colonus and how it reflects the transformative power of tragedy; the *OC* does not just represent death and grief but turns them into art. Inconclusiveness is also a feature of Sophocles' style: see note 103.

140 FIGURING DEATH IN CLASSICAL ATHENS

The play then, puts pressure not just upon what normal might look like in the context of death but also upon the role played by culture in meditating that question. Yes, every death might be idiosyncratic, as might every encounter with another's death (real or represented). But, in the face of that idiosyncrasy, a play like the *OC* can also mediate a shared encounter with death by offering everyone common ingredients, by inviting them to draw analogies, by presenting an instance of death that is spatially and temporally indeterminate—even within the world of the play the location of death is unknown, while the narrated moment not only reoccurs on each re-performance but also participates in an historic-cultic temporality that begins and has already begun, that inhabits a non-mortal (immortal?) temporality.[137] Oedipus (like everyone) is unusual in his death but one of the ways in which his death is unusual also gives it potential to stand not just as an instance but also as an example of death: it is thoroughly known to all.

Figuring Death in Classical Athens: Visual and Literary Explorations. Emily Clifford, Oxford University Press.
© Emily Clifford 2025. DOI: 10.1093/9780198947936.003.0005

[137] See Budelmann (2000a: ch. 2) on the shared perspective invited by Sophocles' characters. On the temporalities, relations, and reflections upon them that are mediated by poetry (specifically Pindar's lyric poetry), see Fearn (2024b).

CONVERSATION THREE

Niobes

One point of emphasis in the previous chapter was on the dying body as an aesthetic object and example to the living. These themes will return in Chapters Four and Five, which probe, respectively, the ways in which sculpted stone bodies mediate reflection on death and the epistemological challenges posed by examples (can you understand what it is like to experience death by observing someone else die and can you extrapolate general principles from instances of death and disease?).

In this third conversation, I want to press the nexus between bodies, stone, and exemplarity, and the generative potential of that nexus for meditation on death. I focus on Niobe—the quintessential mourning woman who saw her twelve or fourteen sons and daughters shot down by the gods Artemis and Apollo and, in her grief, transformed into a grieving rock. Metamorphosis of bodies into stone is central to the myth in its various visual and literary iterations. In *Iliad* 24.602–17, for instance, our earliest surviving rendition of the story, it is not just Niobe who becomes a stone but all the people who might have buried the children. Emphasis in later versions is primarily upon Niobe's petrification, though Roman sarcophagi and the Niobid statue groups present the dying children, together with their mother, as stone objects. Either way, death, grief, and material transformation are running themes. But what is striking for my purposes here is that these bodies-turned-stone prompt reflection not only on what it might be like to die (to transform from a person to a corpse) but also on what it means to see someone else die—in some ways, Niobe's story is about dying vicariously, about observing another's death and, oneself, experiencing a material transformation.

Let us begin with Antigone's words to the chorus in the sung lament that they share before she leaves the stage to her death in Sophocles' tragedy *Antigone*, staged *c.* 441 BCE (*Ant.* 823–33):[1]

> Αν. ἤκουσα δὴ λυγροτάταν ὀλέσθαι
> τὰν Φρυγίαν ξέναν

---

[1] On Sophocles' Antigone and Niobe, see especially Worman (2021: 151–6).

142 FIGURING DEATH IN CLASSICAL ATHENS

> Τανταλου Σιπυλῳ προς ἀ- (825)
> κρῳ, ταν κισσος ὡς ἀτενης
> πετραια βλαστα δαμασεν,
> καὶ νιν ὄμβροι τακομεναν,
> ὡς φατις ἀνδρῶν,
> χιων τ᾽ οὐδαμα λειπει, (830)
> τεγγει δ᾽ ὑπ᾽ ὀφρυσι παγ-
> κλαυτοις δειραδας· ᾆ με δαι-
> μων ὁμοιοταταν κατευναζει.

Antigone: Actually, I heard she died, utterly desolate,
the stranger from Phrygia,
daughter of Tantalus, on the slopes of towering Sipylus;
like intractable ivy
a growth of rock overpowered her,
and, as she dissolves in tears, rain,
they say,
and snow never leave her,
and she pours water over the ridges
from brows that always weep: just like her am I,
as the god lulls me to sleep.

Like Niobe, Antigone will be encased in stone—walled up in a rocky tomb. Like Niobe, her snow-white body will be drenched in fluid (exchanging tears for Haemon's blood: 1236–9). The circumstances of Antigone's future death are thus literally analogous with Niobe's; both deaths are stony, isolated, helpless, and liquid. Moreover, the analogies that she draws between the two situations sketch, in a more exploratory way, what it might feel like to die. Death is, once again, a veil—or, rather, a blanket (of snow), chilling the body, smothering the senses. The rock that sheds tears, too, expresses not just enduring grief but also the paradoxical materialities of the corpse—stiff and still; liquid and flowing.[2] Death stills and chills, divides and dissolves.

But bundled together in Antigone's image of Niobe's death, and in the wider song that she shares with the chorus (who wept in turn to see Antigone: ἰσχειν δ᾽|οὐκετι πηγας δυναμαι δακρυων, 802–3), is the possibility of contagion—an iteration of bodily transformations that transmit, through the affective power of grief, one person's experience of death to another.[3] First, we have the slaughtered children—unmentioned here except insofar as Niobe is the paradigm of maternal grief. Her supreme desolation, her perpetual tears, respond implicitly

---

[2] On this point, see especially Wohl (2018: 19–20) on how death both turns bodies into 'an inert thing' and 'releases a vitality latent within the inanimate'. See further Brown (1987: 192–3) on the paradox of the stone as dead and living (it 'grows').

[3] See further Macintosh (1994: 173–4) on the situation of mourners in Greek tragedy as a kind of death; Rimell (2024) on the pressure Niobe exerts on relational ethics.

to others' deaths that now become her own: the bodies of the children that, as Homer's Achilles told Priam, lay for nine days in their blood (οἱ μὲν ἄρ' ἐννῆμαρ κέατ' ἐν φόνῳ, *Il.* 24.610) become the rain- and tear-soaked landmark of Niobe. Sophocles' play, too, began with a family corpse—the corpse of Antigone's brother Polynices. And again, the 'dripping, clammy' (μυδῶν, 410) body that Antigone mourns becomes her own. What we have, then, in Antigone's self-identification with Niobe—a self-identification that spreads to the chorus—is an example that unravels the epistemological problems probed elsewhere in this book: death just might become knowable from another's experience.

I now turn to my second example, an Attic red-figure mixing bowl (column krater) held in the Museo Civico Archeologico in Caltanissetta and dated to *c*. 450 BCE (Figures C3a and b).[4] Each side of the pot features three figures. On one, a female figure is shown in a mostly frontal position, with her head turned in profile to the left (Figure C3a). Her arms, bent at the elbows, are raised to the sky, while her lower torso is concealed behind or within a cloud-like mass with wavy edges, over which has been scrawled a thin wash of dark paint—this appears to be a rock, leading several viewers to conclude that this is one of our earliest depictions of the transformation of Niobe, and a rare Attic example (the scene is

FIGURES C3A and B. The Caltanissetta krater (both sides). Attic red-figure column krater. *c*. 450 BCE. Height: 23.8 cm. Found in Sabucina, Sicily. Museo Civico Archeologico, Caltanissetta: S 2555. Image: courtesy of the Regional Department of Cultural Heritage and Sicilian Identity—Gela Archaeological Park.

---

[4] *BAPD* 9024586. On this pot, see Robertson (1988: 113); Green (1995: 108); Todisco (2002: 52); Catucci (2003: 56, 369 no. A27, pl. XI), (2009).

more popular on South Italian pots of the fourth century BCE). To the left is a bearded figure shown in profile, bending inwards towards Niobe and wrapped, head-to-toe, in fabric. To the right, a second bearded figure moves away to the right but looks back towards Niobe, grasping what appears to be a stick in his right hand, arm bent at the elbow.[5] On the pot's other side, we again encounter three figures (Figure C3b): this time it is the central figure that is densely wrapped in fabric, looking, again, to the left; this figure is framed by two figures shown in profile, who each look inwards towards him, extending one arm, bent at the elbow. On each side the figured scene is bordered to the left and right with a double strip of bands featuring black dots (another double strip traces the pot's rim), while repeated decorative motifs encircle the pot's neck and shoulders.

Half rock, half woman, and apparently still alive, the woman in Figure C3a is caught in her final moment. And, as in the play, her death unfolds as a material transformation of figured flesh. But the violence with which this happens—a violence that Sophocles' language communicates with a verb of forcing, taming, conquering ($\delta\acute{\alpha}\mu\alpha\sigma\epsilon\nu$) and an adjective of intractability ($\mathring{\alpha}\tau\epsilon\nu\acute{\eta}s$)—is now visual.[6] Niobe's body is not just petrifying, she is losing her coherence: the rock that is her lower half is presented in disarray, as a partially obscured lump encased in squiggly lines. The neat stripes of dots that decorate her clothing reinforce the contrast; this well-organized body is loosening into an amorphous muddle.[7] In fact, the repetition of the decorative dots at the borders of the image and the body of the pot (not just its rim but also its sides, when Niobe is viewed front on), presses the suggestion further. With her dotted, decorated torso and her arms raised symmetrically on each side of her head like the krater's two handles, Niobe appears to transform not just into a rock but also into a pot.[8] This is a twofold suggestion of the material transformation effected by death—body turned stone and body turned clay.[9] Indeed, the implications are not just material

[5] For the details of these two figures' heads, see the reconstruction in Catucci (2009: fig. 3).

[6] On the virility associated with the language, see Griffith (1999: 269) on 826–7.

[7] For a more extreme version of how a loss of figuration might generate ideas about death as materially and ontologically different from life, see John Golding's abstract painting *Niobe* (1966), held in the Metropolitan Museum of Art, New York.

[8] In fact, this suggestion can also be observed on fourth-century South Italian pots, which position the transforming body of Niobe alongside what appear to be funerary urns—more explicitly reflexive versions of the funerary pot on which they are painted. See, for instance, an Apulian amphora of *c.* 340 BCE held in the Museo Archeologico Nazionale, Taranto (8935) and an Apulian hydria of *c.* 330 BCE held in the Musée d'Art et Histoire, Geneva (HR 282bis). See further Trendall (1972); Schmidt et al. (1976: 40–50) (arguing that the images show Niobe being gradually released from petrification); Keuls (1978a); Taplin (2007: 74–9); Comay (2024: 44–6).

[9] Compare Alexey von Jawlensky's *Mystical Heads: Niobe* (1917), held in the McNay Art Museum, Texas. This is a work created through encaustic, by daubing pigmented wax onto the surface. The thick, sticky, thoroughly physical way of producing Niobe's image prompts, in its own way, reflection on her bodily substance—simultaneously viscous and solid, like hot and cold wax. On wax and weeping tragic bodies, see further Worman (2021: 135–6).

but ontological: this woman is turning into an artefact—something altogether different from a living body.

Equally interesting is the visual attention to the physical effect of Niobe's death on those around her. Notable here is the left-hand figure, whose muffled appearance is characteristic of intense grief (compare how Phaedo covered himself with his veil on Socrates' drinking the hemlock: see page 38). In his distress, this painted figure has turned himself into a mirror image of Niobe, encased not in rock but in his own smothering clothes. Observe too the bent arm of the figure that departs to the right, a visual echo of Niobe's own gesture. Then consider what happens if we turn the pot around: the wrapped body has now moved into the centre, compositionally adopting not just the position of Niobe and her situation as a focal point of attention but also, implicitly, her dying moment. As in the *Antigone*, where bodies that observed death seemed to experience it not just vicariously but also physically, reproducing the material transformation in their own body, this krater suggests the possibility of virtual experience in response to an example. With that in mind, let us turn to some flesh-and-rock bodies on the Athenian Acropolis rendered not in words or painted clay, but in carved stone.

Figuring Death in Classical Athens: Visual and Literary Explorations. Emily Clifford, Oxford University Press.
© Emily Clifford 2025. DOI: 10.1093/9780198947936.003.0006

FOUR

Victory, Victory, Victory?

Encountering Death in the West Frieze of the Temple of Athena Nike

I. THING OF BEAUTY

No longer conceived of as a *mimesis* of a unique event (albeit with universal implications), the narrative here becomes a repeated affirmation, a rhetorical statement and restatement of a single abstract concept: victory, victory, victory.

—Andrew Stewart[1]

The Temple of Athena Nike melds history and myth in a hymn of victory. From the shields captured from the Spartans recently affixed to the bastion, to the battles against the Persians, to the mythic exploits on the west and north friezes, the imagery illustrates continuous Athenian success.

—Nathan Arrington[2]

The temple of Athena Nike is covered in slaughter and stone-cold corpses. Despite this, it is generally considered a thing of beauty: the 'pearl of the Acropolis'.[3] Now, there is a difference between wanting to look at actual corpses—a matter for shame and disgust, 'look for yourselves, you wretches, and take your fill of the beautiful sight!'[4]—and wanting to look at sculptures of dead bodies.[5] But the two experiences are not entirely distinct;[6] just because death is

---

[1] Stewart (1985: 67).   [2] Arrington (2015: 176).

[3] A 'jewel box': Goette (2001: 22). Note, too, Brouskari (2001: 73) [1997]: 'The small temple of Athena Nike seems to hang in the light, a miniature masterpiece high on the bastion at the south-west edge of the Acropolis. A lighter note in the heroic symphony of the Propylaea nearby, a smile answering its sobriety, it blends harmoniously with that monument.'

[4] Pl. *Resp.* 4.440a3–4.

[5] The complexities of representation, reality, and cruelty (encompassing the art of death): Nelson (2011). Aestheticization of the shocking in the arts and Euripides' commentary upon it: Shirazi (2018: 109).

[6] Sometimes there are troubling crossovers. Consider the plaster casts of the dead from Pompeii, displayed in the Ashmolean exhibition 'Last Supper in Pompeii' (July 2019–January 2020) but segregated from the other artefacts.

VICTORY, VICTORY, VICTORY?   147

not 'really there' on a temple frieze—what is there is stone, paint, and images—does not mean that it is out of the mental picture. And there is no ignoring death in the sanctuary of Athena Nike. It is sculpted into a temple built on land that was ravaged by the Persians,[7] a temple doubly wreathed in scenes of slaughter—battle on its friezes, sacrifice on its balustrade.

Nevertheless, most viewers agree on one thing: this temple complex is all about victory, whether martial, political, cultural, or ethical—'victory, victory, victory' in the words of Andrew Stewart (presumably riffing off Churchill).[8] Traditional approaches tend to focus on two points—the temple's construction and reconstructions (and when they took place),[9] and the subject matter of its friezes (are they mythological or historical, and to which play, myth, battle, or event should they be matched?)[10]—but no one has interrogated its triumphant message.

[7] Memorializing and forgetting on the Acropolis after the Persian destruction (and representations of the cost of victory in its sculpture): Kousser (2009). She does not focus on the temple of Athena Nike.

[8] See e.g. Michaelis (1862: 252–4); Boulter (1969: 133); Mattingly (1982: 384); Stewart (1985: esp. 67); Simon (1997); Palagia (2005: 190); Lippman et al. (2006); Martin-McAuliffe and Papadopoulos (2012: 346); Trundle (2013: 124); Shear (2016: 351–8); Athanassaki (2023). Ethical victory on the west frieze: Harrison (1997: 121); Karakas (2002: 53–5, 157); Arrington (2015: 172–6).

[9] Ancient construction: Michaelis (1862: 260–7); Travlos (1971: 148–9); Miles (1980: 323–5); Wesenberg (1981); Mattingly (1982), (2000); Childs (1985) (mostly focuses on the temple on the Ilissos); Mark (1993) (detailed); Shear (1999: 120–5); Gill (2001); Furtwängler (2010: 442–51) [1895]; Shear (2016: 27–35). The dates of the authorization, planning, and construction of the temple have provoked considerable debate, with some preferring an earlier date for a decree authorizing construction and the appointment of a priestess (*IG* 1³ 35, dated in *OR* 137 to 438–435 or 450–445) and for initial work on the bastion (see e.g. Shear (2016: 341–7)). Others (see especially Gill (2001)) propose that the temple was anticipated during construction of the Propylaea but that construction took place in the 420s and so was contemporaneous with not just a decree organizing payment of the priestess' salary (*IG* 1³ 36) but also the one mentioned above, if that decree can be downdated (*IG* 1³ 35). However, while *IG* 1³ 36 can be dated with some confidence to 424/3 (see *OR* 156), the date of *IG* 1³ 35 has attracted more debate (though *OR* 137 is confident that it should be dated before *c.* 437 BCE). History of the temple site, alterations, and restoration issues: Giraud (1994). A reconstruction history: de Bree (2010).

[10] Evelyn Harrison has written extensively on the frieze subjects: (1972c) (south frieze) (the battle of Marathon), (1972a) (north frieze) (the battle of Plataea), (1997: esp. 117–22). Some further interpretations: Blümel (1950/51) (Greeks versus Persians on the south; Greeks versus Greeks on the north and west); Pemberton (1972: esp. 304–7) (Athenian defeat of the Corinthians at Megara on the west frieze); Felten (1984: 123–31, esp. 128–9) (mythological themes on the north and west sides, specifically the fight between Achilles and Memnon in the Trojan War, with the weighing of Achilles' and Memnon's souls on the east); Simon (1985: 275) (victories on the north and west friezes, respectively, over Boeotians and Peloponnesians in general); Stewart (1985: 55–67, esp. 55, table 1) (universalizing, allegorical rhetoric in the temple complex); Palagia (2005) (birth of Athena on the east frieze, Athenian victory over Spartans on the west); Schultz (2009) (supporting Harrison's interpretation of the north frieze as representing the battle for the Herakleidai); Furtwängler (2010: 445–50) [1895] (the battle of Plataea on north, west, and south friezes); Shear (2016: 351–5) (providing a comprehensive summary of proposals and favouring specific, but no longer identifiable, historical battles). These discussions form an important backdrop to my discussion but mostly have a different focus. Note, in contrast, Hölscher (1997: 146), arguing for more generic battles (albeit Greek versus Persian or Greek versus Greek) on the friezes. See

148 FIGURING DEATH IN CLASSICAL ATHENS

This approach accords with a dominant thread in scholarship on the Classical Acropolis more generally (especially the Parthenon), namely that its sacred space is a place of Athenian self-definition, self-promotion, and self-celebration.[11] This socio-political goal is (implicitly or explicitly) compatible with a sacred purpose of celebrating the goddess of the city. But we can meaningfully refine the picture by paying closer attention to death. It is surely uncontentious to propose that a temple covered in struggling, dying, and dead bodies prompted reflections on death, but this is not the usual approach, especially to the temple of Athena Nike. Notable exceptions are Nathan Arrington's work on the fallen warrior and Rachel Kousser's article on mourning and memory on the Acropolis.[12] There is, however, much more to be said both specifically on the temple of Athena Nike and generally on how temple sculpture involves viewers in meditation on death.

My slant here seeks to fill this gap, and it does so in two ways. First, I wish to complicate the ways in which this temple deals with victory, which is not a flat concept but rather bound up with defeat and death (especially when viewed in a wartime context).[13] This latter point is not controversial,[14] but seems to have been lost in responses to the temple. In addition, I wish to place a question mark over the specificity of the temple's sculptural representations—to think in terms of plausible possibilities. It is the productive nature of the images that makes them so powerful a springboard for thanatological meditations.[15] Instead of focusing on the purpose of the monument and on what its images were meant to represent, I am going to explore some ways in which interactions with the sculptures generate encounters with death.

First, some context. Completed in the mid-420s—during the Peloponnesian War, in a decade of triumph, defeat, confidence, and despair—the small and ornate temple of Athena Nike perches upon a bastion at the south side of the Propylaea gateway, on the west side of the sacred citadel of Athens (Figure 4.1).[16]

further Osborne (2017: 449) on how the Nike south frieze conjures 'the broad nature of the conflict' not particular individuals.

[11] See e.g. Rhodes (1995: esp. 1–2, 115–16); Hurwit (1999: 230); Schwab (2005).

[12] Kousser (2009); Arrington (2015).

[13] Compare Shear (2016: 358): 'the image of Athenian triumph conveyed by the battle friezes of the Nike temple seems increasingly out of touch with the realities of contemporary warfare, as the long years of the Peloponnesian War dragged on.' Perhaps it is the reception of the temple that is out of touch.

[14] Victory and defeat as 'fluid conditions': Turner and Clark (2018: 6). See further Foster (2018: 100–3), who, as part of an argument that much of the visual and verbal media of Classical Athens (historiography excluded) avoids direct mention of defeat, acknowledges that temple decoration shows what was endured for the sake of victory (page 101). See note 7.

[15] Relevant here (though more focused on how art expresses and communicates ideas than how it generates them) is Hölscher (1997: 157–63) on 'konzeptuelle Bildsprache' on the Nike balustrade.

[16] For a general history of the Acropolis, with an overview of the temple, see Goette (2001: 5–16, 21–3). See further Brouskari (2001: 71–87) [1997]. The precise dating of the conception, authorization, design, building, and completion of the temple does not change my argument here (see note 9): I am interested in responses to the temple once built—in the years that followed all those original moments.

Figure 4.1. Photograph of the temple of Athena Nike taken from the northwest, showing the view of the west frieze from below. Image: Chris Hellier/Alamy Stock Photo.

150 FIGURING DEATH IN CLASSICAL ATHENS

Designed with four-columned porticoes on eastern and western ends (tetrastyle amphiprostyle), it was decorated on its exterior with four continuous friezes in high relief (one on each side); sculptures in both pediments; and gilded bronze statue groups (acroteria) on the apex and corners.[17] Within it stood a cult image of Athena Nike,[18] and around it, enclosing the sanctuary on three of its boundaries to the north, south, and west, ran a balustrade sculpted in relief with images of Nike figures bringing offerings towards seated Athenas.[19] The bastion may have been clad in shields captured from the Spartans at Sphakteria in 425 BCE, rendering the whole structure akin to a monumental trophy.[20]

In this chapter, I focus on the west frieze, the first set of images that you would see on approaching the Acropolis.[21] I probe, first, the relationship between visibility and visualization of death: what does it take to notice death in a sculpted battle scene? How does the stone medium prompt reflection on the imaginative nature of encountering death? Then, turning to the frieze's immediate and wider settings in Classical Athens, including details from the rest of the temple and sanctuary complex,[22] I consider how the sacred-mythological backdrop contributed to thanatological and epistemological meditation. Finally, I discuss the image of a trophy, which is set within an ongoing battle scene. How does this trophy draw attention to existential stakes within, and beyond, the figured scene?

II. WHAT DOES IT TAKE TO NOTICE DEATH IN A TEMPLE FRIEZE?

Consider the sculptural representations on the west frieze (Figures 4.2a–h).

---

[17] Acroteria: see Schultz (2001), rejecting the previous reconstruction in Boulter (1969). Pediments: Despinis (1974); Brouskari (1989); Ehrhardt (1989). See further Shear (2016: 355–6). On the friezes, see note 10.

[18] Nike, an abstract concept (victory), was often associated with other divinities such as Athena and Zeus but was also a deity in her own right: Hamdorf (1964: 58–62); Lonis (1979: 231–61); Ducrey (1985: 264). Note the narrower view in Baudrillart (1894: 5–21, esp. 7) that Nike was an 'offshoot' of Athena, qualified in Daly (1953). There is some evidence for a cult of Athena Nike in the early sixth century (an Archaic statue base and later references in Heliodoros and Pausanias to a xoanon of a wingless Athena Nike): Mark (1993: 123–5). Evidence for the independent cult of Nike dates later than the fifth century: Daly (1953: 1124). The Nike figure in Greek art: Isler-Kerényi (1969) (Archaic period); Gulaki (1981) (Classical period).

[19] The balustrade: Michaelis (1862); Kekulé (1869), (1881); Simon (1985: 280–6), (1997); Jameson (1994); Hölscher (1997); Brouskari (1998).

[20] See Lippman et al. (2006).

[21] Two central blocks (*i* and *k*) are in the British Museum: 1816,0610.160 and 1816,0610.161. The corner blocks are in the Acropolis Museum: 18143 and 18139.

[22] Any temple sculpture is part of a larger entity: not just the temple building but also sanctuary space, including, for example, altars, boundaries, and votive statues. It therefore exists in a sacred space that frames responses to it. The rhetorical unity of the 'sculptural program' of the temple's friezes, pediments, acroteria, and balustrade: Stewart (1985).

FIGURE 4.2A. Corner block *h* from the west frieze of the temple of Athena Nike (Scene 1). 426–421 BCE. Length 52 cm. Acropolis Museum, Athens: Acr. 18143 (west side). Image: © Acropolis Museum, 2018, photographer: Yiannis Koulelis.

FIGURE 4.2B. Block *i* from the west frieze of the temple of Athena Nike (Scenes 2, 3, 4, and 5). 426–421 BCE. Length 205 cm, Height 44.45 cm. British Museum, London: 1816,0610.160. Image: © The Trustees of the British Museum.

FIGURE 4.2C. Block *k* from the west frieze of the temple of Athena Nike (Scenes 5, 6, 7, and 8). 426–421 BCE. Length 205 cm, Height 44.45 cm. British Museum, London: 1816,0610.161. Image: © The Trustees of the British Museum.

152   FIGURING DEATH IN CLASSICAL ATHENS

FIGURE 4.2D. Corner block *l* from the west frieze of the temple of Athena Nike (Scene 8). 426–421 BCE. Length 50 cm. Acropolis Museum, Athens: Acr. 18139 (west side). Image: © Acropolis Museum, 2018, photographer: Yiannis Koulelis.

FIGURE 4.2E. Detail (left half) from block *i* (Scenes 2 and 3). See caption for Figure 4.2b. Image: © The Trustees of the British Museum.

VICTORY, VICTORY, VICTORY? 153

FIGURE 4.2F. Detail (right half) from block *i* (Scenes 4 and 5). See caption for Figure 4.2b.
Image: © The Trustees of the British Museum.

FIGURE 4.2G. Detail (left half) from block *k* (Scenes 5 and 6). See caption for Figure 4.2c.
Image: © The Trustees of the British Museum.

FIGURE 4.2H. Detail (right half) from block *k* (Scenes 6, 7, and 8). See caption for Figure 4.2c.
Image: © The Trustees of the British Museum.

154 FIGURING DEATH IN CLASSICAL ATHENS

Together, the images form a continuous whole (a typical feature of an ionic frieze): they show a battle scene in progress. In tension with this high-level cohesion is the composition of the frieze in vignettes, local scenes that play out between individuals amidst the wider political conflict (see Table 4.1). In the fourth part of this chapter (IV. Life and Death in the Balance), I will examine how the episodic format puts a distinctive spin on existential reflection; for the moment, let us take a closer look at some of the scenes and how they generate exploration of death.

TABLE 4.1 Scenes on the west frieze of the temple of Athena Nike

Scene	Figure	Object	Representation
1	4.2a	Block *h*	Two figures with hoplite shields move towards the right (into battle). Death is conceivable as a future event.
2	4.2b, 4.2e	Block *i*	Two nude figures with hoplite shields lunge away from one another above a nude figure upon the ground. This figure appears to be wounded or in a vulnerable position; he may be dying.
3	4.2b, 4.2e	Block *i*	Two nude figures with hoplite shields face one another above a nude body outstretched behind a rock, and apparently dead.
4	4.2b, 4.2f	Block *i*	One nude figure leaps above another that lies upon the ground, his torso partly raised upon his left elbow. It is unclear whether the latter is falling or getting back up. Behind the figures is a trophy consisting of a shield upon a tree.
5	4.2b, 4.2c, 4.2f, 4.2g	Blocks *i/k*	Two figures leap and run towards the right; another is braced against them. These figures are vigorous and very much alive. They are about to meet in conflict: death is conceivable (especially since the confrontation is unequal).
6	4.2c, 4.2g, 4.2h	Block *k*	There are six figures in total. Three figures, one nude, two draped, leap and lunge. They fight over the outstretched body of a nude warrior (wounded, perhaps dying, perhaps dead). Another nude figure bends to lift the body; another arcs with his shield above the body, perhaps protecting it from attack.
7	4.2c, 4.2h	Block *k*	Two figures lunge above another nude figure that kneels, braced upon the ground, and raises his shield in defence. The latter is in a vulnerable position.
8	4.2c, 4.2d, 4.2h	Block *l*	One draped figure moves to the right, apparently to support another, who is locked shield-to-shield with his opponent.

It is worth stressing now that it is not a stretch to think about death in response to this frieze. Death is present throughout, not just because some bodies are visibly dead or dying, but because most figures are striving to kill and not be killed. All figures on this frieze face an existential crisis. As elsewhere in this book, my question is not whether death is relevant here (it manifestly is) but how the sculptural medium shapes encounters with it.

I begin at the obvious end of the spectrum, with bodies of the dead and dying. The prelude to or aftermath of death is visibly represented by the presence of three fallen bodies in Scenes 2, 3, and 6 (see especially Figures 4.2e and g). (I set aside, for now, the figure below the trophy, who is supporting himself on his left elbow and is unambiguously alive but may be wounded and is in a precarious position.) These bodies are differentiated by their languid inertia and sprawling vulnerability. Other figures stride and lunge, attack and defend, wield weapons and shields, their bodies clear to see and set against waves of rippling drapery and circular shields. These three, by contrast, are relaxed, the curving lines of their bodies forming gentle hollows; those on either end are lifted into a concave dish, the second curls inwards towards the viewer.[23] The flowing curves of their bodies echo the undulations of the drapery: these figures look like men but behave (or, rather, respond) like objects. This passivity dovetails with their vulnerability: they must be screened from attack by the bodies and shields of those above them. Whether dead (most scholars think they are) or incapacitated, they are shown on point of departure from their sculpted world: the first and the last are lifted from the ground; the other sinks out of view, partially concealed by a rock. To the extent that a corpse marks death, death is clear to see and uncomplicated.

But visualizations of death here transcend the visible spectacle of the corpse. Consider the fallen figure in Scene 3 (Figure 4.2e). This body lies outstretched behind a rock, his nude torso twisted and curled, his legs and genitals in a frontal view, and his chest tilted away so the upper body sprawls on its back. Partial concealment of his body complicates the relationship between perception and knowledge. The corpse—visible evidence that death has occurred—is somewhat obscured from view. But does this concealment make it more or less difficult to know that this figure has died? Observing in his doctoral thesis that corpses hold a less central position on the Nike friezes than on the Parthenon metopes, Nathan Arrington commented, 'Here, death is cloaked, concealed, or transformed.'[24] Is this true? As Socrates jokes in the *Phaedo*, corpses are not necessarily good to think with when it comes to the concept of death ('[bury me] any way you

---

[23] There is a similar distinction between living and dead among the extant copies of defeated figures in the Attalid dedication on the Athenian Acropolis of *c.* 200 BCE: see Osborne (2017: 445–6).

[24] Arrington (2010: 103) (on the west frieze). The absence of this point in Arrington (2015: 172–6) suggests that he revised his opinion. Either way, the leap from less obvious corpses to less obvious death is perilous.

156 FIGURING DEATH IN CLASSICAL ATHENS

like—if you can catch me, that is, and I don't slip through your fingers!' 115c).
How concrete a symbol do we need to notice death on this temple?

The rock that cloaks and conceals operates like a visible, material metonym for
the metaphorical veil that covers a warrior's eyes at death's conclusion, smothering his senses, as when Sarpedon dies in the *Iliad* (16.502–3):[25]

> Ὣς ἄρα μιν εἰπόντα τέλος θανάτοιο κάλυψεν
> ὀφθαλμοὺς ῥῖνάς θ'·
>
> He spoke and in that moment the completion of death covered
> his eyes and nostrils...

The sculpted stone medium adds to this effect because stone is not just what
conceals the corpse but also what reveals it—even constitutes it. Put bluntly, this
represented corpse is just as much of a stone as the represented stone in front of
it. Even allowing for paint, which would have clarified the distinction between
three different stone ontologies (background, body, and rock), the overlap suggests a permeability between different cold, inert, and senseless layers.[26] Body as
rock simulates person as object.[27] The very medium presents death as stone-
like—a material transformation in a person that has died.[28]

Moreover, by both showing and hiding a corpse in its sculpted representations
and within the substance of its marble fabric, the frieze turns attention upon the
imaginative processes at play in contemplating death and the dead in response to a
perceptible object. Like a real or painted funerary monument and painted figures at
the grave (see Chapter Two, section III), the sculpted presence of the corpse on this
frieze offers viewers a sensory and affective encounter with a person (not this
sculpted ex-person, necessarily, but a person, perhaps a loved one that will fight, is
fighting, has fought in battle—who might die, might have died, or has died). The
rock that blocks reminds viewers that this encounter is fleeting, contingent upon
their relationship with the image. The represented body is visible and invisible, present and absent. The corpse that sinks out of view thus echoes an epistemological
problem with a sensory one. Is this death? Would it make a difference if we could
see the whole body? Would it make a difference if the body was real, not graven?

Let us turn to a scene in which no dead bodies are shown: Scene 7 (Figures
4.2c and 4.2h). Positioned at the far-right end of block *k*, the scene should be

---

[25] There is also a similar idea in the veiling of Socrates in Plato's *Phaedo* (page 41) and of Ajax on the
Getty cup (pages 63–4). For Hector's death (in similar words), see page 100.

[26] The killing force that 'turns a man into a stone': Weil (2005: 5) [1989].

[27] See Nelson (2011: 175): 'The spectre of our eventual "becoming object"—of our (live) flesh one
day turning into (dead) meat—is a shadow that accompanies us throughout our lives.'

[28] On the complexities of this statement in the light of new materialist critique, see Wohl (2018: 20)
on the death of Astyanax in Euripides' *Trojan Women*, 'while death reduces living beings to inert matter,
it also releases a vitality latent within the inanimate'.

VICTORY, VICTORY, VICTORY?   157

visualized either near the south end of the frieze or just left of the centre.[29] Viewers are presented with a cluster of three fighting male figures. On the left, one nude figure, shown in three-quarters view from the rear, moves swiftly towards the right, his left arm outstretched and covered by his cloak (chlamys), which ripples in waves from his shoulder, indicating his motion.[30] Head tilted forwards, he directs his gaze down upon another nude figure who squats in rear view, resting on his right knee with his left foot braced upon the ground and his shield held up between them.[31] Behind the crouched figure another stands tall, stretching his torso and two arms upwards with his left elbow bent back over his head to deliver a killing blow. To the right, a clothed fourth figure is discernible, and appears to move away from the group, but the top part of the frieze is lost so the composition is unclear.[32] There is an object upon the ground beside one of his feet (a rock, a helmet, a head?).

Corpses are not present or visible in this snapshot. All figures are vigorously alive and the scene is one of rippling muscles and fabric. But it would be pedantic to insist that the concept of death is absent. It is suggested by the precarious imbalance of the scene: two against one, the disadvantage of the lower position, the defensive raise of the shield. Death is hinted to be in the minds of the sculpted figures: the determined purpose of the would-be killers, the dreaded experience from which the victim strives to defend himself—in the words of Simone Weil, 'this person becomes a corpse before anybody or anything touches him.'[33] The possibility of death is sculpted into the scene and anticipated by viewers in response.

The image carries further connotations of death when set against other battle scenes in the visual repertoire of Classical Athens. As Arrington observes, the conspicuous presence of dead humans (especially dead Greeks) on sacred sculpture in the fifth century BCE is, in itself, novel and remarkable.[34] Whether or not the bodies are visually prominent, and whether or not they are subjected to violence, their inclusion indicates that dead and dying figures wrought in stone were considered suitable for mortal and divine contemplation and might well have caught viewers' attention. The fact that fallen bodies on the west frieze seem to be catalysts for the battle that unfolds around them is particularly striking;[35]

---

[29] This block is usually visualized on the right-hand side of the west frieze in accordance with the 1787 reconstruction drawings by J. Stuart and N. Revett (followed, for example, in Blümel (1923: 27–30, pls. I–III)) and the current display of the originals in the British Museum and copies *in situ*. However, the 1994 study undertaken by Dimosthenis Giraud argues in favour of switching blocks *i* and *k* such that the right-hand end of block *k* would reach the centre of the frieze: Giraud (1994: 315–16).

[30] On rippling cloaks and motion in Graeco-Roman art, see Hutchinson (2020a: 8–10).

[31] This is one of only three shields on the frieze that show their exterior to the viewer.

[32] I include this fourth figure in Scene 8; see Table 4.1.   [33] Weil (2005: 5) [1989].

[34] Arrington (2015: 125–33).

[35] Important here is the argument in Saunders (2006), a doctoral thesis on the beautiful death in Archaic and Classical Athenian pottery, that the duel over the body and the retrieval of a warrior's body from the battlefield were more popular motifs on black-figure pots than on red-figure pots; David

the imagery does not just celebrate the living for their treatment of the dead,[36] it marks the dead as valuable.[37]

The composition, too, is significant: clusters of leaping and languid bodies—figures engaged in fierce activity around and about the dead or dying—echo scenes of mythological battle and mass slaughter on rocky terrain in wider painting and sculpture.[38] Let us pull out some of these common threads. Notable is the Amazonomachy that plays out across a fragmentary shield belonging to a statuette in Patras (Figure 4.3), a mid-second century CE Roman version in marble

FIGURE 4.3. Patras shield. Fragmentary shield relief in marble belonging to an Athena Parthenos statuette, mid-second century CE. Diameter 45 cm. Archaeological Museum of Patras: 6. Archaeological Museum of Patras/© Hellenic Ministry of Culture and Sports/Ephorate of Antiquities of Achaea. Image: © German Archaeological Institute at Athens (D-DAI-ATH-1973/2291), photographer: Hartwig Koppermann.

Saunders suggests, in relation to the appearance of these themes on the Nike west frieze, 'Their appearance in architectural sculpture illustrates what seems to be the Athenian *polis*' appropriation of a once élite-associated ideal' (246).

[36] See especially Arrington (2015: 174–6): the Nike west frieze is distinctive for its focus on the recovery of the Greek dead, a slant that gives prominence to the ethical victory of the Athenians in their treatment of the dead. See further note 8.

[37] See Saunders (2006: 274): what matters (for the purposes of a beautiful death) is that dead and dying warriors are 'seen to be valued'.

[38] The evidence that follows is problematic in that the argument is largely based on re-imagining fifth-century material based on ancient descriptions and copies and modern reconstructions. Nevertheless, congruent details give a sense of the sorts of images with which Classical Athenians would have been familiar.

of Phidias' Athena Parthenos, dated to *c.* 440 BCE.[39] As on the west frieze, the relief on the Patras shield is filled with action, with struggling figures displayed in a variety of poses, interspersed with bodies of the wounded and dead. Particularly remarkable is the nude corpse of a male figure, stretched out at the bottom of the scene. In this version he lies alone but it now seems clear that the fifth-century shield featured two corpses alongside one another—a nude Greek and a clothed Amazon—as seen on the Nashville replica, which broadly follows the 1981 reconstruction by Evelyn Harrison (Figure 4.4).[40]

FIGURE 4.4. Nashville Parthenon shield. Modern replica by Alan LeQuire, constructed 1982–1990, gilded and painted in 2002. Nashville, Tennessee. Image: domonabikeUSA/Alamy Stock Photo.

---

[39] For discussions and reconstructions of the shield exterior, see Brommer (1957: fig. 6); Jeppesen (1963: 2–23, esp. 9, fig. 3); Schlörb (1963: esp. 166, fig. 1); Harrison (1966: esp. pl. 38), (1981: esp. 297, fig. 4); Strocka (1967: esp. fig. 43), (1984: 192, fig. 4); Leipen (1971: 41–7, fig. 82); Hölscher and Simon (1976: esp. 122, fig. 1 and 139, fig. 2); Floren (1978: esp. 42, fig. 1); Meyer (1987: esp. 317, fig. 7); Gauer (1988: esp. 29, fig. 1); Davison (2009: 94–110); Arrington (2015: 154–66). See further Paus. 1.17.2 and 1.24.7; Plin. *HN* 36.18–19; Plut. *Per.* 31.4.

[40] See Harrison (1981: 287, fig. 4), brought to life by Alan LeQuire in the Nashville Parthenon (with more images available on the Nashville Parthenon website). An important difference: in Harrison's 1981 reconstruction, though the male corpse is left (like his counterpart on the Nike west frieze) in comparative peace, the clothed body of the Amazon has either been recently subjected to violence at spearpoint or is close to that end; this is also the case on the Strangford shield (images available on the British

160 FIGURING DEATH IN CLASSICAL ATHENS

But compositional affinities run deeper. The pose of the figure upon the ground in Scene 2 of the Nike frieze (Figures 4.2b, 4.2e) seems to be in dialogue with that of the wounded figure in the so-called 'helper group', a group included with slight variations in several versions and reconstructions of Phidias' shield: consider the Patras shield (lower right edge), a Roman relief in the Vatican museum (the 'Lateran relief', Figure 4.5), and the Nashville replica (far right, Figure 4.4).[41] Though the figure upon the ground in the Nike frieze is arranged in mirror

FIGURE 4.5. Lateran relief. Roman relief in marble, c. 125–140 CE. Height 95 cm, Width 128 cm. Lateran Museum, Rome: 10461. Image: GRANGER—Historical Picture Archive/Alamy Stock Photo.

Museum website), where the Amazon is shown pinned beneath the foot of the figure wielding the spear. This detail is not reproduced in the Nashville replica. As Arrington points out (2015: 160–1), the juxtaposition of a nude Greek corpse in 'undisturbed repose' and a clothed Amazon subjected to a 'violent death' proposes a contrast familiar to viewers in the fifth century BCE. To the extent that the humiliating alternative—Vernant's (1991a) 'disfigured corpse'—lurks in the background to the treatment of the dead and dying on the Nike frieze, the imagery taps into a vernacular of non-violent, beautiful death.

[41] The 'helper group' also seems to appear on a terracotta version of the shield from the Athenian agora and other fragmentary reliefs: for discussion see Harrison (1966: 121, nos. 6–7, 132–3, no. 1, pl. 40b), (1981: 307–8), the latter noting the similarity of the motif to that on a sarcophagus fragment in Brescia that has been thought to reflect the Marathon painting in the Stoa Poikile (see Harrison (1972b: 359, pl. 77, fig. 16)); Strocka (1967: 36–7, 50–3, 105, no. 2); Floren (1978: 53–4); Davison (2009: 98–9). Harrison (1997: 120) also saw an attempt to lift a fallen man in this image on the west frieze, which she compared to a similar group on the Bassai frieze (fig. 20).

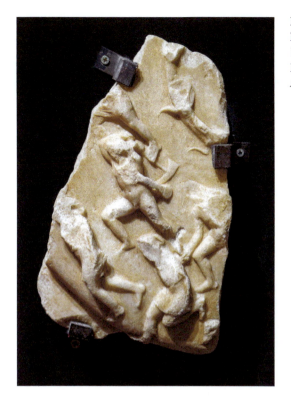

Figure 4.6. Conservatori shield. Fragmentary shield relief in marble, 150–200 CE. Museo Nuovo Capitolino, Rome: 916. Image: Stefano Ravera/Alamy Stock Photo.

image of his equivalent in the various 'helper groups', there are several echoes: notice the head lolling forwards, the legs extended with a slight bend in the knees, the torso lifted beneath the shoulder and turned outwards towards the viewer, one arm extended at the side, the other lying loosely forwards over his knees. For that matter, the would-be victor in Scene 7 of the west frieze (Figures 4.2c, 4.2h), arms bent back behind his head for a killing blow, might echo (softly, and again in mirror image) the Greek figure wielding an axe that is seen most clearly on the Conservatori shield, another fragmentary second-century CE Roman version in marble (Figure 4.6), and which has been included to the left of the Gorgon on the Nashville replica (Figure 4.4).[42] Coincidences in pose raise the possibility that ancient viewers of the Nike west frieze might have noticed not just the content (bodies fighting, dying, retrieving, and so on) but the form—

---

[42] The Greek axe-wielding figure is placed to the left of the Gorgon in several reconstructions: see e.g. Jeppesen (1963: 9, fig. 3); Harrison (1966: 125, no. 24, with pl. 38), (1981: 297, fig. 4); Strocka (1967: fig. 43), (1984: 192, fig. 4); Hölscher and Simon (1976: 122, fig. 1 and 139, fig. 2); Floren (1978: 59–60, with fig. 1); Gauer (1988: 29, fig. 1). Meyer (1987) reconstructed the Greek figure with a spear instead. An 'axe-swinging' pose has sometimes been associated with Theseus and appears in fifth-century Centauromachy scenes: see esp. Barron (1972: esp. 26–8), who suggests an origin for the motif in a fifth-century wall painting at Athens, probably the Centauromachy that was in the Theseion. See further Woodford (1974: 163); Cohen (1983: 175, with figs. 12.3 and 12.4).

162   FIGURING DEATH IN CLASSICAL ATHENS

subtle echoes of not just another battle but also an *artist's version* of a battle. The possibility is epistemologically significant because it defines reflection on death in response to the west frieze as culturally, artistically mediated.

Support for this point arises from the likelihood that there is not a direct one-to-one conversation here (between the Nike frieze and the shield of a cult statue nearby on the Acropolis) so much as a tapestry of imagery brimming with stylistic coincidences. The suggestion of rocky terrain over which the hoplite in Scene 5 leaps (Figures 4.2b, 4.2f) and behind which the nude corpse of Scene 3 recedes (Figures 4.2b, 4.2e), may have put the Nike battle scene, like that on the shield of Athena Parthenos,[43] in dialogue with paintings, such as those that are known to have existed in the Theseion and Stoa Poikile.[44] One important object here is the Niobid krater, a mixing bowl dated to 460–450 BCE and sometimes thought to recall wall painting in its incorporation of landscape elements, multiple groundlines, and distinctive abdominal features (Figures 4.7a and b).[45] Though the poses are different, there is a shared discourse on death between the nude body of the painted Niobid boy, who sinks behind a rock or hill, legs partially concealed in drapery, and the part-exposed, part-hidden nude corpse in Scene 3 of the Nike frieze.[46] Indeed, there is a similar combination of falling and fallen Niobid bodies with rocky terrain in multiple levels on a circular Roman relief (Figure 4.8), which might offer us a glimpse of the Niobid slaughter that, according to Pausanias, featured on the throne of Phidias' statue of Zeus at Olympia.[47]

[43] On the indication of terrain on the shield, see esp. Strocka (1967: 130), (1984: 195) (supporting a more subtle indication of terrain, in contrast to the more elaborate features proposed by Evelyn Harrison).

[44] Paintings on walls in the Stoa Poikile and Theseion are mentioned in Paus. 1.15 and 1.17.2–6. Stoa Poikile: Robert (1895: 1–45); Wycherley (1957: 31–45); Thompson and Wycherley (1972: 90–4); Hölscher (1973: 50–84); Shear (1984: 5–19); Castriota (1992: 76–89, 127–30); De Angelis (1996); Cruciani and Fiorini (1998: 19–76); Stansbury-O'Donnell (1999: 142–5), (2005); Dietrich (2010: 238–40). Theseion: Robert (1895: 46–52); Barron (1972); Cohen (1983: 175–6); Knauer (1986); Castriota (1992: 33–63). See further Arrington (2015: 199–203). Harrison (1972c) has argued for a relationship between the Nike south frieze, the shield of Athena Parthenos, and the Marathon painting in the Stoa Poikile.

[45] *BAPD* 206954; Beazley (1925: 338.9); *ARV*[2] 601.22, 1661; *Para* 395; *Add*[2] 266. See e.g. CVA Louvre 2, France 2: III *I d*, pls 1–4 (pls France 95–8) (E. Pottier), 'très beau style dit polygnotéen'. On how multiple levels and groundlines on pots may reflect wall paintings, see Barron (1972: 24); Davison (2009: 105); Neils (2009a: 113–14). See further Gardner (1889: 121), Six (1919: 130–1), and Denoyelle (1997: 16) on the arrow that has fallen near the handle on the Niobid side as suggestive of the unseen in a manner reminiscent of Mikon (though Gardner in fact associates the pot's style with Polygnotus). The argument is particularly strong for the Herakles side, where an unusual anatomical detail (a fourth abdominal line) may suggest that the Niobid painter closely followed another composition: Barron (1972: 23–4); Osborne (1998: 166–7). On the stylistic influence on the Marathon side, see further Six (1919); Simon (1963: 43–54); Barron (1972: 41–4); Harrison (1972b); Denoyelle (1997: 24–5, 27–8, 30, 32–4, 40–1); Boardman (2005: 69–71). On the Niobid side and the likelihood that it, too, is stylistically influenced by wall painting, see esp. Denoyelle (1997: 16–17).

[46] See further Arrington (2015: 162–6) for subtle compositional affinities between the Niobid krater, the shield of Athena Parthenos, and the Niobids on the throne of Phidias' Zeus at Olympia. For discussion of groundlines, rock-hills, and space on the Niobid krater, see Dietrich (2010: esp. 230–62).

[47] Paus. 5.11.2. On the Niobids on the throne of Zeus: Vogelpohl (1980: esp. 225); previous note.

(a)

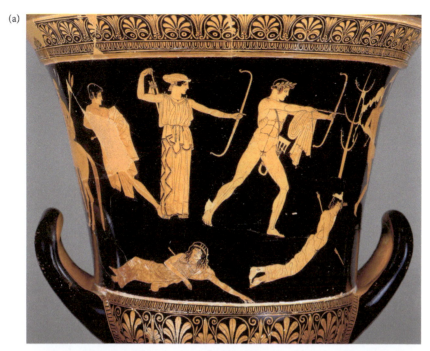

(b)

FIGURES 4.7a and b. Niobid mixing bowl (calyx-krater) (two sides). Attic red-figure krater, attributed to the Niobid Painter. *c.* 460–450 BCE. Height 54 cm, Diameter 51.5 cm. Found in Orvieto. Musée du Louvre, Paris: G 341. Image: © 1994 RMN-Grand Palais (musée du Louvre)/Hervé Lewandowski.

FIGURE 4.8. Niobid relief. Roman circular relief in marble, probably first century CE. Diameter 95 cm. British Museum, London: 1877,0727.1. Image: © The Trustees of the British Museum.

Though his legs are bent, the nude figure curled towards the viewer in the bottom right of the circular Niobid relief is even more alike the nude corpse on the Nike frieze than his painted equivalent on the pot.

An invitation to grapple with one image (and event) in terms of another was a regular feature of fifth-century culture. It is encouraged in this case by the pot's combination of Niobid slaughter on one side with a mysterious scene often thought to evoke the Athenian camp in the sanctuary of Herakles before the battle of Marathon (Figure 4.7b), prompting viewers to draw, and to probe, an analogy between the Niobids and the war dead—an analogy between the distant and more recent past that was also suggested in the Stoa Poikile, which combined scenes of Amazonomachy and the Trojan War with the battle at Marathon.[48]

---

[48] On the unity that is suggested by the continuity of lines from one side of the pot to another, see Gardner (1889: 121–2). Of course, the differences in kind between the deaths represented and anticipated

On the Nike temple too, the multiple resonances of the friezes—scenes that, even if recognized as mythological, also resonate with more recent battles and the contemporary environment—encourage a viewing predicated upon making links.[49]

As a result, while representation of the dead is differently inflected in each context (a slant that has been thoroughly explored by Arrington),[50] more significant for my purposes here is the extent to which imagery on the west frieze might have looked familiar—the possibility that viewers might have noticed common features and reflected upon the artistic framework that mediated their thinking. The corpse behind the rock is not just comparatively beautiful, concealed, peaceful, and so on; it is a reconfiguration of 'slaughtered nude on rocky ground', a reoccurring image—in its various permutations—in fifth-century Athenian painting and sculpture.[51]

The cultural framework within which the corpse lies compounds the invitation to see or not to see a body behind the rock, to see marble as alternatively sculpted body and sculpted rock, and to encounter death in a perceptible object or in the poses and imputed affective state of sculpted bodies. The implications are ethical and theological as well as epistemological. As Richard Neer argues in his discussion of the Procne and Itys group by Alcamenes:

> the centrality or marginality of animal sacrifice does not seem to be quite the issue; the moral dilemmas swirl not around the violence we do to animals, but around the violence we do to people when we regard them as no different from animals (or pieces of meat, or lumps of marble).[52]

When it comes to the temple of Athena Nike, missing death on the west frieze is, in itself, ethically problematic.[53] This is all the more poignant because some have interpreted it as a frieze that celebrates the Athenians for their ethical victory in

in these scenes are undeniable: in the scene of Niobid slaughter there are no efforts to retrieve the dead and the killers are unopposed divinities.

[49] On the relations between myth and history in Greek painting see e.g. Hölscher (1973: 71–3). See further Arrington (2015: 146–54). On the implications of analogical viewing for meditation on death in a different context, see Clifford (2023).

[50] See Arrington (2015: 133–76) for detailed analysis of representations of the war dead in a variety of sacred contexts (including on the Parthenon metopes, the shield of Athena Parthenos, the throne of Zeus at Olympia, the friezes on the temple of Hephaestus in the Athenian agora, and the friezes on the temple of Athena Nike).

[51] For meditation on the implications of coincidences between subject matter and style in a different medium (photography), see Dyer (2005).

[52] Neer (2012: 118). The point made in Elsner (1996: 529) (in the context of religiousness and ritual) is also applicable here, 'The represented is not just in the image, the represented *is* the image.'

[53] Comparable here is emphasis in Greek tragedy on the visuality of bodies that are about to die: see page 129, note 91. Consider, too, images on pots of Achilles and Penthesilea, where the moment of violence, death, and division is simultaneously one of beauty, desire, and longing: for example, *BAPD* 211565 and 310389. See further Spivey (2018: 220, fig. 72) on the questionable ethics of seeing a murder victim as a 'masterpiece' (*The Death of Marat*, by Jacques-Louis David).

166 FIGURING DEATH IN CLASSICAL ATHENS

respect for the dead (for treating the dead not as meat, not as aesthetically valuable, but as people).[54]

Consider, moreover, the wider visual ensemble within which the west frieze must have been viewed. Since the balustrade touched the west side of the temple,[55] there was little space for viewers to stand directly beneath the temple frieze. It must therefore have primarily been seen from far below, from the base of the bastion or the ascending approach through the Propylaea gateway. As a result, any viewers of the west frieze could not help but encounter, at the same time, another sort of death below it: another victim, an animal set prominently in the centre of the western face of the balustrade and shown in the moment of its slaughter.[56] An imperative to notice not just sacrifice but—unusually and prominently—the act of killing dovetails with the invitation to recognize a person's death above it. The combination is provoking and complicates ideas about victory as much as ideas about death.[57] Carved in rock, picked out in paint, positioned on the west end of the Acropolis, the sculpted corpse puts death in the picture. Slipping behind the represented rock, dissolving into its own stone-medium, positioned (in Classical Athens) high up upon the bastion above a sacred victim, it puts pressure on what viewers are supposed to do with it.

Visibility is important. But perhaps, in this case, not so much the visibility of corpses as overall visibility, and what this does for visual impact. The 'viewing and obscuring' of temple friezes is a notorious point of debate,[58] and the west frieze is in a particularly elevated position, perched on a cliff edge. Photographs such as the one in Figure 4.1 indicate that the view was not bad—the frieze was visible (probably even more so in colour)—but visual impact may have been more impressionistic, with compositional suggestions (the multiple associations of lifting the dead, for example, or visual analogies between one part of the temple complex and another) carrying greater resonance than the absence or presence of a cloak type.[59] Proximity aside, the west end of the temple is unquestionably

---

[54] See note 36.

[55] See Simon (1997: 129–33) on the cuttings in the back of the west balustrade blocks for the temple steps.

[56] On the emphatic placement of sacrificial slaughter here, see Jameson (1994: 317–19), with notes 78 and 79 below. See the next section of this chapter for further discussion of the sacred framework within which the west frieze is set.

[57] Indeed, as Osborne (1994b: 85–6) argues, the balustrade sculpture, with its female bodies presented and concealed in folds of drapery, frustrates viewers, unravelling the promise of victory even as it is constructed: 'both what representation is and what Victory is are questioned'. This also leads me to question the confidence with which victory is justified here as the goal; compare Stähli (2005: 43) on Archaic and Classical pot painting, 'Es geht nicht darum, Gewalt als solche, sondern das Ziel, zu dem sie eingesetzt wird, zu rechtfertigen.'

[58] See especially Osborne (1987); Hölscher (2009); Marconi (2009).

[59] The significance of the exomis (one-shouldered tunic) for identification of mythological or historical subjects on friezes (and, especially, its indication on the north and west friezes that these are 'old deeds', παλαιὰ ἔργα): Harrison (1997: 117, note 40). The probability of subject identifications: Pemberton (1972: 304),

prominent: this is what confronted viewers as they approached the Classical Acropolis. It demands to be noticed.

That viewers do encounter death in the frieze is unproblematic. More problematic is the nature of those encounters. The sculpted dead body is partially perceptible, materially and ontologically complex, aesthetically, ethically, and theologically complicated: it generates encounters that are imaginatively contingent and epistemologically challenging.

III. A SACRED ART OF DEATH

Now let us delve deeper into the dialogues between sculptural representations on the west frieze and the cultural frameworks within which they sit, the religious-mythological-artistic vernacular of ancient Athens. This time, I focus upon Scene 6, which features a six-figure group with a wounded or dead body at its centre (Table 4.1, Figures 4.2c, 4.2g, and 4.2h), and the mythological foil presented by Sarpedon.

On the left, a nude male figure lunges to the right in three-quarters view, the arc of the shield on his left arm forming a downward swooping curve that meets the arch of a second nude figure, who bends double to grasp a fallen nude figure about the chest and shoulders. The latter body is lifted into a semi-reclined position, and the crescent formed by his torso and thighs continues the undulating flow of lines that cascade from the first figure's shield, over the second's bent back, and through the body spread upon the ground.[60] In mirrored counterpart, a fourth nude figure to the right forms a convex protective arch, twisting from a rear view to hold his shield to the left above the fallen body and reaching with his right arm to grasp it by the ankle. Above, roughly in the centre of the group, a fifth warrior (this time clothed) leaps to meet him, cloak streaming behind. To the right, the sixth, again clothed, is shown from the rear, either protecting the fallen figure by opposing the leaping warrior or else joining his attack. Conceivably, the distinction between clothing and nudity might signify sides of the battle. (This might have been further indicated by painted cloaks, shield motifs, and helmet types, little of which survives.) That said, the predominance of nude

'the west frieze is virtually complete and a subject should be found [...]. One can only conclude that the average Athenian was sufficiently well informed about the battle and its history to identify it easily.' In fact, our evidence from one, admittedly later, ancient viewer, Pausanias, suggests that the decoration may not have been the most obvious thing for comment in response to this temple. Pausanias' only observation (*Description of Greece* 1.22.4): 'From there the sea is visible, and there, so they say, Aegeus threw himself to his death.' Then follows a brief account of Aegeus' suicide on thinking Theseus was dead. The significance of the view *from* the Acropolis (the framing of Salamis by the Propylaea): Martin-McAuliffe and Papadopoulos (2012).

[60] The unusual nature of the flowing curves in this scene: Blümel (1923: 29).

168 FIGURING DEATH IN CLASSICAL ATHENS

figures and shield interiors suggests that looking for 'who's who' misses much of this frieze's impact, especially with respect to death.

One striking compositional feature here is the central image, which recalls the popular Sarpedon motif, now best known from the red-figure mixing bowl (calyx-krater) in the Museo Nazionale Cerite, potted, painted, and signed by Euphronios and dated to the second half of the sixth century (Figure 4.9).[61] The outstretched nude body, loose and heavy in the arms of a hunched figure (or two) is, in both representations, displayed at the heart of the composition with one arm reaching or dangling to the ground. On the krater, the retrieval of the body is framed by two spectating warriors in profile, standing sentry; on the frieze, by two poised fighters in mirror reflection, one displaying his nude torso in a frontal position, the other clothed and seen from the back.

Even more similar is the pose of Sarpedon's corpse on a mug held in the Merseyside Museum in Liverpool and dating to the second half of the fifth century:[62] as on the frieze, the corpse's torso is raised to form a gentle s-shaped wave from the scoop of his torso through the bend of his knees (Figure 4.10).

My point is not that the figure on the west frieze *is* Sarpedon: as explored by Nigel Spivey,[63] the dead-body motif is popular in the sixth and fifth centuries and beyond, with the Sarpedon tradition bleeding into representations of Memnon,[64] and later unnamed men and women on white-ground funerary jugs.[65] The representation on this frieze is, rather, in dialogue with all these various images and figures.

Let us consider some features of the Sarpedon motif in the Greek cultural tradition, before probing how they might shape encounters with death in the west frieze. The divine frame in which Sarpedon's death unfolds is important. On Euphronios' krater (Figure 4.9), for example, the presence of the immortals Hypnos, Thanatos, and Hermes, escort of the dead and messenger of Zeus, around the dead hero taps into theological and thanatological problems at the core of the myth. In the *Iliad* (16.419–683), too, the 'completion of death' (τέλος θανάτοιο, 16.502) that shrouds Sarpedon's sensory perception not only distinguishes mortals from immortals (as usually emphasized in discussion of death, mortality, and immortality) but also unites them in mutual impotence and sorrow. The problem of Sarpedon's mortality is also a problem for his immortal father Zeus, who is bound by the need for cosmic balance (16.440–9). Consider the troubling image with which Zeus' decision to allow Sarpedon's death is marked (16.458–61):

---

[61] *BAPD* 187. Compare a similar set-up, though framed by two goddesses in motion, on a red-figure cup in the British Museum (1841,0301.22), dated 510–500 BCE: *BAPD* 201052. On this vase and especially the dead-body motif ('the afterlife of an image'), see Spivey (2018: esp. 157–9, and chs. 7 and 8).

[62] *BAPD* 17489.   [63] See note 61.   [64] See page 62, note 27.

[65] For example: *BAPD* 212420; 216353. See pages 81 and 96 (including notes 93 and 148).

FIGURE 4.9. Red-figure mixing bowl (calyx-krater), painted by Euphronios. *c.* 515 BCE. Museo Nazionale Cerite, Cerveteri. Image: GRANGER—Historical Picture Archive/Alamy Stock Photo.

FIGURE 4.10. Red-figure mug fragments. 450–400 BCE. Liverpool, Merseyside Museum: 50.42.12. Image: © National Museums Liverpool.

170 FIGURING DEATH IN CLASSICAL ATHENS

Ὣς ἔφατ’, οὐδ’ ἀπίθησε πατὴρ ἀνδρῶν τε θεῶν τε·
αἱματοέσσας δὲ ψιάδας κατέχευεν ἔραζε
παῖδα φίλον τιμῶν, τόν οἱ Πάτροκλος ἔμελλε
φθίσειν ἐν Τροίῃ ἐριβώλακι τηλόθι πάτρης.

So Hera spoke, and the father of men and gods did not disobey;
but he poured down bloody drops upon the earth,
honouring his beloved son, whom, to his sorrow, Patroclus was about
to waste in Troy with its rich soil, far from his fatherland.

Fact or metaphor, the shower of blood from Zeus is infused with horror, pathos, and honour alike: the gory reality of the drops of Sarpedon's blood that will soak the dust (κόνιος . . . αἱματοέσσης, 486) from his thudding heart (ἁδινὸν κῆρ, 481); the tears of regret and futility that represent Zeus' grief over the loss of his son in tearful war (μάχης . . . δακρυοέσσης, 436), with the fleeting suggestion of father–son separation in 'far from his fatherland' (τηλόθι πάτρης, 461); and, perhaps, early hints of bloody offerings from kin that the hero Sarpedon will receive in Lycia, granted by Zeus (674–5).[66] Buried in the literary and visual mythological traditions of Sarpedon is the overweening power of death, and mortal and immortal impotence, grief, regret, and honour.

On that note, it is striking that the west and east friezes present contrasting scenes of male strife and death on one end, and a congregation of figures, many of whom are female, on the other.[67] Traditional interpretations understand the east frieze as a divine assembly, possibly the birth of Athena.[68] Following these, the contrasts of motion, dress, and mortality might support either a distinction between two realms (human strife versus divine freedom from care),[69] or else divine attendance at or supervision of mortal battle from afar (as in the *Iliad*), perhaps bringing or celebrating victory. But it is worth thinking about what it does to frame a temple with contrasting groups of static seated or standing draped female figures and leaping and falling nude male hoplites. The war scenes on three sides of the temple layer new meaning upon the domesticity of the pre-dominantly female-gendered space on the east frieze, imbuing it with the pride, fear, loss, memories, and mourning that define the emotional state of those left at home and other battle survivors (see Figures 4.11a–c).[70]

---

[66] For this infusion, see especially Lateiner (2002).

[67] Analysis of divine figure identities: Harrison (1997: 110–16).   [68] See note 10.

[69] Harrison (1997: 110), 'This gathering of powers is timeless, while the battles have their separate places in the past.'

[70] I note here Pemberton (1972: 309–10): though she focused on suitable identities for the divinities rather than their visual impact, she emphasized that the gathering of gods honoured the war dead (along with Athena Nike and Poseidon, representatives of land and sea power).

FIGURE 4.11A. Corner block *a* from the east frieze of the temple of Athena Nike. 426–421 BCE. Length 48 cm. Acropolis Museum, Athens: Acr. 18135 (east side). Image: © Acropolis Museum, 2018, photographer: Yiannis Koulelis.

FIGURE 4.11B. Block *b* from the east frieze of the temple of Athena Nike. 426–421 BCE. Length 204.5 cm. Acropolis Museum, Athens: Acr. 18136 (east side). Image: © Acropolis Museum, 2018, photographer: Yiannis Koulelis.

These associations are strengthened by the wider visual landscape in which Athenians were immersed: congregations of mourning figures in the Theatre of Dionysus; gatherings of mourners on funerary ware;[71] the frontality associated with both votive and funerary statue types in the Archaic period;[72] and the 'seated woman' motif and frontal gaze in the new wave of private funerary relief sculpture

---

[71] See page 62, including note 28.

[72] On the frontality of an Archaic kouros and the existential reflection that it generates, see Osborne (1988: 6–9); Elsner (2006: 73–86).

172 FIGURING DEATH IN CLASSICAL ATHENS

FIGURE 4.11c. Block *c* from the east frieze of the temple of Athena Nike. 426–421 BCE. Length 173.5 cm. Acropolis Museum, Athens: Acr. 18138 (east side). Image: © Acropolis Museum, 2018, photographer: Yiannis Koulelis.

that emerges in the last quarter of the fifth century.[73] Indeed, others have remarked on the thanatological significance of the 'figure seated upon a rock', an instance of which can be seen on block *b* and which occurs in other contemporary Athenian art in scenes associated with the underworld (Figure 4.11b).[74]

Amidst this wealth of visual connections, the figures in the eastern tableau, comparatively motionless and comprised of mostly frontal bodily poses, invite viewers to pause, contemplate, and reflect (mentally as well as bodily, mirroring the frontal poses of the figured women with their own).[75] On the Acropolis, a sacred space that was a site of Persian defeat and destruction, the divinities on one side of the temple of Athena Nike reflect upon slaughter with regret and remembrance (as well as, conceivably, triumph). The image of the fallen hoplite is loaded with divine and mortal sorrow and the consolation of the lasting memorial and the honour it brings,[76] as well as more positive themes of Athenian military, political, and ethical victory. To focus on victory alone misses the more complicated way in which death in sacred space brings two realms together.

Moreover, the bloody libation with which Zeus marks the death of Sarpedon in the *Iliad* points towards the other occasion of death that comes to mind when the slain warrior on the west frieze is viewed as one part of a sacred whole

---

[73] For the 'seated woman' motif, see the grave stele of Hegeso: Athens, National Archaeological Museum 3624, dated 410–400 BCE. For frontality, see the 'cat stele': Athens, National Archaeological Museum 715, dated 430–420 BCE.

[74] See Palagia (2005: 181–2) on the motif of the seated figure on a rock on the temple at Ilissos, in Polygnotos' Nekyia painting in the Lesche of the Knidians at Delphi, and on various painted pots. Though Palagia compares the 'sad introspection' of the Ilissos friezes with the more 'triumphal mood' of the Nike temple (page 190), making sense of both against the backdrop of the early years of the Peloponnesian War, I think such 'sad introspection' can also be found in, and is provoked by, the Nike east frieze.

[75] On the possibilities and constraints of a temple's different sculpted spaces and the impact of frontality upon its viewers, see Osborne (2009).

[76] In parallel with the exempla of funeral orations, many of which, as Nathan Arrington argues, may be illustrated on this temple: see Arrington (2015: 175–6).

FIGURE 4.12. North slab IV from the balustrade of the temple of Athena Nike. *c.* 410 BCE. Length 123 cm, Height 105 cm, Width 37 cm. Acropolis Museum, Athens: Acr. 972. Image: © Acropolis Museum, 2018, photographer: Yiannis Koulelis.

comprised of the temple, its sanctuary space (including two altars and votive offerings), and the framing balustrade: sacrifice.[77] Consider block north IV from the balustrade, which depicts two winged Nike figures with a sacrificial victim, possibly for Athena, possibly for another god or a hero such as Theseus (Figure 4.12).[78]

As observed above, one important link between the images on the balustrade and those on the temple is death: specifically, death in a sacred context.[79]

---

[77] Though I focus on killing and death, I do not claim that bloodshed was central to ancient sacrifice per se, as food, killing, or expiation, for instance, as in e.g. Burkert 1983 [1972]; Detienne and Vernant (1989); Girard (2013) [1972]. More recently, scholarship has sought to de-emphasize killing and eating as aspects of ancient Greek sacrifice: see e.g. Faraone and Naiden (2012); Naiden (2015).

[78] The species and gender of cattle on the balustrade has provoked debate. Cows or other offerings to Athena: Kekulé (1869: 28, 33–4), (1881: esp. 4) (though Kekulé had only seen the sculpted animal that could be a bull or a cow). Bulls, indicating chthonic rites to a hero (e.g. Theseus): Simon (1985: 282–5), (1997: 135–40), followed in Hurwit (2004: 190); bulls as part of the 'Niketeria' (thanksgiving celebrations for victory): Hölscher (1997: esp. 153–6). σφάγια for battle victory sought and won: Jameson (1994: 317–19).

[79] Other visual links between animal and human sacrificial victims on the Acropolis (real animals led to the Altar of Athena Polias in the Panathenaia; the sculpture of Procne and Itys): Barringer (2005: 169). On movements of the Nike figures as invitations to viewers to imitate: Simon (1997: 133). On 'divine reflexivity'—divine ritual activity as a catalyst for their cult in the mortal realm: Patton (2009: 170–80).

174 FIGURING DEATH IN CLASSICAL ATHENS

Representations of sacrifice on the balustrade are in dialogue not just with the peaceful procession of the Parthenon's continuous frieze but also with the battles fought in its metopes, in the friezes and pediments of the Athena Nike temple, and also (more problematically) with dramatic representations of explicit human sacrifice in the Theatre of Dionysus.[80] In fact, if the north frieze of the temple of Athena Nike was, indeed, understood to represent the expulsion of Eurystheus from Attica,[81] it too—in a mythological vernacular infused with memories of Euripides' tragic version of the story around 430 BCE (*Children of Herakles*)—might recall the sacrifice of Herakles' daughter (and ultimately, too, the death of Eurystheus), and the divine support these bought as a necessary precondition to victory. In a cultural imagination where gods and heroes might require the lives of young girls (Iphigenia, Polyxena, Erechtheus' daughter) and do often require animals, and where the community requires the lives of young men and the support of the gods, the balustrade sculpture, often celebrated for its charm, beauty, jollity, and frivolity, taps into an altogether more serious tone on the Acropolis.[82]

The west frieze of the Athena Nike temple is not just about Athenian superiority (martial victory on the field; ethical victory in attention to the dead) but also about the deaths out of which mortal and divine outcomes are built.[83] The fallen figures spread across the bottom of the west frieze appear visually and metaphorically as the ground upon which the living fight for victory and survival. Just as Zeus' own bloody libation that honours and grieves for Sarpedon also marks

---

[80] This is not to say that human sacrifice was, in fact, practised but that it was prevalent, as Dennis Hughes (1991: 185) puts it, '*as an idea*'. On the overlap in tragedy between sacrifice and murder (as an ethical commentary not on sacrifice but on murder): Henrichs (2012). As Albert Henrichs observed, Burkert (1966) goes too far in his suggestion that human sacrifice stands behind animal sacrifice more generally (he is also hampered by his emphasis on the origins of the genre, rather than the contemporary dialogues in which it participates). Nevertheless, his linking of human with animal sacrifice and emphasis on 'human existence face to face with death' is relevant and works across media as well as within them (in his case, tragedy) (see esp. pages 111–13, 116–21). See further Henrichs (2006). Human sacrifice was implicitly represented on the Acropolis. Consider the late fifth-century BCE statue of Procne and Itys, discussed in e.g. Barringer (2005) and Neer (2012).

[81] As argued in Harrison (1997: 117–20) and supported, with further analysis, by Schultz (2009).

[82] The tone is both more serious and fractured by uncertainty: see Osborne (1994b: 86) with note 57 above. See further Athanassaki (2023), who proposes a link between Euripides' *Erechtheus* and the temple of Athena Nike (among other monuments) but takes the view that the temple 'sent a confident message of victory' (page 182) and so argues that Euripides' play, in promoting peace, responded to the temple with a 'sceptical note' (page 184).

[83] For similar emphasis on mortal–divine relations in the context of sacrifice, see Kroll (1979: 352) on the Parthenon frieze as a votive relief that expresses the bond forged between human and god; Bremmer (2007: 139–41) on sacrifice as ordering relationships not marking hierarchy; Osborne (2016: 247–8) for emphasis on sharing and the assumed similarities between gods and men in sacrifice; Gaifman (2018: esp. 151) on imagery of libation and 'affirmation of ties and hierarchies among mortals and immortals'. Contrast the emphasis in Vernant (1989: esp. 21–38) on how sacrifice and meat consumption position men *between* gods and beasts (focusing upon Hesiod's foundation myth in *Theogony* 535–57).

VICTORY, VICTORY, VICTORY? 175

and initiates his death, so the wider sacrificial environment—including the visual-material presence of the decorated temple and any bloodless offerings within the sanctuary space—suffuses the fallen hoplite with the weight of necessity, together with gratitude and celebration. The figured bloody deaths are simultaneously bloodless offerings to Athena Nike (ἀγάλματα):[84] they make death a valuable part of what it is to be an Athenian on the sacred Acropolis.[85]

Now, it is important that the fallen figure is not only Sarpedon. He could be Sarpedon but he could also be Memnon, or another mythological, historical, or contemporary figure. Scholarship has put considerable effort into identifying the subject matter of the west frieze, agreeing (implicitly, at least) on four points: the theme is Athenian 'victory'; all the figures are Greek; a specific battle can be identified; the identity of that battle matters. While interpretations disagree as to which battle is depicted (mythological or historical, distant or recent) the goal is to identify the subject (and so the meaning) of the representation and find in it a celebration of Athens. But much of the power of the fallen warrior in Scene 6 lies in his lack of specificity (or multiple possibilities).[86] It is not just that his death can stand for all war deaths, but that his translatability—and, especially, the ambiguity as to his national allegiance—signals the destructive power of death, what Elaine Scarry calls the 'unmaking' of the human being:

> The "unmaking" of the human being, the emptying of the nation from his body, is equally characteristic of dying or being wounded, for the in part naturally "given" and in part "made" body is deconstructed.[87]

The bodiliness of death is about more than sensory experience, or sensory deprivation, and the evidential proof of the corpse; it is also about the bodiliness of

---

[84] For this idea, see especially Neer (2012) on how sculptures such as the Calf-Bearer and Procne and Itys put pressure on the distinction between blood sacrifice and bloodless gift. See further Comella (2002: 31–2, fig. 19, 'Atene 7') on an Archaic votive relief that represents (and constitutes) an artisan's bloodless sacrifice; Elsner (2012b) (on the visibility of sacrifice in late Roman art). On the theologies of visual evidence, see Gaifman (2015), (2016).

[85] Though, to some extent, the temple structure frames its friezes and so separates them from the world of viewers, as explored in Osborne (2017), the figural sculpture also narrativizes the space around it in the way discussed by Neer and Kurke (2019: 69–72) (though, as preserved, the continuous west frieze does not encroach upon the space of viewers so clearly as, say, the Dying Warrior on the east pediment of the temple of Aphaia at Aegina, discussed by Neer and Kurke on page 70, fig. 2.23). Important here is Marconi (2004b) on temple *kosmos* as a system of adornment that participated in organization of the world, including cultural and social identity and relations with the gods. See further Neer (2013: 458): 'orderly architecture might provide a *model* for at least some Greek conceptions of a cosmically ordered universe'. The sacred frame of the temple and thanatological order: Arrington (2015: 133).

[86] This is true of other images and scenes on the temple. On the south frieze, the impact of the battle operates on a scale of specificity from 'war scene' to 'battle with Persians' to 'the battle of Marathon/Plataea'. Several possibilities coexist, as evidenced by the fact that different scholars have identified differently suitable historical and mythological themes for friezes on the temple.

[87] Scarry (1985: 121–4, citation at 122).

176 FIGURING DEATH IN CLASSICAL ATHENS

being just a body, a self-less mass.[88] In the *Iliad*, the moment of Sarpedon's slaughter is compared to the felling of a tree axed for ship's timber (16.482–4):

ἤριπε δ' ὡς ὅτε τις δρῦς ἤριπεν ἢ ἀχερωΐς,
ἠὲ πίτυς βλωθρή, τήν τ' οὔρεσι τέκτονες ἄνδρες
ἐξέταμον πελέκεσσι νεήκεσι νήϊον εἶναι·

He fell, like when some man fells an oak or poplar
or tall pine, which wood-working men on the mountains
cut down with whetted axes to serve as ship's timber.

This simile works in numerous ways—the contrast of constructive work (and the art of poetic language) with the destructive craft of war; the echoes of the fleet that brought Patroclus to Troy; the ordinariness of Sarpedon's climactic end—but at least one way is in how the poetic medium expresses the brutality of Sarpedon's 'unmaking' in the translation of his self into an artefact, effected by the killing blow: the 'force' that turns person to 'thing'.[89] He becomes in death not just an inanimate object but also matter for craft. A similar permeability can be observed on the west frieze and points both to the violence inherent in sacrificial and martial killing and to the cultural processes that not only represent but also generate, and so constitute, ideas about death.[90] Here, a man unfolds like a garment (Scene 6, Figures 4.2c and 4.2g); elsewhere, a body slips back and forth between rock, body, and stone, the sculptural matter of the temple's fabric (Scene 3, Figures 4.2b and 4.2e). Like Sarpedon, whose slaughter at the hands of another man's skill is fashioned with words and an axe into poetic art and boat-building material, death-turned-*kosmos* on a temple frieze turns attention upon the ways in which ideas about death are built out of carved stone in sacred space.

IV. LIFE AND DEATH IN THE BALANCE

I turn now to a scene that has been foundational to some interpretations of the representational content and significance of the west frieze: Scene 4 (Figures 4.2b and 4.2f). On the left, a nude male figure in frontal view is caught in motion, balanced with his weight on his right leg and his left extended to the right, apparently stamping downwards: the line of his thigh meets the upturned face of

---

[88] Though this may not be how the body is viewed by others. Note, for example, *Il.* 16.568, where Sarpedon is referred to as Zeus' dear son: Sarpedon still holds value as a person in the eyes of Zeus.

[89] In the translated language of Simone Weil (2005: 26) [1989]. Though she is focused on what force does to men before they die, either transforming them to 'the level of inert matter' or 'blind force', what she notices in the similes also works for the result of such force: death.

[90] See especially Tatum (2003: 116–35) on the poetry in and of killing.

the partially draped nude male figure on the ground beneath him, and traces of his foot are discernible on that man's abdomen. But this fallen figure is not yet defeated. The arrangement of his body sets him in mirror image to the triumphant figure above: bracing his left elbow and right foot upon the floor, possibly attempting to rise, he too presents one leg straight, one leg bent, and the concave sweep of his body echoes the gentle curve of the torso above that leans in towards its falling opponent. Each cloak (chlamys), too, billows in arches that follow the rounded shoulders and backs of the two figures, framing their bodies as a twofold composition. These figures are locked in mortal combat.

Faintly discernible in the space between them is what appears to be a tree with a shield mounted upon it: a battle trophy. In the classical period, a trophy ($\tau\rho\acute{o}\pi\alpha\iota o\nu$) might be erected by the victors on the site of a battle's decisive turning point ($\tau\rho o\pi\acute{\eta}$), the watershed moment in a battle where the enemy turned and fled.[91] Here, however, figures across the frieze are still fighting; the struggle is ongoing. How, then, can a trophy already be present?[92] One argument is that this trophy sets the visible scene of combat on the site of a former battle,[93] but this interpretation prioritizes a narrative reading over a consideration of what it does to combine a picture of a trophy with a raging battle scene.

Surely the crucial point here is that it is not clear which way this struggle (and the wider battle) will go.[94] The man balancing upon one leg just might be tipping backwards; the one on the ground could be getting back up. In fact, this latter possibility is supported by interpretations that claim that the figured trophy is what marks the overall scene on the west frieze as specific, as a representation of the mythological recovery by Athenians of the corpses of the seven warriors

---

[91] Trundle (2013: 126): 'All sources agree that the name *tropaion* derived from the turning point—the *trope*—of the battle...' On the ancient Greek battle trophy: Woelcke (1911); Janssen (1957); Picard (1957: 16–64); West (1965: xxxix–xlii), with catalogue; Pritchett (1974: 246–75); Lonis (1979: 129–46); Stroszeck (2004); Trundle (2013); Duffy (2018: 30–4); Kinnee (2018: chs. 4 and 5); Nováková and Šályová (2019). Trophies in the fifth century were often temporary structures constructed on the battlefield from the armour of the defeated. There is also evidence for more permanent marble structures in the Classical period at Salamis, Marathon, and Plataea (on which see Vanderpool (1966); West (1969); Beschi (2002); Stroszeck (2004: 320–1); Shear (2016: 13–14)) and sculptural representations of trophies in sanctuaries (see Stroszeck (2004: 303)). See further Orlandos (1922), (1958a), (1958b), (1961a), (1961b) for the excavation and restoration of a fourth-century stone monument at Leuctra. Note especially the proximity of some permanent trophies to tombs, especially the Marathon trophy to the tombs of the fallen (Stroszeck (2004: 317); Nováková and Šályová (2019: 197–8)) and the affinity between columnar permanent trophies and columnar funerary monuments (Beschi (2002: 90, 94)).

[92] Janssen (1957: 81–2) points out that this composition mostly appears on Roman sarcophagi from the second century CE.

[93] For example: Pemberton (1972: 304); Harrison (1997: 120–1); Shear (2016: 353) (arguing that the frieze shows the aftermath of a battle).

[94] See Hurwit (1999: 231–2) in support: 'it may be the struggle, rather than the conquest, that is at the core of the Acropolis's imagery and ideology' (page 231).

178 FIGURING DEATH IN CLASSICAL ATHENS

that fought against Thebes from the site of that former battle (which is marked by the trophy—soon to be replaced by a new one).[95] The position of the fallen but not dead figure beneath the trophy has then been held to have an impact on the narrative flow of the frieze, with the man (identified as Theseus) initiating renewed vigour among the Athenians on the south end of the frieze.[96]

But even accepting the possibility that this figure could be Theseus (which is plausible but needs knowledge and considerable work from viewers to find it), a focus on story seems to miss a meaningful *lack* of narrative. It is not obvious that this is a turning point for the better. Rather, the symbol of a turning point appears alongside a figure in crisis who might have lost or might be getting back up: his life hangs in the balance at its own existential watershed. Combined with a precarious fight, this trophy does not symbolize victory obtained (a retrospective assessment) but the potential for a decisive turn in either direction. The trophy, with its circular shield, acts like an axle about which both men spin.[97]

The precarious possibilities that inhere in this scene fit with the 'rhetoric of struggle' that Nathan Arrington has identified in public casualty lists.[98] One of the few surviving figural reliefs from the top of a casualty list, dated to the second half of the fifth century and held in Oxford (Figure 4.13),[99] shows the fragmentary remains of two figures, one of whom is seated nude upon the ground, while the other lunges towards him, apparently clothed.[100] This is a beautiful death of the sort discussed by Jean-Pierre Vernant in his essay on Homer's *Iliad*:[101] the

[95] Evelyn Harrison (1997) argues that the west frieze depicts the recovery of the bodies of the seven (drawing on Eur. *Supp.* 647–8). Stewart (1985: 56) agrees that the detail of the trophy indicates that a specific battle is meant but reserves judgement on what it might be.

[96] Harrison (1997: 120–1): 'Then comes the turn of the tide of battle, the *trope*, appropriately in front of the trophy of the former battle' (page 120).

[97] This fits with imagery of death as a turning point elsewhere in Athenian culture. For example, looking ahead in time to Sophocles' *OC*, discussed in the previous chapter, metaphorical images of death as the turning post in a race (*OC* 91), or the turn/fall of the scales (*OC* 1508), or even the 'down-turning' of his life that Oedipus requests from the Eumenides (*OC* 102–3) have a counterpart here in the visualized 'turning point' of the battle and the figure that tips over at a kick of a foot like a set of scales. Rachel Bespaloff's essay on the *Iliad* offers an interesting slant on this point (2005: 50) [1947], 'Who is good in the *Iliad*? Who is bad? Such distinctions do not exist; there are only men suffering, warriors fighting, some winning, some losing.' On preservation of the defeated in artistic representations, see Henderson (1994: 129): 'it only brings them closer than ever to your own warmest, most comradely, heart'.

[98] Arrington (2011), (2015: 104–8).

[99] Clairmont (1983: 202–3); Arrington (2011: 197–8), (2015: 101–3, 107, fig. 3.3); Goette (2009: 189–90).

[100] The impact is similar to that of the grave stele that marked the cenotaph of Dexileos, dated 394/3 BCE and held in the Kerameikos Museum in Athens: Kerameikos Museum P 1130. (Though note that Arrington (2011: 196–202) emphasizes the difference between private and public reliefs—the former showing 'complete conquest', the latter articulating struggle. He associates the 'complete conquest' on private reliefs with the moment of rout.) On the Dexileos monument, see Osborne (2010).

[101] Vernant (1991a). See further Loraux (1982) on the shift from the 'beautiful dead' (heroes only) to the Classical Athenian civic concept of 'beautiful death' that is mediated by the funeral oration: on this

Figure 4.13. Fragmentary Attic relief crowning a casualty list. 450–400 BCE. Ashmolean Museum, Oxford: ANMichaelis.85. Image: © Ashmolean Museum.

combination of victorious and fallen warriors operates a double-edged image of excellence (ἀριστεία), excellence in battle and excellence in death as memorialized and compensated by the stone monument; *both* figures can be the mourned and celebrated deceased.[102] Crucially, the sculpted part of the Ashmolean monument does not re-articulate death as a victory or defeat (or part of a wider victory or defeat) after the event. The figures are depicted *in mediis rebus*, at the very turning point of life. The casualty list, which would have collated and memorialized many, even all, of the deaths of that year (regardless of whether the particular battle in which they had died was considered to be an Athenian victory or defeat),

---

public casualty list we seem to be somewhere in the middle; the bodies of the named dead are concealed but nameless bodies in the image are singled out and on display. For reconsideration (and support) of Loraux's argument from a pictorial perspective (Athenian vase painting of 600–400 BCE), see Saunders (2006).

[102] As Arrington (2015: 107) emphasizes, casualty lists are not simple victory statements but are replete with '"struggle" or "undecided contest"'. Complexities of defeat and victory on casualty lists: Low (2010: esp. 346). See further Muth (2006: 291–3) on the 'emotional openness' ('emotionaler Offenheit', page 293) of the Greeks that permitted simultaneous admiration of the victor and compassion for the defeated.

180 FIGURING DEATH IN CLASSICAL ATHENS

heads that inscribed cohort with an image of two alternative trajectories at a point where matters are not yet certain.[103] One point, I think, is that every man always has the potential in battle to be one or the other; every man is both of these men; both these men (like all the inscribed fallen) are the same.[104]

Likewise, in the scene on the west frieze (Scene 4), both winner and loser are presented in perennial struggle (ἀγών).[105] The vignette of single combat between two warriors, their bodies in mirror reflection about a trophy, visualizes a moment of existential crisis, a 'turning point' in which lives are at stake. This is enhanced by intimations of agonistic activity elsewhere on the frieze. Men fight to retrieve the wounded or dead (Scenes 3 and 6), are locked shield-to-shield (Scene 8), or prepare to deliver a killing blow (Scene 7). Most of all, consider the scene to the right of the trophy group in which a nude figure armed with a shield races over rocky terrain, cloak billowing behind (Scene 5, Figures 4.2b and 4.2f). The composition (a nude figure running in armour) is reminiscent of the hoplitodromos, as depicted on a red-figure cup held at Harvard University (see especially the figure in the top left of Figure 4.14).

Athletic contest is appropriate in the context of death (especially memory of death). Ancient aetiological explanations for the Panathenaic games linked their foundation with funeral honours, and games were one way in which the Athenian war dead were commemorated.[106] Nike herself was associated with athletic as

[103] Goette (2009: 192) suggests that the state often produced *two* casualty lists, one for the fallen in general, and one for the cavalry. Osborne (2010: 248, with note 14) observes that sometimes a stele makes no discrimination between the battles in which the war dead fell, sometimes it separates the names by battle. However arranged, lists might include the names of both those that fell in what was overall a victory, and (presumably in greater numbers) those that fell in what was overall a defeat.

[104] This argument also holds for the monument of Dexileos: see note 100. Most scholars read one or the other of the figures as Dexileos. See e.g. the argument in Cohen (2000: 102) that the 'idealized victor' is the deceased, not the fallen warrior. But Dexileos can be seen in both the fallen soldier and the horseman. Comparable are approaches to Aeschylus' *Persians* that have focused on Athenian empathy with the Persians and reflection on the self through the other. I note especially Casey Dué's analysis, in which she demonstrates that, in their grief, the enemy are both distinguished from Athenians and resemble them, such that the play is neither a 'victory song' nor 'a universalization of the experience of defeat': Dué (2006: ch. 2). See, in contrast, Harrison (2019: 103–15) for the view that the play is a patriotic glorification of Athens. On defining oneself not just against but also *in* the other, see Henderson (1994).

[105] See notes 98, 100, and 102. See further Clairmont (1983: 203) on the stylistic similarity between the Ashmolean relief and the friezes on the temple of Athena Nike; Goette (2009: 197) on links between iconography of the demosion sema and the Nike temple. The trophy as a statue of Zeus, arbiter of the contest: Lonis (1979: 136–9). (Lonis's interpretation that all trophies were statues of Zeus seems too restrictive but a looser association with Zeus and contests is persuasive.) It is significant that viewers are shown the interior of the shield in Scene 4 on the west frieze: it is unclear to whom the shield belonged—or might belong.

[106] See, for example, Hyde (1921: 9–14) on the funerary origins of the Panathenaic games. On games as a feature of ancient burial (for which little evidence survives), see Low (2010: 342, 348–9). Moreover, athletes, like fallen battle heroes, could win immortality. On heroization of historical figures (noting that the Marathonomachai are not called 'heroes' in Classical sources): Ekroth (2015: 386–7). On hero cult

FIGURE 4.14. Red-figure cup (kylix), attributed to Onesimos, showing preparation for the hoplitodromos (armed race). 490–480 BCE. Diameter 23.0 cm (31.3 cm with handles), Height 9.9 cm (10.1 cm with handles). Harvard Art Museums/Arthur M. Sackler Museum, Cambridge, Bequest of Frederick M. Watkins: MA: 1972.39. Image: © President and Fellows of Harvard College.

well as military competition.[107] More loosely, the competing figure caught in perpetual motion furthers the impression of ongoing crisis in the frieze's various battle scenes. Like other figures on the frieze, he is caught in a moment of isolated physical endeavour. He will win, or lose, as an individual. The trophy thus underpins not just the one-on-one struggle with which it is compositionally grouped but also the outcomes for or against which all figures on the frieze strive.

This impression is reinforced by the episodic format of the frieze. Taken together, the scenes do not cohere into a narrative in which one collective body

of, among others, the war dead and athletes in Classical Athens (including heroization in life as well as death), see Currie (2005: esp. 89–119, 120–57). See further Meister (2020: ch. 3) on the possibility of enjoying (momentary) immortality in the celebration of athletic victory. Note, too, the representation of Nike crowning a male figure, possibly an athlete on a fragmentary votive relief from the Acropolis (Acropolis Museum 1329), and the argument in Palagia (2009a: 35–44, with fig. 10) that there was interest in the 'quest for immortality' during the Peloponnesian War.

[107] Lonis (1979: 250–3). On the interchangeability between athletics and warfare, see Lonis (1979: 25–36); Stähli (2005: 28–32), observing, further, a shift in painted imagery from Archaic emphasis on agonal confrontation to Classical emphasis on physical excellence—the Nike west frieze contains both; Arrington (2010: 7–8, 69).

182 FIGURING DEATH IN CLASSICAL ATHENS

of soldiers defeats another. Instead, each vignette shows a climactic moment of individual struggle. The collected images present not a story but a series of moments of excellence (ἀριστεία).[108] Pertinent here is Luuk Huitink's chapter on ancient historiographies of battle: his suggestion that the urge to narrativize battles, 'imply[ing] that [...] [they] can be described in terms of a trajectory of causally and temporally linked events', is a modern phenomenon (by comparison with ancient Greek historiographies of battle, at least) suggests that the composition on the west frieze might be bound up in a distinctively Greek way of thinking about what a battle is and what it means to fight in one.[109] Yes, a trophy would be erected after a battle but it was normally (in origin, at least) far from a retrospective assessment of a 'decisive battle';[110] it gave material form to subjective experience of a local point of crisis. Though it often appears as an attribute of Nike,[111] the temporary trophy (in contrast to the permanent stone monuments that also appear in the Classical period) seems to be less an articulation of 'overall victory' and more a marker of how things seemed to soldiers on the ground, as suggested by instances in which both sides erected a trophy in respect of the same battle (Thucydides mentions several of these, e.g. 4.134).[112]

[108] Moments that have then been granted a monumental reward (ἀριστεῖον) of sorts in the temple. On the ἀριστεῖον in Greek warfare, see Pritchett (1974: 276–90).

[109] Huitink (2024: 73–4). Huitink observes, further, 'It is not too fanciful to suppose that at least some ancient historiographers and their audiences were less optimistic than their modern counterparts that battles, as objects of historical knowledge, could be understood in such terms' and notes, for example, that 'Diodorus [...] attributes the central incident of Cunaxa [...] to chance or fate' (both citations on page 74). See further Lendon (2017) on the conventions of the 'battle piece' in ancient historiography and the absence of a logical chain of events in contrast to modern battle narratives (the point that is emphasized by Huitink). Compare the suggestion in Harari (2007: 262–6) that battles are inherently extraordinary, simplified versions of history, 'Battles are decisive, among other things, because they are staged to be decisive by their participants' (page 263). The episodic nature of this frieze has been noted elsewhere: see Felten (1984: 119) and, especially, Hölscher (1973: 95–6) on parallels between the episodic formats of ancient historiographies of battle and the Nike friezes.

[110] Though, on the fifth-century development of a permanent 'secondary' trophy that was more of a victory monument: West (1969: esp. 18–19). The stone representation on a temple of a trophy in a battlefield sits between these trophy types. See note 91.

[111] For example: *LIMC* s.v. 'Nike' nos. 159–67. On images of Nike nailing weapons to a trophy in Greek art (including on the balustrade surrounding the temple of Athena Nike), see Isler-Kerényi (1970), especially on the ambivalence of the Nike-tropaion combination (page 62), 'So erstrebenswert der Sieg auch ist, der Gedanke der anderen, der tödlichen Alternative, soll nicht verdrängt werden.' See further Brouskari (1998: 93–102) on images of Nike adorning trophies on the balustrade; Schultz (2001: 26–40) for the suggestion that the central acroterion might have been a bronze trophy (or else a tripod or a Paionios-style Nike). Nike as a personification of victory, and the trophy as one of her attributes: Smith (2011: 20).

[112] On the chaotic sensory experience of battle and the trophy as a method by which individuals framed battle experience and narrativized it as 'victory': de Vivo (2014: esp. 173), 'the *tropaion* becomes the narrative'. Though, where Juan Sebastian de Vivo emphasizes the success with which a trophy transformed experience into victory, I emphasize the local and subjective impressions to which it testifies. Compare Lindenlauf (2003) on how Athenians used material culture to construct memory of the Persian Wars.

Consider, too, a trophy's formal properties. What does it do as a physical, visible object? The fabrication of the temporary battle trophy, a monument erected on the battlefield by gathering enemy armour and displaying it upon a tree, implicitly uses an assembled body double, a trunk for a trunk (or trunks), a pseudo-corpse that testifies to all enemy deaths (and the dead bodies that were stripped for armour).[113] It uses one mock corpse to signal the many that were routed, defeated, slaughtered. The principle that a trophy is meant to look like a body is clear to see in a representation of Nike decorating a trophy on a red-figure pelike in the Boston Museum of Fine Arts (Figure 4.15).[114]

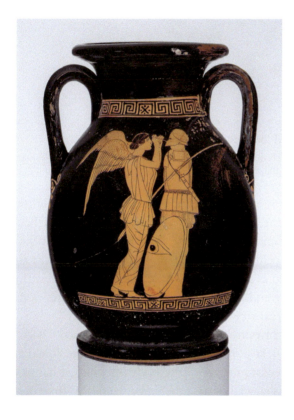

FIGURE 4.15. Attic red-figure two-handled jar (pelike), attributed to The Trophy Painter, depicting Nike setting up a trophy. 450–440 BCE. Height 35.45 cm. Museum of Fine Arts, Boston, MA, Bartlett Collection—Museum purchase with funds from the Francis Bartlett Donation of 1912: 20.187. Image: © 2025 Museum of Fine Arts, Boston.

---

[113] On the trophy as a 'substitute for the opponent himself': Janssen (1957: 40–1, 243), emphasizing the trophy's anthropomorphic form. Woelcke (1911: 142–3) disagreed, arguing that the trophy was all about victory and was erected in gratitude to the god that put opponents to flight. I do not see why we need to choose: these meanings can coexist, even for a single viewer. Stripping the dead for the trophy: Lonis (1979: 129). See Ducrey (1985: 274, fig. 182) for evidence that there were two types of trophy: some were anthropomorphic, some were not (she refers to an image of a pile of weapons on the third-century balustrade of the temple of Athena at Pergamon).

[114] *BAPD* 212473; Beazley (1925: 365.2); *ARV*² 857.2; *Para.* 425; *Add*² 298.

FIGURE 4.16. Attic red-figure mixing bowl (bell-krater), attributed to the Polydektes Painter. 475–425 BCE. From Arnoaldi necropolis, tomb 88. Museo Civico Archeologico, Bologna: inv. MCABo 18109. Image: Courtesy of Bologna, Museo Civico Archeologico.

The arrangement of the armour is anthropomorphic, an effect that is heightened by the eye that stares from the shield as if the inanimate monument has sensory capabilities. The figure of an Athenian citizen on the other side of the pot sets up the trophy, or, more specifically, the making of the trophy, as a visual event: this painted trophy is marked as an object of (triple) visual attention, with the visible painted spectators (Nike and the Athenian citizen) turning attention upon the interaction between the real viewer-handler and the pot.

Compare the impact of a painted trophy on a bell-krater in the Museo Civico Archeologico in Bologna (Figure 4.16).[115] Here, the black hole of the shield's interior draws attention to the insensate matter of the body on which it hangs, an empty vessel. This trophy, too, is viewed by an Athenian citizen (this time the latter's identity as spectator is indicated more explicitly, since he appears on the same side of the pot as the trophy). Moreover, the act of looking at a trophy that is a hollowed-out body is now paired with a scene on the other side of the pot in which Perseus raises the head of the Gorgon and is framed by the figures of Athena and Polydektes. The latter is seated upon a rock, perhaps an indication of his imminent death by petrification upon seeing the head of the Gorgon. Here, as often, the head of the Gorgon is turned outwards towards the viewer.

[115] *BAPD* 214401; Beazley (1925: 408.2); *ARV*² 1069.2, 1681; *Para.* 447.

As explored by Françoise Frontisi-Ducroux and Jean-Pierre Vernant, the frontal stare of the Gorgon on pots implicates the viewer in existential meditation.[116] What is interesting here is that the Gorgon's face is combined with a figure on a rock (Polydektes) and, on the other side, an Athenian citizen looking at a trophy that mimics a dead body with a hollow core. The web of associations connects scenes of viewing bodies (and body parts), viewing objects and viewing viewers, and draws a parallel between all viewers (Polydektes, the painted Athenian viewer, real Athenian viewers). The viewing of objects, especially bodies turned objects, mediates reflection on one's own mortality. Though images of trophies on pots are relatively rare,[117] these two examples do, even on a small scale, indicate that trophies in Classical Athens could be seen as complicated objects, objects that might prompt not just reflections on victory but also on death.[118]

Let us return to the trophy on the west frieze (Scene 4, Figures 4.2b and 4.2f). Several fighting clusters on the frieze are comprised of three figures, often involving two warriors fighting over or above a fallen third.[119] The bare torso of the tree that stands between two fighting figures thus operates like a third party (indeed, the tree's trunk and the chests of the soldiers are comparable in width).[120] The impression that this trophy is not just an object but a body that is built out of defeated bodies (from the armour stripped from the enemy), heightens the urgency that defines this scene of existential crisis. Which fighting body will become the other's trophy?[121]

---

[116] See pages 63 and 64, notes 36 and 39.

[117] A search of the *BAPD* returns nine pots that have been identified as featuring trophies.

[118] Another notable example is a red-figure squat lekythos in the British Museum (1873,0820.298), dated c. 400 BCE: *BAPD* 9031757. This vessel, with its images of Nike constructing an anthropomorphic trophy, a seated warrior, and a woman carrying armour, offers a link between the positive overtones of victory and the regretful undertones of death, loss, and memory. The presence of a woman holding an object beside a monument reframes the more familiar set-up of figures (often women, sometimes with men or warriors) holding objects at graves (see Chapter Two, section III). The association between victory and death would be even more powerful if this lekythos was a grave gift, as many were. Might this object visualize the conceptual continuum between monumentalizing success and memorializing death? Note, further, the juxtaposition of memorials (for example, the architectural fragments incorporated into the walls of the citadel) and monuments (new temples and statues such as the Athena Promachos) on the Acropolis.

[119] This is not true of Scene 1, which only contains two figures (though Praschniker (1924: 23) suggested that these met the left-hand figure of either block *i* or *k*; he also includes an image of a fragment that may have completed block *h*: Acropolis Museum inv. 2422). Scenes 5 and 8 do include three figures, though none are fallen. Scene 6 to some extent combines two sets of three and does include a fallen body.

[120] Moreover, the very material out of which this trophy is built puts pressure on the ontological transformation that is effected by death: this third body is a stone-sculpted representation of a wood-metal-assembled symbol for a collective defeated body. See the discussion above on the corpse behind the rock in Scene 3.

[121] See further Ducrey (1985: 237–55) on the lot of the defeated.

186   FIGURING DEATH IN CLASSICAL ATHENS

The trophy is a composite corpse, one body built from the armour of many, one body to stand for the many defeated bodies that fled in battle, one body to mark a collective. But it also reflects the bodies of all those on the frieze—and beyond.[122] Set within an ongoing battle, it presents the result of a battle, the aftermath of death and defeat (like the corpse behind a rock in Scene 3), and the motivation for one (like the body that comrades fight to retrieve in Scene 6). It speaks to and for all scenes, all figures, on the frieze—and indeed everyone, past, present, and future. It is a universal sounding board, predicated upon the idea that one object, one body, could stand for many or, vice versa, that one man's existential crisis is replicable. In its own singular form, it thus exemplifies the epistemological framework that underpins object-mediated existential meditation.

This turns attention, once more, upon the episodic clusters of which the whole frieze is comprised. The episodic format expands the singular turning point of the trophy into multiple instances, making one man's crisis emblematic of a more general human situation. These instances form a continuous series where any hints of directional imperative or narrative progression towards the right coexist with a sense of transferability and cyclicity.[123] Indeed, the compositional whole is replete with repetitions and reversals of triangular shapes and bodies in mirror image. The nude figures in Scene 3 (Figures 4.2b and 4.2e), for example, one in three-quarter view from the front, one from the back, hunch over towards one another with shields on their left arm: these opponents are each other's twin (an interesting prospect if this frieze invites us to think of the Theban saga and its doubles).[124] The multitude of stone shields with their (represented as) reflecting and refracting metal surfaces reiterates the implicit procreation of images. Consider the warrior pair just described: does each see himself on the surface in his opponent's grasp? Then there is the shield held above the outstretched, fallen

---

[122] In an immediate sense, there were also images of Nikes decorating trophies on the balustrade: see notes 19 and 111. But my point is also a wider one: the trophy speaks not just to figured bodies on the temple complex but also to real Athenian bodies that frequent the Acropolis.

[123] In this respect, the west frieze sits midway between the 'episode' of the metope and the 'continuity and sequence' of the continuous frieze, thereby inviting mixed responses from viewers and not slotting easily into the three approaches summarized in Osborne (2017: 436)—or rather, as he emphasized there and elsewhere, giving viewers a choice (see e.g. Osborne (2000: 242) on how ionic friezes can simultaneously imply directional movement and static viewpoints). It is not so far from cyclicity to the themes of Nemesis that Simone Weil (2005: 11–20, esp. 16) [1989] finds in the *Iliad* and Greek tragedy: 'The progress of the war in the *Iliad* is simply a continual game of seesaw.' Compare, too, Marconi (2013: 430) on the temporality of images on sacred buildings (he focuses on ritual imagery, such as that on the Nike balustrade), which stand as mirrors of the present and commemoration 'for the rest of the time'.

[124] In fact, nudity goes some way towards making many of these figures interchangeable. There is no obvious pattern as to who is nude and who is clothed. This has many effects, perhaps reminding 'of our animal nature and our mortality' (Bonfante (1989: 570) on the power of naked body), perhaps operating as an egalitarian submergence of individuals to the group, as suggested by Stewart (1985: 64). On nudity as a 'costume with various roles', see Hurwit (2007: citation at 57).

Sarpedon-hoplite figure: does the warrior leaning from above see his own reflection on the surface that covers a dead or dying body? Meanwhile the two fighters on the south corner of the frieze are shown in mirror image behind the double surfaces of their shields (Scene 8, Figure 4.2d).

Across the frieze, mirror images—shown and suggested—intimate one response invited from viewers. Friend or foe, the sculpted bodies that fight for life and death together constitute a mirror in which real people on the Acropolis might see and lament their own past, present, and future losses.[125] The trophy does not say (or does not only say) 'this is Theseus' or 'the Athenians are winners', but 'win or lose, the deaths that you encounter here might be your own'.[126]

This becomes still more significant when we consider the incorporation of the west frieze not just into a temple but also into what was effectively a monumental trophy, comprising the temple complex and the bastion upon which it was set. This permanent trophy, set prominently at the entrance to the Acropolis, visible from the Classical agora to the northwest (notably from the Stoa Poikile itself, also decorated in images of Greeks at war and shields captured from Athenian enemies),[127] was built out of real and represented bodies—the figured dead and fighting bodies that flow across the west frieze, the real bodies of the Athenians that frequented the sanctuary space, and the absent bodies of the warriors (probably Spartans) whose shields covered the bastion.[128] Encounters with death ripple outwards from the Acropolis, swelling across the heart of Athens.

[125] Henderson (1994) is important here; the 'arguments' and 'modulations' about the self and the other that he finds in the 'dynamic, "*artefactory*", space of pottery' (page 136) can also be found on a temple—as Robin Osborne demonstrates in his chapter on temple centauromachies in the same volume (1994a). Though Henderson accepts the '(structuralist) *simplicity*' in public art (page 137), it serves as an uninterrogated foil against which his observations about the pluralistic discourse in which a private object participates can be defined more sharply: perhaps he might have found similar debate if he had written on a temple frieze. Indeed, both take as their subject the quintessential, generalizable others of the Amazon and centaur. But the same general questions arise and become more, not less, urgent when fighting men look the same—here I disagree with Osborne's claim that unless the context of a battle (such as the one on the west Nike frieze) can be divined from iconographical details, 'little generalisable impact can be made on any viewer' (page 83). Absence of information as to which man is the 'other' is precisely what makes the scene so (problematically) powerful. See further Estrin (2018: 120–1) on the existential reflection that is prompted by interaction with another's funerary monument. On the ritual implications of shields (for receiving libations or covering sacrificial victims), see Ekroth (2010: 164–7). Shields seem to have been associated with death in the context of sacrifice as well as battle.

[126] On death as an individual defeat (even when the side for which they had fought was victorious), see Arrington (2010: 7). See further Lendon (2005: esp. 65–7) on the lack of distinction made by Classical Greeks between Iliadic-heroic fighting and hoplite fighting.

[127] See Martin-McAuliffe and Papadopoulos (2012: 348–52, esp. figs. 18 and 19) on the sightlines from the Classical agora, 'more than any place else, [...] a locus for civic viewing' (page 348).

[128] See note 20.

188 FIGURING DEATH IN CLASSICAL ATHENS

V. CONCLUSION

Victory was undeniably a central theme of Athena Nike's temple. Nevertheless, I have approached the west frieze from a different angle, as a visual exploration of death. Thoughts of death and dying are compatible with thoughts of victory—they are sometimes two sides of the same coin—but focus on victory has dominated responses to this temple to such an extent that it has left little room for death.

Death cannot be ignored on this temple. Always a larger concept than its visible traces, it is encountered in the fallen bodies that might be dying and might be dead, in the scenes of struggle that cite motifs loaded with deathly associations, and in the porosity, across the frieze, between the body as person and the body as corpse, matter, and object. It is encountered in dialogues between the frieze and the cultural frameworks within which it was embedded: a Sarpedon motif, for instance, frames an image of a fallen soldier in mythological, artistic, literary, theological terms, and generates encounters with death that are defined by loss and necessity as well as celebration. The figured trophy exemplifies the outcomes for and against which all figures struggle. It draws attention to the porosity between individuality and generality that characterizes attitudes to death and processes of encountering death in others' examples. And it sets those processes of grappling with death within a sacred context, at the centre of Athens.[129]

My approach in this chapter has been to treat images on the west frieze not as illustrations of specific subjects but as compositions with multiple associations and significances, viewed as part of a broader Athenian cultural repertoire. Just as we now view war art on the frieze through the prism of Wilfred Owen's 'Dulce et Decorum Est' (a lens that is difficult, and perhaps inadvisable, to remove), it is hard to imagine that Athenian viewers would have seen the retrieval of a fallen warrior without memories of Sarpedon, or a battle trophy without awareness of the defeated human trunks from which its spoils were stripped. These resonances interacted with other possibilities, allowing the sculptural representations to shift between mythological and historical, general and specific.[130] Creative engagement with the images on the frieze was essential to exploratory thought.

---

[129] Indeed, there is a certain overlap between the trophy and the temple in that trophies, like temples, might be dedicated to a god. On dedication of the trophy to a god (and its consequent sanctity), see e.g. Pritchett (1974: 273, 275). See further Picard (1957: 24–36); Stroszeck (2004: 319–20). On temples as trophies, see Shear (2016: 4–5).

[130] Mythology, the general, and the specific—a 'mythic-analogic outlook': Castriota (1992: 3–16, 179–80), though he interprets 'the monuments and their imagery as finely tuned vehicles of an official ideology' (page 12).

Nevertheless, it is worth considering what specificity itself contributes. Perhaps an ancient viewer identified the frieze's subject matter as a historical battle between the Athenians and the Peloponnesians or Corinthians, or a more distant one in which Athenians, led by Theseus, seek to retrieve the bodies of the seven that fought against Thebes. These possibilities would have reinforced the urgency with which the frieze mediated existential reflection because the bodies that fight and the bodies that die could be Athenian. Moreover, how could a cultural framework do any work if viewers did not notice, even subconsciously, compositional details such as a 'helper group' motif, the body of Sarpedon, or the body-like appearance of a trophy? It is not necessary (or likely) that every viewer noted every possibility but some recognition is required to build significance.

The power of the frieze as a visual mediator of exploratory thought derived from its potential to be abundantly specific. Coexistent possibilities (a figure that might simultaneously be Sarpedon, the war dead, and any family member or friend) encouraged the sort of analogical viewing that underpins example-based existential meditation. Repetitions and correspondences, too, encouraged by the episodic format, allowed viewers to slip between identities and, in forging or unravelling connections, to extrapolate generic principles that might or might not resonate more personally. In this respect, the profusion of arguments in favour of one or another specific historical or mythological narrative on the frieze (and also arguments in favour of a generic battle scene) marks its success. The potential for so many stories to be found in the frieze allowed viewers to make those stories their own.

Conceivably, this sort of argument might be made for any frieze (namely, that its visual language combines the specific with the generic). But consider what makes this one unusual. One surprising feature of the west frieze is that all the warriors, whoever they might be, are so ordinary, so interchangeable. Where are the Amazons, Centaurs, Giants, and combats between Heracles or Theseus and variously monstrous figures that are common elsewhere (on the Parthenon and the statue inside it, for instance, or on the temple at Bassai)? The deaths here are uncomfortably real—scenes of killing and being killed between somewhat homogeneous human figures that could easily be Athenian. And the frieze is not tucked out of view; it is positioned at the gateway to the Acropolis. This temple makes death personal and familiar.

This is not surprising when we consider the original historical backdrop. In the 420s, plague and war made death urgently present for Athenians. Themes of war, death, and immortality have generally been observed in late fifth-century art, and it is from roughly 430 that we see renewed efforts to monumentalize death in other Athenian material culture—in figured grave reliefs and stone lekythoi. The west frieze can be understood not just as a work that celebrates victory or acknowledges its cost but also as one that grapples with a situation that refused

190 FIGURING DEATH IN CLASSICAL ATHENS

to be pushed aside, that threw norms into disarray and confounded logic (see Chapter Five). This remains true even if the new temple complex was planned and constructed in a period of comparative optimism (for instance, in response to the Athenian victory at Sphakteria in 425 BCE).[131] Even in a (short-lived) time of triumph, the temple imagery engages insistently with a problem that, for all the heightened horror of the years that frame it, never wholly went away—death. And in fact, in setting up a way of viewing and thinking predicated upon drawing analogies and recognizing oneself in another, the temple invited a double take. Shields on the bastion might have looked Spartan but they might also, at any point, turn Athenian.[132]

This gives the west frieze its chronic punch. It does not *just* show the battle of X; it was not *just* viewed on the Acropolis in the late 420s. The goddesses on the east frieze and the balustrade mourn deaths of the past, receive deaths in the present, preside over deaths in the future, just as the temple is a celebration of a past victory and present Victory and a gift to present Victory for victories future.[133] In these hyper-temporal and hyper-spatial respects, the imagery on the frieze does not so much '[illustrate] continuous Athenian success', as mediate continual Athenian crisis. Like Thucydides' *History of the Peloponnesian War*, the frieze is not a conflict to be understood in one place and at one moment but a possession for all time.

Figuring Death in Classical Athens: Visual and Literary Explorations. Emily Clifford, Oxford University Press.
© Emily Clifford 2025. DOI: 10.1093/9780198947936.003.0007

---

[131] See note 20.

[132] This conceptual possibility becomes more significant if the shields were, indeed, designed to be available for emergency use: see Lippman et al. (2006).

[133] The figured trophy on the west frieze has a similar temporal complexity to a temple when considered in the light of evidence for more permanent fifth-century trophies—at Marathon, for instance (note 91), and implicitly on the Athenian Acropolis (comprising the temple and bastion complex). On the west frieze, it is ambiguous whether the represented trophy is meant to be a temporary organic marker or permanent monument because it has been monumentalized by its representation in stone (note 110); it, like the temple of which it used to form part, could not be limited to one point in time. Trophies, like victory itself (or herself), are difficult to pin down: see note 57.

FIVE

Death and the Plague in Thucydides'
History of the Peloponnesian War

I. HISTORY, PLAGUE, AND KNOWLEDGE

Dr Sam Parnia, director of critical care and resuscitation research at NYU
Langone School of Medicine in New York City, said dying is 'very comfortable'.[1]

—*The Daily Express (online)*, 15 July 2020

According to Dr Sam Parnia, as reported in *The Daily Express*, dying is 'very
comfortable'. Dr Parnia's authority to comment on what death is like comes not
from personal experience but from scientific observation and study: he is a doctor and academic researcher in medicine including consciousness, near-death
experiences, and recalled experiences of death.[2] Whatever conclusions we might
draw generally as to the reliability of his claim, the trust that we might be inclined
to place in his opinion here is modulated not just by his credentials and research
record but also by the status of the source that cites him: *The Daily Express*—not,
traditionally, an acceptable source of authority in an academic book. But it is the
combination of these factors that makes my epigraph an effective way into a
chapter on death and the plague in Thucydides' *History of the Peloponnesian
War*, a work written in the final decades of the fifth century BCE and published
(unfinished) at the turn of the century.[3] The conflation of scientific detail, the
weight of authority, and witness statements from patients who have got as near
to a death experience as it gets, combined with the frame in which information
is reported, offers a window onto the themes of observation, experience,

---

[1] Martin (2021). [2] See, for example, Parnia (2014); Parnia et al. (2022).

[3] When precisely Thucydides was writing and revising his *History* within that period is subject to
debate but he tells us himself that he began work on it at the start of the Peloponnesian War. It was still
incomplete when he died *c.* 400 BCE (though he may have made some of it available before finishing the
whole). For the purposes of this chapter, I envisage readers/listeners of the early fourth century and
beyond, some of whom would have had primary experience of events such as the Athenian plague, the Sicilian
expedition, and more recent events under the Thirty Tyrants, some of whom would have encountered
those events in the memories of others and/or through Thucydides' words.

192 FIGURING DEATH IN CLASSICAL ATHENS

exemplarity, and medium (and the epistemological challenges that these raise)
that underpin my analysis of one writer's efforts to report the historical truth,
specifically the truth about disease and death.

In this chapter, I will focus upon Thucydides' account of the first outbreak of
the plague of Athens (*History* 2.47–54).[4] Thucydides' description begins with
the plague's geographical spread, reputedly from Ethiopia. After explaining that
he will describe its progress and symptoms, but not talk of its origins, he states
that he himself experienced the disease and observed others with it. He describes
its features and effects on the afflicted. Emphasizing that he will focus on its
general nature, he moves on to the widespread fatalities and the helplessness and
despair of the Athenians, recounting the horror as corpses piled up in Athens and
anarchy broke out. He concludes with an oracle that may, or may not, have foretold the plague.

Though this passage has been extensively discussed, there has, perhaps
surprisingly, been little attention to death and dying. Instead, work has circled
around identification of the disease,[5] the influence of the Hippocratic corpus on
Thucydides and his awareness (and incorporation) of technical medical
terminology,[6] and where this passage fits within his political history of the war,[7]
in particular its impact when set against the positive vision of a cohesive Athenian
society that immediately precedes it in Pericles' funeral oration,[8] and its value as
a foil to the social disintegration at Corcyra.[9]

Here, by contrast, I treat Thucydides' account of the plague as exemplary of a
wider historiographical and epistemological discourse—a discourse that has

---

[4] Overviews of the plague: Kohn (1995: 250); Hays (2005: ch. 1).

[5] For example, Crawfurd (1914: 31–5); Page (1953: 110–19); Cunha and Cunha (2008: 4–9);
Papagrigorakis et al. (2008). For discussion and synthesis of some suggestions and approaches to identification: Gomme (1956: vol. 2, 150–3) on 2.48.3. Cautioning against attempts to identify the disease
(chasing a 'will-o'-the-wisp'): Holladay and Poole (1979), (1982), (1984: esp. 485 for the citation);
Holladay (1986).

[6] Cochrane (1929: 14–34); Page (1953: 97–110); Weidauer (1954); Momigliano (1987: 13–15);
Jouanna (2005: 13–17) (though see note 10), as well as work by Holladay and Poole (see previous note).
Note Thomas (2006: esp. 103) on Thucydides' independence, originality, and different objectives and
interests: 'Thucydides was producing his own medical theory, and probably in rivalry to the doctors.'
More recently, Robin Lane Fox has argued that *Epidemics* 1 and 3 were written in the 460s BCE by
Hippocrates and so predated Thucydides, who read or heard them: Lane Fox (2020: 273–82, esp. 282).
Morgan (1994) acknowledges Thucydides' exposure to medical vocabulary but emphasizes his literary
goals (and resulting 'medical inexactness', page 201), while Demont (1983: 352) and Marshall (1990)
emphasize his political ones (defence of Pericles).

[7] Mittelstadt (1968), for example, argues that Thucydides offers his plague description as 'a kind of
symbolic program for the whole work' (page 154), for his *History* as a pathological study of ambition and
its effects. See further Lloyd (2003: 122), 'the detailed description of the plague stands as a model for what
[Thucydides] claims for his whole work. Both are validated on the assumption that they deal with *natures*...'.

[8] See, for example, Keys (1944: 35); Macleod (1983: 151–3); Winton (1992); Morgan (1994: 207–8);
Taylor (2010: 68–9). Recurring patterns in the plague, funeral speech, and Sicilian disaster: Joho (2016).

[9] Orwin (1988), (1994: 173–84) (in which he connects plague, stasis, and the funeral speech).

implications not just for the knowability of death but also for its suitability as a topic in Thucydidean history. In the first place, Thucydides' empirical approach to disease highlights the challenge of accessing a patient's experience of disease from observation and description and a general account of disease from diverse particulars. His account of plague thus models the conceptual problem that drives this book: how to understand what dying is and is like from the perspective of the living.[10] Also integral to this chapter, though, is the distinctive way in which Thucydides' historiography mediates reflection on this epistemological problem. As a historian, Thucydides faced a challenge: to understand and communicate 'what happened' in the plague and the war based on his observations, including those based on his enquiries and (limited) personal experience. This means that the challenges of exteriority and generality that beset reflection on plague are bound up with methodological anxiety about the relationship more generally between perception and knowledge, the concrete and the abstract. Historiographical and disease-mediated epistemological challenges map onto the challenge of extrapolating from observation and (limited) personal experience to build a thesis as to what death is and is like. The historian and the doctor, like the living, are troubled (and blessed) by distance from the object of study.[11] Add to this Thucydides' register in this passage—imagery that sets his account of plague within a poetic-artistic tradition of mythological stories—and epistemological reflection compounds. Are there some subjects that resist, more than others, the sort of history that Thucydides wanted to write? Thinking with Thucydides about history, disease, and death is a threefold, mutually illuminative discourse.

These ideas press a theme that many readers have emphasized before: Thucydides' interest in the human condition, the general, and the abstract.[12]

---

[10] Jouanna (2005: 20–5) is notable here for his discussion of the metaphorical power of medicine in historical writings, but he focuses on cause and crisis and, crucially, on whether Thucydides adopts medical terminology (concluding that direct transposition of the concepts is difficult to establish). On the powerful metaphoricity of disease in Athens (focusing upon the language of plague in Greek tragedy), see Mitchell-Boyask (2008: ch. 3).

[11] Distance and history: Hedrick (1993: esp. 18). In fact, Thucydides' writing has, at different times and by different people, been praised both for objectivity and for vividity. Potentiality for vicarious experience (and ἐνάργεια, 'vividness') in Thucydides was emphasized in Plutarch *De glor. Ath.* ch. 3 (*Mor.* 347A). See further Connor (1985: 9–12); Walker (1993); Grethlein (2013: 92). Robinson (1985: 20–1) argues, by contrast, that this vividity (characteristic of the plague account) can detract from Thucydides' credibility as a historian.

[12] Greenwood (2006: ix): 'a prominent theme in the *History* is the patterns in the human condition that shape events.' See further Ponchon (2017) for emphasis on Thucydides as a (political) philosopher and his 'tragic rationality'. Indeed, Thucydides' development of abstract language, and 'the process of abstraction that seems to lie behind [his] method of composition' supports a reading that looks for more theoretical meditation: see Allison (1997: citation at 2). See further Parry (1970: esp. 19–20) on Thucydides' abstract language and the struggle between human intellect and the παράλογον (something that defies reason); de Romilly (1990: 61–104), (2005: 89–94) on generality in Thucydides; Goldhill (2002: 36), 'History, for Thucydides, is important because of what it can show of the general and the abstract.'

194 FIGURING DEATH IN CLASSICAL ATHENS

But where I look at how Thucydides' account of the plague builds a picture of death and foregrounds the challenges inherent in that endeavour, others have focused more on Thucydides the historiographer, assessing, for better or worse, his objectivity and shaping power over his narrative.[13] Insofar as this scholarship is fundamental to any appreciation of Thucydides as a historian and his work as a history, it lays the foundations for my discussion of where death fits within Thucydides' endeavour. But there is more to be said about what thinking about plague—and thinking about a survivor's account of plague (as part of a history of war)—does for thinking about death.

In the first part of this chapter, I consider how Thucydides foregrounds the problem of exteriority when thinking about disease. I do this by analysing his emphasis on observation and experience, and the possible mismatch between visibility and knowability. Important here is where a history of plague sits within pain discourse, the problem of interiority, and the power of words to communicate subjective experience. This first section is not specifically about death (as opposed to disease) but it provides an important backdrop for later parts of the chapter. Indeed, the disease is so virulent, so frightening, and so extensively fatal that it renders life and death subjects of urgent and consuming importance not just in the minds of Athenians who suffered from and survived the plague but also in the minds of Thucydides' readers, even when explicitly reading about disease. I then turn to questions of generality: to what extent can (and should) incidences of disease and death be subsumed into a single account? Central to this section is a consideration of mass death and the distinctive way in which it might shape epistemological reflection. Finally, I consider the poetics of Thucydides' account. What does it do to combine a literary register worthy of τὸ μυθῶδες with an empirical one, and how far might this combination turn attention upon the nature of the subject matter and the epistemological challenges that it poses?

II. BEYOND RECKONING

γενόμενον γὰρ κρεῖσσον λόγου τὸ εἶδος τῆς νόσου τά τε ἄλλα χαλεπωτέρως ἢ κατὰ τὴν ἀνθρωπείαν φύσιν προσέπιπτεν ἑκάστῳ καὶ ἐν τῷδε ἐδήλωσε μάλιστα ἄλλο τι ὂν ἢ τῶν ξυντρόφων τι.

---

[13] Thucydides the writer (how Thucydides writes): Cornford (1907); Hunter (1973); Hornblower (1987), (2010) [1994]; Allison (1997); Gribble (1998); Rood (1998), (2004); Dewald (2005), (2009: 128–47) [1999]; Greenwood (2006); de Romilly (2017) [1956]. The inextricable connection of Thucydides' history and writing: Macleod (1983: esp. 145–6); Loraux (1986b: 139), 'la pure transitivité'; Goldhill (2002: 31–44). The 'writtenness' of Thucydides' text: Gentili and Cerri (1988: 11–13); Yunis (2003: 198–204); Greenwood (2004); Edmunds (2009) [1993]. Morrison (2004), however, sees Thucydides as a transitional figure between oral and written culture. Note that Rubincam (1991), who makes the war dead her subject, focuses not on death but on Thucydides' research methods and the reliability of his casualty numbers.

> For the form of the disease was beyond reckoning; for the most part it fell upon each person more grievously than human nature can bear, and then in each specific case it very much showed itself to be something different from any of the diseases with which we are familiar.
>
> *History* 2.50.1

Let us begin with how Thucydides foregrounds exteriority and the limitations of extrapolating from observation in his description of the plague. This is most overt in paragraph 49, in which Thucydides describes the symptoms of the plague and the impact it had on the bodies of its victims. By establishing a thematic opposition between the exterior and the interior, between what can be observed and what must be experienced, he sets a question mark over the extent to which a third party can come to know and understand another's predicament.[14] How relevant is visibility (or, more generally, perceptibility)? How reliable is observation?

In the initial section of 2.49, Thucydides emphasizes symptoms of the plague that are identifiable to the senses of an external party. Some are visible, such as redness of eyes (τῶν ὀφθαλμῶν ἐρυθήματα, 2.49.2), bloody/blood-red throat and tongue (ἥ τε φάρυγξ καὶ ἡ γλῶσσα, εὐθὺς αἱματώδη ἦν, 2.49.2), vomited bile (ἀποκαθάρσεις χολῆς, 2.49.3), and spasms (σπασμὸν [...] ἰσχυρόν, 2.49.4); others assail with smell (πνεῦμα ἄτοπον καὶ δυσῶδες, 2.49.2) or sound (πταρμὸς καὶ βράγχος, 2.49.3; βηχὸς ἰσχυροῦ, 2.49.3; λύγξ [...] κενή, 2.49.4). Thucydides explicitly speaks of the appearance of the parts within (τὰ ἐντός, 2.49.2), and it is significant that so much of this is observable from without: certainly the throat and tongue (which can be examined) but also, perhaps, the breast (τὰ στήθη, 2.49.3) and heart (τὴν καρδίαν, 2.49.3). The implication is that one person's internal situation *can* be recognized by another's perception—by contemplation (σκοπῶν, 2.48.3) and sight (ἰδών, 2.48.3).[15]

It is significant that none of these details give information as to the patient's experience. Little attention is paid to pain, for example, beyond one reference to the exertion or suffering (ὁ πόνος, 2.49.3) that descends with violent coughing into the breast.[16] Instead, the object of Thucydides' description is the disease

---

[14] On the body and its hidden interior in Hippocratic thought (including by comparison with early Greek texts), see Holmes (2018: 67–79). See further Holmes (2010: esp. ch. 3) on disease, symptoms, and the unseen; King (2017: 11–17) on changes in the imperial period, with more detailed anatomical knowledge about the internal body.

[15] Indeed, following the argument in Holmes (2007), visual evidence (such as blood) might contribute to representation of unseen pain.

[16] Note a corresponding absence of detail on suffering in the Iliadic plague, discussed in Holmes (2007: esp. 53). In Hippocratic texts such as *Epidemics* 1 and 3, there are several references to the fact of pain but little insight into what that pain was like.

196 FIGURING DEATH IN CLASSICAL ATHENS

itself and 'what sort of thing it became' (οἷόν [...] ἐγίγνετο, 2.48.3).[17] What he focuses on, in paragraph 49 at least, is its impact on the body. But attention to the perceptible corporeal features of another's predicament diverts attention from that person's experience of disease, deconstructing the person into body parts for study. Indeed, others have commented upon Thucydides' emphasis on the head-to-toe movement of the disease, which may suggest a methodical description of symptoms characteristic of novice doctors rather than bearing any sort of meaningful relationship to the disease's progress or patient experience.[18] If this is correct, the experience that is offered to readers is one of medical observation, the external perspective, as opposed to vicarious experience of disease.[19] In this respect, Thucydides' description is similar to the observation-based approaches in some of the Hippocratic texts such as in *Epidemics* 1 and 3 (a resemblance that has been discussed elsewhere, and that I analyse further below).[20]

Crucially, however, Thucydides *is* interested in subjective experience of disease. Though his declared purpose is to speak of 'what sort of thing it was/became' (2.48.3), the nature or quality of the plague, that is, rather than what it felt like to have it, he emphasizes that his evidence comes from personal experience *and* observation of others (αὐτός τε νοσήσας καὶ αὐτὸς ἰδὼν ἄλλους πάσχοντας, 2.48.3), implying that one of these two would be inferior to their combination.[21]

---

[17] There is a conceptual similarity between objectification of pain for the purposes of demonstrating power, as discussed in Scarry (1985: 27–59), and objectification that turns a suffering body into symptoms, the 'disease itself', for the purposes of medical analysis.

[18] This seems consistent with the descriptive mode of 'Thucydides the Painter' in Allan (2013). See further Bakker (1997: 37–9), who sees this part of the description as a typical example of what he calls 'mimetic discourse'—in that it is 'presented from the internal standpoint of the observer'—but acknowledges that it is here characterized by '*generic remembering*', a 'specific universality'. On the head-to-toe approach as characteristic of 'a neophyte modern medical student', see Morgan (1994: 203–4). A similar approach in a different context: Ov. *Am.* 1.5.19–22. Contrast, though, Craik (2001): the Thucydidean plague's progress accords with theories of bodily flux and fixation in some Hippocratic texts.

[19] This distinction is important: however much Thucydides may 'enmesh' his readers in his past (see Grethlein (2013: 114–18) on the 'presence' of Thucydides' past), the resulting experience is characterized by exteriority. (In fact, I am sceptical more generally of whether Grethlein's emphasis on how Thucydides experientially enmeshes his readers in the past works for the plague description: the description also works in (and is designed to work in) the present: each experience, and re-experience, is fresh: see note 119.)

[20] The sophistic defence of medicine in the Hippocratic treatise called *The Art* makes a running theme of visibility; what is visible must exist (para. 2), what can be 'seen' (by eyes *or mind*) can be healed (para. 11), and so on: disease is obscure, and the art of medicine is reliant on communication by the sick and observation and reasoning by doctors (para. 11). See further Perilli (2018) on Hippocratic epistemologies; Thumiger (2018) on doctor–patient communication in Hippocratic medicine; note 14. On the affinity between medical observation and spectatorship (as articulated by later critics), see Lane Fox (2020: 212).

[21] Emphasis on first-person experience is unusual in Thucydides but is characteristic of medical texts such as *Epidemics* 1 and 3: see Thomas (2006: 101–2). See further Marincola (1997: 67–9) on Thucydides' claims to authority as a historian and, especially, his guarantee of autopsy and inquiry (and rigorous analysis of the evidence provided by both).

Moreover, he moves on in paragraph 49 to set up an antithesis between what was felt and seen from the outside (τὸ μὲν ἔξωθεν, 2.49.5) and sensation on the inside (τὰ δὲ ἐντός, 2.49.5).[22] To the doctor, or observing historian, victims' bodies were not excessively hot to the touch or pale: their bodies' surfaces were reddish, livid, and flowering with blisters and sores. By contrast, what was felt within was 'burning' heat (ἐκάετο, 2.49.5), unremitting thirst (τῇ δίψῃ ἀπαύστῳ, 2.49.5). To some extent it was possible to deduce internal experience from observation of patients' behaviour: the fact that victims stripped their bodies naked and actually threw themselves into water containers implies that they felt an uncomfortable heat. But more subjective details provided by Thucydides claim omniscient knowledge of others' motivation, discomfort, pleasure, and appetite: even light or linen clothing was 'unendurable' (μήτε [...] μηδ' [...] ἀνέχεσθαι, 2.49.5); throwing themselves into cold water 'would bring the most pleasure' (ἥδιστά τε ἄν, 2.49.5); drinking deeply or sparingly 'made little difference' (καὶ ἐν τῷ ὁμοίῳ καθειστήκει τό τε πλέον καὶ ἔλασσον ποτόν, 2.49.5). Inability to rest or sleep 'lay upon' (ἐπέκειτο, 2.49.6) the victims, and sometimes, on recovery, complete amnesia, which 'took hold' (ἐλάμβανε, 2.49.8). Thucydides hints not just at a medical situation but at the experience of victims, who felt attacked, oppressed, manhandled.

There are several possible sources for Thucydides' apparent knowledge of internal experience of the plague.[23] His knowledge may reflect details communicated by patients during the illness; it may be derived from Thucydides' personal experience of the disease; it may (as stated above) be conjecture based on observing patient behaviour. Regarding the first two of these, it is striking that Thucydides emphasizes the internal sensation of not just heat but fire: the insides are 'on fire' (ἐκάετο, 2.49.5); the body is not 'quenched' (ἐμαραίνετο, 2.49.6) by the disease but continues in strength until the seventh or ninth day when it is destroyed by 'the internal burning heat' (τοῦ ἐντὸς καύματος, 2.49.6).[24] The metaphorical language of fire to communicate pain felt within (a pain that was not connected to any real heat that could be detected by touching the body) is characteristic of the figurative language used to communicate indescribable pain. Consider the vocabulary gathered in the McGill Pain Questionnaire discussed by Elaine Scarry, where patients talk of pain as 'burning', 'hot', 'flickering', 'searing', and so on.[25] Though consistencies in language (in Thucydides, the 'thermal'

---

[22] Antithesis and Thucydides' prose style: Denniston (1952: 13, 73–4); Parry (1970: 6–12).

[23] This is an example of Thucydides' apparent knowledge of others' thoughts. On this phenomenon, see, for example, Rengakos (2006: 281–4) on 'internal focalisation' (and its Homeric and Herodotean ancestry).

[24] On fieriness as a feature of *Epidemics* 1 and 3: Lane Fox (2020: 228–30).

[25] Scarry (1985: 6–9). For recent reflections upon *The Body in Pain* and its legacies, see Dawney and Huzar (2019). See further, Budelmann (2006: 137–8) on metaphorical language in Sophocles' *Philoctetes*

198 FIGURING DEATH IN CLASSICAL ATHENS

theme and, possibly, a 'temporal' theme of continuous pain that is not 'quenched') do communicate meaningful information that might be helpful for diagnosis and treatment,[26] the symbolic nature of the language (not this, but something *like* this) indicates the obstacles to sharing an experience.[27] As Scarry says, 'To have pain is to have *certainty*; to hear about pain is to have *doubt*.'[28] The language of what was felt within, whether drawn from Thucydides' own experience, from the words of the victims he observed, or both, must be imaginative and approximate, however suggestive. For sufferers, let alone observers, the experience defies language or reason.[29]

Thucydides' description is thus simultaneously characterized by observation and description and by an attention to exteriority that provokes epistemological reflection. In this respect, his account resembles medical treatises. Putting aside the question of influence or familiarity with medical terminology,[30] the authority that he draws from first-person experience and his detailed account of symptoms and the disease's progress gives his description a medical style and method akin to that in *Epidemics* 1 and 3.[31]

More interesting within the context of this chapter, however, is Rosalind Thomas's discussion of Thucydides' emphasis on the helplessness of the medical profession and his declaration that he, unlike the doctors (and others), will not

similar to that in the McGill questionnaire; Clarke et al. (2023) on the articulation and representation of subjective experience in Graeco-Roman writing, especially the chapters by Daniel King and Orly Lewis.

[26] See previous note. The utility of the diagnostic tool and categories such as 'temporal' and 'thermal' are discussed by Scarry at pages 7–8. Her wider point is the inexpressibility of pain (pages 3–11).

[27] Though see Budelmann (2006: 128–33) on the paradox of pain, inherently understandable (he cites Terry Eagleton) and uncommunicable (he cites Virginia Woolf and the prevalence of metaphorical language in pain description).

[28] Scarry (1985: 13), rephrasing Wittgenstein (1953: 89 (I.246)).

[29] The problematic nature of attempts by patients to report their illnesses is also discussed in *The Art*, para. 11. Compare King (2017: 17–21) on pain, language, representation, and experience in the imperial period, including discussion of Kleinman et al. (1997) at pages 18–19, and note 47 (of his Introduction) on eighteenth-century debates on pain and language. Kleinman et al. (1997) emphasizes the social and cultural aspects of pain and suffering (see especially page xiii of the Introduction by the editors).

[30] Discussed in Page (1953); rejected in Parry (1969); revisited with nuance in Thomas (2006: 95–7).

[31] On this resemblance, see especially Thomas (2006: 95–104), noting her emphasis (pages 93–5) on the diversity of the Hippocratic corpus, which includes texts written by different authors in different styles at different times (from the late fifth century to the fourth). Indeed, *Epidemics* 1 and 3 contain material of different sorts: 'constitutions' and case histories. The case histories, especially, differ in style from Thucydides' *History*. The constitutions are more akin to history in that they summarize the year's weather and ailments, but differ in that they, like the case histories, include details in brief and ungrammatical note form. Compare the flowing prose with which Thucydides treats his account and the political event with which he opens it (in contrast to the weather statements that punctuate case studies); these distinguish his writing as narrative history within a military-social-political frame. Thucydides' discussion of the social impact of the plague has a similar effect: see Thomas (2006: 105). Thomas also notes that Thucydides does not (unlike some Hippocratic writers) mention the plague's causes (page 100).

DEATH AND THE PLAGUE IN THUCYDIDES   199

discuss its origins and causes.[32] Though his explicit purpose is to describe the disease such that others can identify it in the future, his implicit aim, or at least his overriding interest, appears less medical and more epistemological: his point is that the plague defies treatment or understanding (discussed further below).[33] In this respect, as Thomas observes, in some ways his narrative has more in common with a tragedy than a medical treatise.

The dramatic characteristics of the plague have been explored elsewhere, notably by Adam Parry.[34] But one important *difference* between representations of sickness and death in Thucydides' *History* and in a tragedy such as Sophocles' *Women of Trachis* is that the dramatic format and interests of the latter both accommodate and make a feature of interaction between spectators and suffering individuals. In staging the excruciating death of Herakles at the end of the play, Sophocles gives space not just to Herakles' real time efforts to communicate his pain but to the affective responses of his observers.[35] At 1023–43, for instance, Herakles screams in an alternating rhythm of lyrics and hexameters, mingling guttural shrieks 'e e!' ($\check{\epsilon}\ \check{\epsilon}$), protracted groans 'io io' ($i\dot{\omega}\ i\dot{\omega}$), and pressured speech characteristic of frenzy, as in $\dot{\alpha}\pi o\tau i\beta\alpha\tau o\varsigma\ \dot{\alpha}\gamma\rho i\alpha\ \nu\acute{o}\sigma o\varsigma$, a rapid string of light syllables.[36] Herakles still communicates his pain in metaphors: the disease leaps and darts ($\theta\rho\dot{\omega}\sigma\kappa\epsilon\iota\ [\ldots]\ \theta\rho\dot{\omega}\sigma\kappa\epsilon\iota$, 1027); it mauls him ($\lambda\omega\beta\hat{\alpha}\tau\alpha\iota$, 1031); it has eaten his flesh ($\beta\acute{\epsilon}\beta\rho\omega\kappa\epsilon\ \sigma\acute{\alpha}\rho\kappa\alpha\varsigma$, 1054) and drunk his blood ($\alpha\hat{i}\mu\acute{\alpha}\ \mu o\upsilon\ |\ \pi\acute{\epsilon}\pi\omega\kappa\epsilon\nu$, 1055–6); it is like a wild animal. But the chorus' reaction hints at an affective response that is physical as well as emotional: 'I shudder to hear the misfortune' ($\kappa\lambda\acute{\upsilon}o\upsilon\sigma$' $\check{\epsilon}\phi\rho\iota\xi\alpha$ $\tau\acute{\alpha}\sigma\delta\epsilon\ \sigma\upsilon\mu\phi o\rho\acute{\alpha}\varsigma$, 1044).[37] There appears to be some limited transference of bodily experience.

---

[32] Thomas (2006: 102).

[33] Indeed, Thucydides' focus on incomprehension and helplessness might communicate psychological pain: see Budelmann (2006: 130–1) on pain narratives and the interaction of body and mind in pain.

[34] Parry (1969: 113–16). On Thucydides and tragedy, see further Cornford (1907: esp. ch. 8) (Aeschylus); Finley (1967: 1–54) (Euripides); Macleod (1983: ch. 13); Alsina (1984) (Sophocles); Ponchon (2017: 193–203) (on Thucydides' tragic use of medical discourse to unveil the chaotic nature of the world and the intrinsic weakness of human nature).

[35] On representation of pain on the tragic stage, see Budelmann (2006, esp. 134–41), (2010: 111–13). The bibliography on the art of pain and suffering is extensive and spans thousands of years: consider Seneca's imaginary account of how Parrhasios tortured a slave to provide a model for his painting of Prometheus (Sen. *Controv.* 10.5) or the canonical status of the statue of Laocoon in the Vatican museums and the debate that it stirred between Winckelmann and Lessing in the eighteenth century. For more recent discussions of art and pain, see Spivey (2001); Nelson (2011) (on cruelty); Sontag (2019) [2003]. See further King (2017: 6–10) on Perkins (1995) and Coakley (2007), two studies that emphasize the cultural and historical aspects of pain, and note 19 of his Introduction for further scholarship on representations of pain in Archaic and Classical art.

[36] His pain is also conveyed by the 'excited series of commands, questions and exclamations': Easterling (1982: 200) on 1004–43.

[37] Though see Cairns (2016) on $\phi\rho i\kappa\eta$ (shivering fear) as an emotion-metaphor founded upon a physical symptom.

200 FIGURING DEATH IN CLASSICAL ATHENS

In Thucydides' account of the plague, by contrast, those among the living who feel most pity for the dying and suffering are those who have previously experienced and recovered from the plague *and who consider themselves to be immune* (2.51.6). The latter detail is crucial. Personal experience of the disease (an impossibility in the case of death) might make it easier for survivors to feel pity, but what prevented even relatives from visiting those dying from the plague was in many cases fear, not lack of pity (or, at least, fear outweighed pity) (2.51.5). Though Thucydides tells us that some, motivated by a sense of shame (αἰσχύνη) and a desire to be virtuous (οἱ ἀρετῆς τι μεταποιούμενοι, 2.51.5),[38] did visit the diseased despite not being immune (and so died), it appears that for the most part the responses of the living to the suffering and dying were conditioned by self-interest.

To some extent, this account of the Athenian people's responses to the predicament of the diseased opens a window onto another sort of exteriority that governs response to the plague in Thucydides' account: the exteriority that underpins Thucydides' methodological approach in the *History*. Thucydides says that his purpose in describing the plague is to enable others to recognize it in the future (not, crucially, to enable others to sympathize or empathize; not to provide others with a vicarious experience of the disease). Reducing a diseased or dying person to an object of and for another's study leaves little space for acknowledgement of or vicarious encounter with that person's experience.

On this note, I return to the epigraph of this part of my chapter (*History* 2.50.1):

> γενόμενον γὰρ κρεῖσσον λόγου τὸ εἶδος τῆς νόσου...
>
> For the form of the disease was beyond reckoning...

With these words, Thucydides seems to acknowledge the challenge posed by a chasm latent within the word εἶδος.[39] What he seeks to capture in his writing is the very essence of the disease, that which distinguishes it from other diseases and which will enable others in the future to recognize it, should it reoccur. But εἶδος also holds a less abstract meaning, a meaning that is more superficial, as it were: 'appearance', 'visible shape'. The word εἶδος shifts between what *can be observed* and what *is*, the essence, 'pattern', 'nature', 'kind' that might be extrapolated from its aspects.[40] This shift is problematic and is (in diverse ways) at the heart of Thucydides' treatment of the plague.

---

[38] Gomme (1956: vol. 2, 157) on 2.51.5 suggests 'primarily courage and a sense of duty, not kindliness'. See further Hutchinson (2013b: 211–12) on Thucydides' 'elegant dilemma on care' in these lines.

[39] Compare Marshall (1990: 167–70), who suggests that this phrase defends Pericles' reputation.

[40] The object of historical enquiry is, like all objects, elusive: see page 57, note 9. Indeed, the word (εἶδος) brings its own ancient philosophical discourse: Plato's use of the word to communicate the ideal, unchanging world of the Forms. This seems to be another example of how the new Socratic philosophy drew upon cultural ideas surrounding viewing and sight to differentiate its purpose and methodology

The plague account thus draws attention to a problem with which Thucydides grappled more widely as a historian. Consider one section of his 'archaeology' of Greek history in Book 1, in which he advances his methodology (*History* 1.10.2):

Λακεδαιμονίων γὰρ εἰ ἡ πόλις ἐρημωθείη, λειφθείη δὲ τά τε ἱερὰ καὶ τῆς κατασκευῆς τὰ ἐδάφη, πολλὴν ἂν οἶμαι ἀπιστίαν τῆς δυνάμεως προελθόντος πολλοῦ χρόνου τοῖς ἔπειτα πρὸς τὸ κλέος αὐτῶν εἶναι [...] Ἀθηναίων δὲ τὸ αὐτὸ τοῦτο παθόντων διπλασίαν ἂν τὴν δύναμιν εἰκάζεσθαι ἀπὸ τῆς φανερᾶς ὄψεως τῆς πόλεως ἢ ἔστιν.

For if the Spartans' city were to be deserted, but the temples and the foundations were left, I think that, after a lot of time had gone by, there would be great disbelief in their power amongst future generations when faced with their renown [...] whereas if the Athenians suffered the same fate, their power would be judged double what it actually is, based on the visible appearance of the city.

There is a difference between what can be seen and what can be known.[41] Nevertheless, Thucydides professes confidence in his ability to communicate the 'sort of things' (τοιαῦτα) that happened in the early history of the Athenians (1.21.1). But the challenge remains, and it permeates the contemporary history that comprises the primary object of his enquiry. There, too, the 'clear truth' that his account will offer relies upon the painstaking way (ἐπιπόνως) in which he discovered it from conflicting reports (1.22.3–4). The gap between perception and knowledge caused Thucydides, like many in the fifth and fourth centuries (and earlier), anxiety. His account of the plague thus offers a microcosm of a larger historiographical problem; indeed, it magnifies the problem by opposing not just truth and appearance (what the plague 'is' versus what it looked like) but also appearance and experience (the distance between the symptom and the subject).[42] This coincidence generates a distinctive sort of encounter with death, an encounter charged with epistemological anxiety.

III. MISSING THE TREES FOR THE WOOD

I now turn to another epistemological point raised by Thucydides' account of the plague: the potential divergence between truth for the purposes of his history, and truth from the individual perspectives of those that suffered and died, not just in the plague, but in the war. What is at stake in summarizing a disease

from that of the Presocratics: see Nightingale (2004) on θεωρία (pilgrimage, spectatorship, spectacle, contemplation) and 'spectacles' of truth. See further Petraki (2024) on Plato's use of sculptural language to articulate the creative process of philosophical thought; note 73.

[41] On this passage and Thucydides' critique of oral sources versus material culture, see Hedrick (1993: 27–8).

[42] On the symptom and its relationship with (and shaping of) the subject, see Holmes (2010).

202 FIGURING DEATH IN CLASSICAL ATHENS

(or a battle)—in painstakingly producing one account from many?[43] This section of the chapter continues to align the epistemological problems raised by Thucydides' account of plague with his reflections on his historiographical practice but delves more directly into what these parallels do for reflection on death by folding in other parts of his history in which death comes to the fore.

Let us begin with the impact of the plague upon a multitude of bodies and the collective body politic.[44] Emphasis has been placed by other readers on Thucydides' representation of the socio-cultural *fragmentation* that results from the plague.[45] Indeed, the civil disorder in the wake of the plague has been aligned with the social disintegration at Corcyra in Book 3 and both, together, have been treated as a foil to the vision of cohesive Athenian society in Pericles' funeral oration.[46] Here, I want to emphasize the opposite: the homogenizing force of the plague. The plague's homogenizing force is deep-set in Thucydides' description— few escape, weak or strong, whether or not under medical care. Though the picture that emerges towards the end of Thucydides' account of the plague is unarguably one of dissolution, there is also considerable emphasis on massing, piling, agglomeration—not cohesion, as such, but amorphous solution.[47]

Consider the grim spectacle in paragraph 52:

Ἐπίεσε δ' αὐτοὺς μᾶλλον πρὸς τῷ ὑπάρχοντι πόνῳ καὶ ἡ ξυγκομιδὴ ἐκ τῶν ἀγρῶν ἐς τὸ ἄστυ, καὶ οὐχ ἧσσον τοὺς ἐπελθόντας. οἰκιῶν γὰρ οὐχ ὑπαρχουσῶν, ἀλλ' ἐν καλύβαις πνιγηραῖς ὥρᾳ ἔτους διαιτωμένων ὁ φθόρος ἐγίγνετο οὐδενὶ κόσμῳ, ἀλλὰ καὶ νεκροὶ ἐπ' ἀλλήλοις ἀποθνῄσκοντες ἔκειντο καὶ ἐν ταῖς ὁδοῖς ἐκαλινδοῦντο καὶ περὶ τὰς κρήνας ἁπάσας ἡμιθνῆτες τοῦ ὕδατος ἐπιθυμίᾳ. τά τε ἱερὰ ἐν οἷς ἐσκήνηντο νεκρῶν πλέα ἦν, αὐτοῦ ἐναποθνῃσκόντων· ὑπερβιαζομένου γὰρ τοῦ κακοῦ οἱ ἄνθρωποι, οὐκ ἔχοντες ὅτι γένωνται, ἐς ὀλιγωρίαν ἐτράποντο καὶ ἱερῶν καὶ ὁσίων ὁμοίως. νόμοι τε πάντες ξυνεταράχθησαν οἷς ἐχρῶντο πρότερον περὶ τὰς ταφάς, ἔθαπτον δὲ ὡς ἕκαστος ἐδύνατο. καὶ πολλοὶ ἐς ἀναισχύντους θήκας ἐτράποντο σπάνει τῶν ἐπιτηδείων διὰ τὸ συχνοὺς ἤδη προτεθνάναι σφίσιν· ἐπὶ πυρὰς γὰρ ἀλλοτρίας φθάσαντες τοὺς νήσαντας οἱ μὲν ἐπιθέντες τὸν ἑαυτῶν νεκρὸν ὑφῆπτον, οἱ δὲ καιομένου ἄλλου ἐπιβαλόντες ἄνωθεν ὃν φέροιεν ἀπῇσαν.

What squeezed them all the more, on top of the distress they already suffered, was also the crowding from the fields into the city, and this had just as much of an impact on the incomers. For since there were not enough houses, and since, instead, they were living in huts that were stifling at that time of year, there was no order to

---

[43] This echoes the point made about battle narratives in John Keegan's *The Face of Battle*, which has proved so influential on debates surrounding the ontology and ethics of battle historiography: Keegan (1991: esp. 62–73) [1976]; he cites Thucydides with approval. For a recent engagement with this discourse with reference to the ancient historiography of battle, see Huitink (2024), discussed on page 182, including note 109.

[44] See Brock (2000) on the metaphor of sickness for political disorder in Greek literature.

[45] See Winton (1992: 206–7), for example.   [46] See note 9.

[47] Compare here Bruzzone (2017) on how Thucydides writes within a literary tradition of 'compound misfortune' (war and plague or famine, and so on). Death piles up on multiple levels.

DEATH AND THE PLAGUE IN THUCYDIDES   203

the death, but corpses were even lying upon one another as they died, and they were rolling about in the streets and around all the fountains, half-dead, desperate for water. And the temples in which they were camped were full of corpses, as people were dying right there inside them; for, since the disaster was forcing itself violently upon them, the people, with no idea what would become of them, turned to contempt of both sacred and profane alike. And all the customs that previously they would observe in burials were confounded, and they began burying as each one could, and many turned to shameful modes of burial for want of resources because so many of their family had already died; for, getting to other people's pyres first, ahead of those that had raised them, some, putting their own corpse on it instead, set it alight, whereas others, if another pyre was already burning, threw the corpse that they were bringing on top of the other and went away.

Things fall apart: funerary customs and respect for the laws of men and the gods (this escalates in paragraph 53). But the destruction has a thoroughly centripetal force. Crammed into the city, confined in suffocating huts and temples, bodies squeeze together living, dying, and dead. Death comes with a choking pressure: the influx of people that weighs down upon (ἐπίεσε) the Athenians; their containment in huts that are described as 'stifling' (καλύβαις πνιγηραῖς, 2.52.2). These are situations of ambiguous metaphor—literal death or unbearable suffering—and both are claustrophobic. Thucydides piles up detail upon detail with καί after καί (eight in total, nine following Gomme's suggested emendation).[48] A profusion of compound words (words such as 'half-dead' ἡμιθνῆτες, 'already-dead' προτεθνάναι, and 'dying-right-there' on the spot ἐναποθνῃσκόντων)—to which we can add three instances of 'corpse' or 'dying person' (νεκροί, νεκρῶν, νεκρόν)—intensifies the feeling of agglomeration; this is a literary foil to the heaped pyres on which the living toss their dead.

In part, this contributes to the *exceptional* horror of the plague: the situation is not ordinary and neither are the deaths or the responses to them (this is precisely what makes the treatment of the dead so shocking; it deviates from custom). Indeed, Thucydides culminated his list in Book 1 of the natural disasters that accompanied the war with the plague—more harmful and destructive than all.[49] But the massing of bodies also introduces a more existential point: with the group (especially the disordered group) comes a loss of the individual.[50] The whole paragraph is concerned with dissipation of what makes these people

---

[48] Gomme (1956: vol. 2, 158) on 2.52.2.

[49] 1.23.3: καὶ ἡ οὐχ ἥκιστα βλάψασα καὶ μέρος τι φθείρασα ἡ λοιμώδης νόσος.

[50] See especially Girard (1974: 833–4), 'The plague is universally presented as a process of undifferentiation, a destruction of specificities.' See further Cooke (2009: 2) on the 'social and political dimension' to plague as a 'community affliction' in contrast to illnesses such as cancer, which are seen to afflict individuals (discussed in Sontag (1991) [1978/1989]). For emphasis (in a different context) on how 'epidemic was regarded as a collective experience rather than as individual ailments', see Boeckl (2000: 154) on plague imagery in European art from the late Middle Ages to the twentieth

204 FIGURING DEATH IN CLASSICAL ATHENS

distinctive—distinctive as Greeks, Athenians, and people. The confusion of the social and cultural fabric (in ξυνεταράχθησαν, again, Thucydides emphasizes the coming together, not the falling apart, of things) is combined with loss of agency. The dying (or dead) 'were rolling about' or 'being rolled about' (the Greek word ἐκαλινδοῦντο leaves it ambiguous whether they were doing it themselves or having it done to them). Together with the sense of revolution, there is a general confusion of living and dead, action and inaction. The word νεκροί at one moment seems to mean 'the dead' and at another 'dying people', and participles for death are in the present (ἀποθνῇσκοντες, ἐναποθνῃσκόντων, 2.52.2–3), rendering dying very much a continuum, with some hanging in limbo, 'half-dead' (ἡμιθνῆτες, 2.52.2), while they die.[51] The general sense of disorder (both in arrangement and existential state) renders all, living and dead, in the same situation: all are helpless.

In this respect, though the sheer number of people that die in the plague in a short period of time and from the same cause is extraordinary, the mass confusion puts pressure upon the universalizing force of death. Insofar as death happens to everyone, it *is* universal. But ordinarily people die individually. Can and should deaths be squeezed together like this? The implications of this question are epistemological and historiographical, as well as ethical.

Indeed, having emphasized the extraordinary nature of the plague, it is worth briefly considering what mass deaths look like elsewhere in Thucydides' *History*. Though Thucydides wrote a history of war—a war that he says had a lot of bloodshed (φόνος, 1.23.2)—he spent little time dwelling upon death. His Peloponnesian War is unlike Homer's Trojan War in that we rarely, almost never, see individual soldiers die. We rarely even see groups die, though sometimes victories or defeats acknowledge casualty numbers or the return of the bodies of the dead. Nevertheless, there are other examples in his *History* where he dwells upon slaughter and dying, and it is significant that these situations have much in common with the plague.

Consider that other moment of extreme (and exceptional) Athenian suffering, despair, and mass death: the disastrous end of the Sicilian expedition. In their last stand by the river Assinarus, Nicias' army are forced to move in an impossibly dense mass (ἁθρόοι γὰρ ἀναγκαζόμενοι χωρεῖν, 7.84.3); falling and trampling upon one another, they end up trapped in confusion in a hollow of the river, where they are slaughtered by the Peloponnesians. Finally, Nicias surrendered, 'by which

---

century. For a differently tragic example, see Cole (2023) on a cemetery near Sidiro that commemorates the unidentified dead, a 'cemetery of persons once-known'.

[51] These are combined with imperfect verbs, for example ἔκειντο, ἐκαλινδοῦντο. According to Bakker (1997: esp. 37–9), the imperfects in this scene correspond to an internal viewpoint, description (as opposed to narration) that is characterized by '*generic remembering*' not knowing; see note 18.

time many bodies were lying upon one another' (νεκρῶν τε πολλῶν ἐπ' ἀλλήλοις ἤδη κειμένων, 7.85.1). Later, once the survivors are imprisoned in the marble quarries (7.87.1–2), Thucydides hammers home the cramped conditions, with many (πολλούς) confined in a small and hollow space (ἐν γὰρ κοίλῳ χωρίῳ ὄντας καὶ ὀλίγῳ), a space so small that the dead are piled together all on top of one another (he reiterates the heap with an accumulation of words to communicate amalgamation: καὶ προσέτι τῶν νεκρῶν ὁμοῦ ἐπ' ἀλλήλοις ξυννενημένων). Other things being equal, it might seem unsurprising that Thucydides should dwell upon piles of bodies when describing moments of exceptional devastation: the plague or the defeat in Sicily. But in the context of eight books in which limited space is given to death, these moments stand out, not just for the mass Athenian deaths that they present, but also because they emphasize in a similar way the quantity *and the quality* of the deaths: in both cases, bodies, dead and alive, are pressed closely together in cramped spaces.[52] Just how exceptional are these moments in the *History*? Is death always a leveller or just when something has gone wrong?

Let us compare an encounter with death in the *History* that is, in many ways, the polar opposite of these: Pericles' funeral speech (2.35–46). It is near impossible to think about death and the dead in this speech without recourse to Nicole Loraux and her point that there are no 'beautiful dead' in this speech; the speech and funeral emphasizes not the individual bodies of the dead (which have already been cremated and collated) but the abstraction that they exemplify, the 'beautiful death'.[53] Apart from the fact that most of the speech focuses not on the war dead but on the cultural and political supremacy of Athens, the references to death and the dead are brief and mostly generalized.[54] This is clear in the moment when Thucydides' Pericles offers a window into the minds of hoplites during the battle, on the cusp of death (2.42.4):

[52] See Rood (2012: 159) on the 'dense physicality' of these two descriptions; Joho (2016: 39–41) for further links between Thucydides' accounts of the plague and the imprisonment in the quarries, and the argument that narrative patterning draws attention to the destructive force of human nature: 'human nature has taken the place that mythical thinkers attributed to the divine' (page 48). The slaughter at Corcyra in Book 4.48 is also comparable (though the deaths are not Athenian). Thucydides describes how the members of the defeated Corcyraean group were attacked and slaughtered while contained in a building; at the end of the night, the Corcyraean popular party throw the corpses onto wagons 'like matwork', 'like a basket' or 'arranged cross-wise' (φορμηδόν, 4.48.4). Again, mass death is effected in a small space. This time, the pile of the dead has an order to it that, in its own way, depersonalizes the dead: bodies are treated like matter for craft, woven anew into a cohesive object.

[53] Loraux (1982: 34–5).

[54] Though Pericles does, at the conclusion of the speech, invite his audience to lament their loved ones individually before departing: νῦν δὲ ἀπολοφυράμενοι ὃν προσήκει ἑκάστῳ ἄπιτε (2.46.2). On the contrasts between the language here—and, indeed, the customary behaviour of the Athenians that Thucydides describes in 2.34.7 (μετὰ δὲ τοῦτο ἀπέρχονται)—and the cursory departure of Athenians (ἀπῇσαν, 2.52.4) after using other people's pyres during the plague, see Hutchinson (2013b: 213–15).

206 FIGURING DEATH IN CLASSICAL ATHENS

καὶ ἐν αὐτῷ τῷ ἀμύνεσθαι καὶ παθεῖν μᾶλλον ἡγησάμενοι ἢ [τὸ] ἐνδόντες σῴζεσθαι, τὸ
μὲν αἰσχρὸν τοῦ λόγου ἔφυγον, τὸ δ' ἔργον τῷ σώματι ὑπέμειναν καὶ δι' ἐλαχίστου καιροῦ
τύχης ἅμα ἀκμῇ τῆς δόξης μᾶλλον ἢ τοῦ δέους ἀπηλλάγησαν.

And in the very moment of defending themselves, thinking it better even to suffer
death than to surrender and save themselves, they fled from what might be shameful in words, and submitted to the deed against their body and, in the briefest
moment of their fate, the very pinnacle of renown rather than fear, they departed.

The difference between these deaths (in the words of Thucydides' Pericles) and
the deaths told in Thucydides' account of the plague and the Sicilian defeat is
vast. These men are not destroyed, they 'depart' (ἀπηλλάγησαν); they (appear to)
feel no pain; their bodies do not accumulate in piles. They also, apparently, made
the right choice, the choice to stay and die gloriously, rather than to surrender
and to save themselves.[55] Most importantly, these men have been given due honours: ὁ πάτριος νόμος, their ancestral funerary rights. Insofar as Pericles' speech
generates encounters with death amidst a vision of perfect and idealized civic
cohesion, it sits in contrast to the disorderly deaths of the plague and at Sicily,
which present a mass and nameless equivalent of the Homeric disfigured corpse.[56]

There are, nevertheless, ways of complicating this picture, not so much to
depart from it as to probe its more existential implications. Consider what is
similar about these encounters. All three passages present a loss of the individual
in death: in one case (in the plague and in Sicily), persons are piled into a chaotic
mess of bodies; in the other (the funeral speech), bodies and identities disappear
into a coherent, idealized 'they'.[57] The political implications of the treatment of
the war dead in fifth-century Athens have been much discussed: it was not just in
a funeral speech such as this (apparently in the sort of words, if not the exact
words, that, in Thucydides' opinion, Pericles would have used in his speech)[58]

---

[55] The Athenians in the plague and at the river Assinarus had no such choice—or, at least, they did not
have the option to save themselves. Nevertheless, there may be an implicit ethical comparison here
between the choice made by the war dead and the 'choices' made by some Athenians in the plague.
Indeed, on Jeffrey Rusten's (1986) analysis and translation, Thucydides' Pericles emphasizes the rationality of the hoplites in the very moment that they chose to fight. The rationality underpinning this choice
can be contrasted with the chaos in which choices are made during the plague and in defeat.

[56] The fires of corpses that burn during the plague of Hom. *Il.* 1.52 are also 'close-set'.

[57] On this point, note especially Orwin (1994: 182): 'Stasis and plague concur in suggesting that there
is no greater political misfortune for human beings than to be freed from the constraint posed by their
bodies. Both phenomena thus comment on the Funeral Oration. [...] The Funeral Oration, despite or
because of its genre, consistently abstracts from death and the body. The plague, by contrast, brings home
both the primacy and frailty of the body—as well as its centrality to actual political life in Athens as elsewhere.' See further Ober (2009: 451–4) [2001] on tensions between the individual/few and the many
in Pericles' funeral speech; Taylor (2010: 64–74) on Thucydides' criticism of Pericles' idealized vision of
Athens as 'an immaterial *polis* unbounded by the physical' (page 64) in his funeral speech.

[58] *History* 1.22.1. On Thucydides' claim to ἀκρίβεια (precision) and authority, and the embarrassment
caused him by speeches, see Crane (1996: ch. 2). Though see Wilson (1982), who finds no conflict

that the war dead were stripped of their individuality, but in inscriptions on casualty reliefs, which listed only the name and tribe (not the patronymic or deme), and occasionally the military position held.[59] Emphasis has been placed on the democratic significance of this treatment—a positive vision of equality sustained in death as well as life. On the other hand, Nicole Loraux has explored ways in which this generalized public death (and the associated restrictions that were placed on public display of private mourning) might have been (on its own) emotionally unsatisfactory, with tragedy providing an outlet for the 'mourning voice'.[60]

What, then, does it do to position one sort of state-sanctioned, largely depersonalized mass death (mediated by the funeral oration) alongside an account of plague in which the impersonal treatment of the dead (thrown on any pyre available) is deeply disturbing—and intended to be so? Yes, these can be described as two different sorts of levelling—a levelling *up* (into an edifying abstraction: 'the war dead') and a levelling *down* (into a horrifying mass of bodies). But the sequence from the speech to the plague provokes more than a contrast; it provokes a double take, as it were—reflection on the homogenizing force not just of plague and war but, more significantly, of the fifth-century Athenian treatment of the dead. At a high level, the speech and the plague present *two* situations in which large-scale death puts bodies in an amorphous mass: one apparently good; one manifestly terrifying. The claim is that these are different situations, but the massing of one with the other within the same book (and, in turn, with a tragedy such as the defeat at Sicily within the same work) draws readers' attention to the possibility that they might glimpse the deaths of the plague in the funeral speech and vice versa—the implication being that death is, either way, a loss of the self, a loss of the individual. The possibility is unsatisfactory, not least because the situations are so obviously different: readers are invited both to draw an analogy and to resist generalization, to consider a shift between the individual and the general that (from an existential perspective) is both ethically and epistemologically problematic. What is at stake is not just what death is but whether one can ever know.

---

between Thucydides' practice and his claims and Fornara (1983: ch. 4) on a convention, resulting from 1.22, that speeches in Greek and Roman historiography '[required] accurate reproduction in substance, always with the possibility, when necessary, of expansion, truncation, or reduction' (page 145). See further Wilson (1982).

[59] Note, too, private gravestones such as that of Chairedemos and Lykeas at Salamis (Piraeus Archaeological Museum: 385): these two are named and distinguished, and they have been given a private monument that is separate from the casualty lists in which their names also appear; they are also, however, homogenized, shown as quintessential hoplites despite the possibility that Lykeas was a trierarch. See Arrington (2015: 221–3).

[60] Loraux (2002: esp. 50–3, 87–90). See further Loraux (1986a: 42–56) [1981] on the shift effected by the funeral speech from lament ($\theta\rho\hat{\eta}\nu o\varsigma$) to praise ($\check{\epsilon}\pi a\iota\nu o\varsigma$).

208 FIGURING DEATH IN CLASSICAL ATHENS

On this note, let us revisit my earlier comparison between Thucydides' account of the plague, a treatise such as *Epidemics* 3, and the staging of Herakles' death in the *Women of Trachis*. *Epidemics* 3 includes a series of case studies of individuals, individuals that are occasionally named and often distinguished.[61] Cases 4 and 5, for example, concern Philistis and Chaerion, while 6 concerns the young daughter of Euryanax and 8 a young man who was lying at the Liars' Market. Likewise, Sophocles presents us with an individual: Herakles. In several essential ways Herakles differs, of course, from real Athenian subjects: he is a mythological hero; he will attain immortality; his situation and ontology are exceptional.[62] The subjects that populate the case studies of *Epidemics* 3 are, by contrast, ordinary. But, albeit in different ways, both Herakles and the medical subjects are individual sufferers.

By contrast, there are no individuals in Thucydides' plague. It is striking, for instance, that he does not draw attention, as he might have done, to the vulnerability of the victims as women and children—those who die are indistinguishably 'people' ($\dot{a}\nu\theta\rho\dot{\omega}\pi\omega\nu$, 2.48.2, 2.49.5, 2.54.1).[63] Rather, when it comes to Thucydides' description of plague within a wider frame of war and politics, the individual has been sacrificed in the interests of 'history': Thucydides' declared purpose in describing the disease (or, rather, its 'general nature') was to enable posterity to identify it should it occur again (2.48.3). To some extent, in fact, the value of generalization for Thucydides' historical purpose coincides with its value for social and political response to pandemic in recent history. The general was essential in identifying common symptoms (the goal to which Thucydides' description seems targeted), and in public response, where the interests of society's survival in general were seen to outweigh individual or more localized experiences and liberties. Elaine Scarry's thinking on appropriation of pain for assertion of state power is illuminative here:

> As an actual physical fact, a weapon is an object that goes into the body and produces pain. As a perceptual fact, it lifts the pain out of the body and makes it visible or, more precisely, it acts as a bridge or mechanism across which some of pain's attributes—its incontestable reality, its totality, its ability to eclipse all else, its power of dramatic alteration and world dissolution—can be lifted away from their source,

---

[61] On the lack of interest in individual experience in patient cases of the *Epidemics*, see Thumiger (2018: 264), though in the rest of the chapter she delves deeper into the doctor–patient relationship.

[62] See further my discussion of Oedipus on pages 137–8.

[63] This is in marked contrast to the chorus' description of the Theban plague in Sophocles' *Oedipus the King* (167–88). Though no individuals are mentioned by name, attention is drawn to the vulnerability of the sufferers: to the agonies of women in childbirth and the children that die and depart in a visual spectacle—a multitude of individuals, each like a well-winged bird ($\check{a}\lambda\lambda o\nu$ δ' $\ddot{a}\nu$ $\check{a}\lambda\lambda\dot{a}$ $\pi\rho o\sigma\acute{\iota}\delta o\iota s$ $\check{a}\pi\epsilon\rho$ $\epsilon\check{v}\pi\tau\epsilon\rho o\nu$ $\check{o}\rho\nu\iota\nu$ | $\kappa\rho\epsilon\hat{\iota}\sigma\sigma o\nu$ $\dot{a}\mu a\iota\mu a\kappa\acute{\epsilon}\tau o\nu$ $\pi\nu\rho\grave{o}s$ $\check{o}\rho\mu\epsilon\nu o\nu$ | $\dot{a}\kappa\tau\grave{a}\nu$ $\pi\rho\grave{o}s$ $\dot{\epsilon}\sigma\pi\acute{\epsilon}\rho o\nu$ $\theta\epsilon o\hat{\nu}$, 175–7).

can be separated from the sufferer and referred to power, broken off from the body and attached instead to the regime.[64]

Though there is clearly no equivalence between the power to absorb individuals into a social group (whether through statistics or policy treatment) and the power to harness another's pain by torture, there is a common thread in terms of whether representation of a widespread experience can do justice to individual incidence. At a granular level, Thucydides' 'general picture' has generated a flood of scholarship attempting (and failing) to identify the medical term by which we would now refer to the Athenian plague; tellingly, the sticking point in each case seems to be the mismatch of one or two specific symptoms.[65] From a more macro perspective, the problem of representing disease is a much larger one of possibility (overcoming subjective experience) and methodology. The specific problem of accessing and representing an individual's plague experience opens onto a wider discourse as to the challenges of drawing general principles or patterns applicable to a larger group; the problem of subjectivity and the dubious value of generalization carry implications both for Thucydides' declared objectives as a historian and for more existential questions regarding what it is like to die.[66]

These are questions with which Thucydides grapples explicitly as a historiographer of plague. He acknowledges that he has omitted many symptoms of the disease that were more 'unusual' (ἀτοπίας, 2.51.1) because the plague's effect was distinct for different people (ὡς ἑκάστῳ ἐτύγχανέ τι διαφερόντως ἑτέρῳ πρὸς ἕτερον γιγνόμενον, 2.51.1).[67] What he offers is 'the general picture'

---

[64] Scarry (1985: 56).   [65] See note 5.

[66] Relevant here is Ober (2009, esp. 446–7) [2001] on tensions between 'Thucydides *Histōr*' and 'Thucydides *Theōrētikos*' (though he focuses on state power). See further de Romilly (2005: 15–30) on the relationship between generality and particularity in Thucydides, especially page 20 on the plague; Kallet (2006: 353–6) on Thucydides' explicit emphasis on generalization here as part of his pedagogical undertaking to his readers. Compare the accounts in Herodotus 1.105 (also 4.67) of the 'female disease' (θήλεαν νοῦσον) and Xenophon *Anabasis* 4.5.7–9 of 'cow hunger' (ἐβουλιμίασαν). Though there are notable differences in the types, declared origins, and treatability of these diseases, and both historians at least gesture towards uncertainty, it is interesting that both appear confident in generalizing about the disease (and, in Xenophon's case, about its cause and cure). Herodotus is clear that the disease can be observed among the Scythians but undercuts the reliability of its divine cause (Aphrodite) with his formulation 'they say' (Lloyd (2003: 116–17) underemphasizes this formulation, though he is right that Herodotus does not explicitly reject divine involvement). Xenophon emphasizes his initial ignorance as to what the disease was but then gives two general statements as to its treatability akin to Hippocratic aphorisms (see note 71): a future vivid construction 'if they eat something, they will get up again' and a generic statement 'whenever they ate something, they would stand up and carry on marching'. Neither historian draws attention to the methodological problem of generalization.

[67] Compare 2.51.2, ἕν τε οὐδὲ ἓν κατέστη ἴαμα ('Absolutely no single remedy established itself', Hornblower's translation). There was no universal cure.

210 FIGURING DEATH IN CLASSICAL ATHENS

(τοιοῦτον ἦν ἐπὶ πᾶν τὴν ἰδέαν, 2.51.1).[68] The word ἰδέα in particular, as a form, semblance, sort, kind, or idea, communicates that what Thucydides can represent is an impression, something similar in nature to the specific but only an approximation for the situation of each individual patient.[69] The dubious extent to which generalization can accommodate a diverse set of phenomena is at the heart of the challenge of representing a widespread human experience, whether epidemic or death. The problem is already there in tragedy and in the Hippocratic corpus, each of which present exemplary deaths. Sophocles' Herakles is exceptional but he also offers an icon, not for admiration as such, but in that he stands as a representative of cultural ideas and associations and so can mediate reflection upon social concerns such as suffering and death.[70] The medical subjects are individuals but the premise of the treatise is that they are members of a group and, through resemblance to one another as patients, can facilitate recognition and comprehension of medical conditions.[71] Thucydides skips the individuals altogether; if anything, it is the plague itself, and not its victims, that has exemplary force. But he invites readers to notice the tension between general and particular as part of a methodological reflection.[72]

Thucydides experienced the disease himself and he observed others with it. But how illuminating can personal testimony be? How helpful is anyone's example even in a circumstance where plague (or death) happens to affect all in the same way? Can one man's experience hold for another? In fact, given that a victim's ability to grasp and describe their own subjective experience seems to falter in the face of plague, it is doubly questionable how close even a personal insight can bring readers to an understanding of what it was generally like to have the disease. This returns us to the statement in 2.50.1 with which Thucydides

---

[68] Lloyd (2003: 126) observes that this distinguishes him from the authors of the *Epidemics* but does not delve into the methodological problems. See Allison (1997: 65–73) on abstraction in Thucydides' plague description and the move from observed evidence to words and concepts, 'from event to *logos*'. Thucydides' predilection for abstract expression: Denniston (1952: 28, 40). Thucydides' interest in 'the human and the generic, the constants, and the larger general rules behind the observable world': Thomas (2006: 87). See note 12.

[69] See further the discussion of εἶδος above with notes 40 and 73.

[70] Compare King (2017: 157–8) on how literary genres in Greek imperial culture reformulated ideas about pain and its language.

[71] On the feedback loop between primary evidence and generalizations and aphorisms in the Hippocratic corpus, see Langholf (1984: esp. 133–4). On the Hippocratic triangle of doctor, patient, and illness, and the circle of similarity, difference, and generalization, see Perilli (2018: 130, 136–9). See further Lane Fox (2020: 218–19). De Romilly (1990: 121–3) also comments on how the approaches of the Hippocratics and Thucydides are both founded on identifying general principles from observations, concluding, 'Thucydide écrit l'histoire en clinicien'.

[72] This problem is also raised in Book 1. Consider the discussion of 1.22.3–4 above: Thucydides says that he offers a clear view (τὸ σαφὲς σκοπεῖν) gleaned from the painstaking review of eyewitness reports that did not say the same things (οὐ ταὐτὰ περὶ τῶν αὐτῶν ἔλεγον), either from bias or memory failure.

DEATH AND THE PLAGUE IN THUCYDIDES   211

crowns his description (see above). What the plague was, its nature, was not just beyond Thucydides' powers of description or reasoning as a historian but also beyond any human reckoning.[73] The sense of the unfathomable is part of what prompts reflection on the inaccessible mystery of death.[74]

IV. FAIR WORDS

What about the well-recognized artistry of Thucydides' writing? Thucydides' account of the plague is neither mythical in content nor ostentatiously 'poetic' in manner.[75] But it *does* engage profoundly with a visual and verbal landscape of mythological devastation, rendering its content 'storylike'—akin to the entertaining accounts found in other visual and literary media. And it can hardly be described as stylistically 'flat'.[76] Adam Parry and, more recently, Pantelis Michelakis have broken important ground here with their detailed discussions of the literary aspects of Thucydides' description and the connections that Thucydides' language forges with other literary plagues such as those in the *Iliad* and *Oedipus the King*.[77] But how does Thucydides' use of imagery in his treat-

[73] This flips Cochrane's optimistic account of Thucydides' 'science of history' (and kinship with Hippocratic writers) into a pessimistic account of the limitations of an empirical approach: see Cochrane (1929). See Thomas (2006: 104), 'the Plague is presented as an exception to rational explanation' and Cooke (2009: 43) on the 'creative endeavour' of writing plague. Compare Weidauer (1954: 21–31) on the meaning of εἶδος in Thucydides and Hippocratic texts ('Zustand' and 'Verfassung', 'condition' and 'constitution'): 'Daß so Außen und Innen für den beobachtenden Arzt zusammenfallen und mit ein und demselben Eindruck erfaßt werden können, zeigen noch folgende Beispiele [...]' (the following examples show that outside and inside coincide for the observing doctor and can be grasped in one and the same impression) (page 28). Note especially his comments on how the singular εἶδος represents a collective sickness (page 31). Michelakis (2019: 389–97) makes the point that the specific and paradigmatic nature of the plague does not just facilitate abstraction but generates it.

[74] On the link between an experience that challenges social paradigms (specifically, the Black Death) and a society's reconception of the world: Tuchmann (1979: 123) [1978].

[75] While the boundaries between prose and poetry are not clear-cut (beyond the basic point that only the latter is metrical—in the ancient world, at least), we can loosely distinguish them in terms of content and form: subject matter that is 'mythological' tends to fall within the remit of poetry—it is in poetry that we encounter relations between gods, heroes, and mortals, for instance—and such 'fantastic' subject matter is often combined with more elaborate language and imagery—metaphor, simile, striking words, and so on. Any of these features can be described as 'poetic', even when they appear in a non-metrical work such as Thucydides' *History*.

[76] See Graff (2005) on poetry, prose, and the probing of their porosity in Classical theories (including the descriptors 'excessive'—ὑπὲρ τὸ ἀξίωμα—and 'flat'—ταπεινός—that were employed by Aristotle).

[77] On 'the plague as a *literary* phenomenon' see especially Michelakis (2019: citation at 382). See further Mittelstadt (1968) (see notes 7 and 81); Parry (1969); Morgan (1994: 205–6). On literary aspects of Thucydides' writing more generally, see, for example, Lateiner (1977) on pathos in Thucydides. For a history of scholarship on Thucydides, which has swung between emphasis on his *History* as science and emphasis on it as art, see Murari Pires (2006). Epic and tragic echoes in Thucydides: Joho (2017). Herodotus' influence upon Thucydides: Rood (1999). Thucydides' narrative legacy from Herodotus and

212 FIGURING DEATH IN CLASSICAL ATHENS

ment of plague and death contribute to the epistemological discourse that I unpack in this chapter? Well, this is a writer who declares, from the outset (1.22.4), that 'the fabulous'—τὸ μυθῶδες, 'a good story'—is absent from his *History* and that his work is not a 'competition piece'—ἀγώνισμα—something deliberately engaging and embellished in style (like an epideictic speech or a tragedy).[78] A writer who claims that all this makes his work less appealing but gives it greater utility. Given his methodological reflections and the aspects of his approach that chime with those in the Hippocratic corpus, the poetic-artistic-storylike qualities of the language in his plague account are not just evocative but polemical.[79] In this section of the chapter, I dig deeper into some of these qualities before proposing one way in which they prompt reflection on the knowability of death.

A figurative mode of thought pervades the account, associating war, plague, and death.[80] The partnership of 'war and plague' is established from the start,

---

Homer: Rengakos (2006). Thucydides' 'agonistic intertextuality': Corcella (2006: 56). Emphasizing the dynamic nature of historiographical genres in antiquity and that each historiographical work 'both comprehends and challenges' genre: Marincola (1999: citation at 321). See further Ponchon (2017: pt. 1) on Thucydides' intellectual and generic debts (historiographical, scientific, epic, tragic). But see Greenwood (2006: 7) on Thucydides' '[strenuous suppression of] the fame and influence of [Homer, Herodotus, and other] authors in his work'. Historians as 'writing something at odds with the temper of the time': Gabba (1981: 52).

[78] τὸ μυθῶδες is difficult to define precisely, but I broadly follow Gomme (1945: vol. 1, 149) on 1.22.4: τὸ μυθῶδες refers to a 'story-telling element' as opposed to mythology (though mythology makes a good story). Compare the narrower view in e.g. Flory (1990), who reads τὸ μυθῶδες as referring specifically to patriotic, idealistic anecdotes. In my view, the latter, too, make a 'good story' and that is partly because they gain, in the telling and remembering, a legendary and exemplary status: consider the inclusion in funeral speeches (and probably on the temple of Athena Nike) of not just distant (more obviously 'mythological') stories of Amazons, Thebes, and Eurystheus, but also more recent past exploits also worthy of pride and emulation such as victories in the Persian Wars (see page 172, note 76). 'Mythological content' cannot be neatly differentiated from real content. Mythical elements in Thucydides, born of an Athenian conception of the world ('Thucydides Mythistoricus'): Cornford (1907) (note especially page 131 on the oral tradition and how 'fact shifts into legend, and legend into myth [...] The story is moulded and remoulded by imagination'). The relationship between myth and history in early Greece and the 'atmospheric saturation achieved by myth in the thoughtworld in which Herodotus and Thucydides were implicated': Cartledge (1993: 18–35, citation at 27). Note further White (1981), who unpacks the value of narrativity in historiography and representation of reality; Moles (1993) on the melding of fact and fiction in the genre of historiography. On the differences between fictional and factual narratives, see especially Genette (1990); Hornblower (2010) [1994]. Pre-history of history in epic: Hartog (2000: esp. 394), 'Like the bard, the historian deals with memory, oblivion, and death'. For the argument that Thucydides does not reject poetic embellishment so much as claim that his subject does not need it, and that his graphic, realistic accounts are an *alternative* to mythologized narrative: Woodman (1988: 7–9, 23–8).

[79] On Thucydides' suppression of intertextual resonances as part of his historiographical agenda: Greenwood (2006: 6–11).

[80] Connection between plague and war in Thucydides (two παράλογα—phenomena beyond human reason): Parry (1969: 115–16). See further Allison (1983: 18) on parallels between war and plague and death as their 'common denominator'; Jouanna (2006: 198–9). Thucydides writes himself into a plague/war tradition (Homer, Aeschylus, Sophocles): Woodman (1988: 32–3); note 47. Thucydides rewrites a relationship in the literary tradition between civil war and plague: Demont (1990: 154–5). Associations

DEATH AND THE PLAGUE IN THUCYDIDES   213

with the first outbreak of the plague following fast upon an invasion of the Peloponnesians with their allies (2.47.1–3). At a macro level, this association is reaffirmed in the ring-composition with which Thucydides concludes his narrative, reflections on the double scourge—plague and war—that squeezed Athens within and without (ἀνθρώπων τ' ἔνδον θνῃσκόντων καὶ γῆς ἔξω δῃουμένης, 2.54.1), and which seemed to confirm the words of the oracle: 'A Dorian war will come, and a plague with it' (ἥξει Δωριακὸς πόλεμος καὶ λοιμὸς ἅμ' αὐτῷ, 2.54.2).

But the figurative overlap runs deeper, with each disaster comprising a foil to the other: the plague in this account is a war; the Peloponnesian War is a plague. As Tim Rood has argued, the geographical movement of the plague down from Ethiopia picks up the movement of its symptoms down through the body; this not only turns attention upon the threat posed to Athens by the spatial reach of the war (as Rood suggests),[81] but also turns the plague into a destructive force akin to an invading army. The plague sweeps into Athens with remarkable speed and violence; it is a force from abroad, from Ethiopia beyond Egypt, that 'descends' (κατέβη, 2.48.1) via Egypt, Libya, and Persia. Moreover, Thucydides furthers the impression of hostile incursion with the explicit links that he draws between the events of the plague and the war. He assembles, at the start of his description, an analogous series of firsts: the plague's first appearances (ἡ νόσος πρῶτον ἤρξατο, 2.47.3), first origins (ἤρξατο δὲ τὸ μὲν πρῶτον, 2.48.1), first attacks (τὸ πρῶτον ἐν τῷ Πειραιεῖ ἥψατο τῶν ἀνθρώπων, 2.48.2), and the invasion of the same numbers of Spartan forces and her allies as 'first' assembled against Athens the previous year (ὥσπερ καὶ τὸ πρῶτον ἐσέβαλον ἐς τὴν Ἀττικήν, 2.47.2).

The plague is then given a life of its own: like the Peloponnesian military forces that 'cut down', 'slay', 'waste' the Attic land (ἐδῄουν τὴν γῆν, 2.47.2; γῆς ἔξω δῃουμένης, 2.54.1), the plague is violent.[82] It 'dives into' Athens (ἐσέπεσε, 2.48.2),[83] lays physical touch on the men of the Piraeus (ἥψατο, 2.48.2), and

---

with war perfuse plague literature more extensively. On connections between plague and war in the *Iliad*, see Blickman (1987). Note, too, the agonistic and military language in which authors of Hippocratic texts talk of fighting incurable diseases: von Staden (1990: 97–102), 'Disease and healer, contestants in the agon for incurability and health, respectively, thus both are living, active agents' (page 99). See further Mitchell-Boyask (2008: 39–41) on the idea of disease as an attack from outside in early Greek thought. The disease-war or disease-fight metaphor is thus not particular to Thucydides' description but has particular effect in the context of his history of war. Beyond antiquity, we find war-plague associations in the literature of Early Modern England: Miller (2016: 161–81). Note, too, Alessandro Manzoni's representation of the outbreak of the 1630 plague in Milan (and more widely in Italy) in chapter 31 of *I Promessi Sposi* (1827): this begins, like Thucydides' account, with a feared invasion of German troops.

[81]   Rood (2012: 159). See further Mittelstadt (1968) on parallels between the progress of the disease through the body and the destruction of the Athenian empire (page 151) and, more generally, on the figurative significance of the plague in Thucydides' *History*.

[82]   War and injuring: Scarry (1985: 63–81). War and force: Weil (2005) [1989].

[83]   On medical use of compound words in πιπτ- see Hornblower (1991: 481) on 3.82.2.

214 FIGURING DEATH IN CLASSICAL ATHENS

'squeezes' the Athenians (ἐπιέζοντο, 2.54.1). Its symptoms 'seize' (ἐλάμβανε, 2.49.2), 'overturn' (ἀνέστρεφε, 2.49.3), 'fall upon' (ἐνέπιπτε, 2.49.4), 'burn' (ἐκάετο, 2.49.5), 'oppress' (ξυνεχόμενοι, 2.49.5), 'attack' with a 'seizure' (τῶν γε ἀκρωτηρίων ἀντίληψις αὐτοῦ ἐπεσήμαινεν. κατέσκηπτε γὰρ ἐς αἰδοῖα...2.49.7–8). Men are 'destroyed' and 'defeated' by it (διεφθείροντο, νικώμενοι, 2.51.5). Indeed, the first victims of the plague, those in the Piraeus, initially believe the force that kills them *is* a military one, substituting one cloak-and-dagger aggressor, the Spartans (who, they think, have thrown poison into their cisterns), for another, the plague.[84] The plague's advent is sudden and furtive (ἐξαπιναίως ἐσέπεσε, 2.48.2; τοὺς δὲ ἄλλους ἀπ' οὐδεμιᾶς προφάσεως, ἀλλ' ἐξαίφνης [...] ἐλάμβανε, 2.49.2). So are its weapons, which pierce the men like arrows, transfixing them like the sickness that 'runs right through' the body of the Athenian diseased (διεξῄει, 2.49.7).[85] The Athenian plague has vitality, agency, and ferocious strength.

Integral to the metaphorical power of Thucydides' imagery here is the cultural tradition through which he writes.[86] At least some Athenians (including Thucydides) must have recalled the plague of the *Iliad*, if not during the fifth-century plague itself, then when considering it in retrospect.[87] The language of the ambiguous oracle cited by Thucydides, 'A Dorian war will come, and a plague with it' (see page 213), calls to mind another war and plague that together ravaged another people cramped in temporary shelter (albeit a military camp, rather than pop-up huts and cabins): the Achaean camp in Homer's *Iliad* 1; in the words of Achilles, war and plague together/at once, will break the Achaeans (εἰ δὴ ὁμοῦ πόλεμός τε δαμᾷ καὶ λοιμὸς Ἀχαιούς, *Il*. 1.61).[88]

Apollo, too descended from elsewhere (βῆ δὲ κατ' Οὐλύμποιο καρήνων, *Il*. 1.44) and shot his arrows from far off (ἕζετ' ἔπειτ' ἀπάνευθε νεῶν, μετὰ δ' ἰὸν ἕηκε, *Il*. 1.48); echoes of his wrath (χωόμενος and χωομένοιο, *Il*. 1.44, 46) and stealth (ὁ δ' ἤϊε νυκτὶ ἐοικώς, *Il*. 1.47)[89] underscore the deadly force of the Athenian plague, which is seen only in the damage that it inflicts.[90] This damage, blisters and sores

---

[84] On accusations of well poisoning in other times of plague: Tuchman (1979: 115–16) [1978].

[85] Apollo, plague, and the 'arrows of pestilence': Crawfurd (1914: 4–9).

[86] See especially Gehrke (1994) on the porosity between history and myth (in the modern world as much as the ancient world), on myth as intentional history ('intentionalen Geschichte'), and on the self-discovery and identity consolidation (as individuals, groups, nations, and so on) that the construction of history and creation of myths facilitates. See further Atkinson (2001: 35–45), who applies Charles Rosenberg's (1992: ch. 13) argument that epidemics have a 'dramaturgic form' to Thucydides' account of the plague.

[87] Linking the birds and dogs of *History* 2.50 with the mules and dogs of *Il*. 1.50: Woodman (1988: 38).

[88] Parry (1969: 115) notes that the style of the language at the beginning of *History* 2.54 seems to echo these words of Achilles at *Il*. 1.61.

[89] Michelakis (2019: 402) comments on the 'military stealth technology' of Apollo's plague archery.

[90] Though Apollo is audible even if not visible: his arrows rattle upon his shoulders (*Il*. 1.46).

that 'flower' like war wounds upon the diseased (φλυκταίναις μικραῖς καὶ ἕλκεσιν ἐξηνθηκός, *History* 2.49.5), is infused with the affective (even erotic) imagery that Casey Dué has traced through epic, lament, love song, and Aeschylus' *Persians*, with images of warriors cut down in their prime:[91] the mass slaughter is loaded with savage beauty, horror, loss, and grief.

Intimations of pain and grief call to mind, in turn, the exemplary story of mourning group death: Niobe and the Niobids.[92] The angered archer-god lurks in the cultural background to Thucydides' plague as unassailable perpetrator of mass slaughter, not just in plague or war but also in divine nemesis against mortals.[93] The Athenian plague annihilates everything together (πάντα ξυνῄρει, 2.51.3) like the slaughter of the Niobids—helpless and unprotected beneath the arrows of the gods. These, too, in the Iliadic tradition at least, were left unburied by their kin in a gory spectacle (*Il.* 24.610–12). Even more than the Achaeans, the Niobids stand for vulnerability: defined by childhood and lack of strength, weapons, or initiative to defend themselves, they are quintessential victims. This vulnerability is present in Thucydides' imagery: his Athenians die in simile: like cattle, flocks, herds, animals for the slaughter (ὥσπερ τὰ πρόβατα ἔθνῃσκον, 2.51.4);[94] like the mules (οὐρῆας, *Il.* 1.50) on which Apollo first directs his arrows in the *Iliad*. The impression is of mass, thick-set death in groups, weak beneath a more powerful force. The helplessness of the Athenian people—men turned animals (in physical and moral frailty) before the violence of the plague—takes on cosmic significance when set against the mythological backdrop, where divine arrows massacre men, children, and beasts.

---

[91] Dué (2006: ch. 2, esp. 64–70). Though Page (1953: 107) argues that there is an 'unmistakable' medical background to Thucydides' use of the verb ἐξανθεῖν, he acknowledges similar uses in fifth-century poetry. Parry (1969: 112) also links to the *Persians*. Note, for instance, Aesch. *Pers.* 59–60 where the men that have departed from the Persian land are described as an ἄνθος, a 'blossom' or 'flower'.

[92] While Niobe and the Niobids seem to have featured in multiple visual and verbal media—from the *Iliad* to Greek tragedy (Aesch. *Niobe*, Soph. *Niobe*), from pots to temple sculpture and the throne of Zeus at Olympia (see pages 162–5 with Figures 4.7a and b and 4.8)—the surviving evidence is fragmentary and uncertain. It has been argued by Dinsmoor (1939), for example, that the group of wounded Niobids found at the Gardens of Sallust in Rome might represent some of the lost south-pediment sculptures from the temple of Apollo at Bassae. If that temple was indeed built for Apollo in thanks for his help during a time of plague (as Pausanias suggests in *Description of Greece* 8.41.7–8), then the Niobids might have been associated not just with divine slaughter but also with plague. However, much of this is conjecture.

[93] See especially Parry (1969: 114, 116) and Michelakis (2019: 385–7). Parry, for instance, notes (page 114) the poetic quality of ἐγκατασκῆψαι—used to describe the plague's (or something similar's) possible earlier outbreaks. His point that it is suggestive of a lightning bolt supports the broader association of the plague with daimonic interference. Michelakis explores at greater length the plague's 'hostile, non-human agency'—it is associated with daimonic and elemental forces, birds of prey and material objects. See further Crawfurd (1914: 22–3) and Michelakis (2019: 387–8) on the cosmic significance of plague in the tragic tradition, as in Sophocles' *Oedipus the King*, performed in the early 420s.

[94] Discussion of literal/metaphorical meaning here: Hornblower (1991: 324–5) on 2.51.4.

216 FIGURING DEATH IN CLASSICAL ATHENS

Associations between war, plague, and death, drawn explicitly in the oracle cited by Thucydides and more suggestively in the mythological tradition, are numerous and carry multiple implications. At a literal level, loss of manpower may have been one actual or perceived reason for Athens' weakness and eventual defeat in the war. More figuratively, the plague offers a foil for the events of Thucydides' *History* (and vice versa): the mass casualties in Sicily; the honour and burial of the fallen in Pericles' funeral speech. In a loose sense, echoes in word and concept communicate the macro, epic significance of both plague and war in the minds of the Athenians.[95]

More important within the context of this book, however, is how Thucydides' poetics turn attention upon the epistemological parameters that define representation of and response to mass death. Parry touches upon this in his emphasis on Thucydides' representation of the plague as daimonic, irrational, incalculable, as a 'violent challenge to the Periclean attempt to exert some kind of rational control over the historical process'.[96] The daimonic power of the plague is, indeed, important. But so is Thucydides' poetic register and the cultural tradition with which he is in discourse. The combination of the two (echoes of Apollo; echoes of a mythological tradition) is provocative and cannot only be seen as a natural or accidental result of the historian's unconscious immersion within his own cultural paradigm.[97] Rather, the whole account is a cultural katabasis of sorts, akin to the geographical and biological 'katabasis' of the plague ($\kappa\alpha\tau\epsilon\beta\eta$, 2.48.1; $\kappa\alpha\tau\epsilon\beta\alpha\iota\nu\epsilon\nu$, 2.49.3):[98] it is a literary descent into an underworld inhabited by mass deaths—the war-plague of the *Iliad*, the slaughters of Niobids, and so on.

This is suggested by the fact that the poetics of the plague narrative produce exactly the sort of history that Thucydides purports to reject. Consider, first, his exclusion of the 'legendary' or 'fabulous' ($\tau\grave{o}$ [...] $\mu\upsilon\theta\hat{\omega}\delta\epsilon\varsigma$, 1.22.4) in his reflections upon the methodology and style that underpin his *History*: his account may bring listeners less pleasure but it will offer a clear view.[99] Though the emphasis in his plague account on observation of symptoms accords with his historiographical promise of something visually vivid, the stories and supremely pleasurable poetry through which he also writes complicate any sort of neat differentiation in register or aesthetic appeal.

---

[95] Note Greenwood (2006: 7): Thucydidean references to Homer (explicit or implicit) assimilate the cultural authority of epic generally.

[96] Parry (1969: 115–16). See notes 12 and 80.

[97] See especially Cornford (1907) on 'Thucydides Mythistoricus'.

[98] Page (1953: 104) observes that this verb is common in medical writings. It is, however, not an exclusively medical term. The descent of the plague is not literally a 'katabasis' but words such as $\kappa\alpha\tau\epsilon\beta\eta$ and $\kappa\alpha\tau\epsilon\beta\alpha\iota\nu\epsilon\nu$ might conceivably bring the deathly associations of $\kappa\alpha\tau\alpha\beta\alpha\sigma\iota\varsigma$ to mind.

[99] See note 78.

DEATH AND THE PLAGUE IN THUCYDIDES 217

Note, too, Thucydides' treatment of the oracle at the conclusion of his plague account (2.54.2–3):

ἐν δὲ τῷ κακῷ οἷα εἰκὸς ἀνεμνήσθησαν καὶ τοῦδε τοῦ ἔπους, φάσκοντες οἱ πρεσβύτεροι πάλαι ᾄδεσθαι 'ἥξει Δωριακὸς πόλεμος καὶ λοιμὸς ἅμ' αὐτῷ.' ἐγένετο μὲν οὖν ἔρις τοῖς ἀνθρώποις μὴ λοιμὸν ὠνομάσθαι ἐν τῷ ἔπει ὑπὸ τῶν παλαιῶν, ἀλλὰ λιμόν, ἐνίκησε δὲ ἐπὶ τοῦ παρόντος εἰκότως λοιμὸν εἰρῆσθαι· οἱ γὰρ ἄνθρωποι πρὸς ἃ ἔπασχον τὴν μνήμην ἐποιοῦντο. ἢν δέ γε οἶμαί ποτε ἄλλος πόλεμος καταλάβῃ Δωρικὸς τοῦδε ὕστερος καὶ ξυμβῇ γενέσθαι λιμόν, κατὰ τὸ εἰκὸς οὕτως ᾄσονται.

And in the disaster, as is fitting, they remembered this oracle, the more senior among them asserting that of old it was sung: 'a Dorian war will come and a plague with it'. So then a quarrel arose amongst the people, arguing that it was not 'plague' that was specified in the oracle by the ancients, but 'famine', but suitably the 'plague' reading prevailed given the situation. For people shaped their memory according to what they suffered. And, in fact, I think that if ever another Dorian war lays hold of Athens after this one and it so happens that there is a famine, people will chant the oracle as such, as appropriate.

This has been interpreted as a wry comment, at the conclusion of his account, upon the popular tendency to look to the gods, or to some larger explanation for suffering (whereas in his *History*, by contrast, divine explanations are noticeably absent).[100] The paragraph is also about memories of hexameter (τοῦδε τοῦ ἔπους), people's readiness ('as is appropriate in difficult times') to account for their own suffering by reference to stories from the past and, crucially, the creativity inherent in memory formation (or re-formation), a creativity underpinned by a desire to find pattern, meaning, and consolation.[101] This could, again, be a critical commentary on the flimsy foundations upon which popular explanations can hang: people's needs and expectations shape what they remember. Taken together with his rejection of 'a good story' in Book 1, it seems that Thucydides decries exactly the sort of engaging account and pervasive attitude that he has just produced in his own semi-poetic response to the plague, a μῦθος of sorts infused with memories of hexameter (the Iliadic plague) and other stories from the past (the Niobids), stories at home in media that seek, in part, to entertain, emote, and enthral.

---

[100] Marinatos (1981: 139), for example, argues that Thucydides attacks not oracles per se but people's interpretations of them. See further Dover (1988: 65–73), arguing for a lack of contempt in Thucydides' discussion of the oracle in 2.54 and a change in his attitude towards oracles over the course of his life. Compare the 'elimination of the supernatural' as an 'epistemologically acceptable empirical attitude' in early Hippocratic treatises, discussed in Mansfeld (1980: esp. 378–81) (he finds roots for this change in the influence of early Presocratic natural philosophy). See further Lloyd (1987: 11–21) on attempts by the Hippocratic writers to demystify disease—a 'rationalist takeover' (page 20).

[101] There is an interesting nexus between the creativity underpinning memory and its relationship to the present and 'virtual history', as discussed in Ferguson (1997).

218 FIGURING DEATH IN CLASSICAL ATHENS

We are thus confronted with an account that is steeped in a mythological tradition of daimonic force and framed in terms that are critical of that tradition and its engaging medium. One possibility is that Thucydides sets up a deliberately agonistic discourse.[102] He draws attention to how he has appropriated a poetic register and rewritten it with a crucial difference: the cultural echoes may be there but the gods are not (except in popular interpretation).[103] But this does not do full justice to the coincidence of register and content. Why this register (and self-reflexive commentary) here? Is it, in some way, *fitting*? It is surely important that Thucydides is not overtly critical of the popular response to disaster (it is not explicit, I think, that Thucydides is not, himself, a member of the category he calls οἱ ἄνθρωποι).[104] Might the condescension that has been found in his references to 'the people's' fitting willingness to fit oracular words to their situation have been sung in tune with scholarly expectations that a daimonic reading would not be fitting in Thucydides' account?[105]

Thucydides was hyper-aware of register and methodology. For most of the *History* he sustains not just an account that is fairly free of descriptions of dying (considering that his topic is war) but also one that eschews supernatural explanations.[106] In his plague account, however, he mingles an objective, clinical description of the plague with a more metaphorical, poetic register and a suggestion that, when it comes to existential disaster, people tend to think with gods and poetry. Intentions aside, his combination suggests that, for all their unsatisfactory methodological implications, 'fair' words are a fair response to mass death.[107]

---

[102] Though, as observed above, he claimed not to compose his *History* as an agonistic feat (ἀγώνισμα) for listeners' instant gratification (τὸ παραχρῆμα) (1.22.4).

[103] On the invention of prose as a contest of authority, see Goldhill (2002: esp. 1–9). See further Demont (1990: 152–3), who points out that Thucydides has reversed cultural associations regarding the causal relationship between failure to bury or respect the dead and plague (as divine punishment for that failure), which might suggest that he reworks daimonic patterns in more realistic terms.

[104] Kallet (2013), at least, thinks Thucydides leaves the possibility of divine intervention as a 'co-combatant', page 373) open, though she does describe Thucydides' treatment of the oracle in 2.54.2–3 as '"comfort-zone" Thucydides'. Compare (as representative of the more standard view) Thomas (2006: 87) on Thucydides' '[implicit rejection of] any idea that the divine might play a part in either individual actions, or the larger patterns of history'. Though a certain superiority seems perceptible in the suggested distance between himself and οἱ ἄνθρωποι, it is important, and acknowledged in Thucydides, that the gods and oracles *do* have a part to play in social conceptualization of disaster and 'the larger patterns of history'. Note evidence for fluctuation in religious activity and feeling during and after the plague: Mikalson (1984).

[105] Kallet (2013: 356) makes a similar point.

[106] See for example Lane Fox (2020: 274, 279–80).

[107] Kitto (1966: 273) observed, 'of the passages of free description, a remarkable number—very remarkable in "a cold and scientific historian"—have to do with death and destruction'. See further Michelakis (2019), who argues that the linguistic and conceptual associations and cross-contaminations in plague narratives reflect and perform its real force. On the balance in Thucydides' *History* between tragic and rational conceptions of the world (and the affinity of this balance with Democritean theories), see Hussey (1985).

The result is that Thucydides' account can readily be situated within a wider discourse about death that often, for good reason, puts not just the gods but a sense of spectacle at the centre. It is highly relevant, then, that Thucydides' account has not only spurred historians of medicine and disease to analyse and re-analyse the symptoms of the Athenian plague,[108] but has also inspired a vibrant cultural reception (including Lucretius' reworking at the conclusion of *de rerum natura* and painted plagues such as Michael Sweerts's *Plague in an Ancient City, c.* 1652–4)[109] and so claimed a spot in canonical world literature and art history of plague.[110]

An uneasy impression that mass death might inherently invite an imaginative response coincides with the methodological reflections on exteriority and generality that I discussed earlier in this chapter. Perhaps this is one reason why there is not more emphasis on dying, especially mass dying, in Thucydides' *History*. Perhaps the historian's excision of death flows not just from a greater interest in the political picture but also from a sense that mass death is difficult to treat in the methodological way he deemed appropriate for the sort of history that he wanted to write.[111]

V. CONCLUSION—AND A SIMILE

Thucydides chose the Peloponnesian war as his subject because he believed it would be great ($\mu\acute{\epsilon}\gamma\alpha\nu$) and most worthy of mention ($\dot{\alpha}\xi\iota\circ\lambda\circ\gamma\acute{\omega}\tau\alpha\tau\circ\nu$) of all wars that had gone before (1.1.1). But he is also clear from the outset that there had never been so much bloodshed ($\varphi\acute{o}\nu\circ\varsigma$, 1.23.2), and that the plague contributed greatly to the human cost (1.23.3). Death may be elusive in the *History*—it is

---

[108] See King and Brown (2015) on the medical reception history of Thucydides' plague description.

[109] Lucr. *de rerum natura* 6.1138–286. See, for example, Finnegan (1999: 31–5). There are further echoes in Giovanni Boccaccio's fourteenth-century account of the Black Death (and especially its impact on customs and morals) in his introduction to the Prima Giornata (First Day) of the *Decameron*.

[110] See Rusten (1989: 179), 'The scientific value of the description is less notable than its literary impact.' Emphasizing 'plague's position within cultural memory': Cooke (2009: 4).

[111] The spectacular and the horrible: Sontag (2019: esp. 66) [2003] on the anxieties raised by photographs that depict suffering, 'The photograph gives mixed signals. Stop this, it urges. But it also exclaims, What a spectacle!' We might think in terms of Thucydides' uncomfortable position within a 'super-genre' of mass death representation; on ancient conceptions of super-genres, see Hutchinson (2013a). Though note, in contrast, Greenwood (2006: 22–4) on Thucydides, the theatre of war, and the 'paradigmatic quality of Athenian drama' vis-à-vis the relationship between sight and insight: visuality is not inherently problematic, especially in a 'theatrical culture' such as Athens. Is it possible, then, that the sight of *death* invites the *wrong sort of viewing* for Thucydides' historiography—absorption and surprise at the expense of clarity? Note here, too, Marincola (1997: 127) on two reasons why 'the mythic' comes to be seen as inappropriate—its 'marvellous or exaggerative' nature and the methodological challenges it poses. Both these reasons seem transferable to death.

220 FIGURING DEATH IN CLASSICAL ATHENS

rarely brought into the foreground as it is in the *Iliad*, especially at an individual level (no one's soul flies groaning to Hades, death cloaks no one's eyes)—but it cannot be ignored. This is especially true at points where Thucydides deals explicitly with massive fatalities—in the plague or Sicily, for instance.

What is fascinating for the purposes of this study is how Thucydides' treatment of plague probes death's epistemological implications. An immediate discourse surrounding the knowability of another's experience of disease and the possibility of generalizing from particulars dovetails with a wider historiographical discourse—one also interested in knowability and generality. Together, these frame how readers think about death and, especially, how they grapple with the epistemological problems that it poses. Add the poetic qualities of his plague description—echoes of mythological mass deaths at the hands of the gods, figurative language, and imaginative ways of grappling with disaster—and we are left with the impression that there is something problematic about death from Thucydides' perspective. Is it inherently entertaining and spectacular? Does it resist explanation and comprehension, demanding creative, not empirical, ways of thinking? 'Death is hard to know and hard to show' (see my prologue)— especially in the sort of history that Thucydides wants to write.

Much of this is encapsulated in Thucydides' simile: the Athenians 'were dying like livestock' (ὥσπερ τὰ πρόβατα ἔθνῃσκον, 2.51.4). To some extent, the analogy tends to collapse the distance between Thucydides' readers and the deaths that occurred in the plague by reframing the extraordinary death of multitudes in more familiar terms (at least, in terms that might have been more familiar to more of Thucydides' readers than readers today). The point, perhaps, is that lots of them died at once.[112] Or that they were vulnerable beneath a stronger force (man, god, plague). Or that they lost their identity in death, shifting from Athenian citizens to a nameless mass of animals. The simile invites movement from observation to reflection, to meditation on what death is and is like.

But the simile also reframes death in terms that draw attention to the epistemological challenges posed by reflection on death. What do people know of the death of sheep? Surely the comparison makes these deaths more, not less, alien? (Does this simile, in fact, point towards the mystery that surrounds *all* death—of sheep or Athenians?) And how comparable are these deaths? The poetic register launches readers into an iterative series of literary comparisons: Thucydides' Athenians die like sheep, like Achaean mules, like Danaans, like Niobids, like flowers. Observation-based reflection on death is founded upon analogy, an imaginative and artistic mode of thought, and it brings readers close,

---

[112] See Rusten (1989: 188) on 2.51.4, 'the point of the comparison lies in the more numerous fatalities associated with diseases of livestock'.

but not too close.[113] In this respect, the invitation to figurative thought that is made by Thucydides' use of a classic literary device—a device that is characteristic of Homer—turns attention back upon the imaginative process that underpins his more empirical approach to disease. Extrapolating a generalized account of disease is founded upon comparison, upon extracting the essential features that make one situation like another.[114] The simile speaks to section III of this chapter (Missing the Trees for the Wood), to the epistemological (and ethical) problems that surround generalizing about disease or death.[115]

But the simile also speaks to section II (Beyond Reckoning). The invitation to poeticize, and mythologize, the Athenians when they die of the plague raises another epistemological problem at the heart of a history of mass death (in war or plague): to what extent does observation of another's predicament permit vicarious experience and, indeed, empathy?[116] What is at stake in seeing dying Athenians as sheep, or as subject matter for poetry (this is a point that I also discussed in Chapter Four)? The relationship between art and suffering, disease, and death, is ethically problematic. But, to the extent that knowledge of death is predicated upon perceiving it happen, the relationship also has epistemological implications. Perhaps spectacle and poetry are integral to appreciation of the existential significance of dying Athenians—to seeing them as more than medical specimens. In this respect, the comparison is not just a simile and does not just compare dying Athenians to dying sheep; it calls to mind the cultural framework through and against which existential reflection might take place.

Thucydides wrote carefully and deliberately. He made a choice to use this simile, to tap into a recognizably poetic register. In the immediate context of his plague account, and the wider context of his *History* (and, especially, his methodological and stylistic reflections), the choice has an impact akin to Socrates' adoption of a more imaginative register in his ecphrasis at the conclusion of Plato's *Phaedo*. Thucydides' enquiry, unlike Plato's, is not self-consciously philosophical (or, at least, not in the same way), and his immediate subject was not

---

[113] Compare the distance that Kathleen Miller identifies in Samuel Pepys's account of the Great Plague: Miller (2016: 174). See further Barker (2004: 668) on *The Plague of Ashdod* and Poussin's creation of 'fictive distance between the spectator and the image'.

[114] Compare Arist. *Poet.* 1457b6–33 on the categories of metaphor, three of which involve notions of genus (γένος) and species (εἶδος). In *Rh.* 1406b20–6, he considers metaphor little different from a simile.

[115] Indeed, it seems that it was this combination in Thucydides (under the influence of Hippocratic medicine) of observation with psychology, the 'unchanging rule which governs the relations between events', that Collingwood found so repugnant: 'In reading Thucydides I ask myself, What is the matter with the man, that he writes like that? I answer: he has a bad conscience. He is trying to justify himself for writing history at all by turning it into something that is not history.' See Collingwood (1993: 29–30) [1946].

[116] Note further Budelmann (2006: 146–7) on staged pain as simultaneously emotive and thought-provoking as part of a larger narrative and an object of fascination in its own right.

222 FIGURING DEATH IN CLASSICAL ATHENS

death (except insofar as a history of war is also a history of death). But his explicit engagement with the challenges surrounding movement from observation to knowledge, and from the particular to the general, invites readers to reflect not just on the existential implications of a deadly plague that accompanies and is like a deadly war, but on the epistemological problems that frame that meditation. Indeed, an epistemological process is at the heart of his stated purpose (2.48.3):[117]

> ἐγὼ δὲ οἷόν τε ἐγίγνετο λέξω, καὶ ἀφ' ὧν ἄν τις σκοπῶν, εἴ ποτε καὶ αὖθις ἐπιπέσοι, μάλιστ' ἂν ἔχοι τι προειδὼς μὴ ἀγνοεῖν, ταῦτα δηλώσω...

> But I will say what sort of thing it became, and I will make details visible from which someone, on close inspection (if ever it even attacks again), might have the best chance of not failing to recognize it, having seen it before...

Should the plague occur again, Thucydides hopes that double observation of the particulars he describes and the particulars that resurface might give his readers some hope of knowing it for what it is. He offers his account of the plague as a simile of sorts—a mirror, or potential mirror, in which his audience, whoever and whenever they are, might observe and come to recognize their own deaths.[118] This is a more intensely aesthetic version of his wider historiography—a 'sight of death' that opens new encounters and new explorations (a new 'politics', as T. J. Clark put it) on readings and re-readings[119]—because it is the only way to do death and also, given his aspirations to speak to posterity,[120] the right way to do it.

Figuring Death in Classical Athens: Visual and Literary Explorations. Emily Clifford, Oxford University Press.
© Emily Clifford 2025. DOI: 10.1093/9780198947936.003.0008

---

[117] The construction here is characteristically complex. For the suggestion that the complexity of Thucydides' expression 'replicates the intractability of historical experience', see Connor (1985: 7–8).

[118] The words of Ulrich von Wilamowitz-Moellendorff (1908: 25) on reception as, inevitably, a contamination of history, take on life here, 'We know that ghosts cannot speak until they have drunk blood; and the spirits which we evoke demand the blood of our hearts. We give it to them gladly; but if they then abide our question, something from us has entered into them; something alien, that must be cast out, cast out in the name of truth!'

[119] This is the sort of engagement and response explored by T. J. Clark (2006) before Poussin's *Landscape with a Man Killed by a Snake* in 2000—a visual experience that generated thousands of words and still resisted description.

[120] See Bakker (2006: 118–23) on the monument and 'eternal process' (page 122) of Thucydides' text—it constitutes not just an enduring monument but an enduring point of encounter, a 'dynamic permanency' (page 122); Greenwood (2006: 1–11) on the 'fiercely anticontextualist' nature of Thucydides' writing (citation at 3)—he wrote for posterity; Nicolai (2009) [1995] for an overview of the modern and ancient reception of Thucydides' words at 1.22.4 on the purpose of his *History*. Compare Lendle (1990: 235, 242), who proposes a more modest reading of Thucydides' goal for his text as of intellectual interest to his contemporary readers for their lifespan (rather than for momentary pleasure). A middle ground can be found in an opposition between 'lasting' (for *any* reader) versus 'momentary'.

CONVERSATION FOUR

Figuring (Out) Death

I. VISUAL AND LITERARY EXPLORATIONS

This book has been about an ancient struggle, a struggle with death and its knowability. What I have sought to do is build a picture of how ancient art and literature each, in their own way, helped Athenians with this struggle—helped them grapple with questions like 'What is death?', 'What is it like?', and 'How do I know?' This has taken readers on a journey from a philosopher's deathbed to the symposium; from the Athenian burial ground to the tragic theatre; from the sanctuary of Athena Nike to the devastation wrought by the Athenian plague and Peloponnesian War, a raw and recent backdrop to the construction of that sanctuary's temple.

Here, I want to put all five chapters in conversation, to delve deeper into three selected themes that both pull them together and call attention to some of their differences.

A. Beyond the Body

One thread running through each chapter is distance—in various ways, attention has been drawn to the sense in which death lies beyond the empirical experience of the living. We can, for instance, set the play-within-a-play form of the *Phaedo* alongside the Messenger's speech in Sophocles' tragedy (another ecphrastic recreation of a missed experience of looking at, and ultimately missing, someone else's death from the outside) and the emphasis on the Met lekythos on looking not so much at a site of death as a site in which figures look at a site of death.

Temporality has also had an important contribution to make here. Recall the narrative pull of Socrates' death as 'the end'—a moment either anticipated or remembered by the living but impossible to perceive in the present—and the analogies constructed by repetitions and echoes on the Getty cup, which invited drinkers to contemplate deaths past and future (including their own). In both, the moment of death itself was suggested to be a blank, with a veil lifting to reveal or falling to conceal the aftermath.

224 FIGURING DEATH IN CLASSICAL ATHENS

Indeed, what can and cannot be perceived has emerged, repeatedly, as both an enticing and inadequate means to grapple with death. We might think of the stone body on the west frieze, which simultaneously makes a spectacle of the corpse and recedes from view, the constructive function of negativity in the Messenger's account of what he did not see, and the visible hole in the pictorial field of the Met lekythos—a blank monument standing in for the invisible corpse. Compare, too, how Thucydides foregrounds exteriority in his description of the Athenian plague, pursuing an opposition between observation and experience of disease that is programmatic not just of death but of historiography. Moreover, as on the Nike west frieze (where death is approached by proxy through the image of the trophy), Thucydides' account stages indirectly the exteriority that defines the perspective of the living—through description not of death but of (fatal) disease.

B. One and Many

Another tension permeating this book is that between particularity and generality. The possibility that one person might come to know their own death through another's example is raised in the *Phaedo* and Sophocles' tragedy, each of which presents a death that is singular but that might be exemplary—Socrates' way of dying is offered as a model for emulation and Oedipus comprises a sphinx-like mix of ordinary and extraordinary.

Similar rhetoric emerges in the analogies concocted by drinking cups—in the suggested equivalence not just between two mythological old men (Priam and Phoenix) but between real and mythological scenarios. And the west frieze, too, is replete with iterations and variations both as a matter of content (an episodic collection of climactic moments of individual struggle) and composition (repeated triangles and bodies set in mirror image). The encouragement to generalize from multiple instances extends, in turn, to the real beholder, becoming an invitation to encounter one's own death in the figured scenes.

Most provocative are the explorations mediated by Thucydides' *History* and the Met lekythos. The former probes the epistemological implications of the exemplary death—or deaths—through descriptions of mass deaths, descriptions that turn attention upon the ethical implications of squeezing deaths together, of seeing one death in many (something that Thucydides explicitly says he does in offering a 'general picture' of the plague symptoms). The Met lekythos, by contrast—itself a variation on a theme of the visit to the grave—presents a profusion of images that are almost, but not quite, identical, suggesting an ontology of death as fragility and loss of individuality and an epistemology of death as something that is simultaneously personal and general, a repeating instance.

C. *Virtual Reality*

My final theme is 'virtual reality', by which I mean the status of the art and literature studied here as created artefacts, artefacts that offer a virtual means of encountering and exploring death from the outside. The invitation *almost* to encounter death—to encounter it *virtually*—is powerful for reflection on death, since death is itself associated with distance and absence. Crucial here is the reflexivity that inheres in both visual and verbal culture.

One example that I include in this category is the use of a more fantastic and figurative mode characteristic of τὸ μυθῶδες, 'a good story'. This features in the myth of Er, discussed in Conversation One, and in Socrates' self-confessedly imaginative ecphrasis of the regions within the earth and the land of the dead in the *Phaedo*. Similar in effect (though set less explicitly within an imaginative frame) are the poetic-artistic-storylike qualities of Thucydides' plague description, which engage with a cultural backdrop of mythological devastation.

But also important are the formal qualities of visual and verbal artefacts, which draw attention to their status as aesthetic objects (as well as representations of something else). Here we have the features of the Messenger's speech that re-present what he saw as 'something suitable for wonder', the doubling of painted borders and motifs as decorative and substantive (consider the meanders that yawn before the eyes of Ajax and are crossed by his feet), and the 'real life' scene on the Met lekythos that is noticeably staged for the real beholder. The latter especially, employing a combination of dimensionalities, explores not just the nature of death as absence, lack of substance, and difference but the status of the painted pot as art not life, drawing attention to the creative framework that underpins exploration of death from the perspective of the living.

II. CLASSICAL ATHENS AND BEYOND

Together, the chapters paint a picture not just of preoccupation with death in Classical Athens, but of preoccupation with its knowability. This concern was widespread; it permeated spaces that were private and public, sacred and funerary, elite, demotic, and domestic.

Given the diversity of visual and verbal material, it is worth observing not just *what* but *who* has been the subject. For instance, the intended and actual audience of Plato's *Phaedo* and Thucydides' account of the plague was likely to have been primarily male and intellectual. The theatre audience, on the other hand, though probably male (a point of debate), involved a wider citizenry. And when we turn to

226 FIGURING DEATH IN CLASSICAL ATHENS

the sacred space of the Acropolis, the make-up of visitors becomes still more diverse, encompassing free men and women from a variety of socio-economic backgrounds. Likewise, cups at the symposium may well have been handled not just by male drinkers but by others involved in the party or in its preparations and aftermath—women and the enslaved, for example. This is still more true of the funerary sphere, where anyone who might visit the Kerameikos—women and children as well as men, individuals enslaved as well as free—might respond to objects such as lekythoi.

There is, then, a local history here of widespread meditation on death and its mystery through interaction with Classical Athenian culture. And, as laid out in Conversation One, we can make sense of this local picture against a historical backdrop that was distinctively Athenian and distinctively Classical. In the wars against Persia and the Peloponnesians, the plague, the violence under the Thirty Tyrants, and the vote to condemn Socrates to death by suicide at the end of the century, we can see a series of external and internal shocks to the fifth-century polis wrought by an overwhelming, norm-shattering profusion of death. In fact, though my drinking cups were drawn from the first quarter of the fifth century, the bulk of my material largely clusters around its final three decades. Arguably, this even includes the *Phaedo*, which, though written *c.* 380 BCE, grapples with death and its knowability through the prism of the one extraordinary death that capped the century. It seems that preoccupation with death and its knowability in Athens gathers momentum. As I said in Conversation One, in some ways, this book has been a story of one culture's existential crisis, told through artefacts.

On the other hand, both cups and the theatre take us rapidly beyond Athens, to re-performances, receptions, and funerary contexts in Greece and further afield. Moreover, wider readership seems to have been anticipated by Plato and Thucydides, who, along with Sophocles, spent portions of their life outside Athens (possibly the years in which they wrote the material studied here). And even lekythoi and the west frieze of the temple of Athena Nike, objects that seem most obviously rooted in a thoroughly Athenian context, would have been viewed by non-Athenians—the semi-public nature of the Kerameikos, outside the polis walls and spread about the roads into the city, invited an audience more diverse than the family group. Add to this the fact that fifth-century Athens not only spoke but also responded to a wider intellectual and cultural environment and tradition (see Conversation Two). Thus, though this book makes Athens and Athenians its focus, it is important that the themes and concerns discussed here were not restricted to Athens; Athens is, rather, one piece of a messier puzzle—this is Athens in conversation with wider cultural and intellectual communities (past, present, and future).

III. HARD TO KNOW AND HARD TO SHOW

The claims made above are unlikely to be controversial. But it seems to me that one thornier question lurking in the background here is not so much the historical who as the *transhistorical* who. This book is about a set of cultural artefacts in relationship with historical people. The thinking that it probes was mediated by those relationships—relationships that unfurled within a particular historical framework (the symposium, the Acropolis, and so on). Its focus, and the picture it paints, is culturally specific. A major theme of the last few decades has been the notion of visuality, the sense in which a lekythos, for instance, was not just visible but visually experienced by ancient eyes—eyes that, for all their individual differences, saw in a way that can be collectively distinguished from the way eyes see today. This book embraces that idea.

But, at the same time, the themes that I have extracted here *are* familiar. There is a streak to death that smacks of universality: all bodies die. In fact, given the focus of this book, I would go further. I would emphasize not just the cultural particularity of the Athenian way of grappling with death but the commonality that I suspect could be found across many different times and places in the very necessity of exploring death imaginatively—through the creative arts. As we saw in Conversation Two, culturally mediated exploration of death and its knowability can be observed in Archaic material; the Prologue, meanwhile, pulled together a set of visual and theatrical explorations of death ranging from eighteenth-century France to fifth-century Athens.

The themes are also contemporary. To the interest in near-death experience that I acknowledged in Conversation One we can add interactive work that offers the possibility of 'dying in virtual reality' (still, crucially, 'virtual' and so somewhere on a continuum with the possibility of experiencing death through Alcestis or Socrates) and studies of what it might look like for artificial intelligence to die (another proxy).[1] Recent years have also seen a resurrected fascination with Vanitas in the contemporary art world. Consider especially Trevor Guthrie's *Myself as a Specimen* (Figure C4), which was to be included in the exhibition curated by Donald Kuspit, 'Mortality: A Survey of Contemporary Death Art'.[2]

---

[1] Shaun Gladwell's work *Passing Electrical Storms* (The Ian Potter Centre, Australia) offers the opportunity to experience dying: https://www.ngv.vic.gov.au/melbourne-now/artists/shaun-gladwell/ [Accessed 3 November 2023]. For the art of AI death, see Alexander Weinstein's science fiction short story 'Saying Goodbye to Yang' (2016: 1–22) and *What I Saw Before the Darkness*, by 'the girl who talks to AI': https://futurism.com/the-byte/watch-ai-die-neural-network [Accessed 3 November 2023].

[2] See Kuspit (2020: 5, 6, 28–9). Note especially his comments, 'strangely enough, all skulls look more or less the same, seem impersonally identical [...] any skull could be anybody else's skull' (page 3). The exhibition was planned for 2020 but cancelled because of the coronavirus pandemic and launched via its catalogue. See https://www.american.edu/cas/museum/2020/mortality-a-survey-of-contemporary-death-art.cfm [Accessed 3 November 2023].

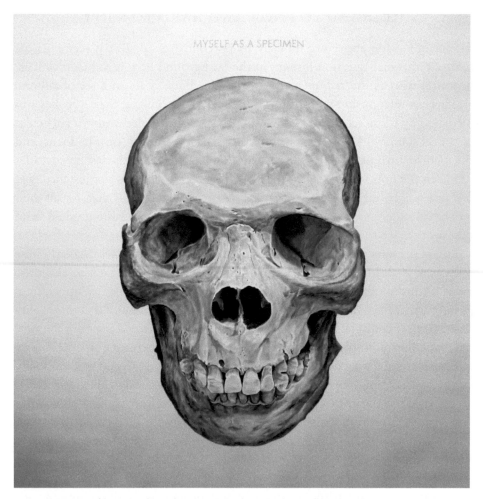

Figure C4. *Myself as a Specimen*, by Trevor Guthrie, 2009, work in charcoal and graphite on paper. 139.7 × 144.8 cm unframed. Private Collection. © Trevor Guthrie. Artwork and photograph reproduced with the kind permission of Trevor Guthrie.

In a morbid variation on the self-portrait, Guthrie presents us, in frontal view, with the blank stare of a monochrome skull. The artist, it seems, saw not himself, but himself as a 'specimen', as the object for display and study that will be left once he (and the rest of his body) has gone. This is Vanitas, a reminder not just of the artist's mortality but the mortality of all viewers; the frontal skull doubles as a representation of someone else's future (Guthrie's) and a mirror reflection of the real beholder. (After all, the words we read here are not 'Guthrie' but 'myself'.) Here, once more, is the possibility of seeing one's own death in another's example. But the 'as' in the title raises the epistemological stakes. Is this meant to be the artist-viewer's future skull (a fantastic visualization of the artist-viewer

CONVERSATION FOUR   229

become specimen) or the artist-viewer rendered 'in the guise of' a specimen?[3] The former is a fantasy; the latter a way of thinking about mortality by proxy (with someone else's skull or a false skull). Either way, the image is creative. It opens a way of exploring mortality but some questions remain. What is death? What is it like? How do we know? For the artist portraying a skull, as for the actor performing Alcestis, faking death is hard.

Figuring Death in Classical Athens: Visual and Literary Explorations. Emily Clifford, Oxford University Press.
© Emily Clifford 2025. DOI: 10.1093/9780198947936.003.0009

[3] The answer is both: the artistic process involved merging an unknown specimen and an X-ray of the artist's skull.

BIBLIOGRAPHY

ADORNATO, G. 2019. 'Kritios and Nesiotes as Revolutionary Artists? Ancient and Archaeological Perspectives on the So-called Severe Style Period'. *American Journal of Archaeology*, 123(4): 557–87.

ALBINUS, L. 1998. 'The Katabasis of Er: Plato's Use of Myths, Exemplified by the Myth of Er'. In *Essays on Plato's Republic*, edited by E. N. Ostenfeld, 91–105. Aarhus.

ALBINUS, L. 2000. *The House of Hades*. Studies in Ancient Greek Eschatology. Aarhus.

ALEXIOU, M. 2002. *The Ritual Lament in Greek Tradition*, second edition, revised by D. Yatromanolakis and P. Roilos. Lanham, MD. [First published in 1974.]

ALLAN, R. J. 2013. 'History as Presence: Time, Tense, and Narrative Modes in Thucydides'. In *Thucydides between History and Literature*, edited by A. Tsakmakis and M. Tamiolaki, 371–89. Berlin and Boston.

ALLAN, R. J. 2020. 'Narrative Immersion: Some Linguistic and Narratological Aspects'. In *Experience, Narrative, and Criticism in Ancient Greece: Under the Spell of Stories*, edited by J. Grethlein, L. Huitink, and A. Tagliabue, 15–35. Oxford and New York.

ALLEN, M. E. 2019. 'Visualizing the Afterlife in Classical Athens: Interactions between the Living and the Dead on White-Ground Lêkythoi'. In *Imagining the Afterlife in the Ancient World*, edited by J. Harrisson, 15–32. London.

ALLISON, J. W. 1983. 'Pericles' Policy and the Plague'. *Historia: Zeitschrift für Alte Geschichte*, 32(1): 14–23.

ALLISON, J. W. 1997. *Word and Concept in Thucydides*. Atlanta.

ALSINA, J. 1984. 'Hippocrate, Sophocle, et la déscription de la peste chez Thucydide'. In *Die hippokratischen Epidemien: Theorie—Praxis—Tradition*, edited by G. Baader and R. Winau, 213–21. Stuttgart.

ANDERSON, M. J. 1997. *The Fall of Troy in Early Greek Poetry and Art*. Oxford.

ANDRIEU, J. 1954. *Le dialogue antique : Structure et présentation*. Paris.

ANNAS, J. 1981. *An Introduction to Plato's Republic*. Oxford.

ANNAS, J. 1982. 'Plato's Myths of Judgement'. *Phronesis*, 27(2): 119–43.

ANTONACCIO, C. M. 1995. *An Archaeology of Ancestors: Tomb Cult and Hero Cult in Early Greece*. Lanham, MD.

ARIAS, P. E. 1962. *A History of Greek Vase Painting*, with photographs by M. Hirmer. London.

ARIETI, J. A. 1991. *Interpreting Plato: The Dialogues as Drama*. Savage, MD.

ARRINGTON, N. T. 2010. 'Between Victory and Defeat: Framing the Fallen Warrior in Fifth-Century Athenian Art'. PhD dissertation, University of California, Berkeley.

ARRINGTON, N. T. 2011. 'Inscribing Defeat: The Commemorative Dynamics of the Athenian Casualty Lists'. *Classical Antiquity*, 30(2): 179–212.

ARRINGTON, N. T. 2014. 'Fallen Vessels and Risen Spirits: Conveying the Presence of the Dead on White-Ground Lekythoi'. In *Athenian Potters and Painters*, volume 3, edited by J. H. Oakley, 1–10. Oxford and Philadelphia.

232 BIBLIOGRAPHY

ARRINGTON, N. T. 2015. *Ashes, Images, and Memories: The Presence of the War Dead in Fifth-Century Athens*. New York.

ARRINGTON, N. T. 2018. 'Touch and Remembrance in Greek Funerary Art'. *The Art Bulletin*, 100(3): 7–27.

ASMIS, E. 1992. 'Plato on Poetic Creativity'. In *The Cambridge Companion to Plato*, edited by R. Kraut, 338–64. Cambridge.

ATHANASSAKI, L. 2023. 'The Politics of Intervisuality: Euripides' *Erechtheus*, the West Pediment of the Parthenon, the Erechtheion, and the Temple of Athena Nike'. In *Intervisuality: New Approaches to Greek Literature*, edited by A. Capra and L. Floridi, 103–20. Berlin and Boston.

ATKINSON, J. E. 2001. 'Turning Crises into Drama: The Management of Epidemics in Classical Antiquity'. *Acta Classica*, 44: 35–52.

AUSLAND, H. W. 1997. 'On Reading Plato Mimetically'. *The American Journal of Philology*, 118(3): 371–416.

BACON, H. H. 1990. 'The Poetry of *Phaedo*'. In *Cabinet of the Muses: Essays on Classical and Comparative Literature in Honor of Thomas G. Rosenmeyer*, edited by M. Griffith and D. J. Mastronarde, 147–62. Atlanta.

BACON, H. H. 2001. 'Plato and the Greek Literary Tradition'. *Transactions and Proceedings of the American Philological Association*, 131: 341–52.

BAKEWELL, G. 2020. '"I Went Down to Piraeus Yesterday": Routes, Roads, and Plato's *Republic*'. *Hesperia*, 89(4): 725–55.

BAKHTIN, M. M. 1981. *The Dialogic Imagination*, edited and translated by M. Holquist, translated by C. Emerson. Austin. [Translated from essays first published in 1975.]

BAKHTIN, M. M. 1990. *Art and Answerability: Early Philosophical Essays*, edited by M. Holquist and V. Liapunov, translation and notes by V. Liapunov, supplement translated by K. Brostrom. Austin. [Contains three essays originally written in 1919 and the 1920s.]

BAKHTIN, M. M. 2004. *Speech Genres and Other Late Essays*, edited by C. Emerson and M. Holquist, translated by V. W. McGee. Austin. [Edition first published in 1986, including essays first published in 1979.]

BAKKER, E. 1997. 'Verbal Aspect and Mimetic Description in Thucydides'. In *Grammar as Interpretation: Ancient Greek Literature in its Linguistic Contexts*, edited by E. J. Bakker, 7–54, Mnemosyne Supplement 171. Leiden.

BAKKER, E. 2006. 'Contract and Design: Thucydides' Writing'. In *Brill's Companion to Thucydides*, edited by A. Rengakos and A. Tsakmakis, 109–29. Leiden and Boston.

BALDASSARE, I. 1988. 'Tomba e stele nelle lekythoi a fondo bianco'. *AION, Sezione di archeologia e storia antica*, 10: 107–15.

BARAD, K. 2008. 'Posthumanist Performativity: Toward an Understanding of How Matter Comes to Matter'. In *Material Feminisms*, edited by S. Alaimo and S. Hekman, 120–54. Bloomington and Indianapolis. [First published in 2003.]

BARDEL, R. 2000. 'Eidôla in Epic, Tragedy and Vase-Painting'. In *Word and Image in Ancient Greece*, edited by N. K. Rutter and B. A. Sparkes, 140–60. Edinburgh.

BARKER, S. 2004. 'Poussin, Plague, and Early Modern Medicine'. *The Art Bulletin*, 86(4): 659–89.

BARRETT, J. 2002. *Staged Narrative: Poetics and the Messenger in Greek Tragedy*. Berkeley.

BARRINGER, J. M. 2005. 'Alkamenes' Procne and Itys in Context'. In *Periklean Athens and its Legacy: Problems and Perspectives*, edited by J. M. Barringer and J. M. Hurwit, 163–76. Austin.

BARRON, J. P. 1972. 'New Light on Old Walls'. *The Journal of Hellenic Studies*, 92: 20–45.

BASSI, K. 2018. 'Morbid Materialism: The Matter of the Corpse in Euripides' *Alcestis*'. In *The Materialities of Greek Tragedy: Objects and Affect in Aeschylus, Sophocles, and Euripides*, edited by M. Telò and M. Mueller, 35–48. London.

BAUDRILLART, A. 1894. *Les divinités de la victoire en Grèce et en Italie d'après les textes et les monuments figurés*. Paris.

BAXANDALL, M. 1988. *Painting and Experience in Fifteenth-Century Italy: A Primer in Social History of Pictorial Style*. Oxford and New York. [First published in 1972.]

BAŻANT, J. 1985. *Les citoyens sur les vases athéniens du 6ème au 4ème siècle av. J.-C.* Prague.

BAŻANT, J. 1986. 'Entre la croyance et l'expérience : Le mort sur les lécythes à fond blanc'. In *Iconographie classique et identités régionales*, edited by L. Kahil, C. Augé, and P. Linant de Bellefonds, *Bulletin de Correspondance Hellénique*, Supplement 14, 37–44. Athens and Paris.

BAZIOTOPOULOU-VALAVANI, E. 2002. 'A Mass Burial from the Cemetery of Kerameikos'. In *Excavating Classical Culture: Recent Archaeological Discoveries in Greece*, edited by M. Stamatopoulou and M. Yeroulanou, 187–201. Oxford.

BEAZLEY, J. D. 1925. *Attische Vasenmaler des rotfigurigen Stils*. Tübingen.

BEAZLEY, J. D. 1938. *Attic White Lekythoi*. Oxford and London.

BECKER, A. S. 1995. *The Shield of Achilles and the Poetics of Ekphrasis*. Lanham, MD.

BECKER, O. 1937. *Das Bild des Weges und verwandte Vorstellungen im frühgriechischen Denken, Hermes*, Einzelschriften 4. Berlin.

BEETS, M. G. J. 1997. *Socrates on Death and Beyond: A Companion to Plato's Phaedo*. Amsterdam.

BENVENISTE, E. 1932. 'Le sens du mot Κολοσσος et les noms grecs de la statue'. *Revue de Philologie*, 6: 118–35.

BENZI, N. 2021. 'Parmenides and the Tradition of *Katabasis* Narratives'. In *Aspects of Death and the Afterlife in Greek Literature*, edited by G. A. Gazis and A. Hooper, 89–104. Liverpool.

BÉRARD, C. 1988. 'Le cadavre impossible'. *AION, Sezione di archeologia e storia antica*, 10: 163–9.

BÉRARD, C. et al. (eds.) 1989. *A City of Images: Iconography and Society in Ancient Greece*, translated by D. Lyons. Princeton. [First published in French in 1984.]

BÉRARD, C. and J.-L. DURAND. 1989. 'Entering the Imagery'. In *A City of Images: Iconography and Society in Ancient Greece*, edited by C. Bérard et al., translated by D. Lyons, 23–37. Princeton. [First published in French in 1984.]

BERGEMANN, J. 1997. *Demos und Thanatos. Untersuchungen zum Wertsystem der Polis im Spiegel der attischen Grabreliefs des 4. Jahrhunderts v.Chr. und zur Funktion der gleichzeitigen Grabbauten*. Munich.

BERGER, J. 1972. *Ways of Seeing*. London.

BERGMANN, B. A. 1996. 'The Pregnant Moment: Tragic Wives in the Roman Interior'. In *Sexuality in Ancient Art: Near East, Egypt, Greece, and Italy*, edited by N. B. Kampen, 199–218. Cambridge.

234 BIBLIOGRAPHY

BERNARD, W. 2001. *Das Ende des Ödipus bei Sophokles. Untersuchungen zur Interpretation des 'Ödipus auf Kolonos'. Zetemata*, 107. Munich.

BERNEK, R. 2004. *Dramaturgie und Ideologie. Der politische Mythos in den Hikesiedramen des Aischylos, Sophokles, und Euripides.* Munich and Leipzig.

BERNSDORFF, H. 2020. *Anacreon of Teos, Testimonia and Fragments*, edited and translated with introduction and commentary. 2 volumes. Oxford.

BESCHI, L. 2002. 'I trofei di Maratona e Salamina e le colonne del Pireo'. *Rendiconti dell'Accademia Nazionale dei Lincei*, 9(13): 51–94.

BESPALOFF, R. 2005. 'On the *Iliad*'. In *War and the Iliad. Simone Weil and Rachel Bespaloff*, with an essay by H. Broch, an introduction by C. Benfrey, and translated by M. McCarthy, 39–100. New York. [First published in French in 1947.]

BIANCHI, E., S. BRILL, and B. HOLMES (eds.) 2019. *Antiquities beyond Humanism.* Oxford.

BILLINGS, J. 2021. *The Philosophical Stage: Drama and Dialectic in Classical Athens.* Princeton and Oxford.

BIRGE, D. 1984. 'The Grove of the Eumenides: Refuge and Hero Shrine in *Oedipus at Colonus*'. *The Classical Journal*, 80(1): 11–17.

BIRK, S. 2013. *Depicting the Dead: Self-Representation and Commemoration on Roman Sarcophagi with Portraits.* Aarhus.

BLANK, D. 1993. 'The Arousal of Emotion in Plato's Dialogues'. *The Classical Quarterly*, 43(2): 428–39.

BLICKMAN, D. R. 1987. 'The Role of the Plague in the *Iliad*'. *Classical Antiquity*, 6(1): 1–10.

BLOCH, E. 2002. 'Hemlock Poisoning and the Death of Socrates: Did Plato Tell the Truth?' In *The Trial and Execution of Socrates: Sources and Controversies*, edited by T. C. Brickhouse and N. D. Smith, 255–78. New York and Oxford.

BLOCH, M. and J. PARRY (eds.) 1982. *Death and the Regeneration of Life.* Cambridge.

BLONDELL, R. 2002. *The Play of Character in Plato's Dialogues.* Cambridge.

BLÜMEL, C. 1923. *Der Freis des Tempels der Athena Nike.* Berlin.

BLÜMEL, C. 1950/51. 'Der Fries des Tempels der Athena Nike in der attischen Kunst des fünften Jahrhunderts von Christus'. *Jahrbuch des Deutschen Archäologischen Instituts*, 65/66: 135–65.

BLUNDELL, M. W. 1989. *Helping Friends and Harming Enemies: A Study in Sophocles and Greek Ethics.* Cambridge.

BLUNDELL, S., D. CAIRNS, and N. S. RABINOWITZ (eds.) 2013. *Vision and Viewing in Ancient Greece*, special issue of *Helios*, 40(1/2): 3–37.

BOARDMAN, J. 1955. 'Painted Funerary Plaques and Some Remarks on Prothesis'. *The Annual of the British School at Athens*, 50: 51–66.

BOARDMAN, J. 1978. *Greek Sculpture: The Archaic Period.* London.

BOARDMAN, J. 1980. 'Posthumous Prospects. Emily Vermeule: *Aspects of Death in Early Greek Art and Poetry*'. *The Times Literary Supplement*, 4009: 97.

BOARDMAN, J. 1988. 'Sex Differentiation in Grave Vases'. *AION, Sezione di archeologia e storia antica*, 10: 171–9.

BOARDMAN, J. 2001. *The History of Greek Vases: Potters, Painters, and Pictures.* London.

BOARDMAN, J. 2005. 'Composition and Content on Classical Murals and Vases'. In *Periklean Athens and its Legacy: Problems and Perspectives*, edited by J. M. Barringer and J. M. Hurwit, 63–72. Austin.

BOCKSBERGER, S. M. 2021. *Telamonian Ajax: The Myth in Archaic and Classical Greece*. Oxford.

BOECKL, C. M. 2000. *Images of Plague and Pestilence: Iconography and Iconology*. Kirksville.

BONFANTE, L. 1989. 'Nudity as a Costume in Classical Art'. *American Journal of Archaeology*, 93(4): 543–70.

BORBEIN, A. H. 2016. 'Die Skulpturen des Parthenon: Wie vollzieht sich Stilentwicklung?' *Jahrbuch des Deutschen Archäologischen Instituts*, 131: 93–147.

BORG, B. 2006. 'Gefährliche Bilder?' In *Gewalt und Ästhetik: Zur Gewalt und ihrer Darstellung in der griechischen Klassik*, edited by B. Seidensticker and M. Vöhler, 223–57. Berlin and New York.

BOSHER, K. (ed.) 2012. *Theater Outside Athens: Drama in Greek Sicily and South Italy*. Cambridge.

BOULTER, P. N. 1969. 'The Acroteria of the Nike Temple'. *Hesperia*, 38(2): 133–40.

BOUVIER, D. 2001. 'Ulysse et le personnage du lecteur dans la *République* : Réflexions sur l'importance du mythe d'Er pour la théorie de la *mimésis*'. In *La philosophie de Platon*, volume 1, edited by M. Fattal, 19–53. Paris.

BOWMAN, L. M. 2007. 'The Curse of Oedipus in *Oedipus at Colonus*'. *Scholia: Studies in Classical Antiquity*, 16: 15–25.

BOWRA, C. M. 1944. *Sophoclean Tragedy*. Oxford.

BRADLEY, M. and S. BUTLER (eds.) 2013–19. *The Senses in Antiquity*. London.

BRANDWOOD, L. 1992. 'Stylometry and Chronology'. In *The Cambridge Companion to Plato*, edited by R. Kraut, 90–120. Cambridge.

BREMMER, J. N. 1983. *The Early Greek Concept of the Soul*. Princeton.

BREMMER, J. N. 2007. 'Greek Normative Animal Sacrifice'. In *A Companion to Greek Religion*, edited by D. Ogden, 132–44. Malden, MA and Oxford.

BRESSON, A. and F. DE CALLATAŸ. 2013. 'Introduction: The Greek Vase Trade; Some Reflections about Scale, Value, and Market'. In *Pottery Markets in the Ancient Greek World (8th–1st Centuries B.C.)*, edited by A. Tsingarida and D. Viviers, 21–4. Brussels.

BRISSON, L. 1998. *Plato the Myth Maker*. Chicago. [First published in French in 1982.]

BROCK, R. 2000. 'Sickness in the Body Politic: Medical Imagery in the Greek Polis'. In *Death and Disease in the Ancient City*, edited by V. M. Hope and E. Marshall, 24–34. London and New York.

BROMMER, F. 1957. *Athena Parthenos*. Bremen.

BRONFEN, E. and S. W. GOODWIN. 1993. 'Introduction'. In *Death and Representation*, edited by S. W. Goodwin and E. Bronfen, 3–25. Baltimore and London.

BROOKS, P. 1984. *Reading for the Plot: Design and Intention in Narrative*. Cambridge, MA and London.

BROUSKARI, M. 1989. 'Aus dem Giebelschmuch des Athena-Nike-Tempels'. In *Festschrift für Nikolaus Himmelmann: Beiträge zur Ikonographie und Hermeneutik*, edited by H.-U. Cain, H. Gabelmann, and D. Salzmann, 115–18. Mainz.

236 BIBLIOGRAPHY

BROUSKARI, M. 1998. Τὸ θωράκιο τοῦ ναοῦ τῆς Ἀθηνᾶς Νίκης. *Archaiologike Ephemeris*, 137. Athens.

BROUSKARI, M. 2001. *The Monuments of the Acropolis*, second edition. Athens. [First edition published in 1997.]

BROWN, A. 1987. *Sophocles: Antigone*. Warminster.

BROWN, N. 2019. 'Phrasikleia. Playing with Signs'. In *Imagining the Afterlife in the Ancient World*, edited by J. Harrisson, 33–48. London and New York.

BROWNE, T. 1958. *Urne Buriall and The Garden of Cyrus*, edited by J. Carter. Cambridge. [First published in 1658.]

BRUZZONE, R. 2017. '*Polemos, Pathemata*, and Plague: Thucydides' Narrative and the Tradition of Upheaval'. *Greek, Roman, and Byzantine Studies*, 57: 882–909.

BRYSON, N. W. 1988. 'The Gaze in the Expanded Field'. In *Vision and Visuality*, edited by H. Foster, 87–114. Seattle.

BUDELMANN, F. 2000a. *The Language of Sophocles: Communality, Communication, and Involvement*. Cambridge.

BUDELMANN, F. 2000b. 'Visual and Verbal Symbolism in Greek Tragedy: The Case of the Uncut Rock in *Oedipus at Colonus*'. In *Theatre: Ancient & Modern*, edited by L. Hardwick, P. Easterling, S. Ireland, N. Lowe, and F. Macintosh, 181–97. Milton Keynes.

BUDELMANN, F. 2006. 'Körper und Geist in tragischen Schmerz-Szenen', translated from the English by R. Knöbl. In *Gewalt und Ästhetik: Zur Gewalt und ihrer Darstellung in der griechischen Klassik*, edited by B. Seidensticker and M. Vöhler, 123–48. Berlin and New York.

BUDELMANN, F. 2010. 'Bringing Together Nature and Culture: On the Uses and Limits of Cognitive Science for the Study of Performance Reception'. In *Theorising Performance: Greek Drama, Cultural History, and Critical Practice*, edited by E. Hall and S. Harrop, 108–22. London.

BUDELMANN, F. 2018. *Greek Lyric: A Selection*. Cambridge.

BUDELMANN, F. and T. PHILLIPS (eds.) 2018. *Textual Events: Performance and the Lyric in Early Greece*. Oxford.

BUDELMANN, F. and E. VAN EMDE BOAS. 2020. 'Experiencing Tragic Messenger Speeches'. In *Experience, Narrative, and Criticism in Ancient Greece: Under the Spell of Stories*, edited by J. Grethlein, L. Huitink, and A. Tagliabue, 59–80. Oxford and New York.

BUNDRICK, S. D. 2019. *Athens, Etruria, and the Many Lives of Greek Figured Pottery*. Madison.

BURIAN, P. 1974. 'Suppliant and Saviour: *Oedipus at Colonus*'. *Phoenix*, 28(4): 408–29.

BURKERT, W. 1966. 'Greek Tragedy and Sacrificial Ritual'. *Greek, Roman, and Byzantine Studies*, 7(2): 87–121.

BURKERT, W. 1983. *Homo Necans: The Anthropology of Ancient Greek Sacrificial Ritual and Myth*, translated by P. Bing. Berkeley, Los Angeles and London. [First published in German in 1972.]

BURN, L. 1985. 'Honey Pots: Three White-Ground Cups by the Sotades Painter'. *Antike Kunst*, 28: 93–105.

BURNET, J. 1911. *Plato, Phaedo*. Oxford.

BUROW, J. 1986. *Corpus Vasorum Antiquorum*, Tübingen 5, Germany 54. Munich.

BURTON, R. W. B. 1980. *The Chorus in Sophocles' Tragedies*. Oxford.

BUXTON, R. G. A. 1984. *Sophocles*. Oxford.

BUXTON, R. G. A. 1987. 'Euripides' *Alkestis*: Five Aspects of an Interpretation'. In *Papers given at a Colloquium on Greek Drama in honour of R. P. Winnington-Ingram*, edited by L. Rodley, 17–31. London.

CAIRNS, D. L. 2014. 'Exemplarity and Narrative in the Greek Tradition'. In *Defining Greek Narrative*, edited by D. L. Cairns and R. Scodel, 103–36. Edinburgh.

CAIRNS, D. 2016. 'Mind, Body, and Metaphor in Ancient Greek Concepts of Emotion'. *L'Atelier du Centre de Recherches Historiques*, 16. https://doi.org/10.4000/acrh.7416.

CALAME, C. 1998. 'Mort heroïque et culte à mystère dans *l'Oedipe à Colone* de Sophocle'. In *Ansichten griechischer Rituale. Geburtstags-Symposium für Walter Burkert*, edited by F. Graf, 326–56. Stuttgart and Leipzig.

CAPRA, A. 2015. *Plato's Four Muses: The Phaedrus and the Poetics of Philosophy*. Washington, DC.

CAPRA, A. and L. FLORIDI (eds.) 2023. *Intervisuality: New Approaches to Greek Literature*. Berlin and Boston.

CARBONI, R. 2007. '"Fu giusto l'onore che ti resi, almeno agli occhi di chi ha mente retta". Morte e miasma nella Grecia antica tra mito e vita reale'. In *Imago: Studi di iconografia antica*, edited by S. Angiolillo and M. Giuman, 9–42. Cagliari.

CAREY, C. 2009. 'The Third Stasimon of *Oedipus at Colonus*'. In *Sophocles and the Greek Tragic Tradition*, edited by S. Goldhill and E. Hall, 119–33. Cambridge and New York.

CARLSON, M. 2001. *The Haunted Stage: The Theatre as Memory Machine*. Ann Arbor.

CARTLEDGE, P. A. 1993. *The Greeks: A Portrait of Self and Others*. Oxford and New York.

CASKEY, M. E. 1976. 'Notes on Relief Pithoi of the Tenian-Boiotian Group'. *American Journal of Archaeology*, 80(1): 19–41.

CASTRIOTA, D. 1992. *Myth, Ethos, and Actuality: Official Art in Fifth-Century B.C. Athens*. Madison.

CATONI, M. L. and L. GIULIANI. 2019. 'Socrates Represented: Why Does He Look Like a Satyr?' *Critical Enquiry*, 45(3): 681–713.

CATUCCI, M. 2003. 'Tempi e modi di diffusione di temi teatrali in Italia attraverso la ceramica di importazione'. In *La ceramica figurata a soggetto tragico in Magna Grecia e in Sicilia*, edited by L. Todisco, 1–97. Rome.

CATUCCI, M. 2009. 'La *Niobe* di Sofocle ed il cratere attico 2555 del Museo di Caltanissetta'. In *La tragedia greca: Testimonianze archeologiche e iconografiche, Atti del Convegno, Roma, 14–16 ottobre 2004*, edited by A. Martina and A.-T. Cozzoli, 63–9. Rome.

CEADEL, E. B. 1941. 'The Division of Parts among the Actors in Sophocles' *Oedipus Coloneus*'. *The Classical Quarterly*, 35(3/4): 139–47.

CHANIOTIS, A. 2022. '"Are You Lonesome Tonight?" Nocturnal Solitude in Greek Culture'. In *Being Alone in Antiquity: Greco-Roman Ideas and Experiences of Misanthropy, Isolation, and Solitude*, edited by R. Matuszewski, 23–39. Berlin and Boston.

CHARALABOPOULOS, N. G. 2012. *Platonic Drama and its Ancient Reception*. Cambridge.

CHILDS, W. 1985. 'In Defense of an Early Date for the Temple on the Ilissos'. *Mitteilungen des Deutschen Archäologischen Instituts, Athenische Abteilung*, 100: 207–51.

CLAIRMONT, C. W. 1983. *Patrios Nomos: Public Burial in Athens during the Fifth and Fourth Centuries B.C.: The Archaeological, Epigraphic-Literary, and Historical Evidence*. Oxford.

CLAIRMONT, C. W. 1993. *Classical Attic Tombstones*. Kilchberg.

CLARK, T. J. 2006. *The Sight of Death: An Experiment in Art Writing*. New Haven and London.

CLARKE, J., D. KING, and H. BALTUSSEN (eds.) 2023. *Pain Narratives in Greco-Roman Writings: Studies in the Representation of Physical and Mental Suffering*. Leiden.

CLARKSON, O. 2017. 'Wordsworth's Negative Way'. *Essays in Criticism*, 67(2): 116–35.

CLAY, D. 1985. 'The Art of Glaukos (Plato *Phaedo* 108D4–9)'. *The American Journal of Philology*, 106(2): 230–6.

CLAY, D. 1988. 'Reading the *Republic*'. In *Platonic Writings, Platonic Readings*, edited by C. L. Griswold Jr., 19–33. New York and London.

CLAY, D. 1992. 'Plato's First Words'. In *Beginnings in Classical Literature*, edited by F. M. Dunn and T. Cole, 113–29. Cambridge.

CLAY, D. 2000. *Platonic Questions: Dialogues with the Silent Philosopher*. University Park, PA.

CLIFFORD, E. 2023. 'Death by Analogy: Identity Crises on a Roman Sarcophagus'. *The Journal of Roman Studies*, 113: 107–36.

CLIFFORD, E. and X. BUXTON (eds.) 2024a. *The Imagination of the Mind in Classical Athens: Forms of Thought*. London and New York.

CLIFFORD, E. and X. BUXTON. 2024b. 'Introduction'. In *The Imagination of the Mind in Classical Athens: Forms of Thought*, edited by E. Clifford and X. Buxton, 1–51. London and New York.

COAKLEY, S. 2007. 'Introduction'. In *Pain and Its Transformations: The Interface of Biology and Culture*, edited by S. Coakley and K. K. Shelemay, 1–16. Cambridge, MA and London.

COCHRANE, C. N. 1929. *Thucydides and the Science of History*. Oxford.

COHEN, B. 1983. 'Paragone: Sculpture versus Painting, Kaineus and the Kleophrades Painter'. In *Ancient Greek Art and Iconography*, edited by W. G. Moon, 171–92. Madison.

COHEN, B. 2000. 'Man-Killers *and* Their Victims: Inversions of the Heroic Ideal in Classical Art'. In *Not the Classical Ideal: Athens and the Construction of the Other in Greek Art*, edited by B. Cohen, 98–131. Leiden, Boston, and Cologne.

COLE, T. 2023. 'What Ancient Greek Tragedies Can Teach Us About Grief'. *The New York Times Magazine* (online), 12 September 2023 (updated 13 September 2023). https://www.nytimes.com/2023/09/12/magazine/greek-tragedy.html [Accessed 18 April 2024].

COLE, T. R. 1992. *The Journey of Life: A Cultural History of Aging in America*. Cambridge and New York.

COLLINGWOOD, R. G. 1993. *The Idea of History*, revised edition, with an introduction by J. van der Dussen. Oxford. [First edition published in 1946.]

COLLINS, P. H. 2000. *Black Feminist Thought: Knowledge, Consciousness, and the Politics of Empowerment*, second edition. New York. [First published in 1990.]

COLLOBERT, C., P. DESTRÉE, and F. J. GONZALEZ (eds.) 2012. *Plato and Myth: Studies on the Use and Status of Platonic Myths*, Mnemosyne Supplement 337. Leiden and Boston.

COLVIN, S. 2000. 'The Language of Non-Athenians in Old Comedy'. In *The Rivals of Aristophanes: Studies in Athenian Old Comedy*, edited by D. Harvey and J. Wilkins, 285–98. London.

COMAY, R. 2024. '*Nihil Est in Imagine Vivum*'. In *Niobes: Antiquity, Modernity, Critical Theory*, edited by M. Telò and A. Benjamin, 36–53. Columbus.

COMELLA, A. 2002. *I rilievi votivi greci di periodo arcaico e classico: Diffusione, ideologia, committenza*. Bari.

CONNOR, W. R. 1985. 'Narrative Discourse in Thucydides'. In *The Greek Historians, Literature and History: Papers presented to A. E. Raubitschek*, edited by M. H. Jameson, 1–17. Stanford.

COOKE, J. 2009. *Legacies of Plague in Literature, Theory, and Film*. Basingstoke and New York.

COOLE, D. and S. FROST (eds.) 2010. *New Materialisms: Ontology, Agency, and Politics*. Durham, NC.

COOPER, B. 2016. 'Intersectionality'. In *The Oxford Handbook of Feminist Theory*, edited by L. Disch and M. Hawkesworth, 385–406. New York.

CORCELLA, A. 2006. 'The New Genre and its Boundaries: Poets and Logographers'. In *Brill's Companion to Thucydides*, edited by A. Rengakos and A. Tsakmakis, 33–56. Leiden and Boston.

CORNFORD, F. M. 1907. *Thucydides Mythistoricus*. London.

COSTELLOE, T. M. 2012. 'The Sublime: A Short Introduction to a Long History'. In *The Sublime: From Antiquity to the Present*, edited by T. M. Costelloe, 1–7. Cambridge and New York.

CRAIK, E. M. 2001. 'Thucydides on the Plague: Physiology of Flux and Fixation'. *The Classical Quarterly*, 51(1): 102–8.

CRANE, G. 1996. *The Blinded Eye: Thucydides and the New Written Word*. Lanham, MD.

CRAWFURD, R. H. P. 1914. *Plague and Pestilence in Literature and Art*. Oxford.

CRENSHAW, K. 1989. 'Demarginalizing the Intersection of Race and Sex: A Black Feminist Critique of Antidiscrimination Doctrine, Feminist Theory, and Antiracist Politics'. *University of Chicago Legal Forum*, 1: 139–67.

CRENSHAW, K. 1991. 'Mapping the Margins: Intersectionality, Identity Politics, and Violence against Women of Color'. *Stanford Law Review*, 43(6): 1241–99.

CROTTY, K. M. 2009. *The Philosopher's Song: The Poets' Influence on Plato*. Lanham, MD.

CROWLEY, P. R. 2019. *The Phantom Image: Seeing the Dead in Ancient Rome*. Chicago.

CRUCIANI, C. and L. FIORINI. 1998. *I modelli del moderato: La Stoà Poikile e l'Hephaisteion di Atene nel programma edilizio cimoniano*. Naples.

CRUNK FEMINIST COLLECTIVE. 2010. 'The R-Word: Why "Rigorous" is the New Black'. *Crunk Feminist Collective* (online), 17 November 2010. https://www.crunkfeministcollective.com/2010/11/17/the-r-word-why-rigorous-is-the-new-black/

CUNHA, C. B. and B. A. CUNHA. 2008. 'Great Plagues of the Past and Remaining Questions'. In *Paleomicrobiology: Past Human Infections*, edited by D. Raoult and M. Drancourt, 1–20. Berlin and Heidelberg.

240 BIBLIOGRAPHY

CURD, P. 2020. 'Presocratic Philosophy'. *The Stanford Encyclopedia of Philosophy* (Fall 2020 Edition), edited by E. N. Zalta. https://plato.stanford.edu/archives/fall2020/entries/presocratics/.

CURRIE, B. 2005. *Pindar and the Cult of Heroes*. Oxford.

CURRIE, B. 2012. 'Sophocles and Hero Cult'. In *A Companion to Sophocles*, edited by K. Ormand, 331–48. Malden, MA and Oxford.

CURTIN, A. 2019. *Death in Modern Theatre: Stages of Mortality*. Manchester.

CURTIUS, E. 1895. 'Fragmente einer polychromen Lekythos im Berliner Museum'. *Jahrbuch des Deutschen Archäologischen Instituts*, 10: 86–91.

DALY, L. W. 1953. 'Nike and Athena Nike'. In *Studies Presented to David M. Robinson*, volume 2, edited by G. E. Mylonas and D. Raymond, 1124–8. St Louis.

DAVIES, D. J. 2019. 'The Death-Turn: Interdisciplinarity, Mourning, and Material Culture'. In *The Materiality of Mourning: Cross-Disciplinary Perspectives*, edited by Z. Newby and R. E. Toulson, 245–60. London.

DAVIES, M. I. 1973. 'Ajax and Tekmessa: A Cup by the Brygos Painter in the Bareiss Collection'. *Antike Kunst*, 16: 60–70.

DAVISON, C. C. 2009. *Pheidias: The Sculptures and Ancient Sources*. London.

DAWE, R. D. 1996. *Sophocles, Oedipus Coloneus*, third edition. Stuttgart and Leipzig.

DAWNEY, L. and T. J. HUZAR. 2019. 'Introduction: The Legacies and Limits of *The Body in Pain*'. In *The Body in Pain: A Re-engagement*, edited by L. Dawney and T. J. Huzar, special issue of *Body & Society*, 25(3), 3–21.

DAY, J. W. 2018. 'The "Spatial Dynamics" of Archaic and Classical Greek Epigram: Conversations among Locations, Monuments, Texts, and Viewer-Readers'. In *The Materiality of Text: Placement, Perception, and Presence of Inscribed Texts in Classical Antiquity*, edited by A. Petrovic, I. Petrovic, and E. Thomas, 73–104. Leiden and Boston.

DE ANGELIS, F. 1996. 'La battaglia di Maratona nella Stoa Poikile'. *Annali della Scuola Normale Superiore di Pisa. Classe di Lettere e Filosofia*, 1: 119–71.

DE BREE, E. 2010. 'The Interventions on the Temple of Athena Nike: A Study of Restoration Techniques and Guidelines based on the Interventions on the Temple of Athena Nike on the Athenian Acropolis'. Master's thesis, University of Bergen.

DE CESARE, M. 1997. *Le statue in immagine: Studi sulle raffigurazioni di statue nella pittura vascolare greca*, with a preface by S. Settis. Rome.

DE JONG, I. J. F. 1991. *Narrative in Drama: The Art of the Euripidean Messenger-Speech*, Mnemosyne Supplement 116. Leiden and New York.

DE JONG, I. J. F. 2004. 'Sophocles'. In *Narrators, Narratees, and Narratives in Ancient Greek Literature*, Studies in Ancient Greek Narrative, volume 1, Mnemosyne Supplement 257, edited by I. J. F. de Jong, R. Nünlist, and A. M. Bowie, 255–68. Leiden.

DE JONG, I. J. F. 2006. 'Where Narratology Meets Stylistics: The Seven Versions of Ajax's Madness'. In *Sophocles and the Greek Language: Aspects of Diction, Syntax, and Pragmatics*, Mnemosyne Supplement 269, edited by I. J. F. de Jong and A. Rijksbaron, 73–93. Leiden.

DE JONG, I. J. F. 2007. 'Sophocles'. In *Time in Ancient Greek Literature*, Studies in Ancient Greek Narrative, volume 2, Mnemosyne Supplement 291, edited by I. J. F. de Jong and R. Nünlist, 275–92. Leiden.

DE JONG, I. J. F. 2012. *Homer, Iliad, Book XXII*. Cambridge.

DEMONT, P. 1983. 'Notes sur le récit de la pestilence athénniene chez Thucydide et sur ses rapports avec la médicine grecque de l'époque classique'. In *Formes de pensée dans la collection hippocratique* : *Actes du IVe colloque international hippocratique, Lausanne, 21–26 Septembre 1981*, edited by F. Lasserre, 341–53. Geneva.

DEMONT, P. 1990. 'Les oracles delphiques relatifs aux pestilences et Thucydide'. *Kernos*, 3: 147–56.

DENNISTON, J. D. 1952. *Greek Prose Style*. Oxford.

DENOYELLE, M. 1997. *La cratère des Niobides*. Paris.

DE PUMA, R. D. 1983. 'Greek Myths on Three Etruscan Mirrors in Cleveland'. *The Bulletin of the Cleveland Museum of Art*, 70(7): 290–302.

DE ROMILLY, J. 1990. *La construction de la vérité chez Thucydide*. Paris.

DE ROMILLY, J. 2005. *L'invention de l'histoire politique chez Thucydide*, with a preface by M. Trédé. Paris.

DE ROMILLY, J. 2017. *The Mind of Thucydides*, translated by E. T. Rawlings, edited and with an introduction by H. R. Rawlings III and J. Rusten. Ithaca. [First published in French in 1956.]

DERRIDA, J. 2003. 'Plato's Pharmacy'. In *Deconstruction: Critical Concepts in Literary and Cultural Studies I*, edited by J. Culler, 167–221. London and New York. [Essay first published in 1968.]

DESPINIS, G. 1974. 'Τὰ γλυπτὰ τῶν ἀετωμάτων τοῦ ναοῦ τῆς Ἀθηνᾶς Νίκης'. *Archaiologikon Deltion*, 29: 1–24.

DESTRÉE, P. and R. G. EDMONDS III. 2017a. 'Introduction: The Power—and the Problems—of Plato's Images'. In *Plato and the Power of Images*, Mnemosyne Supplement 405, edited by P. Destrée and R. G. Edmonds III, 1–10. Leiden and Boston.

DESTRÉE, P. and R. G. EDMONDS III (eds.) 2017b. *Plato and the Power of Images*, Mnemosyne Supplement 405. Leiden and Boston.

DETIENNE, M. and J.-P. VERNANT. 1989. *The Cuisine of Sacrifice among the Greeks*, translated by P. Wissing. Chicago and London.

DE VIVO, J. S. 2014. 'The Memory of Greek Battle: Material Culture and/as Narrative of Combat'. In *Combat Trauma and the Ancient Greeks*, edited by P. Meineck and D. Konstan, 163–84. New York.

DEWALD, C. 2005. *Thucydides' War Narrative: A Structural Study*. Berkeley, Los Angeles, and London.

DEWALD, C. 2009. 'The Figured Stage: Focalizing the Initial Narratives of Herodotus and Thucydides'. In *Thucydides: Oxford Readings in Classical Studies*, edited by J. S. Rusten, 114–47. Oxford and New York. [First published in 1999.]

DHUGA, U. S. 2005. 'Choral Identity in Sophocles' *Oedipus Coloneus*'. *American Journal of Philology*, 126(3): 333–62.

DIETRICH, N. 2010. *Figur ohne Raum? Bäume und Felsen in der attischen Vasenmalerei des 6. und 5. Jahrhunderts v. Chr.* Berlin and New York.

DIETRICH, N. 2017. 'Pictorial Space as a Media Phenomenon: The Case of "Landscape" in Romano-Campanian Painting'. *Mondes Anciens*, 9: 1–27.

DIETRICH, N. and M. SQUIRE (eds.) 2018. *Ornament and Figure in Graeco-Roman Art: Rethinking Visual Ontologies in Classical Antiquity*. Berlin.

242 BIBLIOGRAPHY

Díez de Velasco, F. 1989. 'La iconografía griega de Caronte: Un análisis puntual del LIMC'. *Gerión*, 7: 297–322.

Díez de Velasco, F. 1995. *Los caminos de la muerte: Religión, rito e iconografía del paso al más allá en la Grecia antigua*. Madrid.

Dinsmoor, W. B. 1939. 'The Lost Pedimental Sculptures of Bassae'. *American Journal of Archaeology*, 43(1): 27–47.

Dorion, L.-A. 2011. 'The Rise and Fall of the Socratic Problem'. In *The Cambridge Companion to Socrates*, edited by D. R. Morrison, 1–23. Cambridge and New York.

Dorter, K. 1970. 'The Dramatic Aspect of Plato's *Phaedo*'. *Canadian Philosophical Review*, 8: 564–80.

Dorter, K. 1982. *Plato's Phaedo: An Interpretation*. Toronto.

Dover, K. J. 1988. *The Greeks and their Legacy. Collected Papers*, volume 2, *Prose Literature, History, Society, Transmission, Influence*. Oxford and New York.

Dubel, S. 2015. 'Avant-propos : Théories et pratiques du dialogue dans l'Antiquité'. In *Formes et genres du dialogue antique*, edited by S. Dubel and S. Gotteland, 11–23. Bordeaux.

Dubel, S. and S. Gotteland (eds.) 2015. *Formes et genres du dialogue antique*. Bordeaux.

Ducrey, P. 1985. *Guerre et guerriers dans la Grèce antique*. Paris.

Dué, C. 2006. *The Captive Woman's Lament in Greek Tragedy*. Austin.

Duffy, X. 2018. *Commemorating Conflict: Greek Monuments of the Persian Wars*. Oxford.

Dunn, F. M. 1992. 'Introduction: Beginning at Colonus'. In *Beginnings in Classical Literature*, edited by F. M. Dunn and T. Cole, 1–12. Cambridge.

Dunn, F. M. 2009. 'Sophocles and the Narratology of Drama'. In *Narratology and Interpretation: The Content of Narrative Form in Ancient Literature*, edited by J. Grethlein and A. Rengakos, 337–55. Berlin and New York.

Dyer, G. 2005. *The Ongoing Moment: A Book About Photography*. Edinburgh and London.

Easterling, P. E. 1982. *Sophocles, Trachiniae*. Cambridge.

Easterling, P. E. 1993. '*Oedipe à Colone* : Personnages et "réception"'. In *Sophocle : Le texte, les personnages. Actes du colloque international d'Aix-en-Provence, 10, 11 et 12 janvier 1992, Aix-en-Provence*, edited by A. Machin and L. Pernée, 191–200. Aix-en-Provence.

Easterling, P. E. 1999. 'Plain Words in Sophocles'. In *Sophocles Revisited: Essays Presented to Sir Hugh Lloyd-Jones*, edited by J. Griffin, 95–107. Oxford.

Easterling, P. E. 2006. 'The Death of Oedipus and What Happened Next'. In *Dionysalexandros: Essays on Aeschylus and his Fellow Tragedians in Honour of Alexander F. Garvie*, edited by D. Cairns and V. Liapis, 133–50. Swansea.

Easterling, P. E. 2009. 'Sophocles and the Wisdom of Silenus. A Reading of *Oedipus at Colonus* 1211–48'. In Ἀντιφίλησις: *Studies on Classical, Byzantine, and Modern Greek Literature and Culture in Honour of John-Theophanes A. Papademetriou*, edited by E. Karamalengou and E. Makrygianni, 161–70. Stuttgart.

Easterling, P. E. 2011. 'Sophoclean Journeys'. In *Tradition, Translations, Trauma: The Classic and the Modern*, edited by J. Parker and T. Mathews, 73–89. Oxford.

EBBINGHAUS, S. 2005. 'Protector of the City, or the Art of Storage in Early Greece'. *The Journal of Hellenic Studies*, 125: 51–72.

EDELSTEIN, L. 1962. 'Platonic Anonymity'. *The American Journal of Philology*, 83(1): 1–22.

EDMONDS, R. G. 2004. *Myths of the Underworld Journey: Plato, Aristophanes, and the 'Orphic' Gold Tablets*. Cambridge.

EDMONDS, R. G. (ed.) 2011. *The 'Orphic' Gold Tablets and Greek Religion: Further along the Path*. Cambridge.

EDMUNDS, L. 1996. *Theatrical Space and Historical Place in Sophocles' Oedipus at Colonus*. Lanham, MD and London.

EDMUNDS, L. 2009. 'Thucydides in the Act of Writing'. In *Thucydides: Oxford Readings in Classical Studies*, edited by J. S. Rusten, 91–113. Oxford and New York. [First published in Italian in 1993.]

EHRHARDT, W. 1989. 'Der Torso Wien I 328 und der Westgiebel des Athena-Nike-Tempels auf der Akropolis in Athen'. In *Festschrift für Nikolaus Himmelmann: Beiträge zur Ikonographie und Hermeneutik*, edited by H.-U. Cain, H. Gabelmann, and D. Salzmann, 119–27. Mainz.

EKROTH, G. 2010. '*Theseus and the Stone*: The Iconographic and Ritual Contexts of a Greek Votive Relief in the Louvre'. In *Divine Images and Human Imaginations in Ancient Greece and Rome*, edited by J. Mylonopoulos, 143–70. Leiden and Boston.

EKROTH, G. 2015. 'Heroes—Living or Dead?' In *The Oxford Handbook of Ancient Greek Religion*, edited by E. Eidenow and J. Kindt, 383–96. Oxford.

ELIAS, N. 2001. *The Loneliness of the Dying*, translated by E. Jephcott. London and New York. [First published in German in 1982; first published in English in 1985.]

ELSNER, J. 1996. 'Image and Ritual: Reflections on the Religious Appreciation of Classical Art'. *The Classical Quarterly*, 46(2): 515–31.

ELSNER, J. 1998. 'Ancient Viewing and Modern Art History'. *Mètis*, 13: 417–37.

ELSNER, J. 2002. 'Introduction: The Genres of Ekphrasis'. In *The Verbal and the Visual: Cultures of Ekphrasis in Antiquity*, edited by J. Elsner, special issue of *Ramus*, 31, 1–18.

ELSNER, J. 2004. 'Seeing and Saying: A Psycho-Analytic Account of Ekphrasis'. In *Before Subjectivity? Lacan and the Classics*, special edition of *Helios*, 31(1–2), edited by M. Buchan and J. I. Porter, 157–85.

ELSNER, J. 2006. 'Reflections on the "Greek Revolution" in Art: From Changes in Viewing to the Transformation of Subjectivity'. In *Rethinking Revolutions through Ancient Greece*, edited by S. Goldhill and R. Osborne, 68–95. Cambridge.

ELSNER, J. 2007. *Roman Eyes: Visuality and Subjectivity in Art and Text*. Princeton.

ELSNER, J. 2010. 'Art History as Ekphrasis'. *Art History*, 33: 10–27.

ELSNER, J. 2012a. 'Decorative Imperatives between Concealment and Display: The Form of Sarcophagi'. *Res: Anthropology and Aesthetics*, 61/62: 178–95.

ELSNER, J. 2012b. 'Sacrifice in Late Roman Art'. In *Greek and Roman Animal Sacrifice: Ancient Victims, Modern Observers*, edited by C. A. Faraone and F. S. Naiden, 120–63. Cambridge.

ELSNER, J. 2015. 'Visual Culture and Ancient History: Issues of Empiricism and Ideology in the Samos Stele at Athens'. *Classical Antiquity*, 34(1): 33–73.

244 BIBLIOGRAPHY

ELSNER, J. 2017. 'Transmission'. In *Liquid Antiquity*, edited by B. Holmes and K. Marta, 182–5. Geneva.

ELSNER, J. 2018a. 'The Embodied Object: Recensions of the Dead on Roman Sarcophagi'. *Art History*, 41(3): 546–65.

ELSNER, J. 2018b. 'Ornament, Figure, and *Mise en Abyme* on Roman Sarcophagi'. In *Ornament and Figure in Graeco-Roman Art: Rethinking Visual Ontologies in Classical Antiquity*, edited by N. Dietrich and M. Squire, 353–91. Berlin.

ELSNER, J. and J. HUSKINSON (eds.) 2011. *Life, Death, and Representation: Some New Work on Roman Sarcophagi*. Berlin.

ELSNER, J. and M. SQUIRE. 2016. 'Homer and the Ekphrasists: Text and Picture in the Elder Philostratus' "Scamander" (*Imagines* I.1)'. In *The Archaeology of Greece and Rome: Studies in Honour of Anthony Snodgrass*, edited by J. Bintliff and K. Rutter, 57–99. Edinburgh.

ELSNER, J. and M. SQUIRE. 2024. 'Epilogue: The Ancient Imagination in Retrospect'. In *The Imagination of the Mind in Classical Athens: Forms of Thought*, edited by E. Clifford and X. Buxton, 301–24. London and New York.

ELSNER, J. and H. WU (eds.) 2012. *Sarcophagi*, special issue of *Res: Anthropology and Aesthetics*, 61/62.

EMLYN-JONES, C. and W. PRENDY. 2017. *Plato: Euthyphro, Apology, Crito, Phaedo*. Cambridge, MA and London.

ENGELKE, M. 2019. 'The Anthropology of Death Revisited'. *Annual Review of Anthropology*, 48: 29–44.

ERLER, M. 2013. '"Nur das Gründliche (ist) wahrhaft unterhaltend" (Thomas Mann). Zum Verhältnis lebensweltlicher und philosophischer Wirklichkeit in Platons Dialogen'. In *Der Dialog in der Antike. Formen und Funktionen einer literarischen Gattung zwischen Philosophie, Wissensvermittlung, und dramatischer Inszenierung*, edited by S. Föllinger and G. M. Müller, 367–82. Berlin and Boston.

ERVIN, M. 1963. 'A Relief Pithos from Mykonos'. *Αρχαιολογικόν Δελτίον*, 18: 37–75.

ESCHBACH, N. 2013. 'Ungewöhnliche Helden—eigenartige Formen: Die Giebelskulpturen des Aphaia-Tempels auf Ägina'. In *Zurück zur Klassik. Ein neuer Blick auf das alte Griechenland*, edited by V. Brinkmann, 153–65. Munich.

ESTRIN, S. 2016. 'Cold Comfort: Empathy and Memory in an Archaic Funerary Monument from Akraiphia'. *Classical Antiquity*, 35(2): 189–214.

ESTRIN, S. 2018. 'Memory Incarnate: Material Objects and Private Visions in Classical Athens, from Euripides' *Ion* to the Gravesite'. In *The Materialities of Greek Tragedy: Objects and Affect in Aeschylus, Sophocles, and Euripides*, edited by M. Telò and M. Mueller, 111–32. London.

EUBEN, J. P. 1996. 'Reading Democracy: "Socratic" Dialogues and the Political Education of Democratic Citizens'. In *Demokratia: A Conversation on Democracies, Ancient and Modern*, edited by J. Ober and C. W. Hedrick, Jr., 327–59. Princeton.

FARAONE, C. A. and F. S. NAIDEN (eds.) 2012. *Greek and Roman Animal Sacrifice: Ancient Victims, Modern Observers*. Cambridge.

FARNESS, J. 2003. 'Glaucon's Couch, or Mimesis and the Art of the *Republic*'. In *Plato as Author: The Rhetoric of Philosophy*, edited by A. N. Michelini, 99–121. Leiden and Boston.

FEARN, D. 2024a. 'Imagining Bodies with Gorgias'. In *The Imagination of the Mind in Classical Athens: Forms of Thought*, edited by E. Clifford and X. Buxton, 230–50. London and New York.

FEARN, D. 2024b. 'Pindar and the Nature of Contemplation'. In *Texts, Temporalities, Ideologies: Ancient and Early Modern Perspectives*, edited by B. Xinyue, 107–23. London.

FEHR, B. 2011. *Becoming Good Democrats and Wives: Civic Education and Female Socialization on the Parthenon Frieze*, translated by U. Hoffmann. Zurich and Berlin.

FELDMAN, F. 1991. 'Some Puzzles About the Evil of Death'. *The Philosophical Review*, 100(2): 205–27.

FELTEN, F. 1984. *Griechische tektonische Friese archaischer und klassischer Zeit*. Waldsassen-Bayern.

FERGUSON, N. 1997. 'Virtual History: Towards a "Chaotic" Theory of the Past'. In *Virtual History: Alternatives and Counterfactuals*, edited by N. Ferguson, 1–90. London.

FERRARI, F. 2003. '*Edipo a Colono* 1583: Critica del testo e critica storico-religiosa'. In *Il dramma sofocleo: Testo, lingua, interpretazione*, edited by G. Avezzù, 125–42. Stuttgart and Weimar.

FERRARI, G. 2003. 'Myth and Genre on Athenian Vases'. *Classical Antiquity*, 22(1): 37–54.

FERRARI, G. R. F. 1987. *Listening to the Cicadas: A Study of Plato's Phaedrus*. Cambridge.

FINGLASS, P. J. 2010. 'Sophocles' *Ajax* and the Vase-Painters'. *Omnibus*, 62: 25–7.

FINLEY, J. H. 1967. *Three Essays on Thucydides*. Cambridge, MA.

FINNEGAN, R. 1999. 'Plagues in Classical Literature'. *Classics Ireland*, 6: 23–42.

FISCHER, J. M. and B. MITCHELL-YELLIN. 2016. *Near-Death Experiences: Understanding Visions of the Afterlife*. Oxford.

FLOREN, J. 1978. 'Zu den Reliefs auf dem Schild der Athena Parthenos'. *Boreas*, 1: 36–67.

FLORY, S. 1990. 'The Meaning of τὸ μὴ μυθῶδες (1.22.4) and the Usefulness of Thucydides' *History*'. *The Classical Journal*, 85(3): 193–208.

FÖLLINGER, S. and G. M. MÜLLER (eds.) 2013. *Der Dialog in der Antike. Formen und Funktionen einer literarischen Gattung zwischen Philosophie, Wissensvermittlung, und dramatischer Inszenierung*. Berlin and Boston.

FORMISANO, M. and C. S. KRAUS (eds.) 2018. *Marginality, Canonicity, Passion*. Oxford.

FORNARA, C. W. 1983. *The Nature of History in Ancient Greece and Rome*. Berkeley.

FOSTER, E. 2018. 'Military Defeat in Fifth-Century Athens: Thucydides and His Audience'. In *Brill's Companion to Military Defeat in Ancient Mediterranean Society*, edited by J. H. Clark and B. Turner, 99–122. Leiden and Boston.

FOUCAULT, M. 1969. 'Qu'est-ce qu'un auteur?' *Bulletin de la Société française de Philosophie*, 63(3): 73–104.

FOUCAULT, M. 2002. *The Order of Things*. London and New York. [First published in French in 1966.]

FOWLER, D. 2000. *Roman Constructions: Readings in Postmodern Latin*. Oxford.

FREDE, D. 1992. 'Disintegration and Restoration: Pleasure and Pain in Plato's *Philebus*'. In *The Cambridge Companion to Plato*, edited by R. Kraut, 425–63. Cambridge.

FREDE, M. 1992a. 'Plato's Arguments and the Dialogue Form'. In *Methods of Interpreting Plato and his Dialogues*, edited by J. C. Klagge and N. D. Smith, 201–19. Oxford.

246 BIBLIOGRAPHY

FREDE, M. 1992b. 'Plato's *Sophist* on False Statements'. In *The Cambridge Companion to Plato*, edited by R. Kraut, 397–424. Cambridge.

FREL, J. 1984. *The Death of a Hero*. Malibu.

FRONING, H. 1988. 'Anfänge der kontinuierenden Bilderzählung in der griechischen Kunst'. *Jahrbuch des Deutschen Archäologischen Instituts*, 103: 169–99.

FRONTISI-DUCROUX, F. 1986. 'La mort en face'. *Mètis*, 1(2): 197–217.

FRONTISI-DUCROUX, F. 1988. 'Figures de l'invisible : Stratégies textuelles et stratégies iconiques'. *AION, Sezione di archeologia e storia antica*, 10: 27–40.

FRONTISI-DUCROUX, F. 1989. 'In the Mirror of the Mask'. In *A City of Images: Iconography and Society in Ancient Greece*, edited by C. Bérard et al., translated by D. Lyons, 151–65. Princeton. [First published in French in 1984.]

FRONTISI-DUCROUX, F. 1993. 'La Gorgone, paradigme de création d'images'. *Les Cahiers du collège iconique : Communications et débats*, 1: 71–86.

FRONTISI-DUCROUX, F. 1995. *Du masque au visage : Aspects de l'identité en Grèce ancienne*. Paris.

FRONTISI-DUCROUX, F. 1997. 'L'œil et le miroir'. In *Dans l'œil du miroir*, edited by F. Frontisi-Ducroux and J.-P. Vernant, 51–250. Paris.

FURTWÄNGLER, A. 2010. *Masterpieces of Greek Sculpture: A Series of Essays on the History of Art*, edited and translated by E. Strong. New York. [First published in 1895.]

FURTWÄNGLER, A., E. R. FIECHTER, and H. THIERSCH. 1906. *Aegina: Das Heiligtum der Aphaia*. Munich.

GABBA, E. 1981. 'True History and False History in Classical Antiquity'. *The Journal of Roman Studies*, 71: 50–62.

GAIFMAN, M. 2013. 'Timelessness, Fluidity, and Apollo's Libation'. In *Wet/Dry*, edited by C. S. Wood, special issue of *Res: Anthropology and Aesthetics*, 63/64, 39–52.

GAIFMAN, M. 2015. 'Visual Evidence'. In *The Oxford Handbook of Ancient Greek Religion*, edited by E. Eidinow and J. Kindt, 51–66. Oxford.

GAIFMAN, M. 2016. 'Theologies of Statues in Classical Greek Art'. In *Theologies of Ancient Greek Religion*, edited by E. Eidinow, J. Kindt, and R. Osborne, 249–80. Cambridge.

GAIFMAN, M. 2018. *The Art of Libation in Classical Athens*. New Haven.

GAIFMAN, M., V. PLATT, and M. SQUIRE (eds.) 2018. *The Embodied Object in Classical Antiquity*, special issue of *Art History*, 41(3).

GAISER, K. 1959. *Protreptik und Paränese bei Platon: Untersuchungen zur Form des platonischen Dialogs*. Stuttgart.

GAISER, K. 1984. *Platone come scrittore filosofico: Saggi sull'ermeneutica dei dialoghi platonici*. Naples.

GALLOP, D. 1975. *Plato: Phaedo*. Oxford.

GALLOP, D. 2003. 'The Rhetoric of Philosophy: Socrates' Swan-Song'. In *Plato as Author: The Rhetoric of Philosophy*, edited by A. N. Michelini, 313–32. Leiden and Boston.

GARDINER, C. P. 1987. *The Sophoclean Chorus: A Study of Character and Function*. Iowa City.

GARDNER, E. A. 1889. 'A Vase of Polygnotan Style: M. d. I., XI., 38'. *The Journal of Hellenic Studies*, 10: 117–25.

GARLAND, R. 1989. 'The Well-Ordered Corpse: An Investigation into the Motives behind Funerary Legislation'. *Bulletin of the Institute of Classical Studies*, 36: 1–15.

GARLAND, R. 2001. *The Greek Way of Death*, second edition. Ithaca. [First published in 1985.]

GARVIE, A. F. 2016. *The Plays of Sophocles*, second edition. London and New York. [First edition published in 2005.]

GAUER, W. 1988. 'Parthenonische Amazonomachie und Perserkrieg'. In *Kanon: Festschrift Ernst Berger, zum 60. Geburtstag am 26. Februar 1988 gewidmet*, edited by M. Schmidt, 28–41. Basel.

GEHRKE, H.-J. 1994. 'Mythos, Geschichte, Politik—antik und modern'. *Saeculum*, 45: 239–64.

GENETTE, G. 1990. 'Fictional Narrative, Factual Narrative', translated by N. Ben-Ari, with B. McHale. *Poetics Today*, 11(4): 755–74.

GENTILI, B. and G. CERRI. 1988. *History and Biography in Ancient Thought*. Amsterdam.

GEROULANOS, S. and R. BRIDLER. 1994. *Trauma, Wund-Entstehung und Wund-Pflege im antiken Griechenland*. Mainz.

GILL, C. 1973. 'The Death of Socrates'. *Classical Quarterly*, 23(1): 25–8.

GILL, C. 2002. 'Dialectic and the Dialogue Form'. In *New Perspectives on Plato, Modern and Ancient*, edited by J. Annas and C. J. Rowe, 145–71. Cambridge, MA and London.

GILL, D. W. J. 1988a. 'The Distribution of Greek Vases and Long-Distance Trade'. In *Proceedings of the 3rd Symposium on Ancient Greek and Related Pottery, Copenhagen, August 31–September 4, 1987*, edited by J. Christiansen and T. Melander, 175–85. Copenhagen.

GILL, D. W. J. 1988b. 'The Temple of Aphaia on Aegina: The Date of the Reconstruction'. *The Annual of the British School at Athens*, 83: 169–77.

GILL, D. W. J. 1991. 'Pots and Trade: Spacefillers or *Objets d'art*?' *The Journal of Hellenic Studies*, 111: 29–47.

GILL, D. W. J. 1993. 'The Temple of Aphaia on Aegina: Further Thoughts on the Date of the Reconstruction'. *The Annual of the British School at Athens*, 88: 173–81.

GILL, D. W. J. 2001. 'The Decision to Build the Temple of Athena Nike (*IG* I³ 35)'. *Historia*, 50(3): 257–78.

GIORA, R., N. BALABAN, O. FEIN, and I. ALKABETS. 2005. 'Negation as Positivity in Disguise'. In *Figurative Language Comprehension: Social and Cultural Influences*, edited by H. L. Colston and A. N. Katz, 233–58. Mahwah, NJ.

GIRARD, R. 1974. 'The Plague in Literature and Myth'. *Texas Studies*, 15(5): 833–50.

GIRARD, R. 2013. *Violence and the Sacred*, translated by P. Gregory. London and New York. [First published in French in 1972.]

GIRAUD, D. 1994. Μελέτη ἀποκαταστάσεως τοῦ ναοῦ τῆς Ἀθηνᾶς Νίκης [*Study for the Restoration of the Temple of Athena Nike*], volume 1a. Athens.

GIUDICE, E. 2003. 'Hypnos, Thanatos ed il viaggio della morte sulle lekythoi funerarie a fondo bianco'. *Ostraka: Rivista di Antichità*, 12(2): 145–58.

GIUDICE, E. 2015. *Il tymbos, la stele, la barca di Caronte: L'immaginario della morte sulle lekythoi funerarie a fondo bianco*. Rome.

248 BIBLIOGRAPHY

GIUDICE, F. and I. GIUDICE. 2009. 'Seeing the Image: Constructing a Data-Base of the Imagery on Attic Pottery from 635–300 BC'. In *Athenian Potters and Painters*, volume 2, edited by J. H. Oakley and O. Palagia, and translated by F. Muscolino, 48–62. Oxford.

GIULIANI, L. 2013. *Image and Myth: A History of Pictorial Narration in Greek Art*, translated by J. O'Donnell. Chicago and London. [First published in German in 2003.]

GLYNN, D. 2022. 'The (Un)performability of Death and Violence on Stage'. In *Last Scene of All: Representing Death on the Western Stage*, edited by J. Goodman, 95–108. Cambridge.

GOETTE, H. R. 2001. *Athens, Attica and the Megarid: An Archaeological Guide*. London and New York.

GOETTE, H. R. 2009. 'Images in the Athenian "Demosion Sema"'. In *Art in Athens during the Peloponnesian War*, edited by O. Palagia, 188–206. New York.

GOFF, B. (ed.) 2005. *Classics and Colonialism*. London.

GOLDHILL, S. D. 1987. 'The Great Dionysia and Civic Ideology'. *Journal of Hellenic Studies*, 107: 58–76.

GOLDHILL, S. D. 1994. 'The Failure of Exemplarity'. In *Modern Critical Theory and Classical Literature*, edited by I. J. de Jong and J. J. Sullivan, 51–73. Leiden.

GOLDHILL, S. D. 1996. 'Refracting Classical Vision: Changing Cultures of Viewing'. In *Vision in Context: Historical and Contemporary Perspectives on Sight*, edited by T. Brennan and M. Jay, 15–28. New York and London.

GOLDHILL, S. D. 2000. 'Placing Theatre in the History of Vision'. In *Word and Image in Ancient Greece*, edited by N. K. Rutter and B. Sparkes, 161–79. Edinburgh.

GOLDHILL, S. D. 2002. *The Invention of Prose*. Oxford.

GOLDHILL, S. D. 2006. 'Der Ort der Gewalt: Was sehen wir auf der Bühne?' translated from the English by A. Wessels and B. Seidensticker. In *Gewalt und Ästhetik: Zur Gewalt und ihrer Darstellung in der griechischen Klassik*, edited by B. Seidensticker and M. Vöhler, 149–68. Berlin and New York.

GOLDHILL, S. D. 2007. 'What Is Ekphrasis For?'. In *Ekphrasis*, edited by S. Bartsch and J. Elsner, special issue of *Classical Philology*, 102(1), 1–19.

GOLDHILL, S. D. 2008a. 'Introduction: Why don't Christians do Dialogue?' In *The End of Dialogue in Antiquity*, edited by S. D. Goldhill, 1–11. Cambridge and New York.

GOLDHILL, S. D. (ed.) 2008b. *The End of Dialogue in Antiquity*. Cambridge and New York.

GOLDHILL, S. D. 2012. *Sophocles and the Language of Tragedy*. Oxford and New York.

GOLDHILL, S. D. 2017. 'The Limits of the Case Study: Exemplarity and the Reception of Classical Literature'. *New Literary History*, 48(3): 415–35.

GOLDHILL, S. and R. OSBORNE (eds.) 1994. *Art and Text in Ancient Greek Culture*. Cambridge and New York.

GOMBRICH, E. H. 1968. *Art and Illusion: A Study in the Psychology of Pictorial Representation*, third edition. London. [First published in 1959.]

GOMME, A. W. 1945. *A Historical Commentary on Thucydides*, volume 1. Oxford.

GOMME, A. W. 1956. *A Historical Commentary on Thucydides*, volume 2. Oxford.

GONZALEZ, F. J. 2003. 'How to Read a Platonic Prologue: *Lysis* 203a–207d'. In *Plato as Author: The Rhetoric of Philosophy*, edited by A. N. Michelini, 15–44. Leiden and Boston.

GONZALEZ, F. J. 2017. 'The Power and Ambivalence of a Beautiful Image in Plato and the Poets'. In *Plato and the Power of Images*, Mnemosyne Supplement 405, edited by P. Destrée and R. G. Edmonds III, 47–65. Leiden and Boston.

GOODMAN, J. 2022. 'Death on Stage: A Never-Ending Ending'. In *The Last Scene of All: Representing Death on the Western Stage*, edited by J. Goodman, 1–9. Cambridge.

GÖRGEMANNS, H. 2004. 'Dialogue'. In *Brill's New Pauly: Encyclopaedia of the Ancient World*, edited by H. Cancik and H. Schneider, 352–6. Leiden and Boston.

GOULD, J. 2001. *Myth, Ritual, Memory, and Exchange: Essays in Greek Literature and Culture*. Oxford.

GOWARD, B. 1999. *Telling Tragedy: Narrative Technique in Aeschylus, Sophocles, and Euripides*. London.

GRAF, F. and S. I. JOHNSTON. 2013. *Ritual Texts for the Afterlife: Orpheus and the Bacchic Gold Tablets*, second edition. London and New York. [First edition published in 2007.]

GRAFF, R. 2005. 'Prose versus Poetry in Early Greek Theories of Style'. *Rhetorica*, 23(4): 303–35.

GRAY, C. L. 2011. 'Foreigners in the Burial Ground: The Case of the Milesians in Athens'. In *Living Through the Dead: Burial and Commemoration in the Classical World*, edited by M. Carroll and J. Rempel, 47–64. Oxford and Oakville.

GREEN, J. R. 1995. 'Theatre Production: 1987–1995'. *Lustrum*, 37: 7–202.

GREENWOOD, E. 2004. 'Making Words Count: Freedom of Speech and Narrative in Thucydides'. In *Free Speech in Classical Antiquity*, Mnemosyne Supplement 254, edited by I. Sluiter and R. M. Rosen, 175–95. Leiden.

GREENWOOD, E. 2006. *Thucydides and the Shaping of History*. London and New York.

GREENWOOD, E. 2008. 'Fictions of Dialogue in Thucydides'. In *The End of Dialogue in Antiquity*, edited by S. D. Goldhill, 15–28. Cambridge and New York.

GREGORY, J. 1979. 'Euripides' *Alcestis*'. *Hermes*, 107: 259–70.

GREGORY, J. 1991. *Euripides and the Instruction of the Athenians*. Ann Arbor.

GRETHLEIN, J. 2013. 'The Presence of the Past in Thucydides'. In *Thucydides between History and Literature*, edited by A. Tsakmakis and M. Tamiolaki, 91–118. Berlin and Boston.

GRETHLEIN, J. 2015. 'Vision and Reflexivity in the *Odyssey* and Early Vase-Painting'. *Word & Image*, 31(3): 197–212.

GRETHLEIN, J. 2016. 'Sight and Reflexivity: Theorizing Vision in Greek Vase-Painting'. In *Sight and the Ancient Senses*, edited by M. Squire, 85–106. London and New York.

GRETHLEIN, J. 2017. *Aesthetic Experiences and Classical Antiquity: The Significance of Form in Narratives and Pictures*. Cambridge and New York.

GRETHLEIN, J. 2018. 'Ornamental and Formulaic Patterns: The Semantic Significance of Form in Early Greek Vase-Painting and Homeric Epic'. In *Ornament and Figure in Graeco-Roman Art: Rethinking Visual Ontologies in Classical Antiquity*, edited by N. Dietrich and M. Squire, 73–96. Berlin.

250 BIBLIOGRAPHY

GRETHLEIN, J., L. HUITINK, and A. TAGLIABUE (eds.) 2020. *Experience, Narrative, and Criticism in Ancient Greece: Under the Spell of Stories.* Oxford and New York.

GRETHLEIN, J. and A. RENGAKOS (eds.) 2009. *Narratology and Interpretation: The Content of Narrative Form in Ancient Literature.* Berlin and New York.

GRIBBLE, D. 1998. 'Narrator Interventions in Thucydides'. *The Journal of Hellenic Studies*, 118: 41–67.

GRIEVE, L. C. G. 1898. *Death and Burial in Attic Tragedy, Part 1: Death and the Dead.* New York.

GRIFFIN, J. 2009. *Homer on Life and Death.* Oxford. [First published in 1980.]

GRIFFITH, M. 1999. *Sophocles, Antigone.* Cambridge.

GUIDORIZZI, G., G. AVEZZÙ, and G. CERRI. 2008. *Sofocle, Edipo a Colono*, introduction and commentary by G. Guidorizzi, text edited by G. Avezzù, translation by G. Cerri. Milan.

GULAKI, A. 1981. *Klassische und klassizistische Nikedarstellungen. Untersuchungen zur Typologie und zum Bedeutungswandel.* Bonn.

GUNDERT, H. 1971. *Dialog und Dialektik: zur Struktur des platonischen Dialogs.* Amsterdam. [First published in 1968.]

GÜTHENKE, C. 2020. ' "For Time is / nothing if not amenable"—Exemplarity, Time, Reception'. *Classical Receptions Journal*, 12(1): 46–61.

GÜTHENKE, C. and B. HOLMES. 2018. 'Hyper-Inclusivity, Hyper-Canonicity, and the Future of the Field'. In *Marginality, Canonicity, Passion*, edited by M. Formisano and C. S. Kraus, 57–73. Oxford.

GUTHRIE, W. K. C. 1962. *A History of Greek Philosophy*, volume 1, *The Earlier Presocratics and the Pythagoreans.* Cambridge.

GUTHRIE, W. K. C. 1965. *A History of Greek Philosophy*, volume 2, *The Presocratic Tradition from Parmenides to Democritus.* Cambridge.

GUTHRIE, W. K. C. 1969. *A History of Greek Philosophy*, volume 3, *The Fifth-Century Enlightenment.* Cambridge.

HACKFORTH, R. 1955. *Plato's Phaedo.* Cambridge.

HALL, E. 2018. 'Materialisms Old and New'. In *The Materialities of Greek Tragedy: Objects and Affect in Aeschylus, Sophocles, and Euripides*, edited by M. Telò and M. Mueller, 203–18. London.

HALLAM, E. and J. HOCKEY. 2001. *Death, Memory, and Material Culture.* Oxford and New York.

HALLIWELL, S. 1988. *Plato, Republic 10.* Oxford.

HALLIWELL, S. 2000. 'Plato and Painting'. In *Word and Image in Ancient Greece*, edited by N. K. Rutter and B. A. Sparkes, 99–116. Edinburgh.

HALLIWELL, S. 2002. *The Aesthetics of Mimesis: Ancient Texts and Modern Problems.* Princeton.

HALLIWELL, S. 2007. 'The Life-and-Death Journey of the Soul: Interpreting the Myth of Er'. In *The Cambridge Companion to Plato's Republic*, edited by G. R. F. Ferrari, 445–73. Cambridge.

HALLIWELL, S. 2011. *Between Ecstasy and Truth: Interpretations of Greek Poetics from Homer to Longinus.* Oxford and New York.

HALPERIN, D. M. 1992. 'Plato and the Erotics of Narrativity'. In *Innovations of Antiquity*, edited by R. Hexter and D. Selden, 95–126. New York and London.

HAMDORF, F. W. 1964. *Griechische Kultpersonifikationen der vorhellenistischen Zeit*. Mainz.

HANSON, V. D. 1989. *The Western Way of War: Infantry Battle in Classical Greece*, with an introduction by J. Keegan. Berkeley and Los Angeles and London.

HANSON, V. D. 2005. *A War Like No Other: How the Athenians and Spartans Fought the Peloponnesian War*. New York.

HARARI, Y. N. 2007. 'The Concept of "Decisive Battles" in World History'. *Journal of World History*, 18(3): 251–66.

HARDIE, P. 2002. *Ovid's Poetics of Illusion*. Cambridge.

HARMAN, G. 2005. *Guerrilla Metaphysics: Phenomenology and the Carpentry of Things*. Chicago.

HARMAN, G. 2012. 'The Well-Wrought Broken Hammer: Object-Oriented Literary Criticism'. *New Literary History*, 43(2): 183–203.

HARRISON, E. B. 1966. 'The Composition of the Amazonomachy on the Shield of Athena Parthenos'. *American Journal of Archaeology*, 35: 107–33.

HARRISON, E. B. 1972a. 'A New Fragment from the North Frieze of the Nike Temple'. *American Journal of Archaeology*, 76(2): 195–7.

HARRISON, E. B. 1972b. 'Preparations for Marathon, the Niobid Painter and Herodotus'. *The Art Bulletin*, 54(4): 390–402.

HARRISON, E. B. 1972c. 'The South Frieze of the Nike Temple and the Marathon Painting in the Painted Stoa'. *American Journal of Archaeology*, 76(4): 353–78.

HARRISON, E. B. 1981. 'Motifs of the City-Siege on the Shield of Athena Parthenos'. *American Journal of Archaeology*, 85(3): 281–317.

HARRISON, E. B. 1997. 'The Glories of the Athenians: Observations on the Program of the Frieze of the Temple of Athena Nike'. In *The Interpretation of Architectural Sculpture in Greece and Rome*, Studies in the History of Art 49, edited by D. Buitron-Oliver, 108–25. Hanover and London.

HARRISON, T. 2019. *The Emptiness of Asia: Aeschylus' Persians and the History of the Fifth Century*. London and New York.

HARRISSON, J. (ed.) 2019. *Imagining the Afterlife in the Ancient World*. London.

HARTOG, F. 2000. 'The Invention of History: The Pre-History of a Concept from Homer to Herodotus'. *History and Theory*, 39(3): 384–95.

HASELSWERDT, E. 2019. 'Sound and the Sublime in Sophocles' *Oedipus at Colonus*: The Limits of Representation'. *American Journal of Philology*, 140(4): 613–42.

HAYS, J. N. 2005. *Epidemics and Pandemics: Their Impacts on Human History*. Santa Barbara.

HAYWOOD, C. 1997. *Death in White and Color: An Exhibition of Attic White Lekythoi of the 5th c. B.C.* Dublin.

HEDREEN, G. 2001. *Capturing Troy: The Narrative Functions of Landscape in Archaic and Early Classical Greek Art*. Ann Arbor.

HEDRICK, C. W. 1993. 'The Meaning of Material Culture: Herodotus, Thucydides, and their Sources'. In *Nomodeiktes: Greek Studies in Honor of Martin Ostwald*, edited by R. M. Rosen and J. Farrell, 17–38. Ann Arbor.

252 BIBLIOGRAPHY

HEFFERNAN, J. A. W. 2004. *Museum of Words: The Poetics of Ekphrasis from Homer to Ashbery*. Chicago. [First published in 1993.]

HENDERSON, J. 1994. 'Timeo-Danaos: Amazons in Early Greek Art'. In *Art and Text in Ancient Greek Culture*, edited by S. Goldhill and R. Osborne, 85–137. Cambridge.

HENRICHS, A. 1983. 'The "Sobriety" of Oedipus: Sophocles *OC* 100 Misunderstood'. *Harvard Studies in Classical Philology*, 87: 87–100.

HENRICHS, A. 1993. 'The Tomb of Aias and the Prospect of Hero Cult in Sophokles'. *Classical Antiquity*, 12(2): 165–80.

HENRICHS, A. 2006. 'Blutvergießen am Altar: Zur Ritualisierung der Gewalt im griechischen Opferkult'. In *Gewalt und Ästhetik: Zur Gewalt und ihrer Darstellung in der griechischen Klassik*, edited by B. Seidensticker and M. Vöhler, 59–87. Berlin and New York.

HENRICHS, A. 2012. 'Animal Sacrifice in Greek Tragedy: Ritual, Metaphor, Problematizations'. In *Greek and Roman Animal Sacrifice: Ancient Victims, Modern Observers*, edited by C. A. Faraone and F. S. Naiden, 180–94. Cambridge.

HERRERO DE JÁUREGUI, M. 2013. 'Emar Tode: Recognizing the Crucial Day in Early Greek Poetry'. *Classical Antiquity*, 32(1): 35–77.

HERTZ, R. 1960. *Death and the Right Hand*, translated by R. and C. Needham, with an introduction by E. E. Evans-Pritchard. London and New York.

HESK, J. 2012. '*Oedipus at Colonus*'. In *Brill's Companion to Sophocles*, edited by A. Markantonatos, 167–89. Leiden and Boston.

HESTER, D. A. 1977. 'To Help One's Friends and Harm One's Enemies: A Study in the *Oedipus at Colonus*'. *Antichthon*, 11: 22–41.

HIDALGO DOWNING, L. 2002. 'Creating Things That Are Not: The Role of Negation in the Poetry of Wisława Szymborska'. *Journal of Literary Semantics*, 31(2): 113–32.

HOLLADAY, A. J. 1986. 'The Thucydides Syndrome: Another View'. *New England Journal of Medicine*, 315: 1170–2.

HOLLADAY, A. J. and J. C. F. POOLE. 1979. 'Thucydides and the Plague of Athens'. *The Classical Quarterly*, 29(2): 282–300.

HOLLADAY, A. J. and J. C. F. POOLE. 1982. 'Thucydides and the Plague: A Footnote'. *The Classical Quarterly*, 32(1): 235–6.

HOLLADAY, A. J. and J. C. F. POOLE. 1984. 'Thucydides and the Plague: A Further Footnote'. *The Classical Quarterly*, 34(2): 483–5.

HOLLEIN, H.-G. 1988. *Bürgerbild und Bildwelt der attischen Demokratie auf den rotfigurigen Vasen des 6.–4. Jahrhunderts v. Chr.* Frankfurt am Main.

HOLLOWAY, R. R. 1973. *A View of Greek Art*. Providence.

HOLMES, B. 2007. 'The *Iliad*'s Economy of Pain'. *Transactions of the American Philological Association*, 137(1): 45–84.

HOLMES, B. 2010. *The Symptom and the Subject: The Emergence of the Physical Body in Ancient Greece*. Princeton.

HOLMES, B. 2013. 'Antigone at Colonus and the End(s) of Tragedy'. *Ramus*, 42: 23–43.

HOLMES, B. 2018. 'Body'. In *The Cambridge Companion to Hippocrates*, edited by P. E. Pormann, 63–88. Cambridge.

HOLQUIST, M. 1990. *Dialogism: Bakhtin and his World*. London.

HÖLSCHER, T. 1973. *Griechische Historienbilder des 5. und 4. Jahrhunderts v. Chr.* Würzburg.

HÖLSCHER, T. 1997. 'Ritual und Bildsprache. Zur Deutung der Reliefs an der Brüstung um das Heiligtum der Athena Nike in Athen'. *Mitteilungen des Deutschen Archäologischen Instituts, Athenische Abteilung*, 112: 143–66.

HÖLSCHER, T. 2009. 'Architectural Sculpture: Messages? Programs? Towards Rehabilitating the Notion of "Decoration"'. In *Structure, Image, Ornament: Architectural Sculpture in the Greek World*, edited by P. Schultz and R. von den Hoff, 54–67. Oxford and Oakville.

HÖLSCHER, T. and E. SIMON. 1976. 'Die Amazonenschlacht auf dem Schild der Athena Parthenos'. *Mitteilungen des Deutschen Archäologischen Instituts, Athenische Abteilung*, 91: 115–48.

HOPE, V. M. and J. HUSKINSON (eds.) 2011. *Memory and Mourning: Studies on Roman Death.* Oxford and Oakville.

HORNBLOWER, S. 1987. *Thucydides.* London.

HORNBLOWER, S. 1991. *A Commentary on Thucydides*, volume 1: *Books I–III.* Oxford and New York.

HORNBLOWER, S. 2010. 'Narratology and Narrative Techniques in Thucydides'. In *Thucydidean Themes*, edited by S. Hornblower, 59–99. Oxford and New York. [Revised version of a chapter written in 1994.]

HOUBY-NIELSEN, S. H. 1995. '"Burial Language" in Archaic and Classical Kerameikos'. *Proceedings of the Danish Institute at Athens*, 1: 129–91.

HOUSMAN, A. E. 1988. *Collected Poems and Selected Prose.* London.

HUFFMAN, C. A. 1993. *Philolaus of Croton: Pythagorean and Presocratic. A Commentary on the Fragments and Testimonia with Interpretive Essays.* Cambridge.

HUFFMAN, C. A. 1999. 'The Pythagorean Tradition'. In *The Cambridge Companion to Early Greek Philosophy*, edited by A. A. Long, 66–87. Cambridge and New York.

HUGHES, D. D. 1991. *Human Sacrifice in Ancient Greece.* London and New York.

HUITINK, L. 2020. 'Enargeia and Bodily Mimesis'. In *Experience, Narrative and Criticism in Ancient Greece: Under the Spell of Stories*, edited by J. Grethlein, L. Huitink, and A. Tagliabue, 188–209. Oxford.

HUITINK, L. 2024. 'How Far, How Close? Imagining the Battle of Cunaxa in Greek Historiography'. In *The Imagination of the Mind in Classical Athens: Forms of Thought*, edited by E. Clifford and X. Buxton, 55–84. London and New York.

HUMPHREYS, S. C. 1980. 'Family Tombs and Tomb Cult in Ancient Athens: Tradition or Traditionalism?' *The Journal of Hellenic Studies*, 100: 96–126.

HUNTER, V. J. 1973. *Thucydides: The Artful Reporter.* Toronto.

HUNZINGER, C. 2015. 'Wonder'. In *A Companion to Ancient Aesthetics*, edited by P. Destrée and P. Murray, 422–37. Malden, MA and Chichester.

HURWIT, J. M. 1977. 'Image and Frame in Greek Art'. *American Journal of Archaeology*, 81(1): 1–30.

HURWIT, J. M. 1985. *The Art and Culture of Early Greece, 1100–480 B.C.* Ithaca and London.

HURWIT, J. M. 1992. 'A Note on Ornament, Nature, and Boundary in Early Greek Art'. *Bulletin Antieke Beschaving*, 67: 63–72.

254 BIBLIOGRAPHY

HURWIT, J. M. 1999. *The Athenian Acropolis: History, Mythology, and Archaeology from the Neolithic Era to the Present*. Cambridge.

HURWIT, J. M. 2004. *The Acropolis in the Age of Pericles*. Cambridge.

HURWIT, J. M. 2007. 'The Problem with Dexileos: Heroic and Other Nudities in Greek Art'. *American Journal of Archaeology*, 111: 35–60.

HUSKINSON, J. 1998. '"Unfinished Portrait Heads" on Later Roman Sarcophagi: Some New Perspectives'. *Papers of the British School at Rome*, 66: 129–58.

HUSSEY, E. 1985. 'Thucydidean History and Democritean Theory'. *History of Political Thought* 6: 118–38.

HUSSEY, E. 1990. 'The Beginnings of Epistemology from Homer to Philolaus'. In *Epistemology*, edited by S. Everson, 11–38. Cambridge.

HUTCHEON, L. and M. HUTCHEON. 2004. *Opera: The Art of Dying*. Cambridge, MA.

HUTCHINSON, G. O. 1999. 'Sophocles and Time'. In *Sophocles Revisited: Essays Presented to Sir Hugh Lloyd-Jones*, edited by J. Griffin, 47–72. Oxford.

HUTCHINSON, G. O. 2007. 'The Monster and the Monologue: Polyphemus from Homer to Ovid'. In *Hesperos: Studies in Ancient Greek Poetry Presented to M. L. West on his Seventieth Birthday*, edited by P. J. Finglass, C. Collard, and N. J. Richardson, 22–39. Oxford.

HUTCHINSON, G. O. 2013a. 'Genre and Super-Genre'. In *Generic Interfaces in Latin Literature: Encounters, Interactions, and Transformations*, edited by T. D. Papanghelis, S. J. Harrison, and S. Frangoulidis, 19–34. Berlin and Boston.

HUTCHINSON, G. O. 2013b. *Greek to Latin: Frameworks and Contexts for Intertextuality*. Oxford.

HUTCHINSON, G. O. 2015. 'Appian the Artist: Rhythmic Prose and its Literary Implications'. *The Classical Quarterly*, 65(2): 788–806.

HUTCHINSON, G. O. 2017. 'Repetition, Range, and Attention: The *Iliad*'. In *The Winnowing Oar, New Perspectives in Homeric Studies, Studies in Honour of Antonios Rengakos*, edited by C. Tsagalis and A. Markantonatos, 145–70. Berlin and Boston.

HUTCHINSON, G. O. 2020a. *Motion in Classical Literature: Homer, Parmenides, Sophocles, Ovid, Seneca, Tacitus, Art*. New York and Oxford.

HUTCHINSON, G. O. 2020b. 'Space and Text Worlds in Apollonius'. *Trends in Classics*, 12(1): 114–25.

HYDE, W. W. 1921. *Olympic Victor Monuments and Greek Athletic Art*. Washington, DC.

INVERNIZZI, A. 1965. *I frontoni del tempio di Aphaia ad Egina*. Torino.

IRWIN, T. H. 1992. 'Plato: The Intellectual Background'. In *The Cambridge Companion to Plato*, edited by R. Kraut, 51–89. Cambridge.

IRWIN, T. H. 2008. 'The Platonic Corpus'. In *The Oxford Handbook of Plato*, edited by G. Fine, 63–87. Oxford.

ISLER-KERÉNYI, C. 1969. *Nike: Der Typus der laufenden Flügelfrau in archaischer Zeit*. Zurich.

ISLER-KERÉNYI, C. 1970. 'Nike mit dem Tropaion'. *Antike Plastik*, 10: 57–65.

JACKSON KNIGHT, W. F. 1970. *Elysion: On Ancient Greek and Roman Beliefs Concerning a Life after Death*, with an introduction by G. Wilson Knight. London.

JAMESON, M. 1994. 'The Ritual of the Temple of Nike Parapet'. In *Ritual, Finance, Politics: Athenian Democratic Accounts Presented to David Lewis*, edited by R. Osborne and S. Hornblower, 307–24. Oxford.

JANSEN, S. R. 2013. 'Plato's *Phaedo* as a Pedagogical Drama'. *Ancient Philosophy*, 33: 333–52.

JANSSEN, A. J. 1957. *Het antieke tropaion*, with a summary in English. Ledeberg/Ghent.

JEBB, R. C. 1900a. *Antigone*. Cambridge. [First edition published in 1888.]

JEBB, R. C. 1900b. *The Oedipus Coloneus*, third edition. Cambridge. [First edition published in 1886.]

JEBB, R. C. 2004. *Ajax*, new edition, edited by P. E. Easterling, with an introduction by P. Wilson. London. [First edition published in 1896.]

JEFFERY, L. H. 1962. 'The Inscribed Gravestones of Archaic Attica'. *The Annual of the British School at Athens*, 57: 115–53.

JEPPESEN, K. 1963. 'Bild und Mythus an den Parthenon'. *Acta Archaeologica*, 34: 1–96.

JOHNSTON, S. I. 1999. *Restless Dead: Encounters between the Living and the Dead in Ancient Greece*. Berkeley.

JOHO, T. 2016. 'The Revival of the Funeral Oration and the Plague in Thucydides Books 6–7'. *Greek, Roman, and Byzantine Studies*, 57(1): 16–48.

JOHO, T. 2017. 'Thucydides, Epic, and Tragedy'. In *The Oxford Handbook of Thucydides*, edited by S. Forsdyke, E. Foster, and R. Balot, 587–604. Oxford.

JONES, N. 2015. 'Phantasms and Metonyms: The Limits of Representation in Fifth-Century Athens'. *Art History*, 38(5): 814–37.

JOUANNA, J. 1995. 'Espaces sacrés, rites et oracles dans l'Œdipe à Colone de Sophocle'. *Révue des Études Grecques*, 108: 38–58.

JOUANNA, J. 2005. 'Cause and Crisis in Historians and Medical Writers of the Classical Period.' In *Hippocrates in Context: Papers Read at the XIth International Hippocratic Colloquium: University of Newcastle upon Tyne, 27–32 August 2002*, edited by P. J. van der Eijk, 3–27. Leiden and Boston.

JOUANNA, J. 2006. 'Famine et pestilence dans l'Antiquité grecque : Un jeu de mots sur *limos/loimos*'. In *L'homme face aux calamités naturelles dans l'Antiquité et au Moyen Âge. Actes du 16ème colloque de la Villa Kérylos à Beaulieu-sur-Mer les 14 & 15 octobre 2005*, edited by J. Jouanna, J. Leclant, and M. Zink, 197–219. Paris.

JOUANNA, J. 2018. *Sophocles: A Study of His Theater in Its Political and Social Context*, translated by S. Rendall. Princeton and Oxford. [First published in French in 2007.]

JOYCE, R. A. 2005. 'Archaeology of the Body'. *Annual Review of Anthropology*, 34: 139–58.

KACHUK, A. J. 2021. *The Solitary Sphere in the Age of Virgil*. New York.

KAHN, C. H. 1997. *Plato and the Socratic Dialogue: The Philosophical Use of a Literary Form*. Cambridge.

KALLET, L. 2006. 'Thucydides' Workshop of History and Utility Outside the Text'. In *Brill's Companion to Thucydides*, edited by A. Rengakos and A. Tsakmakis, 335–68. Leiden and Boston.

KALLET, L. 2013. 'Thucydides, Apollo, the Plague, and the War'. *The American Journal of Philology*, 134(3): 355–82.

256 BIBLIOGRAPHY

KAMERBEEK, J. C. 1984. *The Plays of Sophocles, Part VII: The Oedipus Coloneus.* Leiden.

KARAKAS, S. L. 2002. 'Subject and Symbolism in Historical Battle Reliefs of the Late Classical and Hellenistic Periods'. PhD thesis, University of North Carolina, Chapel Hill.

KARDARA, C. P. 1960. 'Four White Lekythoi in the National Museum of Athens'. *The Annual of the British School at Athens,* 55: 149–58.

KAROUZOU, S. 1968. *National Archaeological Museum: Collection of Sculpture.* Athens.

KEARNS, E. 1989. *The Heroes of Attica.* London.

KEEGAN, J. 1991. *The Face of Battle,* first Pimlico edition. London. [First published in 1976.]

KEKULÉ VON STRADONITZ, R. 1869. *Die Balustrade des Tempels der Athena Nike.* Leipzig.

KEKULÉ VON STRADONITZ, R. 1881. *Reliefs an der Balustrade der Athena Nike.* Stuttgart.

KELLEHEAR, A. 2007. *A Social History of Dying.* Cambridge.

KELLY, A. 2009. *Sophocles: Oedipus at Colonus.* London.

KEMP, G. and G. M. MRAS (eds.) 2016. *Wollheim, Wittgenstein, and Pictorial Representation: Seeing-as and Seeing-in.* London.

KERN, P. B. 1999. *Ancient Siege Warfare.* Bloomington and Indianapolis.

KEULS, E. 1978a. 'Aeschylus' *Niobe* and Apulian Funerary Symbolism'. *Zeitschrift für Papyrologie und Epigraphik,* 30: 41–68.

KEULS, E. C. 1978b. *Plato and Greek Painting.* Leiden.

KEYS, T. E. 1944. 'The Plague in Literature'. *Bulletin of the Medical Library Association,* 32(1): 35–56.

KING, D. 2017. *Experiencing Pain in Imperial Greek Culture.* Oxford.

KING, D. 2023. 'Painful Drinks: Poison and Pain Experience in Nicander's *Alexipharmaca*'. In *Pain Narratives in Greco-Roman Writings: Studies in the Representation of Physical and Mental Suffering,* edited by J. Clarke, D. King, and H. Baltussen, 44–65. Leiden.

KING, H. and J. BROWN. 2015. 'Thucydides and the Plague'. In *A Handbook to the Reception of Thucydides,* edited by C. Lee and N. Morley, 449–73. Chichester.

KINNEE, L. 2018. *The Greek and Roman Trophy: From Battlefield Marker to Icon of Power.* Abingdon and New York.

KIRK, G. S. 1974. 'Review: M. L. West, *Early Greek Philosophy and the Orient*'. *The Classical Review,* 24: 82–6.

KIRKWOOD, G. M. 1994. *A Study of Sophoclean Drama,* with a new preface and enlarged bibliographical note. Ithaca and London. [First published in 1958.]

KITCHER, P. 2018. 'Aging Oedipus'. In *The Oedipus Plays of Sophocles: Philosophical Perspectives,* edited by P. Woodruff, 151–82. Oxford and New York.

KITTO, H. D. F. 1966. *Poiesis: Structure and Thought.* Berkeley and Los Angeles.

KLEINMAN, A., V. DAS, and M. LOCK (eds.) 1997. *Social Suffering.* Berkeley and London.

KNAPPETT, C. 2020. *Aegean Bronze Age Art: Meaning in the Making.* Cambridge and New York.

KNAUER, E. R. 1986. 'Still More Light on Old Walls? Eine ikonographische Nachlese'. In *Studien zur Mythologie und Vasenmalerei: Konrad Schauenburg zum 65. Geburtstag am 16. April 1986,* edited by E. Böhr and W. Martini, 121–6. Mainz am Rhein.

KNIGGE, U. 1991. *The Athenian Kerameikos: History, Monuments, Excavations.* Athens. [First published in 1988.]

KNOX, B. 1964. *The Heroic Temper: Studies in Sophoclean Tragedy.* Berkeley and Los Angeles.

KOHN, G. C. (ed.) 1995. *Encyclopedia of Plague and Pestilence: From Ancient Times to the Present.* New York.

KOTIN, J. 2001. 'Shields of Contradiction and Direction: Ekphrasis in the *Iliad* and the *Aeneid*'. *Hirundo*, 1: 11–16.

KOTSONAS, A. 2016. 'Politics of Periodization and the Archaeology of Early Greece'. *American Journal of Archaeology*, 120(2): 239–70.

KOUSSER, R. 2009. 'Destruction and Memory on the Athenian Acropolis'. *The Art Bulletin*, 91(3): 263–82.

KRAUT, R. 1992. 'Introduction to the Study of Plato'. In *The Cambridge Companion to Plato*, edited by R. Kraut, 1–50. Cambridge.

KRIEGER, M. 1992. *Ekphrasis: The Illusion of the Natural Sign.* Baltimore.

KROLL, J. 1979. 'The Parthenon Frieze as a Votive Relief'. *American Journal of Archaeology*, 83: 349–52.

KÜBLER, K. 1976. *Die Nekropole der Mitte des 6. bis Ende des 5. Jahrhunderts*, Kerameikos 7.1. Berlin.

KUHN, H. 1941. 'The True Tragedy: On the Relationship between Greek Tragedy and Plato, I'. *Harvard Studies in Classical Philology*, 52: 1–40.

KUNZE, C. 2005. 'Dialog statt Gewalt. Neue Erzählperspektiven in der frühklassischen Vasenmalerei'. In *Die andere Seite der Klassik: Gewalt im 5. und 4. Jahrhundert v. Chr.*, edited by G. Fischer and S. Moraw, 45–71. Stuttgart.

KUNZE-GÖTTE, E., K. TANCKE, and K. VIERNEISEL. 2000. *Die Nekropole von der Mitte des 6. bis zum Ende des 5. Jahrhunderts*, Kerameikos 7.2. Munich.

KURTZ, D. C. 1975. *Athenian White Lekythoi: Patterns and Painters.* Oxford.

KURTZ, D. C. 1984. 'Vases for the Dead: An Attic Selection, 750–400 BC'. In *Ancient Greek and Related Pottery: Proceedings of the International Vase Symposium in Amsterdam, 12–15 April 1984*, edited by H. A. G. Brijder, 314–28. Amsterdam.

KURTZ, D. C. and J. BOARDMAN. 1971. *Greek Burial Customs.* London.

KUSPIT, D. 2020. *Mortality: A Survey of Contemporary Death Art.* Washington, DC. https://doi.org/10.57912/23856474.v1.

LABORDERIE, J. 1978. *Le dialogue platonicien de la maturité.* Paris.

LAKOFF, G. and M. JOHNSON. 2003. *Metaphors We Live By*, updated edition. Chicago and London. [First published in 1980.]

LAKS, A. 1999. 'Soul, Sensation, and Thought'. In *The Cambridge Companion to Early Greek Philosophy*, edited by A. A. Long, 250–70. Cambridge.

LAKS, A. and G. W. MOST (eds. and trans.) 2016. *Early Greek Philosophy*, Volume IV: *Western Greek Thinkers, Part 1.* Cambridge, MA and London.

LAMARI, A. A. 2009. 'Knowing a Story's End: Future Reflexive in the Tragic Narrative of the Argive Expedition Against Thebes'. In *Narratology and Interpretation: The Content of Narrative Form in Ancient Literature*, edited by J. Grethlein and A. Rengakos, 399–419. Berlin and New York.

258 BIBLIOGRAPHY

LAMM, J. A. 2005. 'The Art of Interpreting Plato'. In *The Cambridge Companion to Friedrich Schleiermacher*, edited by J. Mariña, 91–108. Cambridge.

LANE FOX, R. 2020. *The Invention of Medicine: From Homer to Hippocrates*. London.

LANGHOLF, V. 1984. 'Generalisationen und Aphorismen in den Epidemienbüchern'. In *Die hippokratischen Epidemien: Theorie—Praxis—Tradition*, edited by G. Baader and R. Winau, 131–43. Stuttgart.

LANGLANDS, R. 2015. 'Roman Exemplarity: Mediating between General and Particular'. In *Exemplarity and Singularity: Thinking through Particulars in Philosophy, Literature, and Law*, edited by M. Lowrie and S. Lüdemann, 68–80. London and New York.

LANGLANDS, R. 2018. *Exemplary Ethics in Ancient Rome*. Cambridge.

LAPATIN, K. D. S. 2005. 'Picturing Socrates'. In *A Companion to Socrates*, edited by S. Ahbel-Rappe and R. Kamtekar, 110–55. Oxford.

LARDINOIS, A. 1992. 'Greek Myths for Athenian Rituals: Religion and Politics in Aeschylus' *Eumenides* and Sophocles' *Oedipus Coloneus*'. *Greek, Roman, and Byzantine Studies*, 33(4): 313–27.

LATEINER, D. 1977. 'Pathos in Thucydides'. *Antichthon*, 11: 42–51.

LATEINER, D. 2002. 'Pouring Bloody Drops (*Iliad* 16.459): The Grief of Zeus'. *Colby Quarterly*, 38(1): 42–61.

LATTIMORE, S. 2006. 'From Classical to Hellenistic Art'. In *A Companion to the Classical Greek World*, edited by K. H. Kinzl, 456–79. Oxford and Malden, MA.

LEFKOWITZ, M. R. 1981. *The Lives of the Greek Poets*. London.

LEHRER, K. 2011. *Art, Self, and Knowledge*. New York and Oxford.

LEIPEN, N. 1971. *Athena Parthenos: A Reconstruction*. Toronto.

LENDLE, O. 1990. 'Κτῆμα ἐς αἰεί. Thukydides und Herodot'. *Rheinisches Museum für Philologie*, Neue Folge, 133: 231–42.

LENDON, J. E. 2005. *Soldiers and Ghosts: A History of Battle in Classical Antiquity*. New Haven and London.

LENDON, J. E. 2017. 'Battle Descriptions in the Ancient Historians, Part I: Structure, Array, and Fighting' and 'Battle Descriptions in the Ancient Historians, Part II: Speeches, Results, and Sea Battles'. *Greece & Rome*, 64: 39–64, 145–67.

LESCHER, J. H. 1999. 'Early Interest in Knowledge'. In *The Cambridge Companion to Early Greek Philosophy*, edited by A. A. Long, 225–49. Cambridge.

LESCHER, J. H. 2008. 'The Humanizing of Knowledge in Presocratic Thought'. In *The Oxford Handbook of Presocratic Philosophy*, edited by P. Curd and D. W. Graham, 458–84. Oxford.

LESSING, G. E. 1984. *Laocoön: An Essay on the Limits of Painting and Poetry*, translated by E. A. McCormick. Baltimore. [First published in German in 1766.]

LEWIS, O. 2023. 'Perceiving and Diagnosing Pain According to Archigenes of Apamea'. In *Pain Narratives in Greco-Roman Writings: Studies in the Representation of Physical and Mental Suffering*, edited by J. Clarke, D. King, and H. Baltussen, 145–75. Leiden.

LIEBERT, R. S. 2017. *Tragic Pleasure from Homer to Plato*. Cambridge.

LIFSCHITZ, A. and M. SQUIRE (eds.) 2017. *Rethinking Lessing's Laocoon: Antiquity, Enlightenment, and the 'Limits' of Painting and Poetry*. Oxford.

LINDENLAUF, A. 2003. 'Constructing the Memory of the Persian Wars in Athens'. In *SOMA 2002: Symposium on Mediterranean Archaeology*, edited by A. Brysbaert, N. de Bruijn, E. Gibson, A. Michael, and M. Monaghan, 53–62. Oxford.

LINFORTH, I. M. 1951. 'Religion and Drama in *Oedipus at Colonus*'. *University of California Publications in Classical Philology*, 14: 75–191.

LIPPMAN, M., D. SCAHILL, and P. SCHULTZ. 2006. '*Knights* 843–59, the Nike Temple Bastion, and Cleon's Shields from Pylos'. *American Journal of Archaeology*, 110(4): 551–63.

LISSARRAGUE, F. 2000. 'Jeu d'images : Un nouveau lécythe du peintre de Bosanquet'. *Ktema*, 25: 89–91.

LISSARRAGUE, F. 2001. *Greek Vases: The Athenians and Their Images*, translated by K. Allen. New York. [First published in French in 1999.]

LISSARRAGUE, F. 2009. 'L'image mise en cercle'. In *Dossier : Images mises en forme*, 13–41. Paris.

LLOYD, G. E. R. 1987. *The Revolutions of Wisdom: Studies in the Claims and Practice of Ancient Greek Science*. Berkeley and London.

LLOYD, G. E. R. 2003. *In the Grip of Disease: Studies in the Greek Imagination*. Oxford and New York.

LLOYD, M. A. 1985. 'Euripides' *Alcestis*'. *Greece & Rome*, 32: 119–31.

LLOYD, M. A. 2007. 'Euripides'. In *Time in Ancient Greek Literature: Studies in Ancient Greek Narrative*, volume 2, Mnemosyne Supplement 291, edited by I. J. F. de Jong and R. Nünlist, 293–304. Leiden.

LODGE, D. 1990. *After Bakhtin: Essays on Fiction and Criticism*. London and New York.

LONG, A. A. 1968. *Language and Thought in Sophocles: A Study of Abstract Nouns and Poetic Technique*. London.

LONG, A. G. 2007. 'The Form of Plato's *Republic*'. In *Debating the Athenian Cultural Revolution: Art, Literature, Philosophy, and Politics 430–380 B.C.*, edited by R. Osborne, 224–41. Cambridge and New York.

LONIS, R. 1979. *Guerre et religion en Grèce à l'époque classique : Recherches sur les rites, les dieux, l'idéologie de la victoire*. Paris.

LORAUX, N. 1982. 'Mourir devant Troie, tomber pour Athènes : De la gloire du héros à l'idée de la cité'. In *La mort, les morts dans les sociétés anciennes*, edited by G. Gnoli and J.-P. Vernant, 27–44. Cambridge.

LORAUX, N. 1986a. *The Invention of Athens: The Funeral Oration in the Classical City*, translated by A. Sheridan. Cambridge, MA and London. [First published in French in 1981.]

LORAUX, N. 1986b. 'Thucydide a écrit la Guerre du Péloponnèse'. *Métis*, 1: 139–61.

LORAUX, N. 2002. *The Mourning Voice: An Essay on Greek Tragedy*, translated from the French by E. T. Rawlings, with a foreword by P. Pucci. Ithaca and London.

LORENZ, K. 2016. *Ancient Mythological Images and their Interpretation: An Introduction to Iconology, Semiotics, and Image Studies in Classical Art History*. Cambridge.

LOW, P. 2010. 'Commemoration of the War Dead in Classical Athens: Remembering Defeat and Victory'. In *War, Democracy and Culture in Classical Athens*, edited by D. Pritchard, 341–58. Cambridge.

260 BIBLIOGRAPHY

LOWE, N. J. 2000. *The Classical Plot and the Invention of Western Narrative*. Cambridge and New York.

LOWRIE, M. and S. LÜDEMANN (eds.) 2015. *Exemplarity and Singularity: Thinking through Particulars in Philosophy, Literature, and Law*. London and New York.

LUSCHNIG, C. A. E. 1995. *The Gorgon's Severed Head: Studies in Alcestis, Electra, and Phoenissae*, Mnemosyne Supplement 153. Leiden, New York, and Köln.

McCABE, M. M. 1996. 'Unity in the *Parmenides*: The Unity of the *Parmenides*'. In *Form and Argument in Late Plato*, edited by C. Gill and M. M. McCabe, 5–47. Oxford.

McCABE, M. M. 2008. 'Plato's Ways of Writing'. In *The Oxford Handbook of Plato*, edited by G. Fine, 88–113. Oxford.

McCABE, M. M. 2015. *Platonic Conversations*. Oxford.

MACINTOSH, F. 1994. *Dying Acts: Death in Ancient Greek and Modern Irish Drama*. Cork.

MACINTOSH, F. 2022. 'The Whole Point of Living Is Preparing to Die: Dying into Death in Tragic Drama'. In *The Last Scene of All: Representing Death on the Western Stage*, edited by J. Goodman, 163–75. Cambridge.

McKIM, R. 1988. 'Shame and Truth in Plato's Gorgias'. In *Platonic Writings, Platonic Readings*, edited by C. L. Griswold Jr., 34–48. New York and London.

MACLEOD, C. 1983. *Collected Essays*. Oxford.

McMANNERS, J. 1981. *Death and the Enlightenment: Changing Attitudes to Death among Christians and Unbelievers in Eighteenth-Century France*. Oxford and New York.

McPHERRAN, M. 2010. 'Virtue, Luck, and Choice at the End of the *Republic*'. In *Plato's Republic: A Critical Guide*, edited by M. McPherran, 132–46. Cambridge.

MAN, S.-C. 2020. *Instances of Death in Greek Tragedy*. Newcastle upon Tyne.

MANNACK, T. 2014. 'Beautiful Men on Vases for the Dead'. In *Athenian Potters and Painters*, volume 3, edited by J. H. Oakley, 116–24. Oxford and Philadelphia.

MANSFELD, J. 1980. 'Theoretical and Empirical Attitudes in Early Greek Scientific Medicine'. In *Hippocratica : Actes du Colloque hippocratique de Paris (4–9 septembre 1978)*, edited by M. D. Grmek, 371–90. Paris.

MARCONI, C. 2004a. 'Images for a Warrior: On a Group of Athenian Vases and their Public'. In *Greek Vases: Images, Contexts, and Controversies*, edited by C. Marconi, 27–40. Leiden.

MARCONI, C. 2004b. 'Kosmos: The Imagery of the Archaic Greek Temple'. *Res: Anthropology and Aesthetics*, 45: 211–24.

MARCONI, C. 2009. 'The Parthenon Frieze: Degrees of Visibility'. *Res: Anthropology and Aesthetics*, 55/56: 156–73.

MARCONI, C. 2013. 'Mirror and Memory: Images of Ritual Actions in Greek Temple Decoration'. In *Heaven on Earth: Temples, Ritual, and Cosmic Symbolism in the Ancient World*, edited by D. Ragavan, 425–46. Chicago.

MARCONI, C. 2017. 'The Frames of Greek Painted Pottery'. In *The Frame in Classical Art: A Cultural History*, edited by V. Platt and M. Squire, 117–53. Cambridge and New York.

MARINATOS, N. 1981. 'Thucydides and Oracles'. *The Journal of Hellenic Studies*, 101: 138–40.

MARINCOLA, J. 1997. *Authority and Tradition in Ancient Historiography*. Cambridge.

MARINCOLA, J. 1999. 'Genre, Convention, and Innovation in Greco-Roman Historiography'. In *The Limits of Historiography: Genre and Narrative in Ancient Historical Texts*, edited by C. S. Kraus, 281–324. Leiden and Boston.

MARK, I. S. 1993. *The Sanctuary of Athena Nike in Athens: Architectural States and Chronology*. Princeton.

MARKANTONATOS, A. 2002. *Tragic Narrative: A Narratological Study of Sophocles' Oedipus at Colonus*. Berlin and New York.

MARKANTONATOS, A. 2007. *Oedipus at Colonus: Sophocles, Athens, and the World*, Untersuchungen zur antiken Literatur und Geschichte 87. Berlin and New York.

MARKANTONATOS, A. 2013. *Euripides' Alcestis: Narrative, Myth, and Religion*. Berlin and Boston.

MARLOW, H., K. POLLMANN, and H. VAN NOORDEN (eds.) 2021. *Eschatology in Antiquity: Forms and Functions*. London and New York.

MARSHALL, M. 1990. 'Pericles and the Plague'. In *'Owls to Athens': Essays on Classical Subjects Presented to Sir Kenneth Dover*, edited by E. M. Craik, 163–70. Oxford.

MARTENS, D. 1992. *Une esthétique de la transgression : Le vase grec de la fin de l'époque géométrique au début de l'époque classique*. Brussels.

MARTIN, B. 2016. 'Cold Comfort: Winged *Psychai* on Fifth-Century BC Greek Funerary Lekythoi'. *Bulletin of the Institute of Classical Studies*, 59(1): 1–25.

MARTIN, B. 2020. *Harmful Interaction Between the Living and the Dead in Greek Tragedy*. Liverpool.

MARTIN, S. 2021. 'Life after death: Scientist explains what ACTUALLY happens when you die—VIDEO'. *The Daily Express* (online), 16 October 2021. https://www.express.co.uk/news/science/880461/Life-after-death-what-happens-when-you-die-sam-parnia-afterlife [Accessed 15 July 2020].

MARTINEZ, J. 2013. 'Banishing the Poet: The Pedagogical Function of Mythology in the Dialogues of Plato'. *Emerita*, 81(1): 31–44.

MARTIN-MCAULIFFE, S. L. and J. K. PAPADOPOULOS. 2012. 'Framing Victory: Salamis, the Athenian Acropolis, and the Agora'. *Journal of the Society of Architectural Historians*, 71(3): 332–61.

MATTINGLY, H. B. 1982. 'The Athena Nike Temple Reconsidered'. *American Journal of Archaeology*, 86(3): 381–5.

MATTINGLY, H. B. 2000. 'The Athena Nike Dossier: IG 1³ 35/36 and 64 a–b'. *The Classical Quarterly*, 50(2): 604–6.

MAYS, R. G. and S. B. MAYS. 2017. 'Near-Death Experiences: A Critique of the Fischer and Mitchell-Yellin Physicalist Interpretation'. *Journal of Near-Death Studies*, 36(2): 69–99.

MÉAUTIS, G. 1940. *L'Oedipe à Colone et le culte des héros*. Recueil de la Faculté des Lettres de Neuchâtel 19. Neuchâtel.

MEISTER, F. J. 2020. *Greek Praise Poetry and the Rhetoric of Divinity*. Oxford.

MESKELL, L. 1996. 'The Somatization of Archaeology: Institutions, Discourses, Corporeality'. *Norwegian Archaeological Review*, 29(1): 1–16.

MESKELL, L. 2000. 'Embodying Archaeology: Theory and Praxis'. *The Bulletin of the American Society of Papyrologists*, 37(1): 171–92.

METCALF, P. and R. HUNTINGTON. 1991. *Celebrations of Death: The Anthropology of Mortuary Ritual*, second edition. Cambridge. [First published in 1979.]

262 BIBLIOGRAPHY

MEYER, H. 1987. 'Ein Neues Piräusrelief. Zur Überlieferung der Amazonomachie am Schild der Athena Parthenos'. *Mitteilungen des Deutschen Archäologischen Instituts, Athenische Abteilung*, 102: 295–321.

MEYER, M. 1980. 'Dialectic and Questioning: Socrates and Plato'. *American Philosophical Quarterly*, 17(4): 281–9.

MICHAELIS, A. 1862. 'Die Balustrade am Tempel der Athena Nike auf der Akropolis von Athen'. *Archäologische Zeitung*, 20: 250–67.

MICHELAKIS, P. 2019. 'Naming the Plague in Homer, Sophocles, and Thucydides'. *American Journal of Philology*, 140(3): 381–414.

MICHELINI, A. N. 2003. 'Plato's Socratic Mask'. In *Plato as Author: The Rhetoric of Philosophy*, edited by A. N. Michelini, 45–65. Leiden and Boston.

MIKALSON, J. D. 1984. 'Religion and the Plague in Athens, 431–423 BC'. In *Studies Presented to Sterling Dow on His Eightieth Birthday*, edited by A. L. Boegehold et al., 217–26. Durham, NC.

MILBANK, J. 2024. 'Negation in Poetics and Theology'. *Modern Theology*, 40(1): 228–42.

MILES, M. 1980. 'The Date of the Temple on the Ilissos River'. *Hesperia*, 49(4): 309–25.

MILLER, K. 2016. *The Literary Culture of Plague in Early Modern England*. London.

MINTSI, E. 1997. 'Hypnos et Thanatos sur les lécythes attiques à fond blanc (deuxième moitié du Ve Siècle av. J.-C.)'. *Revue des Études Anciennes*, 99(1–2): 47–61.

MIRTO, M. S. 2012. *Death in the Greek World: From Homer to the Classical Age*. Norman. [First published in Italian in 2007.]

MITCHELL, W. J. T. 1994. *Picture Theory: Essays on Verbal and Visual Representation*. Chicago and London.

MITCHELL-BOYASK, R. 2008. *Plague and the Athenian Imagination: Drama, History, and the Cult of Asclepius*. Cambridge.

MITTELSTADT, M. C. 1968. 'The Plague in Thucydides: An Extended Metaphor?' *Rivista di Studi Classici*, 16: 145–54.

MOLES, J. L. 1993. 'Truth and Untruth in Herodotus and Thucydides'. In *Lies and Fiction in the Ancient World*, edited by C. Gill and T. P. Wiseman, 88–121. Exeter.

MÖLLENDORFF, P. VON. 2013. 'Auctor & Actor. Formen auktorialer Präsenz in antiken Dialogen'. In *Der Dialog in der Antike. Formen und Funktionen einer literarischen Gattung zwischen Philosophie, Wissensvermittlung, und dramatischer Inszenierung*, edited by S. Föllinger and G. M. Müller, 383–419. Berlin and Boston.

MOMIGLIANO, A. 1987. 'History between Medicine and Rhetoric'. In *Ottavo contributo alla storia degli studi classici e del mondo antico*, edited by A. Momigliano, 13–25. Rome.

MONTHÉARD, O. 2020. 'Negation and Poetic Capability in Keats's Odes'. *Etudes anglaises*, 73(2): 171–85.

MONTIGLIO, S. 2005. *Wandering in Ancient Greek Culture*. Chicago and London.

MOODY, R. A. 2022. *Life after Life*. London. [First published in 1975.]

MOORE, M. B. 1998. *Corpus Vasorum Antiquorum*, Malibu 8, USA 33. Malibu.

MOORS, K. 1988. 'Muthologia and the Limits of Opinion: Presented Myths in Plato's *Republic*'. *Proceedings of the Boston Area Colloquium in Ancient Philosophy*, 4: 213–47.

MORGAN, K. 2000. *Myth and Philosophy from the Presocratics to Plato*. Cambridge.

MORGAN, K. 2002. 'Comments on Gill'. In *New Perspectives on Plato, Modern and Ancient*, edited by J. Annas and C. J. Rowe, 173–87. Cambridge, MA and London.

MORGAN, K. 2012. 'A Prolegomenon to Performance in the West'. In *Theater Outside Athens: Drama in Greek Sicily and South Italy*, edited by K. Bosher, 35–55. Cambridge.

MORGAN, T. E. 1994. 'Plague or Poetry? Thucydides on the Epidemic at Athens'. *Transactions of the American Philological Association*, 124: 197–209.

MORRIS, I. 1989. *Burial and Ancient Society: The Rise of the Greek City-State*. Cambridge. [First published in 1987.]

MORRIS, I. 1992. *Death-Ritual and Social Structure in Classical Antiquity*. Cambridge.

MORRIS, I. 1997. 'Periodization and the Heroes: Inventing a Dark Age'. In *Inventing Ancient Culture: Historicism, Periodization, and the Ancient World*, edited by M. Golden and P. Toohey, 96–131. London and New York.

MORRIS, I. 2000. *Archaeology as Cultural History: Words and Things in Iron Age Greece*. Oxford and Malden, MA.

MORRISON, J. S. 1955. 'Parmenides and Er'. *The Journal of Hellenic Studies*, 75: 59–68.

MORRISON, J. V. 2004. 'Memory, Time, and Writing: Oral and Literary Aspects of Thucydides' *History*'. In *Oral Performance and its Contexts*, Mnemosyne Supplement 248, edited by C. J. Mackie, 95–116. Leiden and Boston.

MOST, G. 1993. 'A Cock for Asclepius'. *The Classical Quarterly*, 43(1): 96–111.

MURARI PIRES, F. 2006. 'Thucydidean Modernities: History between Science and Art'. In *Brill's Companion to Thucydides*, edited by A. Rengakos and A. Tsakmakis, 811–38. Leiden and Boston.

MURNAGHAN, S. 1988. 'Body and Voice in Greek Tragedy'. *Yale Journal of Criticism*, 1: 23–43.

MURRAY, O. 1988. 'Death and the Symposion'. *AION, Sezione di archeologia e storia antica*, 10: 239–57.

MURRAY, P. 1999. 'What Is a Muthos for Plato?' In *From Myth to Reason? Studies in the Development of Greek Thought*, edited by R. Buxton, 251–62. Oxford.

MURRAY, P. 2017. 'Poetry and the Image of the Tyrant in Plato's *Republic*'. In *Plato and the Power of Images*, Mnemosyne Supplement 405, edited by P. Destrée and R. G. Edmonds III, 199–218. Leiden and Boston.

MUTH, S. 2006. 'Als die Gewaltbilder zu ihrem Wirkungspotential fanden'. In *Gewalt und Ästhetik: Zur Gewalt und ihrer Darstellung in der griechischen Klassik*, edited by B. Seidensticker and M. Vöhler, 259–93. Berlin and New York.

MUTH, S. 2008. *Gewalt im Bild: Das Phänomen der medialen Gewalt im Athen des 6. und 5. Jahrhunderts v. Chr.* Berlin and New York.

NAGEL, T. 1970. 'Death'. *Noûs*, 4(1): 73–80.

NAIDEN, F. 2015. 'Sacrifice'. In *The Oxford Handbook of Ancient Greek Religion*, edited by E. Eidenow and J. Kindt, 463–76. Oxford.

NAILS, D. 2005. 'The Trial and Death of Socrates'. In *A Companion to Socrates*, edited by S. Ahbel-Rappe and R. Kamtekar, 5–20. Oxford.

NASH, J. C. 2019. *Black Feminism Reimagined: After Intersectionality*. Durham, NC.

NEER, R. 1995. 'The Lion's Eye: Imitation and Uncertainty in Attic Red-Figure'. *Representations*, 51: 118–53.

264 BIBLIOGRAPHY

NEER, R. 2002. *Style and Politics in Athenian Vase-Painting: The Craft of Democracy, ca. 530–460 B.C.E.* Cambridge.

NEER, R. 2010. *The Emergence of the Classical Style in Greek Sculpture.* Chicago and London.

NEER, R. 2012. 'Sacrificing Stones: On Some Sculpture, Mostly Athenian'. In *Greek and Roman Animal Sacrifice: Ancient Victims, Modern Observers*, edited by C. A. Faraone and F. S. Naiden, 99–119. Cambridge.

NEER, R. 2013. 'Cosmos and Discipline'. In *Heaven on Earth: Temples, Ritual, and Cosmic Symbolism in the Ancient World*, edited by D. Ragavan, 457–63. Chicago.

NEER, R. and L. KURKE. 2019. *Pindar, Song, and Space: Towards a Lyric Archaeology.* Baltimore.

NEHAMAS, A. 1998. *The Art of Living: Socratic Reflections from Plato to Foucault.* Princeton.

NEHAMAS, A. 1999. *Virtues of Authenticity: Essays on Plato and Socrates.* Princeton.

NEILL, M. 1997. *Issues of Death: Mortality and Identity in English Renaissance Tragedy.* Oxford.

NEILS, J. 2009a. 'Beloved of the Gods: Imag(in)ing Heroes in Greek Art'. In *Heroes: Mortals and Myths in Ancient Greece*, edited by S. Albersmeier, 108–19. Baltimore.

NEILS, J. 2009b. 'The "Unheroic" Corpse: Re-reading the Sarpedon Krater'. In *Athenian Potters and Painters*, volume 2, edited by J. H. Oakley and O. Palagia, 212–19. Oxford.

NELSON, M. 2011. *The Art of Cruelty: A Reckoning.* New York and London.

NEWBY, Z. 2016. *Greek Myths in Roman Art and Culture: Values and Identity in Italy, 50 BC–AD 250.* Cambridge.

NEWBY, Z. and R. LEADER-NEWBY (eds.) 2007. *Art and Inscriptions in the Ancient World.* Cambridge.

NEWBY, Z. and R. E. TOULSON. 2019a. 'Introduction: Emotions and Materiality in Theory and Method'. In *The Materiality of Mourning: Cross-Disciplinary Perspectives*, edited by Z. Newby and R. E. Toulson, 1–20. London.

NEWBY, Z. and R. E. TOULSON (eds.) 2019b. *The Materiality of Mourning: Cross-Disciplinary Perspectives.* London.

NICOLAI, R. 2009. '*Ktêma es aei*: Aspects of the Reception of Thucydides in the Ancient World'. In *Thucydides: Oxford Readings in Classical Studies*, edited by J. S. Rusten, 381–404. Oxford and New York. [First published in Italian in 1995.]

NIGHTINGALE, A. 1995. *Genres in Dialogue: Plato and the Construct of Philosophy.* New York.

NIGHTINGALE, A. 2001. 'On Wandering and Wondering: "Theôria" in Greek Philosophy and Culture'. *Arion*, 9(2): 25–58.

NIGHTINGALE, A. 2002a. 'Distant Views: "Realistic" and "Fantastic" Mimesis in Plato'. In *New Perspectives on Plato, Modern and Ancient*, edited by J. Annas and C. J. Rowe, 227–47. Cambridge, MA and London.

NIGHTINGALE, A. 2002b. 'Toward an Ecological Eschatology: Plato and Bakhtin on Other Worlds and Times'. In *Bakhtin and the Classics*, edited by R. Bracht Branham, 220–49. Evanston, IL.

NIGHTINGALE, A. 2004. *Spectacles of Truth in Classical Greek Philosophy*. Cambridge.

NIGHTINGALE, A. 2016. 'Sight and the Philosophy of Vision in Classical Greece: Democritus, Plato and Aristotle'. In *Sight and the Ancient Senses*, edited by M. Squire, 54–67. London and New York.

NOOTER, S. 2012. *When Heroes Sing: Sophocles and the Shifting Soundscape of Tragedy*. Cambridge and New York.

NOVÁKOVÁ, L. and R. ŠÁLYOVÁ. 2019. 'Marking the Victory in Ancient Greece: Some Remarks on Classical Trophy Monuments'. *ILIRIA International Review*, 9(1): 191–201.

NUSSBAUM, M. 2001. *The Fragility of Goodness: Luck and Ethics in Greek Tragedy and Philosophy*, revised edition. Cambridge. [First published in 1986.]

OAKLEY, J. H. 1997a. *The Achilles Painter*. Mainz.

OAKLEY, J. H. 1997b. 'The Bosanquet Painter'. In *Athenian Potters and Painters: The Conference Proceedings*, edited by J. H. Oakley, W. D. E. Coulson, and O. Palagia, 241–8. Oxford.

OAKLEY, J. H. 2004. *Picturing Death in Classical Athens: The Evidence of the White Lekythoi*. Cambridge and New York.

OAKLEY, J. H. 2009. 'Children in Athenian Funerary Art during the Peloponnesian War'. In *Art in Athens during the Peloponnesian War*, edited by O. Palagia, 207–35. Cambridge.

OAKLEY, J. H. 2020. *A Guide to Scenes of Daily Life on Athenian Vases*. Madison.

OBER, J. 2009. 'Thucydides *Theôrêtikos*/Thucydides *Histôr*: Realist Theory and the Challenge of History'. In *Thucydides: Oxford Readings in Classical Studies*, edited by J. S. Rusten, 434–78. Oxford and New York. [First published in 2001.]

OGDEN, D. 2001. *Greek and Roman Necromancy*. Princeton.

OGDEN, D. 2008. *Night's Black Agents: Witches, Wizards, and the Dead in the Ancient World*. London.

ORLANDOS, A. 1922. ῞Εργασίαι ἐν Λεύκτροις τῆς Θεσπικῆς'. Πρακτικά της εν Αθήναις Αρχαιολογικῆς Εταιρείας, 1922–24: 38–40.

ORLANDOS, A. 1958a. ᾿Ανασκαφικὴ ἔρευνα καὶ ἀναπαράστασις τοῦ τροπαίου τῶν Λεύκτρων'. Πρακτικά τῆς εν Αθήναις Αρχαιολογικῆς Εταιρείας: 43–4, pls. 34–7.

ORLANDOS, A. 1958b. 'Λεῦκτρα. Τρόπαιον'. Το Έργον της εν Αθήναις Αρχαιολογικῆς Εταιρείας (Το Έργον): 48–52, figs. 49–54.

ORLANDOS, A. 1961a. ᾿Αναστήλωσις καὶ συντήρησις μνημείων: Λεῦκτρα. Τρόπαιον'. Πρακτικά της εν Αθήναις Αρχαιολογικῆς Εταιρείας: 225, pl. 179.

ORLANDOS, A. 1961b. ᾿Αναστήλωσις καὶ συντήρησις μνημείων: Λεῦκτρα, Τρόπαιον'. Το Έργον της εν Αθήναις Αρχαιολογικῆς Εταιρείας (Το Έργον): 229–31, fig. 245.

ORWIN, C. 1988. 'Stasis and Plague: Thucydides on the Dissolution of Society'. *The Journal of Politics*, 50: 831–47.

ORWIN, C. 1994. *The Humanity of Thucydides*. Princeton.

OSBORNE, C. 1996. 'Space, Time, Shape, and Direction: Creative Discourse in the *Timaeus*'. In *Form and Argument in Late Plato*, edited by C. Gill and M. M. McCabe, 179–211. Oxford.

266 BIBLIOGRAPHY

Osborne, R. 1987. 'The Viewing and Obscuring of the Parthenon Frieze'. *The Journal of Hellenic Studies*, 107: 98–105.

Osborne, R. 1988. 'Death Revisited, Death Revised: The Death of the Artist in Archaic and Classical Greek Art'. *Art History*, 11(1): 1–16.

Osborne, R. 1994a. 'Framing the Centaur: Reading Fifth-Century Architectural Sculpture'. In *Art and Text in Ancient Greek Culture*, edited by S. Goldhill and R. Osborne, 52–84. Cambridge.

Osborne, R. 1994b. 'Looking On—Greek Style: Does the Sculpted Girl Speak to Women Too?' In *Classical Greece: Ancient Histories and Modern Archaeologies*, edited by I. M. Morris, 81–96. Cambridge.

Osborne, R. 1998. *Archaic and Classical Greek Art*. Oxford and New York.

Osborne, R. 2000. 'Archaic and Classical Greek Temple Sculpture and the Viewer'. In *Word and Image in Ancient Greece*, edited by N. K. Rutter and B. A. Sparkes, 228–46. Edinburgh.

Osborne, R. 2004. 'Images of a Warrior: On a Group of Athenian Vases and their Public'. In *Greek Vases: Images, Contexts, and Controversies*, edited by C. Marconi, 41–54. Leiden.

Osborne, R. 2009. 'The Narratology and Theology of Architectural Sculpture, *or* What You Can Do with a Chariot But Can't Do with a Satyr on a Greek Temple'. In *Structure, Image, Ornament: Architectural Sculpture in the Greek World*, edited by P. Schultz and R. von den Hoff, 2–12. Oxford and Oakville.

Osborne, R. 2010. 'Democratic Ideology, the Events of War and the Iconography of Attic Funerary Sculpture'. In *War, Democracy, and Culture in Classical Athens*, edited by D. M. Pritchard, 245–65. Cambridge.

Osborne, R. 2012. 'Polysemy and Its Limits: Controlling the Interpretation of Greek Vases in Changing Cultural Contexts'. In *Vasenbilder im Kulturtransfer: Zirkulation und Rezeption griechischer Keramik im Mittelmeerraum*, edited by S. Schmidt and A. Stähli, 177–86. Munich.

Osborne, R. 2016. 'Sacrificial Theologies'. In *Theologies of Ancient Greek Religion*, edited by E. Eidinow, J. Kindt, and R. Osborne, 233–48. Cambridge.

Osborne, R. 2017. 'How the Gauls Broke the Frame: The Political and Theological Impact of Taking Battle Scenes off Greek Temples'. In *The Frame in Classical Art: A Cultural History*, edited by V. Platt and M. Squire, 425–56. Cambridge.

Osborne, R. 2018. *The Transformation of Athens: Painted Pottery and the Creation of Classical Greece*. Princeton and Oxford.

Page, D. L. 1953. 'Thucydides' Description of the Great Plague at Athens'. *Classical Quarterly*, new series, 3: 97–119.

Palagia, O. 2005. 'Interpretations of Two Athenian Friezes: The Temple of the Ilissos and the Temple of Athena Nike'. In *Periklean Athens and Its Legacy: Problems and Perspectives*, edited by J. Barringer and J. M. Hurwit, 177–92. Austin.

Palagia, O. 2009a. 'Archaism and the Quest for Immortality in Attic Sculpture during the Peloponnesian War'. In *Art in Athens during the Peloponnesian War*, edited by O. Palagia, 24–51. Cambridge.

Palagia, O. (ed.) 2009b. *Art in Athens during the Peloponnesian War*. Cambridge.

PALMISCIANO, R. 2023. 'Intervisuality in the Greek Symposium'. In *Intervisuality: New Approaches to Greek Literature*, edited by A. Capra and L. Floridi, 103–20. Berlin and Boston.

PAPAGRIGORAKIS, M. J., C. YAPIJAKIS, and P. N. SYNODINOS. 2008. 'Typhoid Fever Epidemic in Ancient Athens'. In *Paleomicrobiology: Past Human Infections*, edited by D. Raoult and M. Drancourt, 161–73. Berlin and Heidelberg.

PARKER, L. M. 2007. *Euripides, Alcestis*. Oxford.

PARKER, R. 1983. *Miasma: Pollution and Purification in Early Greek Religion*. Oxford.

PARKER, R. 1999. 'Through a Glass Darkly: Sophocles and the Divine'. In *Sophocles Revisited: Essays Presented to Sir Hugh Lloyd-Jones*, edited by J. Griffin, 11–30. Oxford.

PARKER, R. 2005. *Polytheism and Society at Athens*. Oxford.

PARKER PEARSON, M. 2003. *The Archaeology of Death and Burial*. Stroud. [First edition published in 1999.]

PARNIA, S. 2014. 'Death and Consciousness: An Overview of the Mental and Cognitive Experience of Death'. *Annals of the New York Academy of Sciences*, 1330: 75–93.

PARNIA, S. et al. 2022. 'Guidelines and Standards for the Study of Death and Recalled Experiences of Death: A Multidisciplinary Consensus Statement and Proposed Future Directions'. *Annals of the New York Academy of Sciences*, 1511: 5–21.

PARRY, A. 1969. 'The Language of Thucydides' Description of the Plague'. *Bulletin of the Institute of Classical Studies*, 16: 106–18.

PARRY, A. 1970. 'Thucydides' Use of Abstract Language'. *Yale French Studies*, 45: 3–20.

PATTON, K. C. 2009. *Religion of the Gods: Ritual, Paradox, Reflexivity*. Oxford.

PEIFER, E. 1989. *Eidola und andere mit dem Sterben verbundene Flügelwesen in der attischen Vasenmalerei in spätarchaischer und klassischer Zeit*. Frankfurt am Main.

PELLING, C. 1997. 'Is Death the End? Closure in Plutarch's *Lives*'. In *Classical Closure: Reading the End in Greek and Latin Literature*, edited by D. H. Roberts, F. M. Dunn, and D. Fowler, 228–50. Princeton.

PEMBERTON, E. 1972. 'The East and West Friezes of the Temple of Athena Nike'. *American Journal of Archaeology*, 76: 303–10.

PENNER, T. 1992. 'Socrates and the Early Dialogues'. In *The Cambridge Companion to Plato*, edited by R. Kraut, 121–69. Cambridge.

PEPONI, A.-E. 2012. *Frontiers of Pleasure: Models of Aesthetic Response in Archaic and Classical Greek Thought*. Oxford and New York.

PERILLI, L. 2018. 'Epistemologies'. In *The Cambridge Companion to Hippocrates*, edited by P. E. Pormann, 119–51. Cambridge.

PERKINS, J. 1995. *The Suffering Self: Pain and Narrative Representation in the Early Christian Era*. London and New York.

PETRAKI, Z. 2021. '"Were You There Yourself?" The "Dialectics of the Body" in Plato's *Phaedo*'. In *Framing the Dialogues: How to Read Openings and Closures in Plato*, edited by E. Kaklamanou, M. Pavlou, and A. Tsakmakis, 176–96. Leiden and Boston.

PETRAKI, Z. 2024. 'Plato's Creative Imagination'. In *The Imagination of the Mind in Classical Athens: Forms of Thought*, edited by E. Clifford and X. Buxton, 173–96. London and New York.

268 BIBLIOGRAPHY

PETRIDOU, G. 2013. '"Blessed Is He, Who Has Seen": The Power of Ritual Viewing and Ritual Framing in Eleusis'. In *Vision and Viewing in Ancient Greece*, edited by S. Blundell, D. Cairns, and N. Rabinowitz, special issue of *Helios*, 40(1/2): 309–41.

PHILLIPS, T. 2018. 'Polyphony, Event, Context: Pindar, *Paean 9*'. In *Textual Events: Performance and the Lyric in Early Greece*, edited by F. Budelmann and T. Phillips, 189–209. Oxford.

PHILLIPS, T. 2020. *Untimely Epic: Apollonius Rhodius' Argonautica*. Oxford and New York.

PHILLIPS, T. 2021. 'A Poet's Lives'. In *A Companion to Theocritus*, edited by P. Kyriakou, E. Sistakou, and A. Rengakos, 41–62. Boston and Leiden.

PHILLIPS, T. 2024. 'Vigilance to the Point of Magic'. In *The Imagination of the Mind in Classical Athens: Forms of Thought*, edited by E. Clifford and X. Buxton, 253–70. London and New York.

PICARD, G. C. 1957. *Les trophées romains: Contribution à l'histoire de la religion et de l'art triumphal de Rome*. Paris.

PLATT, V. 2011. *Facing the Gods: Epiphany and Representation in Graeco-Roman Art, Literature, and Religion*. Cambridge.

PLATT, V. 2012. 'Framing the Dead on Roman Sarcophagi'. In *Sarcophagi*, edited by J. Elsner and H. Wu, special issue of *Res: Anthropology and Aesthetics*, 61/62, 213–27.

PLATT, V. 2017. 'Framing the Dead on Roman Sarcophagi'. In *The Frame in Classical Art: A Cultural History*, edited by V. Platt and M. Squire, 353–81. Cambridge. [Revised from an article published in *Sarcophagi*, edited by J. Elsner and H. Wu, special issue of *Res: Anthropology and Aesthetics*, 61/62, 213–27.]

PLATT, V. and M. SQUIRE (eds.) 2017. *The Frame in Classical Art: A Cultural History*. Cambridge and New York.

PONCHON, P. 2017. *Thucydide philosophe : La raison tragique dans l'histoire*. Grenoble.

PORTER, J. I. 2010. *The Origins of Aesthetic Thought in Ancient Greece: Matter, Sensation, and Experience*. Cambridge.

PORTER, J. I. 2012. 'The Value of Aesthetic Value'. In *The Construction of Value in the Ancient World*, edited by J. K. Papadopoulos and G. Urton, 336–53. Los Angeles.

PORTER, J. I. 2015. 'The Sublime'. In *A Companion to Ancient Aesthetics*, edited by P. Destrée and P. Murray, 393–405. Malden, MA and Chichester.

PORTER, J. I. 2016. *The Sublime in Antiquity*. Cambridge.

POSTER, C. 1998. 'The Idea(s) of Order of Platonic Dialogues and Their Hermeneutic Consequences'. *Phoenix*, 52(3/4): 282–98.

POTTIER, E. 1883. *Étude sur les lécythes blancs attiques à représentations funéraires*. Paris.

POTTIER, E. 1923. *Corpus Vasorum Antiquorum*. Louvre 2, France 2. Paris.

POTTS, D. T. 2002. 'The Domestication of Death'. *Review of Archaeology*, 23(1): 17–22.

PRASCHNIKER, C. 1924. 'Zum Friese des Tempels der Athena Nike'. In *Strena Buliciana*, edited by M. Abramić and V. Hoffiller, 19–25. Zagreb and Split.

PRESS, G. A. (ed.) 2000. *Who Speaks for Plato? Studies in Platonic Anonymity*. Lanham and Oxford.

PRINCE, S. 2006. 'The Organization of Knowledge'. In *A Companion to the Classical Greek World*, edited by K. H. Kinzl, 432–55. Oxford and Malden, MA.

PRITCHETT, W. K. 1974. *The Greek State at War, Part 2*. Berkeley, Los Angeles, and London.

PUCCI, P. 2007. 'Euripides and Aristophanes: What Does Tragedy Teach?' In *Visualizing the Tragic: Drama, Myth, and Ritual in Greek Art and Literature*, edited by C. Kraus, S. Goldhill, H. P. Foley, and J. Elsner, 105–26. Oxford.

RABE, H. (ed.) 1913. *Hermogenis Opera*. Leipzig.

RAPP, C. 2015. 'Tragic Emotions'. In *A Companion to Ancient Aesthetics*, edited by P. Destrée and P. Murray, 438–54. Malden, MA and Chichester.

RECKE, M. 2002. *Gewalt und Leid: Das Bild des Krieges bei den Athenern im 6. und 5. Jh. v. Chr.* Istanbul.

REHM, R. 2002. *The Play of Space: Spatial Transformation in Greek Tragedy*. Princeton and Oxford.

REINHARDT, K. 1979. *Sophocles*, translated by H. Harvey and D. Harvey, with an introduction by H. Lloyd Jones. Oxford. [First edition published in German in 1933.]

RENGAKOS, A. 2006. 'Thucydides' Narrative: The Epic and Herodotean Heritage'. In *Brill's Companion to Thucydides*, edited by A. Rengakos and A. Tsakmakis, 279–300. Leiden and Boston.

RETIEF, F. P. and L. CILLIERS. 2006. 'Burial Customs, the Afterlife and the Pollution of Death in Ancient Greece'. *Acta Theologica*, 26(2), Supplement 7: 44–61.

RHODES, R. F. 1995. *Architecture and Meaning on the Athenian Acropolis*. Cambridge.

RHOMAIOS, K. 1930. *Corpus Vasorum Antiquorum*. Athens, National Museum 1, Greece 1. Paris.

RICHARDSON, H. 1926. 'The Myth of Er (Plato, *Republic*, 616b)'. *Classical Quarterly*, 20: 113–33.

RICHARDSON, N. J. 1981. 'Emily Vermeule: Aspects of Death in Early Greek Art and Poetry'. *The Classical Review*, 31(1): 124–5.

RICHTER, G. M. A. 1944. *Archaic Attic Gravestones*. Cambridge, MA.

RICHTER, G. M. A. 1963. *A Handbook of Greek Art*, third edition. London. [First published in 1959.]

RICHTER, G. M. A. 1970. *Kouroi: Archaic Greek Youths. A Study of the Development of the Kouros Type in Greek Sculpture*. London and New York. [First edition published in 1942.]

RICHTER, G. M. A. and M. J. MILNE. 1935. *Shapes and Names of Athenian Vases*. New York.

RIDGWAY, B. S. 1970. *The Severe Style in Greek Sculpture*. Princeton.

RIEZLER, W. 1914. *Weissgrundige attische Lekythen*. Munich.

RIJKSBARON, A. 2006. 'On False Historic Presents in Sophocles (and Euripides)'. In *Sophocles and the Greek Language: Aspects of Diction, Syntax, and Pragmatics*, Mnemosyne Supplement 269, edited by I. J. F. de Jong and A. Rijksbaron, 127–49. Leiden.

RIMELL, V. 2024. 'Philosophers' Stone: Enduring Niobe'. In *Niobes: Antiquity, Modernity, Critical Theory*, edited by M. Telò and A. Benjamin, 69–84. Columbus.

RINGER, M. 1998. *Electra and the Empty Urn: Metatheater and Role Playing in Sophocles*. Chapel Hill and London.

ROBB, J. 2013. 'Creating Death: An Archaeology of Dying'. In *The Oxford Handbook of the Archaeology of Death and Burial*, edited by S. Tarlow and L. N. Stutz, 441–57. Oxford.

ROBERT, C. 1895. *Die Marathonschlacht in der Poikile und weiteres über Polygnot*. Halle.

270 BIBLIOGRAPHY

ROBERTS, D. H. 1989. 'Different Stories: Sophoclean Narrative(s) in the *Philoctetes*'. *Transactions of the American Philological Association*, 119: 161–76.

ROBERTS, D. H. 1997. 'Afterword: Ending and Aftermath, Ancient and Modern'. In *Classical Closure: Reading the End in Greek and Latin Literature*, edited by D. H. Roberts, F. M. Dunn, and D. Fowler, 251–73. Princeton.

ROBERTSON, M. 1988. 'Sarpedon Brought Home'. In *Studies in Honour of T. B. L. Webster*, volume 2, edited by J. H. Betts, J. T. Hooker, and J. R. Green, 109–20. Bristol.

ROBERTSON, M. 1992. *The Art of Vase-Painting in Classical Athens*. Cambridge.

ROBINSON, P. 1985. 'Why Do We Believe Thucydides? A Comment on W. R. Connor's "Narrative Discourse in Thucydides"'. In *The Greek Historians, Literature and History: Papers Presented to A. E. Raubitschek*, edited by M. H. Jameson, 19–23. Stanford.

RODIGHIERO, A. 2007. *Una serata a Colono. Fortuna del secondo Edipo*. Verona.

RODIGHIERO, A. 2012. 'The Sense of Place: *Oedipus at Colonus*, "Political" Geography, and the Defence of a Way of Life'. In *Crisis on Stage: Tragedy and Comedy in Late Fifth-Century Athens*, edited by A. Markantonatos and B. Zimmerman, 55–80. Berlin and Boston.

ROHDE, E. 1925. *Psyche: The Cult of Souls and Belief in Immortality among the Ancient Greeks*, translated from the eighth edition by W. B. Hillis. London and Bradford.

ROISMAN, H. M. 2019. 'Tecmessa'. In *Looking at Ajax*, edited by D. Stuttard, 97–116. London.

ROLLER, M. 2015. '"Between Unique and Typical: Senecan *Exempla* in a List'. In *Exemplarity and Singularity: Thinking through Particulars in Philosophy, Literature, and Law*, edited by M. Lowrie and S. Lüdemann, 81–95. London and New York.

ROLLER, M. 2018. *Models from the Past in Roman Culture: A World of Exempla*. Cambridge.

ROOD, T. 1998. *Thucydides: Narrative and Explanation*. Oxford.

ROOD, T. 1999. 'Thucydides' Persian Wars'. In *The Limits of Historiography: Genre and Narrative in Ancient Historical Texts*, Mnemosyne Supplement 191, edited by C. S. Kraus, 141–68. Leiden, Boston, and Köln.

ROOD, T. 2004. 'Thucydides'. In *Narrators, Narratees, and Narratives in Ancient Greek Literature: Studies in Ancient Greek Narrative*, volume 1, Mnemosyne Supplement 257, edited by R. Nünlist, A. M. Bowie, and I. J. F. de Jong, 115–28. Leiden.

ROOD, T. 2012. 'Thucydides'. In *Space in Greek Literature: Studies in Ancient Greek Narrative*, volume 3, Mnemosyne Supplement 339, edited by I. J. F. de Jong, 141–59. Leiden and Boston.

ROOD, T., C. ATACK, and T. PHILLIPS. 2020. *Anachronism and Antiquity*. London and New York.

ROSENBERG, C. E. 1992. *Explaining Epidemics and Other Studies in the History of Medicine*. Cambridge.

ROSENMEYER, T. G. 1952. 'The Wrath of Oedipus'. *Phoenix*, 6(3): 92–112.

ROUET, P. 2001. *Approaches to the Study of Attic Vases: Beazley and Pottier*, translated by L. Nash. Oxford.

ROWE, C. J. 1993. *Plato, Phaedo*. Cambridge.

ROWE, C. J. 2007. *Plato and the Art of Philosophical Writing*. Cambridge and New York.

RUBENSTEIN, R. 2008. '"I Meant Nothing by the Lighthouse": Virginia Woolf's Poetics of Negation'. *Journal of Modern Literature*, 31(4): 36–53.

RUBINCAM, C. 1991. 'Casualty Figures in the Battle Descriptions of Thucydides'. *Transactions of the American Philological Association*, 121: 181–98.

RUDOLPH, K. 2016. 'Sight and the Presocratics: Approaches to Visual Perception in Early Greek Philosophy'. In *Sight and the Ancient Senses*, edited by M. Squire, 36–53. London and New York.

RÜHFEL, H. 1984. *Das Kind in der griechischen Kunst: Von der minoisch-mykenischen Zeit bis zum Hellenismus*. Mainz.

RUIJGH, C. J. 2006. 'The Use of the Demonstratives ὅδε, οὗτος, and (ἐ)κεῖνος in Sophocles'. In *Sophocles and the Greek Language: Aspects of Diction, Syntax, and Pragmatics*, Mnemosyne Supplement 269, edited by I. J. F. de Jong and A. Rijksbaron, 151–61. Leiden.

RUSTEN, J. S. 1986. 'Structure and Style in Interpreting Thucydides: The Soldier's Choice (Thuc. 2.42.4)'. *Harvard Studies in Classical Philology*, 90: 49–76.

RUSTEN, J. S. 1989. *Thucydides, The Peloponnesian War, Book II*. Cambridge.

RUTHERFORD, I. 1995. 'Theoric Crisis: The Dangers of Pilgrimage in Greek Religion and Society'. *Studi e Materiali di Storia delle Religioni*, 61: 275–92.

RUTHERFORD, R. B. 1995. *The Art of Plato: Ten Essays in Platonic Interpretation*. London.

RUTHERFORD, R. B. 2012. *Greek Tragic Style: Form, Language, and Interpretation*. Cambridge.

RUTTER, N. K. and B. A. SPARKES (eds.) 2000. *Word and Image in Ancient Greece*. Edinburgh.

RYAN, C. 2010. 'Eighteenth-Century Responses to Sophocles' *Oedipus at Colonus*'. PhD thesis, University of Nottingham.

SAÏD, S. 2012. 'Athens and Athenian Space in *Oedipus at Colonus*'. In *Crisis on Stage: Tragedy and Comedy in Late Fifth-Century Athens*, edited by A. Markantonatos and B. Zimmerman, 81–100. Berlin and Boston.

SAUNDERS, D. 2006. 'Sleepers in the Valley: Athenian Vase-Painting 600–400 B.C. and the "Beautiful Death"'. DPhil thesis, Lincoln College, University of Oxford.

SAYRE, K. M. 1995. *Plato's Literary Garden: How to Read a Platonic Dialogue*. Notre Dame and London.

SCARFE, F. 1961. 'Keats's Use of the Negative'. *Études anglaises*, 14(1): 1–9.

SCARRY, E. 1985. *The Body in Pain: The Making and Unmaking of the World*. New York and Oxford.

SCHARFFENBERGER, E. W. 2017. '*Oedipus at Colonus*'. In *Brill's Companion to the Reception of Sophocles*, edited by R. Lauriola and K. N. Demetriou, 326–88. Leiden and Boston.

SCHLÖRB, B. 1963. 'Beiträge zur Schildamazonomachie der Athena Parthenos'. *Mitteilungen des Deutschen Archäologischen Instituts, Athenische Abteilung*, 78: 156–72.

272 BIBLIOGRAPHY

SCHMIDT, M., A. D. TRENDALL, and A. CAMBITOGLOU. 1976. *Eine Gruppe Apulischer Grabvasen in Basel, Studien zu Gehalt und Form der unteritalischen Sepulkralkunst.* Basel.

SCHMIDT, S. 2005. *Rhetorische Bilder auf attischen Vasen: Visuelle Kommunikation im 5. Jahrhundert v. Chr.* Berlin.

SCHMITZ, T. 2008. *Modern Literary Theory and Ancient Texts: An Introduction.* Malden, MA. [First published in German in 2002.]

SCHNAPP, A. 1988. 'Why Did the Greeks Need Images?' In *Proceedings of the 3rd Symposium on Ancient Greek and Related Pottery, Copenhagen, August 31–September 4, 1987*, edited by J. Christiansen and T. Melander, 568–74. Copenhagen.

SCHULTZ, P. 2001. 'The Akroteria of the Temple of Athena Nike'. *Hesperia*, 70: 1–47.

SCHULTZ, P. 2009. 'The North Frieze of the Temple of Athena Nike'. In *Art in Athens during the Peloponnesian War*, edited by O. Palagia, 128–67. New York.

SCHWAB, K. A. 2005. 'Celebrations of Victory: The Metopes of the Parthenon'. In *The Parthenon: From Antiquity to the Present*, edited by J. Neils, 159–97. Cambridge.

SCODEL, R. 1984. *Sophocles.* Boston.

SCODEL, R. 2009. 'Ignorant Narrators in Greek Tragedy'. In *Narratology and Interpretation: The Content of Narrative Form in Ancient Literature*, edited by J. Grethlein and A. Rengakos, 421–47. Berlin and New York.

SCOTT, D. 2006. *Plato's Meno.* Cambridge.

SCOTT, G. F. 1994. *The Sculpted Word: Keats, Ekphrasis, and the Visual Arts.* Hanover and London.

SCULLION, S. 2000. 'Tradition and Invention in Euripidean Aitiology'. In *Euripides and Tragic Theatre in the Late Fifth Century*, Illinois Classical Studies 24/5, edited by M. Cropp, K. Lee, and D. Sansone, 217–33. Champaign, IL.

SEDLEY, D. 1995. 'The Dramatis Personae of Plato's *Phaedo*'. *Proceedings of the British Academy*, 85: 3–26.

SEESKIN, K. 1987. *Dialogue and Discovery: A Study in Socratic Method.* Albany.

SEGAL, C. 1978. '"The Myth Was Saved": Reflections on Homer and the Mythology of Plato's *Republic*'. *Hermes*, 106(2): 315–36.

SEGAL, C. 1981. *Tragedy and Civilization: An Interpretation of Sophocles.* Cambridge, MA and London.

SEGAL, C. 1992. 'Tragic Beginnings: Narration, Voice, and Authority in the Prologues of Greek Drama'. In *Beginnings in Classical Literature*, Yale Classical Studies 29, edited by F. M. Dunn and T. Cole, 85–112. Cambridge.

SEGAL, C. 1993a. *Euripides and the Poetics of Sorrow: Art, Gender, and Commemoration in Alcestis, Hippolytus, and Hecuba.* Durham, NC and London.

SEGAL, C. 1993b. 'Euripides' *Alcestis*: How to Die a Normal Death in Greek Tragedy'. In *Death and Representation*, edited by S. W. Goodwin and E. Bronfen, 213–41. Baltimore and London.

SEGAL, C. 1995. *Sophocles' Tragic World: Divinity, Nature, Society.* Cambridge, MA.

SEGAL, C. 2019. 'The Two Worlds of Euripides' *Helen*'. In *Interpreting Greek Tragedy: Myth, Poetry, Text*, by C. Segal, 222–67. Ithaca. [First published in 1971.]

SEKITA, K. 2015. 'The Figure of Hades/Plouton in Greek Beliefs of the Archaic and Classical Periods'. DPhil thesis, St Anne's College, University of Oxford.

SEKITA, K. 2022. 'Forms of Solitude and Isolation in the Face of Death in Greece'. In *Being Alone in Antiquity: Greco-Roman Ideas and Experiences of Misanthropy, Isolation, and Solitude*, edited by R. Matuszewski, 41–55. Berlin and Boston.

SEKITA, K. 2024. 'Morbid Phantasies: The "After-Death" and the Dead between Imagination and Perception'. In *The Imagination of the Mind in Classical Athens*, edited by E. Clifford and X. Buxton, 103–25. London and New York.

SEN, A. 2006. *Identity and Violence: The Illusion of Destiny*. London.

SENELICK, L. 2022. *The Final Curtain: The Art of Dying on Stage*. London and New York.

SHAKESHAFT, H. 2022. 'Beauty, Gods, and Early Greek Art: The Dedications of Mantiklos and Nikandre Revisited'. *The Art Bulletin*, 104(2): 20–46.

SHAPIRO, G. 2007. 'The Absent Image: Ekphrasis and the "Infinite Relation" of Translation'. *Journal of Visual Culture*, 6(1): 13–24.

SHAPIRO, H. A. 1991. 'The Iconography of Mourning in Athenian Art'. *American Journal of Archaeology*, 95(4): 629–56.

SHAPIRO, H. A. 1993. *Personifications in Greek Art: The Representation of Abstract Concepts, 600–400 B.C.* Zurich.

SHEAR, I. M. 1999. 'The Western Approach to the Athenian Akropolis'. *Journal of Hellenic Studies*, 119: 86–127.

SHEAR, T. L. 1984. 'The Athenian Agora: Excavations of 1980–1982'. *Hesperia*, 53: 1–57.

SHEAR, T. L. 2016. *Trophies of Victory: Public Building in Periklean Athens*. Princeton.

SHIRAZI, A. 2018. 'The Other Side of the Mirror: Reflection and Reversal in Euripides' *Hecuba*'. In *The Materialities of Greek Tragedy: Objects and Affect in Aeschylus, Sophocles, and Euripides*, edited by M. Telò and M. Mueller, 97–109. London.

SILK, M. 2009. 'The Logic of the Unexpected: Semantic Diversion in Sophocles, Yeats (and Virgil)'. In *Sophocles and the Greek Tragic Tradition*, edited by S. Goldhill and E. Hall, 134–57. Cambridge and New York.

SILVERMAN, A. 2003. 'Metaphysics and Individual Souls in the Phaedo'. In *Plato as Author: The Rhetoric of Philosophy*, edited by A. N. Michelini, 267–86. Leiden and Boston.

SIMON, E. 1963. 'Polygnotan Painting and the Niobid Painter'. *American Journal of Archaeology*, 67: 43–62.

SIMON, E. 1985. 'La decorazione architettonica del tempietto di Atena Nike sull'Acropoli di Atene'. *Museum Patavinum*, 3(2): 271–88.

SIMON, E. 1997. 'An Interpretation of the Nike Temple Parapet'. In *The Interpretation of Architectural Sculpture in Greece and Rome*, edited by D. Buitron-Oliver, 127–43. Hanover and London.

SIMON, E. and A. HIRMER. 1976. *Die griechischen Vasen*. Munich.

SIX, J. 1919. 'Mikon's Fourth Painting in the Theseion'. *The Journal of Hellenic Studies*, 39: 130–43.

274 BIBLIOGRAPHY

SJÖBERG, B. L. 2019. 'The Prothesis: A Ritualized Construction of Everyday Social Space in Ancient Greek Society'. In *Family Lives: Aspects of Life and Death in Ancient Families*, edited by K. B. Johannsen and J. H. Petersen, 77–102. Copenhagen.

SLAWISCH, A. 2019. 'Figures in Motion: An Ionian Perspective on the Severe Style'. *The Annual of the British School at Athens*, 114: 145–65.

SMALL, J. P. 2003. *The Parallel Worlds of Classical Art and Text*. Cambridge.

SMITH, A. C. 2011. *Polis and Personification in Classical Athenian Art*. Leiden and Boston.

SMITH, J. E. 1985. 'Plato's Myths as "Likely Accounts", Worthy of Belief'. *Apeiron*, 19: 24–42.

SMITH, R. R. R. 2002. 'The Use of Images: Visual History and Ancient History'. In *Classics in Progress: Essays on Ancient Greece and Rome*, edited by T. P. Wiseman, 59–102. Oxford.

SNODGRASS, A. M. 1998. 'Rural Burial in the World of Cities'. In *Nécropoles et pouvoir: Idéologies, pratiques, interpretations*, edited by S. Marchegay, M.-T. Le Dinahet, and J.-F. Salles, 37–42. Paris.

SNODGRASS, A. M. 2009. 'The Classical Greek Cemetery: A Barometer of Citizenship?' In *Inside the City in the Greek World: Studies of Urbanism from the Bronze Age to the Hellenistic Period*, edited by S. Owen and L. Preston, 99–107. Oxford.

SOFAER, J. R. 2006. *The Body as Material Culture: A Theoretical Osteoarchaeology*. Cambridge.

SONTAG, S. 1991. *Illness as Metaphor and AIDS and Its Metaphors*. New York. [First published as two separate works: *Illness as Metaphor* in 1978 and *AIDS and Its Metaphors* 1989.]

SONTAG, S. 2019. *Regarding the Pain of Others*. London. [First published in 2003.]

SOURVINOU-INWOOD, C. 1981. 'To Die and Enter the House of Hades: Homer, Before and After'. In *Mirrors of Mortality: Studies in the Social History of Death*, edited by J. Whaley, 15–39. London.

SOURVINOU-INWOOD, C. 1983. 'A Trauma in Flux: Death in the 8th Century and After'. In *The Greek Renaissance of the Eighth Century B.C.: Tradition and Innovation*, edited by R. Hägg, 33–49. Stockholm.

SOURVINOU-INWOOD, C. 1987. 'Images grecques de la mort : Représentations, imaginaire, histoire'. *AION, Sezione di archeologia e storia antica*, 9: 145–58.

SOURVINOU-INWOOD, C. 1995. *'Reading' Greek Death: To the End of the Classical Period*. Oxford and New York.

SOUTHWOOD, K. E and K. SEKITA (eds.) 2025. *Death Imagined: Ancient Perceptions of Death and Dying*. Liverpool.

SPARKES, B. A. 1996. *The Red and the Black: Studies in Greek Pottery*. London and New York.

SPIEGEL, N. 1990. *War and Peace in Classical Greek Literature*. Jerusalem.

SPIVEY, N. J. 1994. 'Psephological Heroes'. In *Ritual, Finance, Politics: Athenian Democratic Accounts Presented to David Lewis*, edited by R. Osborne and S. Hornblower, 39–51. Oxford.

SPIVEY, N. J. 1997. *Greek Art*. London and New York.

SPIVEY, N. J. 2001. *Enduring Creation: Art, Pain, and Fortitude*. London.

SPIVEY, N. J. 2005. *How Art Made the World*. London.

SPIVEY, N. J. 2018. *The Sarpedon Krater: The Life and Afterlife of a Greek Vase*. London.

SQUIRE, M. 2009. *Image and Text in Graeco-Roman Antiquity*. Cambridge.

SQUIRE, M. 2016a. 'Introductory Reflections: Making Sense of Ancient Sight'. In *Sight and the Ancient Senses*, edited by M. Squire, 1–35. London and New York.

SQUIRE, M. (ed.) 2016b. *Sight and the Ancient Senses*. London and New York.

SQUIRE, M. 2018a. 'Embodying the Dead on Classical Attic Grave-Stelai'. *Art History*, 41(3): 518–45.

SQUIRE, M. 2018b. '"To haunt, to startle, and way-lay": Approaching Ornament and Figure in Graeco-Roman Art'. In *Ornament and Figure in Graeco-Roman Art: Rethinking Visual Ontologies in Classical Antiquity*, edited by N. Dietrich and M. Squire, 1–35. Berlin.

STÄHLI, A. 2005. 'Die Rhetorik der Gewalt in Bildern des archaischen und klassischen Griechenland'. In *Die andere Seite der Klassik: Gewalt im 5. und 4. Jahrhundert v. Chr.*, edited by G. Fischer and S. Moraw, 19–44. Stuttgart.

STAMPOLIDĒS, N. CHR. 2014. 'The Moment of Death'. In *Beyond: Death and Afterlife in Ancient Greece*, edited by N. Chr. Stampolidēs and S. Oikonomou, 18–25. Athens.

STANSBURY-O'DONNELL, M. D. 1999. *Pictorial Narrative in Ancient Greek Art*. Cambridge.

STANSBURY-O'DONNELL, M. D. 2005. 'The Painting Programme in the Stoa Poikile'. In *Periklean Athens and Its Legacy: Problems and Perspectives*, edited by J. M. Barringer and J. M. Hurwit, 73–87. Austin.

STANSBURY-O'DONNELL, M. D. 2006. *Vase Painting, Gender, and Social Identity in Archaic Athens*. Cambridge and New York.

STEARS, K. 2000. 'Losing the Picture: Change and Continuity in Athenian Grave Monuments in the Fourth and Third Centuries BC'. In *Word and Image in Ancient Greece*, edited by N. K. Rutter and B. A. Sparkes, 206–27. Edinburgh.

STEINER, A. 2007. *Reading Greek Vases*. Cambridge.

STEINER, D. T. 2001. *Images in Mind: Statues in Archaic and Classical Greek Literature and Thought*. Princeton and Oxford.

STEINER, D. T. 2012. 'Drowning Sorrows: Archilochus fr. 13 W. in its Performance Context'. *Greek, Roman, and Byzantine Studies*, 52: 21–56.

STEWART, A. 1985. 'History, Myth and Allegory in the Program of the Temple of Athena Nike, Athens'. In *Pictorial Narrative in Antiquity and the Middle Ages*, edited by H. L. Kessler and M. Shreve Simpson, 53–73. Hanover and London.

STEWART, A. 1990. *Greek Sculpture: An Exploration*. New Haven and London.

STEWART, A. 1997. *Art, Desire, and the Body in Ancient Greece*. Cambridge.

STEWART, A. 2008a. *Classical Greece and the Birth of Western Art*. Cambridge.

STEWART, A. 2008b. 'The Persian and Carthaginian Invasions of 480 BCE and the Beginning of the Classical Style: Part 2, The Finds from Other Sites in Athens, Attica,

Elsewhere in Greece, and on Sicily; Part 3, The Severe Style: Motivations and Meaning'. *American Journal of Archaeology*, 112(4): 581–615.

STEWART, A. 2013. 'Die Invasionen der Perser und Karthager und der Beginn des klassischen Stils'. In *Zurück zur Klassik. Ein neuer Blick auf das alte Griechenland*, edited by V. Brinkmann, 132–43. Munich.

STEWART, D. J. 1972. 'Socrates' Last Bath'. *Journal of the History of Philosophy*, 10(3): 253–9.

STEWART, J. A. 1960. *The Myths of Plato*, edited and introduced by G. R. Levy. London. [First published in 1905.]

STEWART, S. 2009. 'Lyric'. In *The Oxford Handbook of Philosophy and Literature*, edited by R. Eldridge, 45–70. Oxford.

STIEBER, M. 2011. *Euripides and the Language of Craft*, Mnemosyne Supplement 327. Leiden.

STOKES, M. C. 1986. *Plato's Socratic Conversations: Drama and Dialectic in Three Dialogues*. London.

STRAUSS, B. S. 1997. 'The Problem of Periodization: The Case of the Peloponnesian War'. In *Inventing Ancient Culture: Historicism, Periodization, and the Ancient World*, edited by M. Golden and P. Toohey, 165–75. London and New York.

STROCKA, V. M. 1967. *Piräusreliefs und Parthenosschild: Versuch einer Wiederherstellung der Amazonomachie des Phidias*. Bochum.

STROCKA, V. M. 1984. 'Das Schildrelief—Zum Stand der Forschung'. In *Parthenon-Kongress Basel: Referate und Berichte, 4. bis 8. April 1982*, edited by E. Berger, 188–196. Mainz am Rhein.

STROSZECK, J. 2004. 'Greek Trophy Monuments'. In *Myth and Symbol II: Symbolic Phenomena in Ancient Greek Culture. Papers from the 2nd and 3rd International Symposia on Symbolism at The Norwegian Institute at Athens, September 19–22, 2002*, edited by S. des Bouvrie, 303–32. Bergen.

STUPPERICH, R. 1977. 'Staatsbegräbnis und Privatgrabmal im klassischen Athen'. PhD thesis, University of Münster, Münster.

SUKSI, A. 2001. 'The Poet at Colonus: Nightingales in Sophocles'. *Mnemosyne*, 54(6): 646–58.

SULLIVAN, S. D. 1999. *Sophocles' Use of Psychological Terminology: Old and New*. Ottawa.

SWIFT, L. 2019. 'Ajax the Hero'. In *Looking at Ajax*, edited by D. Stuttard, 29–42. London.

SZLEZÁK, T. A. 1999. *Reading Plato*, translated by G. Zanker. London and New York. [First published in German in 1993.]

TANNER, J. 2006. *The Invention of Art History in Ancient Greece: Religion, Society, and Artistic Rationalisation*. Cambridge.

TANNER, J. 2016. 'Sight and Painting: Optical Theory and Pictorial Poetics in Classical Greek Art'. In *Sight and the Ancient Senses*, edited by M. Squire, 107–22. London and New York.

TAPLIN, O. 2003. *Greek Tragedy in Action*, second edition. London. [First edition published in 1978.]

TAPLIN, O. 2007. *Pots and Plays: Interactions between Tragedy and Greek Vase-Painting of the Fourth Century B.C.* Los Angeles.

TARLOW, S. and L. N. STUTZ (eds.) 2013. *The Oxford Handbook of the Archaeology of Death and Burial*. Oxford.

TARRANT, D. 1955a. 'Plato as Dramatist'. *The Journal of Hellenic Studies*, 75: 82–9.

TARRANT, D. 1955b. 'Plato's Use of Extended *Oratio Obliqua*'. *The Classical Quarterly*, 5: 222–4.

TARRANT, H. 2000. 'Where Plato Speaks: Reflections on an Ancient Debate'. In *Who Speaks for Plato? Studies in Platonic Anonymity*, edited by G. A. Press, 67–80. Lanham and Oxford.

TATUM, J. 2003. *The Mourner's Song: War and Remembrance from the Iliad to Vietnam*. Chicago and London.

TAYLOR, C. C. W. and M.-K. LEE. 2020. 'The Sophists'. *The Stanford Encyclopedia of Philosophy* (Fall 2020 Edition), edited by E. N. Zalta. https://plato.stanford.edu/archives/fall2020/entries/sophists/.

TAYLOR, M. C. 2010. *Thucydides, Pericles, and the Idea of Athens in the Peloponnesian War*. Cambridge and New York.

TELÒ, M. and M. MUELLER (eds.) 2018. *The Materialities of Greek Tragedy: Objects and Affect in Aeschylus, Sophocles, and Euripides*. London.

THAYER, H. S. 1988. 'The Myth of Er'. *History of Philosophy Quarterly*, 5(4): 369–84.

THE CAMBRIDGE GREEK PLAY. 2019. https://www.cambridgegreekplay.com/plays/2019/oedipus-at-colonus [Accessed 7 April 2022].

THE COMBAHEE RIVER COLLECTIVE. 2014. 'A Black Feminist Statement'. *Women's Studies Quarterly*, 42(3/4): 271–80. [First published in 1978.]

THOMAS, R. 2006. 'Thucydides' Intellectual Milieu and the Plague'. In *Brill's Companion to Thucydides*, edited by A. Rengakos and A. Tsakmakis, 87–108. Leiden and Boston.

THOMPSON, H. A. and R. E. WYCHERLEY. 1972. *The Agora of Athens: The History, Shape, and Uses of an Ancient City Center*. Agora 14. Princeton.

THUMIGER, C. 2013. 'Vision and Violence in Greek Tragedy'. In *Vision and Viewing in Ancient Greece*, edited by S. Blundell, D. Cairns, and N. Rabinowitz, special issue of *Helios*, 40(1/2): 223–45.

THUMIGER, C. 2018. 'Doctors and Patients'. In *The Cambridge Companion to Hippocrates*, edited by P. E. Pormann, 263–91. Cambridge.

TILG, S. 2004a. 'Die Symbolik chthonischer Götter in Sophokles' *Ödipus auf Kolonos*'. *Mnemosyne*, fourth series, 57(4): 407–20.

TILG, S. 2004b. '"Komm, süsser Tod." Zu den "süßen Eumeniden" in Sophokles' *Ödipus auf Kolonos* v. 106 (γλυκεῖαι παῖδες ἀρχαίου Σκότου)'. *Rheinisches Museum für Philologie*, neue Folge, 147: 19–25.

TODISCO, L. 2002. *Teatro e spettacolo in Magna Grecia e in Sicilia: Testi, immagini, architettura*. Milan.

TRABATTONI, F. 2023. *From Death to Life: Key Themes in Plato's Phaedo*. Leiden.

TRAVLOS, J. 1971. *Pictorial Dictionary of Ancient Athens*. London.

TREHERNE, P. 1995. 'The Warrior's Beauty: The Masculine Body and Self-Identity in Bronze-Age Europe'. *Journal of European Archaeology*, 3(1): 105–44.

TRENDALL, A. D. 1972. 'The Mourning Niobe'. *Revue Archéologique*, new series, 2: 309–16.

TRIMBLE, J. 2018. 'Figure and Ornament, Death and Transformation in the Tomb of the Haterii'. In *Ornament and Figure in Graeco-Roman Art: Rethinking Visual Ontologies in Classical Antiquity*, edited by N. Dietrich and M. Squire, 327–52. Berlin.

TRITLE, L. A. 2007. '"Laughing for Joy": War and Peace among the Greeks'. In *War and Peace in the Ancient World*, edited by K. Raaflaub, 172–90. Oxford.

TRIVIGNO, F. V. 2018. 'The Goodness of Death in *Oedipus at Colonus*'. In *The Oedipus Plays of Sophocles: Philosophical Perspectives*, edited by P. Woodruff, 209–38. Oxford and New York.

TRUNDLE, M. 2013. 'Commemorating Victory in Classical Greece: Why Greek *Tropaia?*' In *Rituals of Triumph in the Mediterranean World*, Culture and History of the Ancient Near East 63, edited by A. Spalinger and J. Armstrong, 123–38. Leiden and Boston.

TSINGARIDA, A. 2012. 'White-Ground Cups in Fifth-Century Graves: A Distinctive Class of Burial Offerings in Classical Athens'. In *Red-Figure Pottery in Its Ancient Setting: Acts of the International Colloquium held at the National Museum of Denmark in Copenhagen, November 5–6, 2009*, edited by S. Schierup and B. B. Rasmussen, 43–57. Aarhus.

TUCHMANN, B. W. 1979. *A Distant Mirror: The Calamitous 14th Century*. London. [First published in 1978.]

TURNER, B. and J. H. CLARK. 2018. 'Thinking about Military Defeat in Ancient Mediterranean Society'. In *Brill's Companion to Military Defeat in Ancient Mediterranean Society*, edited by J. H. Clark and B. Turner, 3–22. Leiden and Boston.

TURNER, S. 2016. 'Sight and Death: Seeing the Dead through Ancient Eyes'. In *Sight and the Ancient Senses*, edited by M. Squire, 143–60. London and New York.

VALAKAS, K. 2009. 'Theoretical Views of Athenian Tragedy in the Fifth Century BC'. In *Sophocles and the Greek Tragic Tradition*, edited by S. Goldhill and E. Hall, 179–207. Cambridge and New York.

VAN ALPHEN, E. 1993. 'Touching Death'. In *Death and Representation*, edited by S. W. Goodwin and E. Bronfen, 29–50. Baltimore and London.

VAN ERP TAALMAN KIP, A. M. 2006. 'Words in the Context of Blindness'. In *Sophocles and the Greek Language: Aspects of Diction, Syntax, and Pragmatics*, edited by I. J. F. de Jong and A. Rijksbaron, 39–49, Mnemosyne Supplement 269. Leiden.

VAN GENNEP, A. 2004. *The Rites of Passage*, translated by M. B. Vizedom and G. L. Caffee, with an introduction by S. T. Kimball. London. [First published in 1960.]

VAN NORTWICK, T. 2012. 'Last Things: *Oedipus at Colonus* and the End of Tragedy'. In *A Companion to Sophocles*, edited by K. Ormand, 141–54. Malden, MA and Oxford.

VAN NORTWICK, T. 2015. *Late Sophocles: The Hero's Evolution in Electra, Philoctetes, and Oedipus at Colonus*. Ann Arbor.

VANCE SMITH, D. 2020. *Arts of Dying: Literature and Finitude in Medieval England*. Chicago.

VANDERPOOL, E. 1966. 'A Monument to the Battle of Marathon'. *Hesperia*, 35(2): 93–106.

VASUNIA, P. 2013. *The Classics and Colonial India*. Oxford.

VATRI, A. 2017. *Orality and Performance in Classical Attic Prose: A Linguistic Approach*. Oxford.

VERMEULE, E. 1979. *Aspects of Death in Early Greek Art and Poetry*. Berkeley, Los Angeles and London.

VERNANT, J.-P. 1982. *The Origins of Greek Thought*, translated from the French. London. [First published in French in 1962.]

VERNANT, J.-P. 1983. *Myth and Thought among the Greeks*. London. [First published in French in 1965.]

VERNANT, J.-P. 1985. *La mort dans les yeux : Figures de l'Autre en Grèce ancienne*. Paris.

VERNANT, J.-P. 1987. 'Dans l'œil du miroir : Méduse'. In *Lo specchio e il doppio: Dallo stagno di Narciso allo schermo televisivo*, edited by G. Macchi, M. Vitali, and M. Antonelliana, 26–32. Milan.

VERNANT, J.-P. 1989. 'At Man's Table: Hesiod's Foundation Myth of Sacrifice'. In *The Cuisine of Sacrifice Among the Greeks*, edited by M. Detienne and J.-P. Vernant, translated by P. Wissing, 21–86. Chicago.

VERNANT, J.-P. 1990. 'Figuration et image'. *Mètis*, 5(1–2): 225–38.

VERNANT, J.-P. 1991a. 'A "Beautiful Death" and the Disfigured Corpse in Homeric Epic'. In *Mortals and Immortals: Collected Essays of Jean-Pierre Vernant*, edited by F. I. Zeitlin, 50–74. Princeton.

VERNANT, J.-P. 1991b. '*Panta kala*: From Homer to Simonides'. In *Mortals and Immortals: Collected Essays*, edited by F. I. Zeitlin, 84–91. Princeton.

VERNANT, J.-P. 1996. 'Death with Two Faces'. In *Reading the Odyssey: Selected Interpretive Essays*, edited by S. L. Schein, 55–61. Princeton.

VICKERS, M. 1985. 'Artful Crafts: The Influence of Metal Work on Athenian Painted Pottery'. *The Journal of Hellenic Studies*, 105: 108–28.

VOGELPOHL, C. 1980. 'Die Niobiden vom Thron des Zeus in Olympia'. *Jahrbuch des Deutschen Archäologischen Instituts*, 95: 197–226.

VON BOTHMER, D. 1969. 'Aspects of a Collection'. *The Metropolitan Museum of Art Bulletin*, new series, 27: 425–36.

VON DEN HOFF, R. 2005. '"Achill, das Vieh?" Zur Problematisierung transgressiver Gewalt in klassischen Vasenbildern'. In *Die andere Seite der Klassik: Gewalt im 5. und 4. Jahrhundert v. Chr.*, edited by G. Fischer and S. Moraw, 225–46. Stuttgart.

VON REDEN, S. and S. GOLDHILL. 1999. 'Plato and the Performance of Dialogue'. In *Performance Culture and Athenian Democracy*, edited by S. Goldhill and R. Osborne, 257–89. Cambridge.

VON STADEN, H. 1990. 'Incurability and Hopelessness: The Hippocratic Corpus'. In *La maladie et les maladies dans la Collection Hippocratique. Actes du VIe colloque international hippocratique*, edited by P. Potter, G. Maloney, and J. Desantels, 75–112. Quebec.

VOUT, C. 2014a. 'The End of the "Greek Revolution"?' *Perspective*, 2: 246–52.

VOUT, C. 2014b. 'The Funerary Altar of Pedana and the Rhetoric of Unreachability'. In *Art and Rhetoric in Roman Culture*, edited by J. Elsner and M. Meyer, 288–315. Cambridge.

WAGNER, C. 2000. 'The Potters and Athens: Dedications on the Athenian Acropolis'. In *Periplous: Papers on Classical Art and Archaeology Presented to Sir John Boardman*, edited by G. R. Tsetskhladze, A. J. N. W. Prag, and A. M. Snodgrass, 383–7. London.

WALKER, A. 1993. '*Enargeia* and the Spectator in Greek Historiography'. *Transactions of the American Philological Association*, 123: 353–77.

WALLACE, N. O. 1979. '*Oedipus at Colonus*: The Hero in his Collective Context'. *Quaderni Urbinati di Cultura Classica*, new series, 3: 39–52.

WALTER-KARYDI, E. 2015. *Die Athener und ihre Gräber (1000–300 v. Chr.)*. Berlin.

WANNAGAT, D. 2003. 'Plötzlichkeit: Zur temporalen und narrativen Qualität fallender Gegenstände'. In *Zum Verhältnis von Raum und Zeit in der griechischen Kunst*, edited by P. C. Bol, 59–77. Möhnesee.

WEBB, R. 2009. *Ekphrasis, Imagination, and Persuasion in Ancient Rhetorical Theory and Practice*. Farnham and Burlington.

WEBSTER, T. B. L. 1939a. *Greek Art and Literature, 530–400 B.C.* Oxford.

WEBSTER, T. B. L. 1939b. 'Tondo Composition in Archaic and Classical Greek Art'. *The Journal of Hellenic Studies*, 59(1): 103–23.

WEBSTER, T. B. L. 1972. *Potter and Patron in Classical Athens*. London.

WEIDAUER, K. 1954. *Thukydides und die Hippokratischen Schriften: Der Einfluss der Medizin auf Zielsetzung und Darstellungsweise des Geschichtswerks*. Heidelberg.

WEIL, S. 2005. 'The *Iliad*, or the Poem of Force'. In *War and the Iliad. Simone Weil and Rachel Bespaloff*, with an essay by H. Broch, an introduction by C. Benfrey, translated by M. McCarthy, 1–37. New York. [First published in French in 1940.]

WEINSTEIN, A. 2016. *Children of the New World*. Melbourne and London.

WESENBERG, B. 1981. 'Zur Baugeschichte des Niketempels'. *Jahrbuch des Deutschen Archäologischen Instituts*, 96: 28–54.

WEST, M. L. 1971. *Early Greek Philosophy and the Orient*. Oxford.

WEST, W. C. 1965. 'Greek Public Monuments of the Persian Wars'. PhD thesis, University of North Carolina, Chapel Hill.

WEST, W. C. 1969. 'The Trophies of the Persian Wars'. *Classical Philology*, 64(1): 7–19.

WESTWOOD, G. 2024. 'Imagining Justice in the Athenian Law Court: Aeschines and Others'. In *The Imagination of the Mind in Classical Athens: Forms of Thought*, edited by E. Clifford and X. Buxton, 152–72. London.

WHITE, H. 1981. 'The Value of Narrativity in the Representation of Reality'. In *On Narrative*, edited by W. J. T. Mitchell, 1–24. Chicago and London.

WHITE, N. P. 1979. *A Companion to Plato's Republic*. Oxford.

WILAMOWITZ-MOELLENDORFF, T. VON. 1917. *Die dramatische Technik des Sophokles*. Berlin.

WILAMOWITZ-MOELLENDORFF, U. VON. 1908. *Greek Historical Writing and Apollo: Two Lectures Delivered Before the University of Oxford June 3 and 4 1908*, translated by G. Murray. Oxford.

WILAMOWITZ-MOELLENDORFF, U. VON. 1920. *Platon. Erster Band. Leben und Werke*. Berlin.

BIBLIOGRAPHY 281

WILES, D. 1997. *Tragedy in Athens: Performance Space and Theatrical Meaning*. Cambridge.

WILLI, A. 2012. 'Challenging Authority: Epicharmus between Epic and Rhetoric'. In *Theater Outside Athens: Drama in Greek Sicily and South Italy*, edited by K. Bosher, 56–75. Cambridge.

WILLIAMS, B. 2006. '*The Women of Trachis*: Fictions, Pessimism, Ethics'. In *The Sense of the Past: Essays in the History of Philosophy*, edited with an introduction by M. Burnyeat, 49–59. Princeton and Oxford.

WILLIAMS, C. J. F. 1969. 'On Dying'. *Philosophy*, 44: 217–30.

WILLIAMS, D. 1980. 'Ajax, Odysseus, and the Arms of Achilles'. *Antike Kunst*, 23(2): 137–45.

WILSON, E. R. 2004. *Mocked with Death: Tragic Overliving from Sophocles to Milton*. Baltimore and London.

WILSON, E. R. 2007. *The Death of Socrates: Hero, Villain, Chatterbox, Saint*. London.

WILSON, E. R. 2012. 'Nikos G. Charalabopoulos, *Platonic Drama and its Ancient Reception*. Cambridge classical studies. Cambridge; New York: Cambridge University Press, 2012'. *Bryn Mawr Classical Review*, 2012.12.62.

WILSON, J. 1982. 'What Does Thucydides Claim for His Speeches?' *Phoenix*, 36(2): 95–103.

WILSON, J. P. 1997. *The Hero and the City: An Interpretation of Sophocles' Oedipus at Colonus*. Ann Arbor.

WINNINGTON-INGRAM, R. P. 1954. 'A Religious Function of Greek Tragedy: A Study in the *Oedipus Coloneus* and the *Oresteia*'. *The Journal of Hellenic Studies*, 74: 16–24.

WINNINGTON-INGRAM, R. P. 1980. *Sophocles: An Interpretation*. Cambridge.

WINTON, R. I. 1992. 'Athens and the Plague: Beauty and the Beast'. *Mètis*, 7(1–2): 201–8.

WITTGENSTEIN, L. 1953. *Philosophical Investigations*, edited by G. E. M. Anscombe and R. Rhees, translated by G. E. M. Anscombe. Oxford.

WOELCKE, K. 1911. 'Beiträge zur Geschichte des Tropaions'. *Bonner Jahrbücher*, 120: 127–235.

WOHL, V. 2018. 'Stone into Smoke: Metaphor and Materiality in Euripides' *Troades*'. In *The Materialities of Greek Tragedy: Objects and Affect in Aeschylus, Sophocles, and Euripides*, edited by M. Telò and M. Mueller, 17–33. London.

WOLLHEIM, R. 1980. *Art and Its Objects*, second edition. Cambridge. [First published in 1968.]

WOLLHEIM, R. 1998. 'On Pictorial Representation'. *Journal of Aesthetics and Art Criticism*, 56(3): 217–26.

WOLLHEIM, R. 2003. 'In Defense of Seeing-In'. In *Looking at Pictures: An Interdisciplinary Approach to Pictorial Space*, edited by H. Hecht, R. Schwartz, and M. Atherton, 3–115. Cambridge and London.

WOODFORD, S. 1974. 'More Light on Old Walls: The Theseus of the Centauromachy in the Theseion'. *The Journal of Hellenic Studies*, 94: 158–65.

WOODMAN, A. J. 1988. *Rhetoric in Classical Historiography: Four Studies*. London and Sydney.

282 BIBLIOGRAPHY

WOODRUFF, P. 2015. 'Mimesis'. In *A Companion to Ancient Aesthetics*, edited by P. Destrée and P. Murray, 329–40. Malden, MA and Chichester.

WORMAN, N. 2021. *Tragic Bodies: Edges of the Human in Greek Drama*. London and New York.

WYCHERLEY, R. E. 1957. *The Athenian Agora: Results of Excavations Conducted by the American School of Classical Studies at Athens. Volume III: Literary and Epigraphical Testimonia*. Princeton.

XENIS, G. A. 2018. *Scholia vetera in Sophoclis Oedipum Coloneum*, Sammlung griechischer und lateinischer Grammatiker 18. Berlin and Boston.

YATROMANOLAKIS, D. 2009. 'Ancient Greek Popular Song'. In *The Cambridge Companion to Greek Lyric*, edited by F. Budelmann, 263–76. Cambridge.

YUNIS, H. 2003. 'Writing for Reading: Thucydides, Plato, and the Emergence of the Critical Reader'. In *Written Texts and the Rise of Literate Culture in Ancient Greece*, edited by H. Yunis, 189–212. Cambridge.

ZEITLIN, F. I. 2009. *Under the Sign of the Shield: Semiotics and Aeschylus' Seven Against Thebes*, second edition. Lanham and Plymouth. [First published in 1982.]

ZEITLIN, F. I. 2013. 'Figure: Ekphrasis'. *Greece & Rome*, 60(1): 17–31.

ZEITLIN, F. I. 2018. 'Constructing the Aesthetic Body in Homer and Beyond'. In *Thinking the Greeks: A Volume in Honor of James M. Redfield*, edited by B. M. King and L. E. Doherty, 53–69. London and New York.

ZUCKERBERG, D. 2018. *Not All Dead White Men: Classics and Misogyny in the Digital Age*. Cambridge, MA and London.

INDEX

Note: Figures are indicated by an italic '*f*', respectively, following the page number.

Since the index has been created to work across multiple formats, indexed terms for which a page range is given (e.g., 52–53, 66–70, etc.) may occasionally appear only on some, but not all of the pages within the range.

absence 27–35, 63–4, 78, 81–3, 119–25, 134–7, 225
abstraction 63–4, 100–1, 104, 192–4, 205, 207
Achilles 64–71, 97, 101, 142–3, 214
actor 107 n.7, 119–20, 133 n.103
Aeschylus
   Agamemnon 82–3, 86–7, 106
   Persians 113 n.29, 180 n.104, 214–15
affect 20–1, 86–7, 100–1, 142–3, 199, 214–15
aftermath 42, 63–4, 106–8, 132, 135–7, 186, 223
Aigina warriors 13–15, 14*f*
Ajax 60–73, 61*f*, 92–3, 97, 225, *see also* Sophocles/*Ajax*
Alcestis ix–xiii, 227, *see also* Euripides/*Alcestis*
Amazons 158–62, 164–5, 187 n.125, 189
analogy 63–4, 69–71, 93–5, 108–9, 138–40, 142, 164–5, 189–90, 220–1
anticipation 35–42, 64–71, 90–1, 107–8, 112–17, 134–5, 223
Apollo 112, 116 n.41, 214–15
Archaic
   death 22–3, 59 n.15, 100–5
   pots 56 n.3, 58 n.13, 62 n.28, 71–2, 81, *see also* Mykonos pithos
   stelai 78, 79*f*, 81–2
   see also kouros
Arrington, Nathan 19–22, 146, 148, 155–8, 165, 178–80
art and text 21–2, 100–5, 141–5, *see also* ecphrasis
ashes 56–7, 82–3, *see also* cremation
Astyanax 66–70, 67*f*, 133 n.106, 156 n.28
Athena 64, 170, 172–3, 184–5, *see also* shield of Phidias' Athena Parthenos
athletics 79–81, *see also* funerary/funerary games
author 33–5, 138–9

authority 45–6, 191–2, 198
autopsy *see* witness

beautiful death 42, 61–2, 99–101, 129–31, 157 n.35, 178–80, 205
belief *see* eschatology
beyond
   beyond Athens 16–17, 226
   beyond comprehension 48–50, 97, 210–11, 223–4
   beyond words 41, 197–8
   the beyond 32–3, 43–51
blood 63–4, 73, 142–3, 170, 172–5, 199, 204
body
   acting bodies 106–7, 117–18
   body as object 40–1, 71–2, 128–32, 141–5, 175–6
   corporeality 106–7
   dead and dying bodies 3–4, 29–30, 56–7, 61–3, 81–3, 107–8, 117–34, 155–6, 162–4
   embodied experience 15–16, 20–1, 120–1
   heroic body 97, 133–8
   object as body 56–7, 73, 78, 81–3, 183–6
   out-of-body experience 115
   see also mass death, war dead
borders 72–3, *see also* frames
Bosanquet Painter 73–96, 74*f*, 75*f*, 76*f*, 88*f*
Browne, Thomas 22, 56–7
Brygos Painter 60–73
burial
   burial in earth 82–3, 104
   burial of kin 135–7, 202–3, 215
   cenotaph 138
   collective burial 11–12, 81–2, 135–7
   hidden burial 135–7
   urn-burial 56–7, 102–3

284 INDEX

casualty lists 178–80, 179*f*
Charon 93–5, 94*f*
clarity 25, 31–3, 201, 216
climax 26–7, 35–42, 64–5, 90
concealment 38–9, 63–4, 103–4, 135–7,
    143–4, 155–6, *see also* invisibility
Corcyra 192, 202
corpse
    absent corpse 82–3, 104, 108,
        135–7, 139
    aesthetic corpse 146–7, 165, *see also*
        Leontius
    concealed corpse 155–6
    material corpse 142
    pseudo corpse x–xi, 78, 106–7, 129–32,
        183, 186
    stone corpse 141–5, 156
    visibility of the corpse 61–3, 158–9,
        162–4
    see also mass death
cremation 4, 81–2, *see also* ashes
crisis 16–17, 112–17, 155, 178–82, 186–7,
    190, 226
cult hero 110, 138
culture as mediator of thought 4–10,
    19–21, 63–4, 104–5, 139–40, 165,
    221, 227

death
    longue durée of dying 129–32
    near-death experience *see* near-death
        experience
    ontology of death 72–3, 83–91, 129,
        144–5, 156, 224
    ordinary death *see* ordinary death
    philosophy of death 51–5
    presence at death 25, 28, 30–1, 77–8,
        119–25
    process of death 3–4, 116–17,
        129–31, 134
    response to death *see* response to death
    The Greek Way of Death see Garland,
        Robert
    time of death 3–4, 4 n.11
    see also ending
departure 36–7, 48, 100–1, 104, 155
difference 11–12, 84–7
disorder 144–5, 203–4

distance 3, 27–35, 46–7, 51, 53–4, 92–3,
    119–25, 192–3, 220–1, 223–4
divergence xii–xiii, 40–1, 115–17
drinking cups 60–73, 96–7, 224

eccyclema 81, 107 n.8
ecphrasis 3, 25, 27–35, 43–51, 117–34,
    223, 225
eidolon 78, 84, 89 n.131
ekphora 61–2
Eleusinian mysteries 6 n.19
Elsner, Jaś 15
embodiment
    disembodied 106–7
    embodied experience 13–16, 20–1
    embodied presence 120–1
emotions 31, 38–9, 47–8, 97–8, 112, 132
empiricism 4, 10, 12–13, 15–16, 51,
    192–3, 223
emptiness x, 71–3, 78, 81–2, 84–6, 126–7,
    184–5
ending 25–6, 30–1, 35–42, 90, 114, 223
environment 20–1, 73, 128, *see also*
    landscape
ephemerality 96–7
episodic 181–2, 186–7, 189, 224
eschatology 17 n.62, 127–8
Estrin, Seth 19–22, 86–7
ethics 133–4, 147, 165–6, 204, 207,
    221, 224
Etruria 57–8, 61*f*, 67*f*
Euphronios krater 15–16, 168, 169*f*
Euripides
    Alcestis x–xiii, 4, 15, 86–7, 93–5, 106–7,
        113 n.30, 114 n.33, 116 n.40,
        129 n.91
    Children of Herakles 173–4
    Hippolytus 106–7, 113
    Iphigenia at Aulis 113
    Trojan Women 86–7, 90
exemplarity 6 n.20, 8–10, 30–1, 54, 97, 99,
    108–10, 137–9, 141–5, 192–3,
    209–10, 224
experience *see* embodiment/embodied
    experience, patient experience, senses,
    vicarious experience
exteriority 3, 15–16, 35–42, 91–2, 117–34,
    192–201, 224

INDEX 285

eyes 29–30, 42, 56–7, 72–3, 116, 132–4, 156, 184

failure 37–8, 41, 43–51
female figures 170, 171*f*, 172*f*, *see also* women
figurative 46, 48–50, 98, 197–8, 212–16, 220–1, 225
final day 39, 47–8, 114, 114 n.33, 129–32
flesh 77–8, 144–5
focalization 117–18, 121–2, *see also* perspective
foreknowledge 108, 113, 113 n.30, 129–31
fragility 37–8, 56–7, 90–1, 95–6, 224
frames 28–9, 43, 61–3, 66–8, 72–3, 77, 81–2, 103, 117–18, 121, 143–4, 168, 170, 184–5, 208
Frontisi-Ducroux, Françoise 19–22, 184–5
funerary
    funeral speech 192, 202, 205–7, 216
    funerary games 180–1
    funerary jug *see* lekythos
    funerary legislation 11–12, 17 n.61
    funerary rites 58–9, 61–2, 81–2, 86–7, 129–32, 135–7

Garland, Robert 3–4, 4 n.12, 65 n.44
generality 10–12, 97, 101, 103, 108–10, 138–9, 186–90, 192–4, 201–11, 224
Gorgon 160–2, 184–5
Greek Revolution 10–11, 13–16, 98–9
grief 38–9, 52–3, 101, 131, 141–5, 170, 214–15
Guthrie, Trevor 227–9, 228*f*

hearsay 3, 32–3, 43 n.80
heat 196–8
Hector 90, 97, 100–1, 103–4
Herakles x, xii, 106–7, 164–5, *see also* Euripides/*Children of Herakles*, Sophocles/*Women of Trachis*
Hermes 168, 169*f*
Hippocratic texts 12–13, 15–16, 192, 195–6, 198, 208–10
historiography 15–16, 181–2, 192–3, 201, 204, 209–10, 216–19, 222

Homer
    Iliad 68–9, 100–1, 103–4, 141, 156, 168–70, 178–80, 211–15
    Odyssey 18–19
horror 39, 52–3, 133–4, 139, 170, 203–4, 214–15
human condition 137–8, 193–4, *see also* mortality
Hypnos and Thanatos 81 n.93, 96 n.148, 168, 169*f*

idiosyncrasy 10, 22, 65–6, 109–10, 140
Iliupersis *see* Trojan War
imagination 10–11, 43–51, 78, 86–7, 93–7, 107–8, 113, 124–5, 156, 219, 227–9
immersion 29–30, 117–21
immortality 16–17, 24–55, 99, 106–7, 168, 170, 189–90, 208
indescribable *see* beyond/beyond words
indirectness 92, 224
individuality 87–9, 101, 138, 188, 203–4, 206–8, 224
insubstantial 85, 87
interiority 13, 15, 194
intermediary 18–19, 27–35
invisibility 11–12, 63, 78, 82–3, 92–3, 135, 156, 224
Iphigenia 113, 129 n.91, 173–4, *see also* Aeschylus/*Agamemnon*

jokes 34, 63 n.33, 155–6
Jones, Nathaniel 19–20, 98–9

katabasis 5 n.16, 216
Kerameikos 77–8, 225–6
kouros 11–12, 78, 80*f*, 81–2, 171–2, *see also* Archaic
krater 143–5, 143*f*, 184–5, 184*f*, *see also* Euphronios krater, Niobid krater
kylix *see* drinking cups

landscape 47, 120–1, 125–8, 132, 162–4
lekythos 73–99, 74*f*, 75*f*, 76*f*, 88*f*, 91*f*, 94*f*
Leontius 52–3, 133–4, 146–7
liminality 134
Loraux, Nicole 205–7

286 INDEX

mass death 132, 202–5, 207, 215–16, 219, 224
materiality 20–1, 104, 126–7, 142, 144–5
memorial 42, 54, 58–9, 82–3, 90, 172, 178–80
miniature 72–3, 82–3, 85, 87–9, 101
mirror 39, 42, 95–6, 98–9, 145, 168, 172, 176–7, 180, 186–7, 222, 224, 228–9
mise en abyme 32–3, 70–1, 87–9
monument 42, 54, 73–96, 156, 178–80, 183–4, 224, *see also* tomb
mortality 70–1, 90–1, 96–7, 168, 184–5, 228–9
mourning 21–2, 37, 65–6, 73–98, 108, 132, 135–7, 141–5, 170–2, 206–7, 215, *see also* ritual lament
μῦθος 43–51, 44 n.85, 211–12, 216–17
Mykonos pithos 102–4, 102*f*
Myth 2 n.7, 65–6, 98
myth of Er 1–4, 32–3, 225

near-death experience 2, 191–2, 227
Neer, Richard 98–9, 165
negation 48–50, 82, 84, 122–4, 224
Nike 150, 172–3, 180–2, 183*f*
Niobe 141–5, 143*f*, 215
Niobid krater 162–5, 163*f*
Niobids 215–17, 220–1
nudity 71–2, 77–81, 84

object *see* body
Odysseus 22, 64–5, 97
oracles 212–14, 216–19
ordinary death 4, 109–11, 114, 137–8, 224
Osborne, Robin 19–22, 98–9

pain *see* patient experience
paradox 48–50, 97–8, 114, 126–8, 131, 135, 142
Parthenon 148, 155–6, 173–4, 189
particularity 10–12, 104–5, 224, *see also* generality, individuality
patient experience 192–201
Patroclus 101, 176
Persian Wars 16–17, 108–9, 146–7, 172, 226
Peloponnesian War 8, 16–17, 108–9, 148, 189, 191–222, 226

perspective 10–11, 15–16, 27–35, 93–5, 116–17, 119–25, 192–3, *see also* focalization
Phoenix 68–71, 69*f*, 96–7
piled bodies *see* mass death
Plato
  Phaedo 24–55, 99, 103–5, 129–31, 139, 145, 155–6, 221–2
  Republic 1–4, 133–4, *see also* Leontius, myth of Er
politics of death 11–12, 222
Polyxena 66–8, 129 n.91, 173–4
Priam 66–71, 67*f*, 96–7, 142–3, 224
privilege 2–3, 5, 45–6, 116, 121–2, 124–5
prophecy 43, 45–6, 116
prothesis 61–2, 81, 129–32

real life 98–9, 120–1, 225
reflexivity 5–6, 58–9, 91–6, 218, 225
reliability xii–xiii, 2, 27–8, 31, 116
remembrance 53–4, 64–6, 92–3, 172, 217
  memory images 86–7
response to death 27–8, 30, 39, 65–6
retrospection 27–35, 64–71, 90–1, 97–8, 119–25, 134–5, 223
revelation 29, 60–4, 103, *see also* visibility
ritual lament 87–9, 101, 131–2

sacrifice 66–8, 126, 166, 172–5
Sappho 87–9
Sarpedon 61–2, 73, 81, 156, 168–70, 169*f*, 175–6
  see also Euphronios krater
Scarry, Elaine 175, 197–8, 208–9
senses 10–13, 29–30, 40–1, 52–3, 77–8, 135, 142, 156
shared 140, 162–4, *see also* universality
shield of Phidias' Athena Parthenos 158–62, 158*f*, 159*f*, 160*f*, 161*f*
shroud x, 63–6, 92–3
Sicilian disaster 108–9, 204–7, 216
'Sight of Death' 222
silence 39, 42, 50–1
simile 176, 215, 220–2
singularity *see* particularity
Socrates 1–4, 16–17, 24–55, 99, 104–5, 129–31, 145, 155–6, 221–7
solitude 46, 50–1

Sophocles
    Ajax 63–4, 113
    Antigone 11–12, 106, 139, 141–3
    Electra 82–3
    Oedipus at Colonus 106–40
    Oedipus the King 211–12
    Women of Trachis 106–7, 199, 208–10
Sourvinou-Inwood, Christiane 18–19, 93–5
Spartans 150, 187, 189–90, 201, 213–14
specificity 47, 148, 175, 189, *see also*
    particularity
spectacle 61–3, 65–6, 112–13, 125–34,
    155–6, 202–3, 215, 218–19, 221
Sphakteria 150, 189–90
stone x–xi, 77–8, 141–5, 156, 165–6
storytelling 2–3, 32–3, 211–19, 225
strangeness *see* wonder
struggle 178–82, 223–4
sublimity 116–17, 127–8, 133–4
sunset 36–7, 43–4
surface 56–7, 62–3, 70–3, 129 n.91, 186–7
symposium 60–73, 96–7, 225–7
symptoms 12–13, 194–201, 208, 213–14

Tartarus 46–50, 70–1
tears 38–9, 142–3, 170
temporality 26–7, 30–1, 64–71, 96–7,
    140, 223
text and art *see* art and text
thanatology 3–4, 20–1
Thanatos *see* Hypnos and Thanatos
Theseus 106–40, 172–3, 177–8
Thirty Tyrants 16–17, 108–9, 226
throne of Phidias' Zeus at Olympia 162–4,
    164*f*
tomb 66–8, 73–96, 125–7, 132, 135–7, 142
transferability 2, 109–10, 186–7
transformation 4, 72–3, 141–5, 155–6
transhistorical 4–6, 227–9
Trojan War 65–71, 100–5, 164–5, 204,
    see also Homer/*Iliad*, Mykonos pithos

trophy 176–87, 183*f*, 184*f*
truth 31, 34–5, 43, 52–5, 201
turning point 113–14, 177–80

uncertainty xii, 1 ('the great unknown')
    10–11, 22–3, 43–4, 97, 115–16,
    123–4, 137–8, 197–8
unfamiliar 48
unfathomable *see* beyond/beyond
    comprehension
universality 87–9, 97–8, 137–8, 204, 227,
    see also shared

Vanitas 227–9
veils 29–30, 38–9, 41, 52, 62–4, 70–2,
    104, 142, 145, 156, 223
Vermeule, Emily 22–3
vicarious experience xii–xiii, 27–35, 52–3,
    78, 97, 112–13, 142–3, 145, 221
virtuality 13, 15, 95–6, 145, 225, 227
    artificial intelligence 227
visibility 61–3, 73–83, 103, 150–67,
    194–201, 224
visuality 6 n.19, 227
visual ontology 85–6, 98–9
vividness 29–30
voice 30, 33–4, 45–6, 100–1, 131,
    206–7
voyeurism 15, 121, 133–4

waiting *see* anticipation
Walter-Karydi, Elena 15, 19–20, 98–9
war dead 11–12, 81–3, 135–8, 164–5,
    180–1, 206–7
washing 129–31, 139
Weil, Simone 157
witness 2–3, 31, 41, 191–2
women 11–12, 39, 58–9, 73–96, 98,
    141–5, 171–2, 208, 225–6, *see also*
    female figures
wonder 39, 47–50, 52–3, 84, 125–34, 225